Angular Boot Camp

Version 10

Angular Boot Camp

© 2022 Kevin Ruse + Associates Inc.

Part Number: 2019ANG4+

Edition Number: 10

ISBN: 978-0-692-96196-4

Author: Kevin Ruse

Disclaimer

Kevin Ruse + Associates Inc. takes care to ensure the accuracy and quality of this courseware and related courseware files. We cannot guarantee the accuracy of these materials. The courseware and related files are provided without any warranty whatsoever, including but not limited to implied warranties of merchantability or fitness for a particular purpose. If anyone's name appears, by accident, in this courseware, please notify Kevin Ruse + Associates Inc. at kevin@kevinruse.com and we will change the name in upcoming printed versions of this courseware. Use of screenshots, product names and icons in this courseware are for editorial purposes only. No such use should be construed to imply sponsorship or endorsement of the book, nor any affiliation of such entity with Kevin Ruse + Associates, Inc.

Third-Party Information

This courseware contains links to third-party web sites that are not under the control of Kevin Ruse + Associates Inc. and we are not responsible for the content on any linked site. If you access a third-party site mentioned in this courseware, then you do so at your own risk. Kevin Ruse + Associates Inc. provides these links only as a convenience, and the inclusion of the link does not imply that Kevin Ruse + Associates Inc. endorses or accepts responsibility for the content on those third-party links. This courseware contains references to tutorials and resources found on the internet and are licensed under the Creative Commons agreement found here: http://creativecommons.org/licenses/by-nc-sa/3.0/. Information in this courseware may change without notice and does not represent a commitment on the part of Kevin Ruse + Associates Inc.

Copyright

All references to the Food Plate are in the public domain and may be found at http://www.choosemyplate. gov/.
If you would like Information regarding the sites policies, see:
http://www.usda.gov/wps/portal/usda/usdahome?navtype=FT&navid=POLICY_LINK.

Help us improve our courseware

Please send your comments and suggestions via email to kevin@kevinruse.com.

Author

Kevin Ruse (Santa Clara, CA) is an enthusiastic instructor who has taught at various community colleges and universities in Silicon Valley, California. He currently provides training to Fortune 500 companies throughout the United States, Europe, Asia and the Middle East. Kevin specializes in Rich Internet Applications and associated languages and technologies including HTML5, CSS3, JavaScript, TypeScript, ActionScript, Flex, XML, XSLT, jQuery, JavaScript, JavaScript frameworks and more. Kevin has taught at Google, Facebook, Hewlett Packard, Cisco Systems, KLA-Tencor, Applied Materials and Avaya as well as the United States Air Force, Canadian Forces and government institutions. He has 40 years' experience in the printing, graphic and design industry from concept to finished product and started designing and building web pages since the world wide web began. He is the author of books, video training and DVDs published by Adobe Press. When not training, Kevin is a Project Manager and Web Developer. Along with training, creating training materials is his passion.

Courseware

As most developers know, frameworks like Angular can and do change frequently. The Angular framework and the Angular CLI tool may change in content and/or behavior at various times during development. In addition to changes within Angular, the tools we use for web development including Node.js, Yarn and NPM change as well. This could result in unexpected behavior when working through this course.

Please note any differences between courseware instructions and expected results with your instructor when implementing any of the following:

- TypeScript code
- Angular CLI commands
- Build process
- Production build process

Instructor Notes

All demo files are optional. They should be noted to the student, but do not have to be completed in class for a successful conclusion to the project.

All practice exercises are optional.

Homework exercises are not intended for completion in class but may be helpful for advanced students who finish the exercises early.

In addition, there are numerous references to web links that contain micro-learning modules (quizzes, games, infographics and so on). While these may be used in-class, they are intended to help the student understand complex and/or time-consuming concepts after class as they will encroach on in-class time that is best used for guided and challenge exercises. Instructors should use discretion when time constrained.

Course Icons

This book uses various icons to help guide you through the course.

	**Q and A/Lecture** (typically between 10-15 minutes)
	**Exercise** Guided, Challenge and Extra-Credit exercises
	**Resource** on the web
	**Quiz** (at the end of chapters)
	**Exercise** to be done in the **FoodPlate-cli project**
	**Exercise** to be done in the **Angular-seed project**
	All **in-class resources and reference URLs** may be found at: https://www.kevinruse.com/resources/angular
Code Files	If you prefer not to type the exercise code in class, you may cut and paste most code from the angular-class-files folder (contains any code that is over approximately 6 lines). For example, when instructed to write: plate.component.ts, look for the file named: plate-component-ts.txt

Using the staged files

Although each exercise in this course builds upon the previous exercise, you may start the course at any chapter you wish. Below are the instructions for using the staged files to begin the exercises at any chapter number.

Step 1 Locate the staged-files folder and find the chapter you would like to begin with. For example, if you would like to start working on Chapter 8 for the CLI project, you should open the 2020-angular-bootcamp-FoodPlate-cli-v6.0.0-chapter-7-finished zip file.

Step 2 Find the foodPlate-cli folder inside the chapter folder and unzip if necessary.

Step 3 Create a new project in your IDE using the foodPlate-cli folder as the project folder.

Step 4 Using a command prompt (built-in to your IDE or you may use node.js), navigate to the project folder

Step 5 Run the command:

```
npm install
```

Note If you run into any problems, run `npm cache clean` then run the command `npm install`.

Step 6 To start the application:

```
ng serve
```

Table of Contents

Chapter 1
Introduction to Angular

Chapter 1: Introduction to Angular

Objectives

- Define Angular as a framework and a platform
- Describe how Angular determines version numbers
- List three helpful Angular resources found on the Internet
- Visit some applications that have been built with Angular
- Download useful Angular extensions for Chrome

Online Resources for Chapter 1

http://kevinruse.com/resources/angular

1.0 What is Angular?

Angular is an open-source MIT-licensed JavaScript framework for building single-page web applications that can be deployed on the web, the mobile web, native mobile and native desktop. Angular was originally written in 2009 by Miško Hevery and Adam Abrons and is now maintained by Google. AngularJS 1.0 was released in 2012. The current release, known simply as Angular, may be written in Dart, TypeScript or JavaScript including the latest version of ECMAScript. The Angular team uses TypeScript when writing the Angular frameworks' source code. For a historical timeline of releases see Appendix C which also includes a comparison of AngularJS and Angular's version 2 release.

1.1 The Angular team considers Angular a platform

The Angular team refers to Angular as a platform because they are attempting to provide more than just a framework. From the language (TypeScript) to CLI tools (AngularCLI) and testing libraries, the team has been working hard to provide developers everything they need to build and maintain enterprise applications.

1.2 The Angular ecosystem

Angular enjoys a large ecosystem that includes not only Google and Microsoft (for TypeScript), but also the "Angular community of developers." Because of this large community Angular developers have access to a variety of tools including IDE plug-ins, browser extensions, performance testing tools and so on. In addition, developers will find a vast array of tutorials, videos and documentation for Angular. For a complete reference to the Angular ecosystem, see Appendix A.

1.3 Why should you choose Angular?

There are a vast number of JavaScript frameworks available today for creating web applications. Many of the features that make Angular a desirable choice can be found in other frameworks including React, Ember, Vue and others. It is the combination of features along with the preferences of your team and the requirements of your project that together make a framework suitable. Below are some of the features of Angular. These features may be debatable, but they have nevertheless been proven in countless projects.

- Angular is scalable which makes it a suitable framework for large enterprise applications.
- Angular has a large ecosystem of tools, browser extensions, and libraries including a UI framework called Material Design that was made specifically for Angular.
- Angular is a full-featured framework that is very opinionated yet provides opportunities for custom configuration. This includes configuring and choosing your own build tools, language choice, UI framework, state management, coding style, and so on.
- Angular ports well to multiple platforms including web browsers, native desktop and native mobile.
- Angular is designed from the ground up with the goal of achieving maximum performance, resulting in Angular applications that provide an experience like a desktop application.

MICROLEARNING LINK

http://kevinruse.com/resources/angular-and-beyond.html

1.4 Angular Versioning

Per Igor Minar, Angular Lead Developer: while the original version of Angular was known as AngularJS and version two quickly became referred to as Angular2, as of December 2012, "it's just Angular." This was announced at the NG-BE, Belgium's first Angular conference on December 8 and 9th of 2016.

For more information visit http://angularjs.blogspot.com/2016/12/ok-let-me-explain-its-going-to-be.html.

Mr. Minar went on to say: "As you might have already guessed, the term 'Angular 2' is also kind of deprecated once we get to version 4, 5 etc. That said, we should start naming it simply 'Angular' without the version suffix. Also, we should start avoiding GitHub/NPM libraries prefixed with ng2- or angular2- *"

To understand more about Angular's use of semantic versioning as well as its history regarding version numbers see Appendix B.

1.5 Angular New Features and Prior Versions

Each new version of Angular introduces bug fixes, performance improvements and new features. In the past, the Angular team has put the focus of a new release on one category of changes such as performance. In more recent versions, we have seen improvements across multiple various categories. For detailed information on newly added features per release version, see Appendix D.

1.5.1 The Angular Update Guide

When migrating your application from an older to a newer version of the framework, Angular provides an Update guide found at the link below. It provides some assistance in refactoring your code to accommodate the framework changes.

https://update.angular.io/

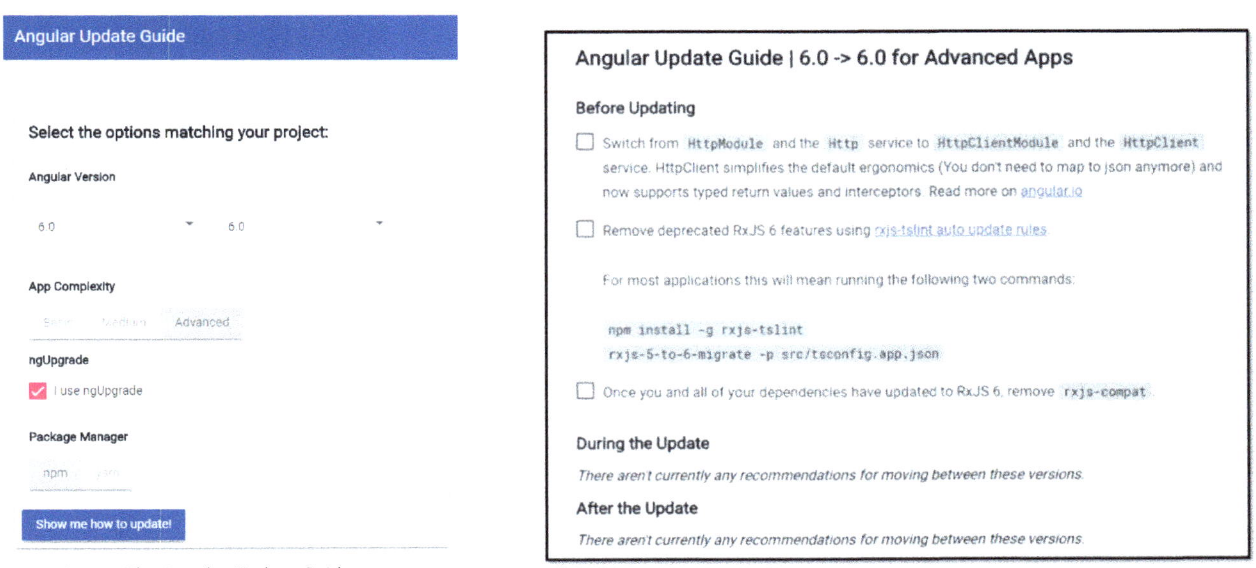

Figure #1: The Angular Update Guide

1—Guided Exercise: (Optional) Useful Angular Resources

Step 1 Launch a web browser and visit and bookmark the URLs shown in the list below.

All the links below can be found by visiting https://www.kevinruse.com/resources/angular

1. Angular documentation:
   https://angular.io
   https://angular.io/docs

2. John Papa Angular Style Guide:
   https://angular.io/guide/styleguide

3. Angular versioning reference and roadmap:
   https://blog.angularjs.org/2016/12/ok-let-me-explain-its-going-to-be.html

4. Angular playground:
   http://plnkr.co/edit/?p=catalogue

   Plunker is an online community for creating, collaborating on and sharing your web development ideas. It may be used throughout the class to test ideas, ask questions and run demos.

5. StackBlitz:
   https://stackblitz.com/

6. JavaScript playground:
   http://jsbin.com

   jsBin is an online JavaScript editor that is helpful for quickly testing and/or demonstrating code that uses JavaScript libraries

7. Additional resources:
   https://blog.angular.io/
   https://twitter.com/angular

8. Websites:
   https://indepth.dev/
   https://medium.com/tag/angular

9. Twitter:
   https://twitter.com/mhevery
   https://twitter.com/bradlygreen
   https://twitter.com/gkalpakas
   https://twitter.com/karaforthewin

10. Tutorials:
    https://code.tutsplus.com/categories/angular:

1 – Demo (optional): Angular examples

Step 1 Launch a web browser and visit the following site built with Angular.
https://www.24ur.com/
https://jsonschema.net/login

Step 2 For more sites built with Angular, visit:
http://angularexpo.com/
https://www.madewithangular.com/

Optional Helpful downloads

Step 1 Install Chrome extensions for detecting the libraries and frameworks used by the websites you visit.

Wappalyzer:
https://www.wappalyzer.com

Frameworks:
https://github.com/kassens/frameworks/

Step 2 Install a Chrome extension for debugging and profiling Angular applications:
Augury
https://augury.angular.io/

Step 3 Redux DevTools Extension
Redux
https://tinyurl.com/h2m9d9d

Step 4 Tooling Options (libraries)
Angular Playground:
https://blog.bitsrc.io/my-top-favorite-tools-for-angular-developers-c2ed96397f6b

Storybook:
https://storybook.js.org/

Angular DevTools
https://tinyurl.com/7akh8ct5

Angular Coding Environment

https://stackblitz.com/edit/angular-playground

Chapter 1 Quiz

https://tinyurl.com/qk5zoop

1) Angular may be written in which language(s)?
   - A. JavaScript only
   - B. Dart only
   - C. TypeScript only
   - D. TypeScript and JavaScript only
   - E. JavaScript or Dart or TypeScript

2) Which of the following are valid versions of Angular?
   - A. AngularJS
   - B. Angular 3.0
   - C. Angular 1.0
   - D. Angular 2.0
   - E. Angular 4.0

3) Angular may be used to develop which of the following?
   - A. Desktop applications
   - B. Mobile applications
   - C. Native mobile applications
   - D. Native desktop applications
   - E. All the above

4) Which of the following represents a best practice guide for Angular?
   - A. Plunker
   - B. John Papa's Style Guide
   - C. Made with Angular
   - D. Wappalyzer

Chapter summary

Angular is:

- an open source framework for developing web applications for:
  - Desktop
  - Mobile
  - Native mobile
  - Native desktop
- considered by the Angular team as a platform
- written in:
  - Dart
  - TypeScript
  - JavaScript
    - ECMAScript 5
    - ECMAScript 6
- originally written in 2009 by:
  - Miško Hevery
  - Adam Abrons
- released:
  - as AngularJS 1.0 in 2012
  - as version 2 in 2016
  - as version 4 in 2017

Tentative release schedule can be found at:

https://angular.io/guide/releases#support-policy-and-schedule

Homework

Step 1 Using the following resources as guides, compare Angular to two other front-end frameworks.

- https://www.safaribooksonline.com/blog/2013/10/16/choosing-a-javascript-framework/
- https://www.safaribooksonline.com/blog/2013/10/14/13-criteria-for-evaluating-web-frameworks/
- https://javascriptreport.com/the-ultimate-guide-to-javascript-frameworks/

Note You may choose any two frameworks you are familiar with. If you are not familiar with any other frameworks compare Angular to:

React https://reactjs.org/
Vue https://vuejs.org/v2/guide/

Step 2 Try this online quiz to help you choose a framework:
https://code.tutsplus.com/articles/quiz-choose-the-right-front-end-javascript-framework-for-your-project--cms-27739

Next Chapter

In the next chapter, you set up a development environment to use throughout the course.

Chapter 2
Class Setup

Chapter 2: Class setup

Objectives

- Confirm the course setup requirements
- Check your machine to confirm the course requirements have been met
- Confirm that you have the prerequisite skills to take this course

Online Resources for Chapter 2

http://kevinruse.com/resources/angular

Introduction

This chapter covers the setup requirements for the course, including:

- Minimal software requirements
- Integrated Development Environments
- Code editors
- Web application development tools available for download on the internet
- Course prerequisites
- What you should know before you take this course

2.0 Requirements (detailed installation instructions are on the next page)

- Integrated Development Environment or code editor
- nodeJS
- npm
- Chrome web browser
- Angular CLI
- Git

2.1 Course Setup Requirements

This course requires the software listed below. All the links can be found at http://www.kevinruse.com/resources/angular under Chapter 2.

2.1.1 Operating System Choices:

Windows version 7 or higher.. https://www.microsoft.com/en-us/software-download/
MacOS version 10.12.5 or higher...https://support.apple.com/downloads/x11_for_mac_os_x_1_0

2.1.2 Web browser

Chrome version 91 or higher .... https://www.google.com/chrome/browser/desktop/index.html

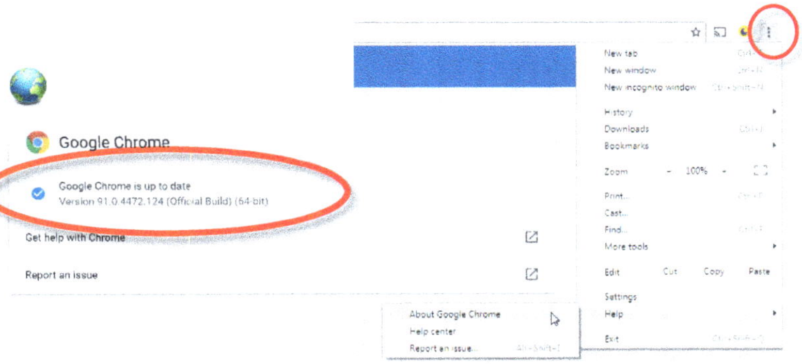

Latest version is recommended.

2.1.3 Chrome Angular DevTools Extension

Angular DevTools https://tinyurl.com/2p8dexrm

https://chrome.google.com/webstore/detail/angular-devtools/ienfalfjdbdpebioblfackkekamfmbnh?hl=en-US

2.1.4 Node.js JavaScript runtime

Node.js versions 14.17.0.. https://nodejs.org/download/release/v14.17.0/

Index of /download/release/v14.17.0/

../	
docs/	11-May-2021 18:56
win-x64/	11-May-2021 18:11
win-x86/	11-May-2021 18:07
SHASUMS256.txt	11-May-2021 23:13
SHASUMS256.txt.asc	11-May-2021 23:13
SHASUMS256.txt.sig	11-May-2021 23:13
node-v14.17.0-aix-ppc64.tar.gz	11-May-2021 18:40
node-v14.17.0-darwin-x64.tar.gz	11-May-2021 18:30
node-v14.17.0-darwin-x64.tar.xz	11-May-2021 18:31
node-v14.17.0-headers.tar.gz	11-May-2021 18:56
node-v14.17.0-headers.tar.xz	11-May-2021 18:56
node-v14.17.0-linux-arm64.tar.gz	11-May-2021 19:19
node-v14.17.0-linux-arm64.tar.xz	11-May-2021 19:22
node-v14.17.0-linux-armv7l.tar.gz	11-May-2021 19:12
node-v14.17.0-linux-armv7l.tar.xz	11-May-2021 19:13
node-v14.17.0-linux-ppc64le.tar.gz	11-May-2021 18:08
node-v14.17.0-linux-ppc64le.tar.xz	11-May-2021 18:09
node-v14.17.0-linux-s390x.tar.gz	11-May-2021 18:11
node-v14.17.0-linux-s390x.tar.xz	11-May-2021 18:12
node-v14.17.0-linux-x64.tar.gz	11-May-2021 18:14
node-v14.17.0-linux-x64.tar.xz	11-May-2021 18:15
node-v14.17.0-win-x64.7z	11-May-2021 18:12
node-v14.17.0-win-x64.zip	11-May-2021 18:12
node-v14.17.0-win-x86.7z	11-May-2021 18:07
node-v14.17.0-win-x86.zip	11-May-2021 18:07
node-v14.17.0-x64.msi	11-May-2021 18:12
node-v14.17.0-x86.msi	11-May-2021 18:07
node-v14.17.0.pkg	11-May-2021 19:26
node-v14.17.0.tar.gz	11-May-2021 18:48
node-v14.17.0.tar.xz	11-May-2021 18:53

A. Go to the download site and download the .msi file for your operating system and bit architecture. See the screenshot above pointing to the Windows 64-bit version: node-v14.17.0-x64.msi.

   a. Accept the License Agreement.
   b. Choose the location for the installation.
   c. Accept the defaults options in the custom setup. Make sure you keep the default "Add to PATH" option
   d. Do ***not*** check the Tools for Native Modules option: Automatically install the necessary tools.

B. Launch nodejs command prompt.

C. Type: `node --version` (or `node -v`) to confirm that you have installed version 14.17.0

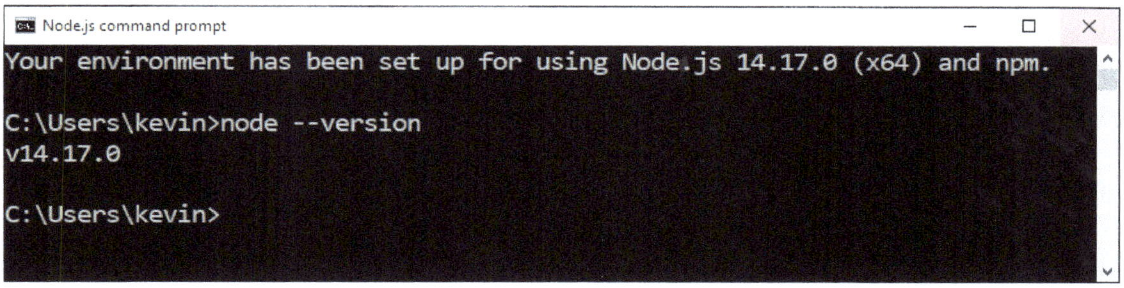

At publication time, the latest Long Term Support (LTS) version for Windows is 16.13.1 and the latest current version for Windows (with the latest features) is 17.3.0. You should have downloaded and installed version 14.17.0.

2.1.5 npx

npx makes it easy to use CLI tools and other executables hosted on the registry.

npx package runner .... https://www.npmjs.com/package/npx

A. `npm install -g npx`

B. Type: `npx --version`

2.1.6 Node Package Manager

npm version 6.14.13 .... https://docs.npmjs.com/getting-started/installing-node#updating-npm

npm *should be installed automatically along with the node.js installation.*

A. You can update npm with the command: `npm install -g npm`

B. Launch node.js command prompt

C. type: `npm --version` (or `npm -v`)

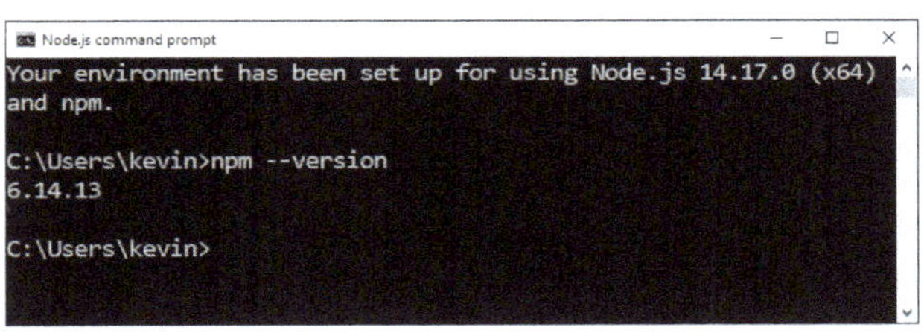

At publication time, the latest version of npm is 8.1.2. The version you install should be 6.14.13.

2.1.7 Angular CLI tool

Angular CLI .... https://github.com/angular/angular-cli

A. Use a node.js command prompt to install and verify the Angular CLI tool using the commands below.

```
npm install -g @angular/cli@10.0.3
```

B. Type: `ng --version`

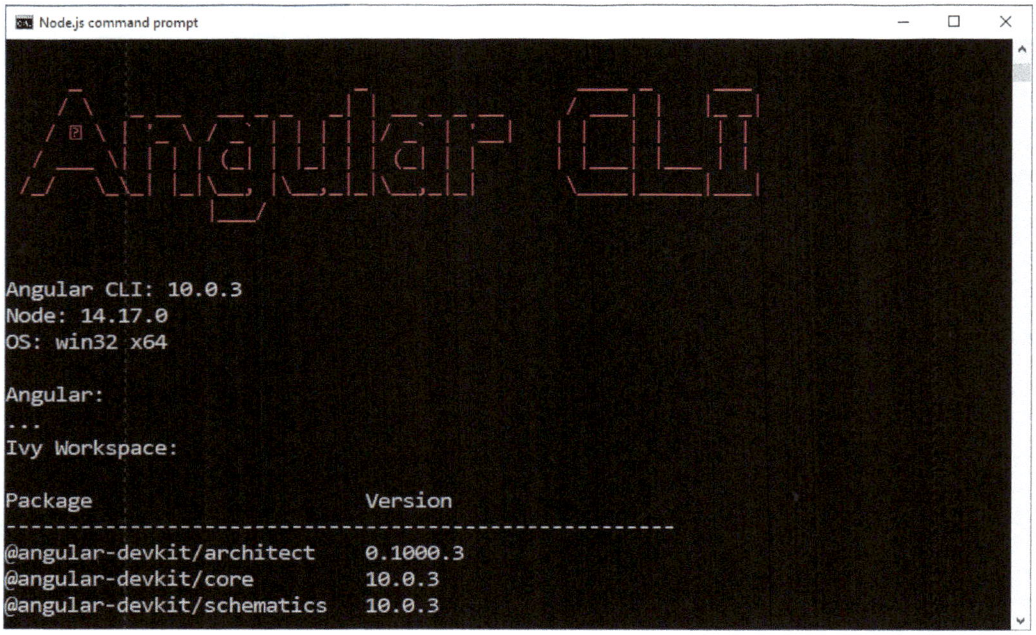

At publication time, the version of the CLI associated with Angular 10 was version 10.0.3.

2.1.8 Git

Git .... https://git-scm.com/downloads

A. Go to the download site and download the git for your operating system.
   a. Accept the License Agreement.
   b. Choose the installation location.
   c. Accept the default options.
   d. If prompted, set the "Select Start Menu Folder."
   e. Choose the default editor used by Git (Vim).
   f. Adjust your PATH Environment. Choose "Git from the command line and also from 3rd-party software."
   g. Choose HTTPS transport backend. Choose "Use the OpenSSL library."
   h. Configure the line ending conversions. Choose "Checkout Windows-style, commit Unix-style line endings" which is the recommended setting on Windows.
   i. Configuring the terminal emulator to use with Git Bash. Choose "Use MinTTY (the default terminal of MSYS2).
   j. Configure extra options. Choose
      i. Enable file system caching
      ii. Enable Git Credential Manager
   k. Configuring experimental options. Do not choose any options.

I. Click the “Install” button.

B. Launch node.js command prompt

C. type: `git --version`

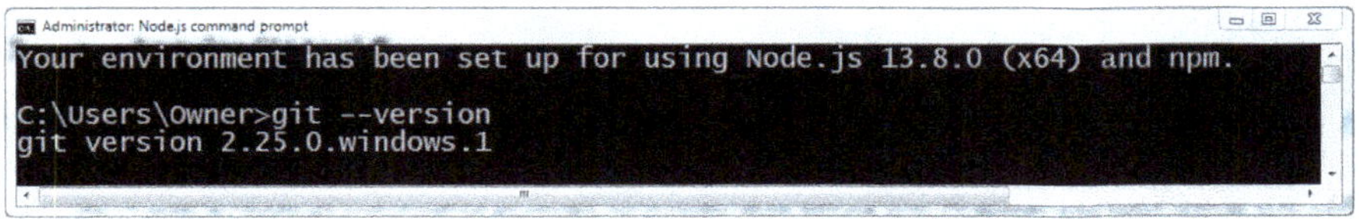

D. You may need to run the following commands

```
git config user.name "<first name> <last name>"
git config email "<email address>"
```

At publication time, the latest version of Git is 2.32.0 for Windows and 2.31.0 for Mac.

2.1.9 Integrated Development Environment

This course works best with the following IDE’s:

- JetBrains WebStorm Version 2017 or higher https://www.jetbrains.com/webstorm/download
- VisualStudio Code (latest version) https://code.visualstudio.com/download
  - At publication time, the latest version is 1.5.7 (user setup)
- Visual Studio 2017 or higher https://www.microsoft.com/en-us/store/b/visualstudio

2.2 Configuring Visual Studio Code for Angular

1. Launch VSCode and click the extensions button on the toolbar on the left side of the screen.

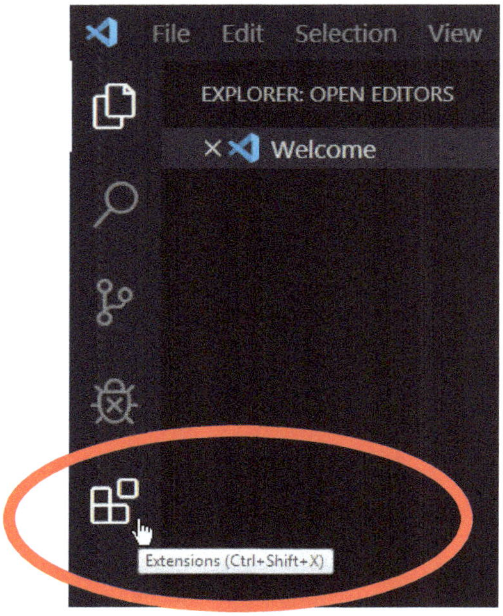

   i. Search for Angular Snippets (Version 9) as shown below.

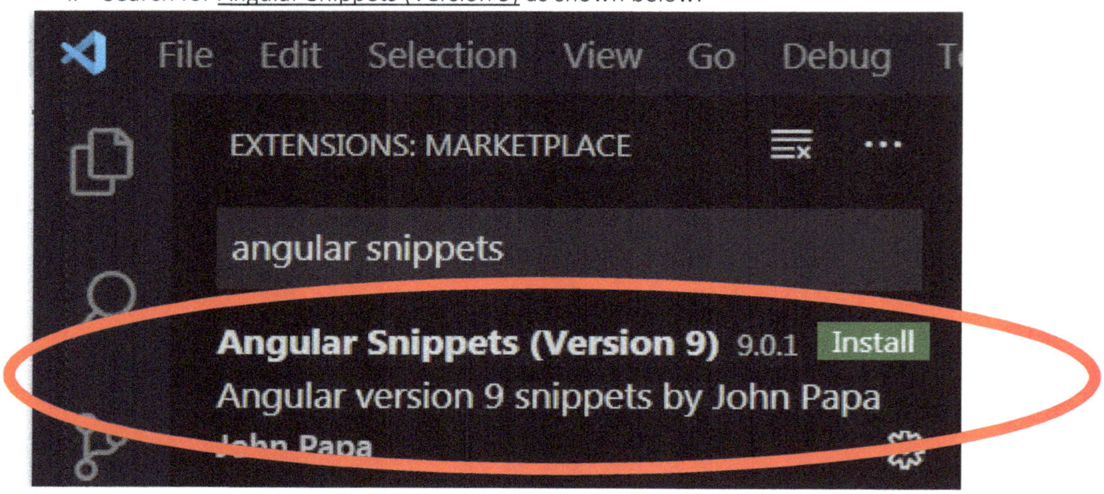

   ii. Click the Green Install button on the right of the extension name.

2. Continue to use the Extension toolbar to search for the remaining extensions in the steps below.
   i. Search for and install Peacock
      1. Subtly change the color of your Visual Studio Code workspace. Ideal when you have multiple VS Code instances, use VS Live Share, or use VS Code's Remote features, and you want to quickly identify your editor.
      2. To use:
         a. Press F1 to open the command palette
         b. Type Peacock
         c. Choose Peacock: Change to a favorite color
         d. Choose one of the pre-defined colors and see how it changes your editor

   ii. Search for and install VSCode simpler icons with Angular

1. Creates icons next to your Angular project files as shown below.

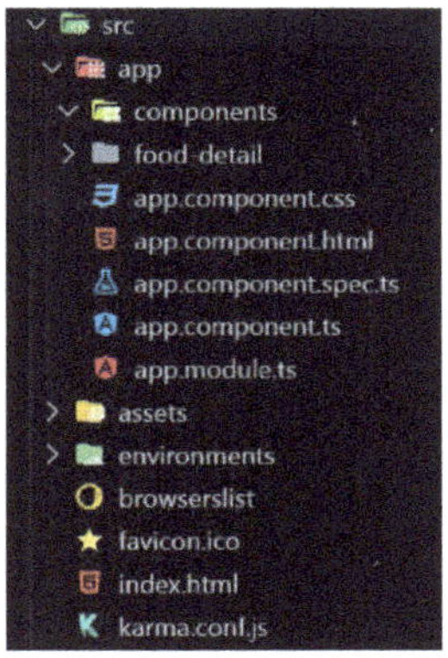

iii. Search for and install Auto Import – ES6 & TS
   1. Automatically finds, parses and provides code actions and code completion for all available imports.
iv. Search for and install Bracket Pair Colorizer
   1. A customizable extension for colorizing matching brackets.
v. Search for and install Angular2 inline
   1. This package is a language extension for Microsoft Visual Studio Code. It extends the JavaScript and Typescript languages to add Angular2 specific features for inline templates and stylesheets. When you define an inline template or inline style sheet using the backtick character(`) the content will be processed by this extension.
   2. The features provided by this extension:
      a. Syntax highlighting of inline html and css.
      b. Code completion, highlighting, and hover information for inline html.
vi. Search for and install Debugger for Chrome
   1. Debug your JavaScript code in the Chrome browser, or any other target that supports the Chrome Debugger protocol.
vii. Search for and install Angular Language Service
   1. This extension provides a rich editing experience for Angular templates, both inline and external templates including:
      a. Completions lists
      b. AOT Diagnostic messages
      c. Quick info
      d. Go to definition

3. Configure the Emmet Extension
   i. Click the settings (gear) icon on the lower left of the screen and choose "Settings"

   ii. Type the command: `emmet.triggerExpansionOnTab: true`

   In the field shown on the next page circled in red.

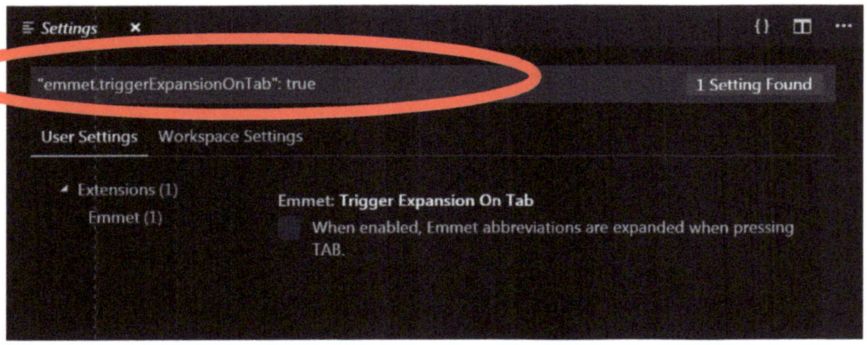

iii. Click the Checkbox shown below circled in red.

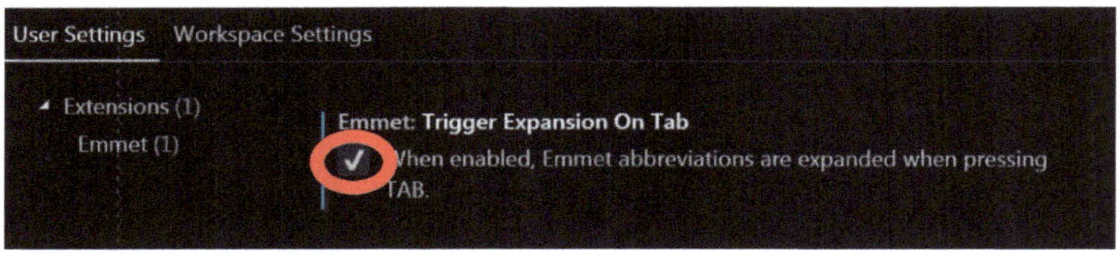

NOTE: be sure to note and/or bookmark the docs for each extension for later reference.

iv. To locate the next setting, type Emmet: Include Languages

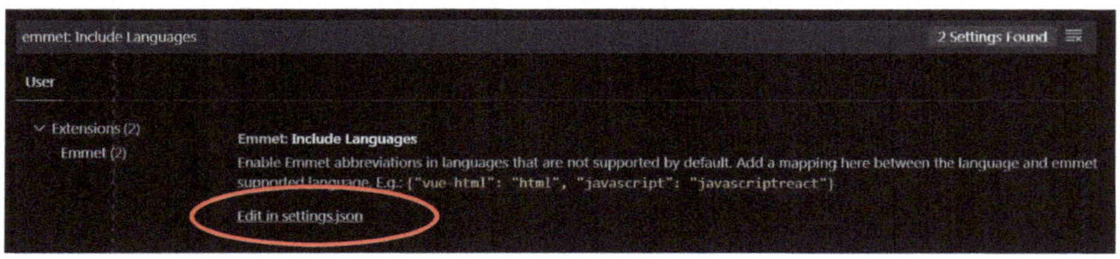

v. Click the "Edit in settings.json" link.

vi. Add the code shown below.

```
"emmet.includeLanguages": {
    "typescript": "html",
}
```

2.3 Chrome Extensions

- Install the Angular DevTools Chrome extension from https://chrome.google.com/webstore/detail/angular-devtools/ienfalfjdbdpebioblfackkekamfmbnh?hl=en-US
    - Tiny URL: https://tinyurl.com/yc825wbf
- Install the Redux DevTools extension from https://chrome.google.com/webstore/detail/redux-devtools/lmhkpmbekcpmknklioeibfkpmmfibljd?hl=en
    - https://tinyurl.com/ybn8hjy6
    - Resources for Redux DevTools: https://codeburst.io/redux-devtools-for-dummies-74566c597d7

2.4 Additional Information

Students should have internet access and administrative permission to install software.

2.5 Course Prerequisites

Students should have a working knowledge of the following languages:

- HTML version 5
- CSS any version
- JavaScript/ECMAScript 2015 or higher
- TypeScript version 2.0 or higher

2.6 Setup questions?

Email: kevin@kevinruse.com

Next Chapter

In the next chapter, you build your first Angular application.

Chapter 3
Building Your First Angular Application

Chapter 3: Building your first Angular application

Objectives

- Describes the leading methodology for building Angular applications
- Create an Angular application by cloning the "Angular Seed Project"
- Create an Angular application by using the Angular CLI tool

Online Resources for Chapter 3

http://kevinruse.com/resources/angular

Introduction

There are several paths a developer might take to build their first Angular application. This course will focus on building your app via tools provided by the Angular team.

3.0 Use Angular tools (recommended method)

The Angular team recommends using the Angular tool created by the team specifically for starting Angular projects called the Angular CLI. The Angular CLI can be built and installed from https://github.com/angular/angular-cli.

Another option is to clone a starter project, which can be made by the lead Angular architect on the team.

3.1 Building Code from scratch (not recommended for Angular applications)

Either method is far more efficient and bug-free than the alternative methods used in the past. For example, you could write all of the Angular boilerplate code (which you will learn in subsequent chapters) from scratch. You will then need to use a large variety of existing tools to complete the remaining tasks of installing libraries and dependencies, install and configure transpilers, vet, install and create a unit testing framework, vet, install and create an end-to-end testing framework, configure and install a module loader, maintain dependencies by writing and maintain a package.json manifest file and so on through configuring development and release builds.

The Angular CLI tool does most of this work for you or at the very least provides the starter and configuration files for these tasks.

Once that work is done, you can continue working on the application using any simple code editor, such as:

- Sublime (https://www.sublimetext.com/)
- Visual Studio Code (https://code.visualstudio.com/)
- Brackets (http://brackets.io/)
- Atom (https://atom.io/)

To maintain the application, you will use existing tools, like: npm, webpack, and so on to build the entire application from scratch, including:

- All configuration files (such as configuring the Typescript transpiler, unit test configurations, module loading configurations, package.json and others)
- index.html
- Cascading Style Sheets
- All TypeScript components, directives, routes, and so on

Today's Integrated Development Environment's (IDEs) provide both native and 3rd party utilities/extensions to facilitate the creation of Angular applications. By using a sophisticated IDE with built-in tooling for creating Angular projects, you can utilize time saving features that mimic the Angular CLI tool. The most popular IDE's are listed below.

- Microsoft Visual Studio IDE (https://www.visualstudio.com/)
  - https://angular.io/guide/visual-studio-2015
- JetBrains WebStorm IDE (https://www.jetbrains.com/webstorm/)
  - https://blog.jetbrains.com/webstorm/2016/04/angular-2-workflow-in-webstorm/
- Microsoft Visual Studio Code (a free IDE)
  - https://code.visualstudio.com/download

2–Guided Exercise: Cloning a repo to create your first Angular Application

Introduction

In this exercise, you clone a Github repository also known as a repo. Github is a web-based hosting service that allows developers to version control and manage their source code. Github hosts in excess of 5 million code repositories.

In prior versions of Angular, this was a common method for starting an Angular project. A popular repo at that time was Minko Gechev's Angular Seed Project written while he was a member of the Angular team. The project is described at https://github.com/mgechev/angular-seed below.

The Angular seed provides a stable and robust foundation for local development of Angular projects. The seed project provides a starting app module with an app component as well as a main file which bootstraps the application. The seed project includes many more files which you will learn about throughout the course. It also provides a lightweight development only node.js-based web server called "lite-server" (https://github.com/johnpapa/lite-server), as well as scripts that run the server and serve the application.

NOTE: While the Angular seed project provides fast, reliable and extensible starter for the development of Angular projects, it has been updated from its original version to version 4. The current version of Angular (as of this publication date July 13, 2020) is Angular 10. The angular seed project from Minko Gechev is now deprecated as shown below, however it can be useful to examine the various tools and libraries it utilizes.

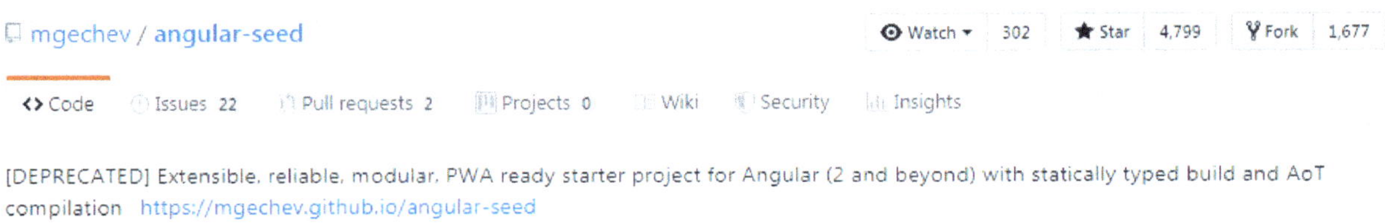

The angular-seed project from Mink Gechev.

For this exercise, you will clone a simple Angular-seed project.

Step 1 Using the node.js command prompt, navigate to your root drive. Use the following command:

```
c:\
```

Step 2 Clone the seed project into your project folder. The - - depth 1 ensures that git will copy only the latest revision of everything in the repository as opposed to every revision of every file commit. This step will result in a newly created folder in your root drive named "angular-seed."

```
git clone -b chapter-3 --depth 1
https://github.com/kevinruse/angular-v10-seed.git
```

Step 3 Change directory into the angular-seed directory created during the clone command in Step 4.

```
cd angular-v10-seed
```

Step 4 Install npm package dependencies used by the seed project (which are stored in the package.json config file) via npm.

```
npm install
```

If necessary execute `npm audit fix`.

For a fast install, use yarn with the command shown below. First, you will have to install yarn for windows from https://yarnpkg.com/en/docs/install.

```
yarn install
```

Step 5 Launch the sample application using the command shown below. This may take time as the project starts up.

```
npm start
```

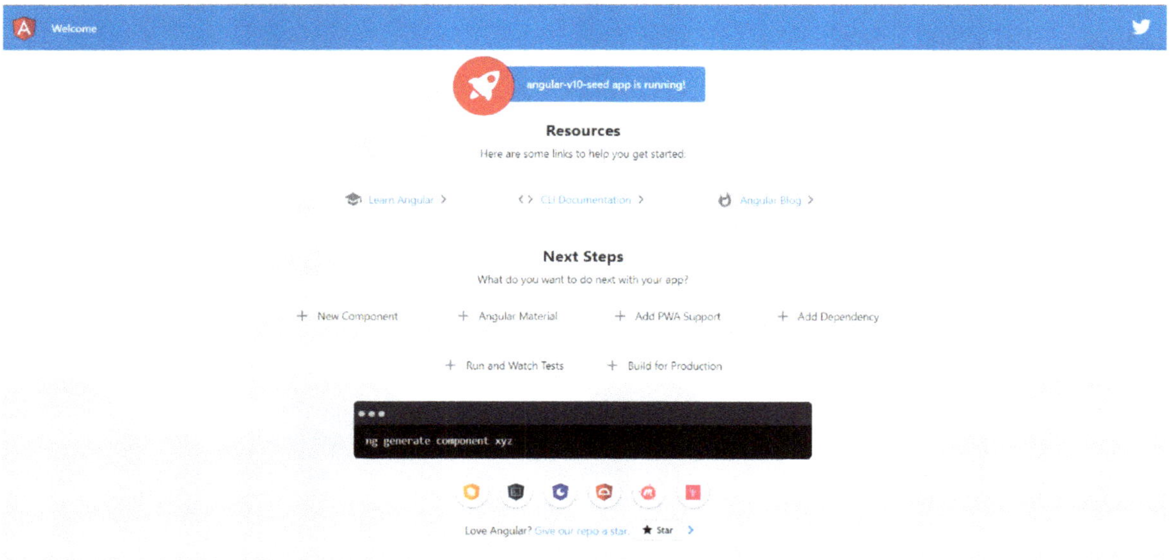

Step 6 To see the application as shown above, launch a web browser and enter the URL: http://localhost:5200.
Step 7 In the Chrome web browser, open the Angular extension and confirm the version of Angular is 10.x.x.

3.2 The Angular-CLI

The Angular-CLI tool is a command line interface used to build Angular applications. In addition to scaffolding the application, the CLI tool also automates the building of Angular constructs such as controllers, directives and others. The tool uses a prescribed methodology for creating development and release builds of your application. It includes a predefined set of tools including Webpack, Broccoli, Karma, Jasmine and others. It supports CoffeeScript, Less, Stylus and Compass. The CLI tool has enhanced functionality for building Angular applications that include additional syntax and JavaScript files.

The Angular-CLI tool can be found at https://github.com/angular/angular-cli
Some of the CLI commands are shown in the screenshot below.

Command Overview

COMMAND	ALIAS	DESCRIPTION
add		Adds support for an external library to your project.
analytics		Configures the gathering of Angular CLI usage metrics. See https://angular.io/cli/usage-analytics-gathering.
build	b	Compiles an Angular app into an output directory named dist/ at the given output path. Must be executed from within a workspace directory.
config		Retrieves or sets Angular configuration values in the angular.json file for the workspace.
deploy		Invokes the deploy builder for a specified project or for the default project in the workspace.
doc	d	Opens the official Angular documentation (angular.io) in a browser, and searches for a given keyword.
e2e	e	Builds and serves an Angular app, then runs end-to-end tests using Protractor.
generate	g	Generates and/or modifies files based on a schematic.

Figure #2: The AngularCLI webpage https://angular.io/cli

From https://angular.io/cli#command-overview

Warning: These tools can and do change frequently, so commands and their behavior may change.

3.2.1 Additional Angular CLI commands

For a complete list of commands and further documentation visit https://angular.io/cli.

`ng new`	Create a new Angular application
`ng serve`	To run the application in the browser
`ng test`	Run unit tests with karma
`ng e2e`	Run end-to-end tests with protractor
`ng get`	Gets values for project
`ng set`	Sets values for project
`ng version`	Get the version of the CLI
`ng lint`	Run codelyzer to analyze code
`ng doc`	Generate docs for your project
`ng eject`	Get access to the webpack configuration files

3.2.2 Angular CLI ng generate options

`--flat`	Don't create the code in its own directory. Files will be added to the current directory.
`--route=<route>`	Specify the parent route (for generating components and routes).
`--skip-router-generation`	Don't create the route config. (for generating routes).
`--default`	The generated route is a default route.
`--lazy`	Specify if route is lazy (default = true).
`--inline-template`	Generates components with inline templates; template markup is generated in the component, not it a separate file.
`--inline-style`	Generates components with inline styles; css is not generated in a separate file.
`--minimal`	Generates a minimal project with inline templates and styles and no test files.
`--spec false`	Generates components without unit testing "spec" files.

3.2.3 Angular CLI ng new options

`--directory`	Specifies the directory the project will be created in.
`--style`	The default extension for files responsible for styling.
	Possible values: css, scss, less, sass, (default = app)
`--prefix`	The prefix to use for all component selectors (default: app)
`--routing`	Generate a routing module (default = false)

3—Guided Exercise: Build a new Angular Application with the Angular CLI tool

Introduction

An alternative to using the Angular Quickstart seed project is the Angular CLI tool. In addition to starting your project, the CLI tool may be used during development as well. Using commands like `ng generate`, you can create many of Angular structures, including components, routes, directives, pipes and more. In addition, the Angular CLI provides commands for creating a build, running unit tests, linting code, preprocessing CSS and more. In this exercise, you will install and use the Angular CLI tool (version 1.7.1 at publication time) to scaffold an Angular application.

Note When executing these commands in the IDE (WebStorm or Visual Studio Code) first, start a new project instance. Thus you will have two IDE windows open throughout class. One for the seed project and one for the following project called FoodPlate.

Step 1 Launch a node.js command prompt and navigate to your root drive with the following command:

```
cd c:\
```

Step 2 Check if you have already installed the Angular CLI tool by typing the command below. The version compatible with this course is 10.0.3.

```
ng --version
```

If the angular-cli tool is NOT installed, follow the instructions below to install it.

A. Install the Angular CLI tool with a global install (`-g` denotes the global install).

```
npm install -g @angular/cli@10.0.3
```

If the angular-cli tool is installed, follow the instructions below to upgrade to the new package @angular/cli.

B. Remove the previous version by typing the commands below.

```
npm uninstall -g angular-cli
npm cache verify
npm install -g @angular/cli@10.0.3
```

C. If you are unable to successfully uninstall your previous version of angular-cli, you may need to perform the install as an administrator. If you still have problems uninstalling, see the following stack overflow for viable solutions: https://stackoverflow.com/questions/39566257/how-to-uninstall-angular-cli

Step 3 To see a list of possible cli commands type:

```
ng -help
```

Step 4 Generate an Angular project called foodPlate-cli

```
ng new foodPlate-cli
```

You will receive prompts to create the new application. Use the responses below.

Would you like to Add routing? N

Which stylesheet format would you like to use? CSS

Step 5 Change directory to "foodPlate-cli"

```
cd foodPlate-cli
```

Step 7 Serve the application using the command below. The - - open will open Chrome and run the application.

```
ng serve --open
```

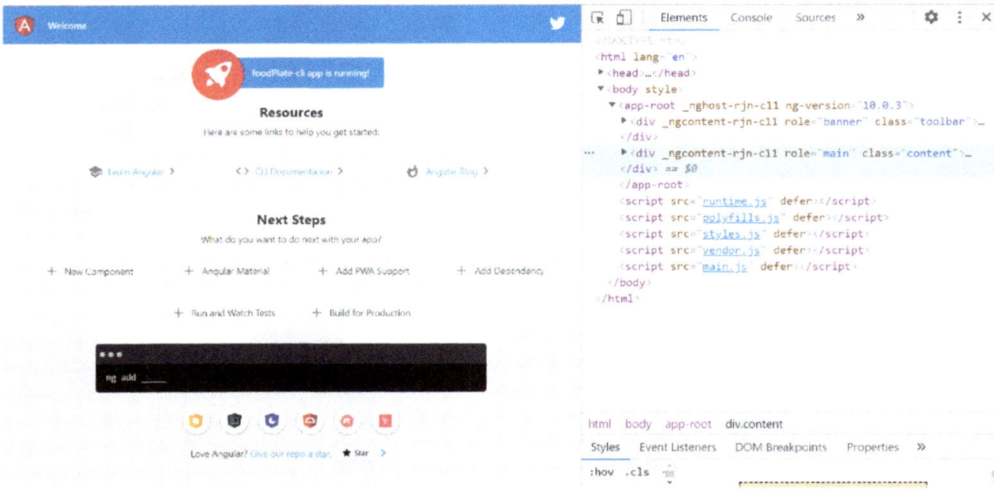

The CLI-generated Angular application running on localhost port 4200.

Your application should now be running at http://localhost:4200. You can check the version of Angular by inspecting the code as shown in the image on the right.

Step 7 Make a new project in your IDE (WebStorm or similar) using the "foodPlate-cli" folder as the root directory of the project.

Step 8 Make a second project in your IDE using the foodPlate-seed folder as the root directory of the project.

Note You will keep both projects open throughout the course.

1 – Practice Exercise: Build a practice project

Step 1 Open the CLI to make a "practice" project to experiment with throughout the class.

Step 2 Name the new project "angular-playground" and save it at a location of your choice.

Chapter 3 Quiz

https://tinyurl.com/uuas9q9

1) True/False The Angular Seed project is located at Github.

2) As of this publication date the fastest way to install dependencies with the seed project is?

   a. Yarn
   b. Npm
   c. Originally, Yarn was typically faster, now it is npm
   d. You must test for the most accurate results.

3) Write the Angular-CLI command for making a new Class called FoodItem

____

Chapter summary

The Angular Quickstart Seed project serves as a starting point for local development. Alternatively, developers can use the Angular CLI tool which provides code generation commands. In addition, to the CLI and the Quickstart Seed tools, many IDE's provide direct access to these tools from their user interface. Explore your IDE's project settings for more information.

Angular applications may be built using:

- Angular Tools
  - Angular Seed project
  - Angular CLI Tool
- Manually using:
  - Code editors
    - Sublime
    - Visual Studio Code
    - Brackets
    - Atom
- Integrated Development Environments with Angular Tooling
  - Microsoft Visual Studio
  - JetBrains WebStorm
  - Visual Studio Code

Homework

Step 1 Refer to the following website for a comparison of Integrated Development Environments for building Angular applications. https://jaxenter.com/angular-2-intellij-netbeans-eclipse-128461.html

Note The article was written with Angular 2 in mind, however, most of the features of the various IDE's have been updated to support the latest version of Angular.

Next Chapter

In this chapter, you built an Angular application but didn't really write any code. Throughout the remainder of this course, you will be writing Angular code and building a web application. It is important to understand the code that was generated in this chapter's exercises. In the next chapter, you will examine and understand the code generated by both the Angular Seed project and the Angular CLI tool. You will understand the basic constructs of Angular applications, how they are bootstrapped and how they work.

Chapter 4
Understanding Angular Architecture

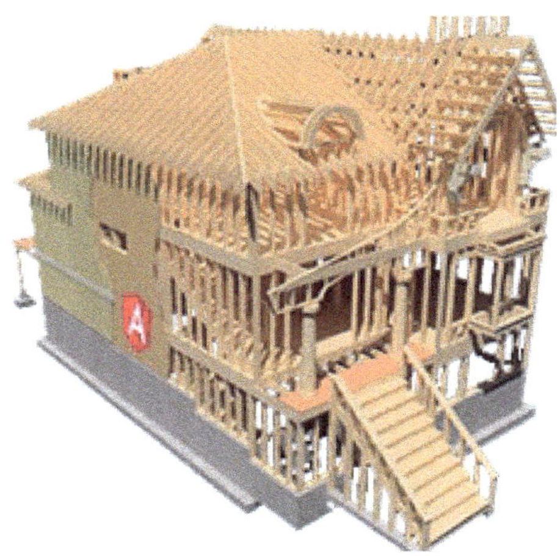

Chapter 4: Understanding Angular Architecture

Objectives

- List the seven keys to Angular
- Define a template as used by Angular
- Define the role of "template strings" as used in Angular
- Describe an Angular component
- Describe the role of modules in Angular
- Define a decorator
- Scaffold an Angular application
- Write an Angular applications app module file with Typescript

Introduction

Angular as a platform includes many structures and constructs in addition to implementing a variety of web application concepts. This introductory course will focus on the "Seven keys to Angular" shown below. This chapter specifically covers modules, templates and components at an introductory level. These topics will get more advanced coverage later in the course as will the remaining topics: databinding, structural directives, services and dependency injection. This chapter begins by defining an Angular application.

The Seven Keys to Angular

- Modules
- Components
- Templates
- Databinding
- Structural directives
- Services
- Dependency injection

4.0 What is an Angular application?

Put simply, an Angular application is a tree of components. These components are comprised of a compilation of templates that are managed by component classes. Angular's application logic is written inside of services. Services, components and other structures are boxed inside of modules. Let's start with components.

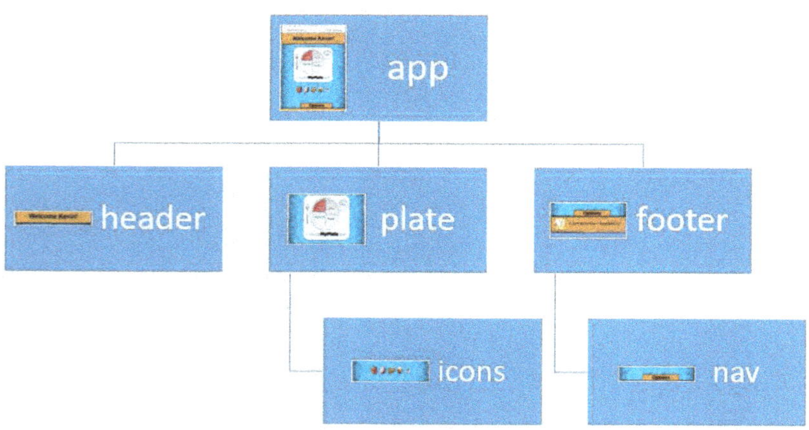

Figure #3: An Angular tree of components.

4.1 What is a component?

Remember that Angular is basically a tree of components. A component is simply a part or piece of your application. Components may be optimized for reuse. They can be generic buttons or tabbed panels that can be repurposed with appropriate labels for each use case. Components are meant to be composable such that large components may be composed of smaller components.

Figure #4: An example of components. (https://login.mailchimp.com/)

4.1.1 The root component

At the root of this tree of components is the application component which is itself a component. This is the component that bootstraps the application, and it is composed of the other components in your application. It is customary to name this component class: AppComponent. The components below the root component have a parent/child relationship. When Angular bootstraps an application, it renders the root component and all its children. Likewise, down the ancestor chain of components.

The Augury Chrome Extension

The Augury Chrome extension is an open-source collaboration effort between Google and Rangle.io. Augury helps developers visualize the application's component trees and structure and serves as a visual debugging tool.
The extension can be installed from https://augury.angular.io/.

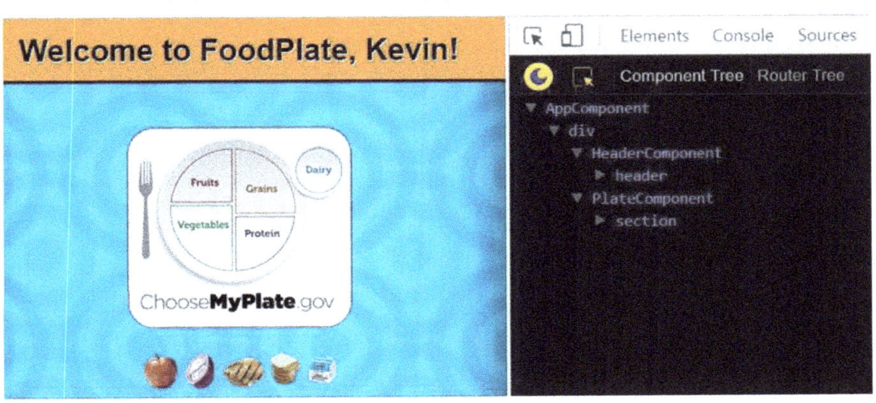

Figure #5: The Augury Chrome extension showing the applications' tree of components.

4.1.2 The component file

The component file begins by importing the necessary Angular core "Component" package. Any other files required by this component would be imported here as well. Below the import statements, the component is created. It is composed of two sections: a decorator and an exported class, but what is a decorator?

4.1.3 What's a decorator?

A decorator is just a function that modifies a JavaScript class from outside the class. You will learn more about decorators in Chapter 6 Understanding Components.

```
export interface ComponentDecorator {
    /**
     * @whatItDoes Marks a class as an Angular component and collects component configuration
     * metadata.
     *
     * @howToUse
     *
     * {@example core/ts/metadata/metadata.ts region='component'}
     *
     * @description
     * Component decorator allows you to mark a class as an Angular component and provide additional
     * metadata that determines how the component should be processed, instantiated and used at
     * runtime.
     *
     * Components are the most basic building block of an UI in an Angular application.
     * An Angular application is a tree of Angular components.
     * Angular components are a subset of directives. Unlike directives, components always have
     * a template and only one component can be instantiated per an element in a template.
     *
     * A component must belong to an NgModule in order for it to be usable
     * by another component or application. To specify that a component is a member of an NgModule,
     * you should list it in the `declarations` field of that NgModule.
     *
```

Figure #6: A snippet from the Angular ComponentDecorator interface

The `@Component()` decorator function is passed a configuration object that includes two very commonly used properties: `selector` and `template`.

The `selector` property's value is a CSS selector that identifies the element, attribute or class that will serve as the custom component. Selector's typically become custom elements. Custom elements are demonstrated in Chapter 6: Understanding Angular Components.

The `template` property's value is the HTML fragment that provides the component's view and is injected into the HTML Document Object Model (DOM). The `template` property's value may be expressed in a single quoted line of HTML or a multi-line HTML snippet enclosed in backticks (`). The template is closely related to HTML template strings. (For a closer look at the template string, see the HTML Template Strings demonstration on the next page.) The `template` property can be exchanged for a `templateUrl` property. The value of the `templateUrl` property is the URL for an .html file that contains the HTML fragment.

4.2 What is an HTML template?

An HTML template is a snippet or fragment of HTML. It is the view referenced by a component.

Figure #7: The HTML template shown inside of the class file that creates a component.

2 – Demo (optional) HTML Template Strings

Template strings, now known as template literals, may contain placeholders for variables using the `$ { }` syntax. See the examples below.

Declaring a variable that holds a string plus two variables:

```
var message = "Hello " + name + ". Your password is " + password + "."
```

Declaring the same variable as above using template string aka template literal:

```
var message = `Hello ${name}. Your password is ${password}.`
```

Step 1 Open the demo file template-strings.html in your IDE and run it in a web browser.

Step 2 Using your web browser, check out the support chart indicating the support for template-strings. The URL is http://kangax.github.io/compat-table/es6/#test-template_literals.

Step 3 Using your IDE examine the script block on the page (shown below).

```
<script>
    let firstName = 'Kevin';
    let lastName = 'Ruse';
    let fullName = `<div>
                        <h1>My name is: </h1>
                        <h1>${firstName} ${lastName} </h1>
                    </div>`;
    document.querySelector('#tmpl').innerHTML = fullName;
</script>
```

JavaScript showing the use of a template string.

Step 4 Note the use of the back ticks as well as the embedded expressions enclosed in curly braces.

References:

https://developer.mozilla.org/en-US/docs/Web/JavaScript/Reference/Template_literals
http://www.ecma-international.org/ecma-262/6.0/#sec-template-literal-lexical-components

4.3 What is a module?

In an earlier section titled "What is an Angular application?" it was noted that "Services, components and other structures are boxed inside of modules." It's time to understand modules. A module is a feature of your application.

Figure #8: A module of the MailChimp application: the login screen. (https://login.mailchimp.com/)

A broader definition of a module might include a set of features (such as the login shown above which includes the sign up as well. Modules can also hold a workflow within your application, or simply, a closely related set of application capabilities. Ultimately, a module is a class file that contains the code that implements this feature or functionality. It is an exclusive block of code dedicated to functionality that has been modularized by the developer.

Like a component, the module is created with a decorator function called `@NgModule()`. The module file also exports the module class similar to the way the component file exports the component class.

Consider the example above: the login feature. It includes several components: the form and its buttons, the logo and the sign-up link. It also includes outside services like the authorization and sign-up processes (perhaps using Twitter and Facebook sign-in options). In addition, it includes functionality like form validation and keeping the user logged in. You may combine all the code needed to implement this feature inside of an Angular module. Thus, you have a bundle of TypeScript objects that together comprise a feature, a workflow and so on.

Angular modules are not the same modules that are used in ECMAScript 6. ES6 modules are a code organization implementation that contain single files that include different imported and exported code that are ultimately combined via a module loader. Angular modules, on the other hand include various Angular constructs such as components, pipes, services and directives. Angular modules serve to organize the entire application, while ES6 modules organize our JavaScript code and make it more reusable.

4.3.1 The application root module

Every Angular application must have a root module (used to bootstrap the application). This module is typically name AppModule. Angular itself is organized by modules which include:

- FormsModule
- HttpModule
- RouterModule
- And more

Third-party libraries are also available as modules, including:

- Material Design (a UI framework)
- AngularFire2 (a Firebase (cloud-hosted NoSQL DB) library)
- And more

4.3.2 How do modules work?

A module declares which components belong to the module (as well as directives and pipes to be learned later). It imports other modules with the components needed by the current module, and it provides services to be used by application components (services will be addressed later in the course). Below is an example of an AppModule class.

A module:

- Imports other modules needed by the current module (classes that you need to reference in this module's components templates)
- Declares components that belong to the module

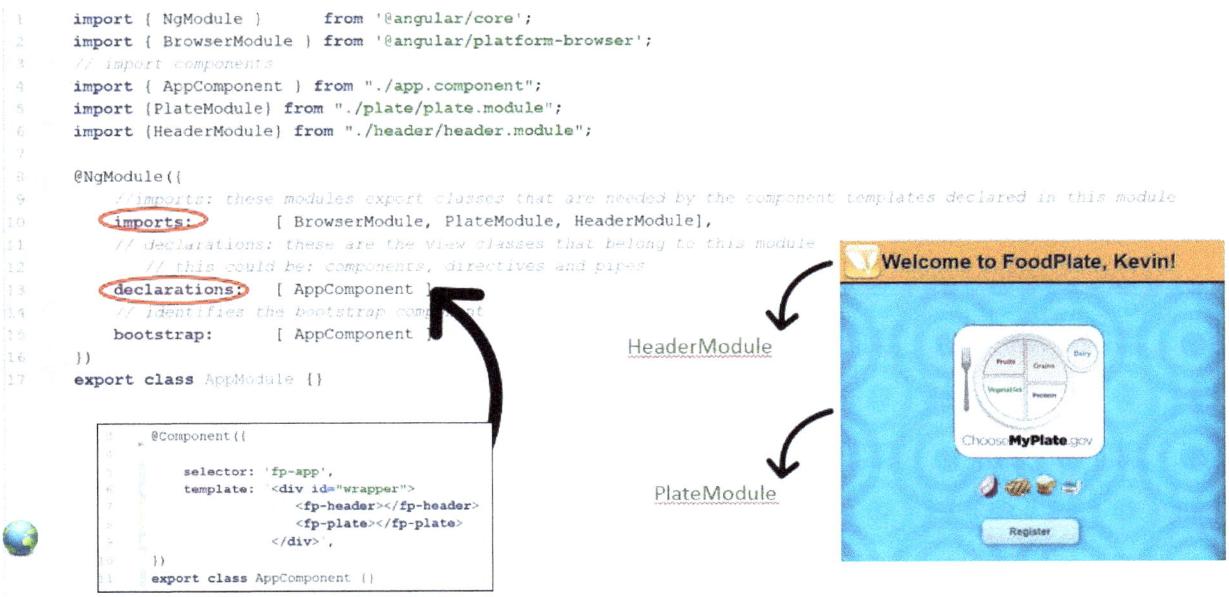

Figure #9: An AppModule example.

A module consists of three main sections:

1. Import statements (that import the modules necessary to the class)
2. The `@NgModule()` function (aka decorator or annotation*)
3. The exported class

*For more information about the difference between an annotation and decorator visit:
http://blog.thoughtram.io/angular/2015/05/03/the-difference-between-annotations-and-decorators.html

4.3.3 The@NgModule() decorator

Property	Description
`declarations`	the *view classes* that belong to this module. Angular has three kinds of view classes: components, directives, and pipes.
`exports`	the subset of declarations that should be visible and usable in the component templates of other modules.
`imports`	other modules whose exported classes are needed by component templates declared in *this* module.
`providers`	creators of services that this module contributes to the global collection of services; they become accessible in all parts of the app.
`bootstrap`	the main application view, called the *root component*, that hosts all other app views. Only the *root module* should set this bootstrap property.

Module summary

Modules

- Express the features of an application in a separate file
- Imported other required modules
- Declare the components required by the module
- Consist of:
- An `@NgModule()` function [annotation/decorator]
- Declares the required components
- Imports necessary modules
- If necessary, assigns a bootstrap component
- An exported class

4—Guided Exercise: Building the app module

In this exercise, you create the module that will bootstrap the application. Angular does not bootstrap from a component, but instead uses a module that points to the component that loads at bootstrap. This file is named app.module.ts. NOTE: you will not make a practice of deleting generated files either in class or in production. This is a one-time operation in class to help better familiarize yourself with the structure and architecture of Angular applications.

Step 1 Using your IDE return to the angular-v10-seed project you created earlier.
If necessary, create a project in your IDE first that points to the angular-seed directory.

Step 2 Delete the following files created from the `git clone` of the Angular seed project:

- angular-seed/src/app/app.module.ts
- angular-seed/src/app/app.component.ts
- angular-seed/src/app/app.component.html
- angular-seed/src/app/app.component.css

Note While it might seem redundant to delete and recreate files, it is important to type these files manually at least once. Ultimately you will rely on Angular's code generation tools to create this and other files. This guided exercise is to help reinforce and understand the Angular architecture.

After deleting the files and folders in step 2, the app will not compile or run in the browser. This is because it is missing its' main module: app.module.ts which is used to bootstrap the application when Angular compiles the application.

Step 3 Using a CLI, run the tests with the command: npm test. The relevant snippet of output is shown below.

```
[10:44:38] Starting 'build.js.dev'...
src\client\app\main.ts(12,27): error TS2307: Cannot find module './app.module'.
TypeScript: 1 semantic error
TypeScript: emit succeeded (with errors)
```

Step 4 Inside of src /app, create a new TypeScript file called app.module.ts file and import the necessary modules:

a. First come the import statements. Your IDE should implement code assist and generate the "`from 'some/module'`" code after you type the `import { Module }` statement. Because you are creating a module you will need to import the `@NgModule()` decorator function. Next, import the BrowserModule which is responsible for rendering the application in a web browser, as opposed to other runtimes.

b. This module will be using one component: the app.component, so you will import that as well. Notice the line break below separating that which is Angular code from that which is our source code. See Best Practice 1 on the following page for more information.

```
import { NgModule }       from '@angular/core';
import { BrowserModule } from '@angular/platform-browser';

import { AppComponent } from './app.component';
```

Best Practice 1: from: https://angular.io/guide/styleguide#style-03-06
Consider leaving one empty line between third party imports and application imports.
Consider listing import lines alphabetized by the module.
Why? The empty line separates your stuff from their stuff. Alphabetizing makes it easier to read and locate symbols.

Step 5 Call the @NgModule decorator function (aka annotation).

```
@NgModule()
```

Step 6 Pass to the NgModule function, the metadata object that tells Angular how to compile and launch the application and export the class "AppModule" (shown below in bold).

```
@NgModule({
            imports:      [ BrowserModule ],
            declarations: [ AppComponent ],
            bootstrap:    [ AppComponent ]
      })

export class AppModule {
}
```

Step 7 Try to compile the application via the command: `ng serve`.

Warning: We haven't built the app.component yet, therefore the application will not compile at this point. Your IDE may warn you that it cannot find module ./app.component.

Metadata object notes:

Every browser-based application must import the BrowserModule because it adds any web related features required by an application that runs in a web browser (a web application).

The following steps will be covered later in the course.

- Import the modules that export classes needed by the component templates declared in this module.
- Declare the view classes, directives and pipes and providers that will be used by this module. In other words, declare all the components we want to make available to this module.
- Identify the component that will bootstrap this application. This creates the component and inserts it into the browser DOM.

Notes to remember about modules:

1. JavaScript imports at the top of the file provide access to properties and methods exported by other files so you can reference them from the current module.
2. The imported modules (in the metadata object) are used when features of the module are required by the current module.
3. Only modules go in the imports array.
4. The declarations array (in the metadata object) are used to tell Angular which components belong to the module as well as pipes and directives, both of which will be covered in a subsequent chapter.

2 – Practice Exercise: Understanding the AppModule

Write the app.module.ts module using the screenshot of the application below.

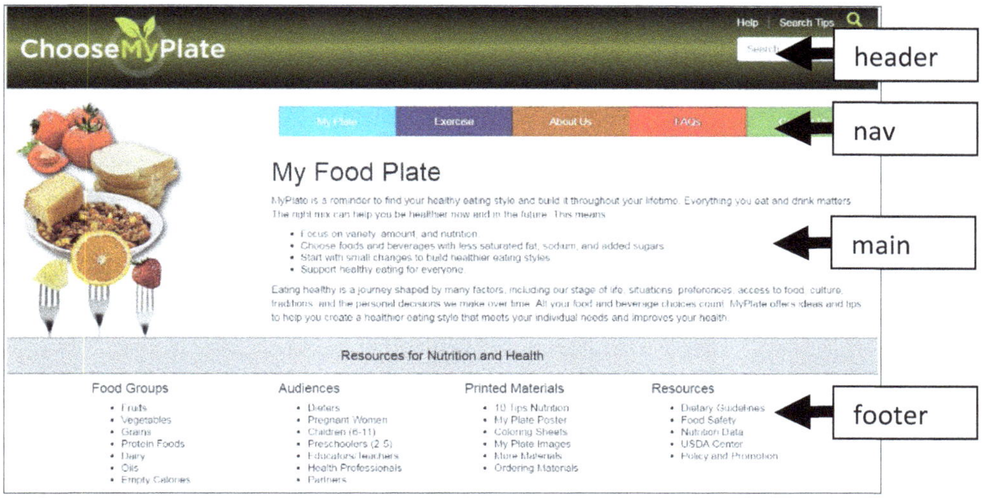

A sample web application for building the app.module.ts file.

Note: You are not building the entire application, just the app.module. Use the graphic above to get a sense of the modules and components the application will require.

Hints: Every Angular application has an application module and an application component.
Refer to the guides on the following pages for naming conventions and best practices.

Step 1 Fill in the missing files in the sample directories below.

src
—app
____
____
____
____
—header
____
____
____
____
—nav
____
____
____
____
—main
____
____
____
____

—footer

____

____

____

____

Step 2 Using your IDE or code editor, open the file "practice/app.module.practice.ts" and fill in the missing code.

```
import { ________________ } from '@angular/core';
import { ________________ } from '@angular/platform-browser';

import { ________________ } from './footer/footer.module';
import { ________________ } from './header/header.module';
import { ________________ } from './main/main.module';
import { ________________ } from './nav/nav.module';


import { ________________ }  from './app.component';

@NgModule({
    imports:       [________________________________________________  ],
    declarations:  [__________,__________,__________,__________,__________,],
    bootstrap:     [________________  )
})
export class AppModule { }
```

A sample finished file is provided, called app.module.practice.ts. It appears on page 50.

When building large enterprise applications creating a folder structure that scales well while maintaining best practices can be challenging. There are many folder options and many developers have blogged about what works for them. The key is that each solution should at least follow the following basic two guidelines:

- Structure the app such that you can locate code quickly
- Have a near-term view of implementation and a long-term vision

With this in mind, consider the following options:

- A single folder for all services
- A page-based approach
- A core folder for universal components and features
- Separating container components from presentation components

Here are a few articles that provide some suggestions for folder structure in Angular projects:

- https://itnext.io/choosing-a-highly-scalable-folder-structure-in-angular-d987de65ec7
- https://medium.com/@motcowley/angular-folder-structure-d1809be95542
- https://www.tektutorialshub.com/angular/angular-folder-structure-best-practices/

Consider the following best practices when naming your modules and components.

Best Practice 2: from https://angular.io/guide/styleguide#style-02-12
Do append the symbol name with the suffix Module.
Do give the file name the .module.ts extension.
Do name the module after the feature and folder it resides in.
Why? Provides a consistent way to quickly identify and reference modules. Upper camel case is conventional for identifying objects that can be instantiated using a constructor. Easily identifies the module as the root of the same named feature.
Best Practice 3: https://angular.io/guide/styleguide#style-04-08
Do create an Angular module in the app's root folder (e.g., in /src/app).
Why? Every app requires at least one root Angular module.
Consider naming the root module app.module.ts.
Why? Makes it easier to locate and identify the root module.
Best Practice 4: https://angular.io/guide/styleguide#style-04-09
Do create an Angular module for all distinct features in an application (e.g. Heroes feature).
Do place the feature module in the same named folder as the feature area (example: app/heroes).
Do name the feature module file reflecting the name of the feature area and folder (e.g. app/heroes/heroes.module.ts)
Do name the feature module symbol reflecting the name of the feature area, folder, and file (e.g. app/heroes/heroes.module.ts defines HeroesModule)
Why? A feature module can expose or hide its implementation from other modules.
Why? A feature module identifies distinct sets of related components that comprise the feature area.
Why? A feature module can easily be routed to both eagerly and lazily.
Why? A feature module defines clear boundaries between specific functionality and other application features.
Why? A feature module helps clarify and make it easier to assign development responsibilities to different teams.
Why? A feature module can easily be isolated for testing.

Consider the application scaffold when naming files and assigning them to directories. Use the following best practices as a guide.

Best Practice 5: https://angular.io/guide/styleguide#style-04-06
Do start small but keep in mind where the app is heading down the road.
Do have a near term view of implementation and a long-term vision.
Do put all the app's code in a folder named src.
Consider creating a folder for a component when it has multiple accompanying files (.ts, .html, .css and .spec.ts).
Why? Helps keep the app structure small and easy to maintain in the early stages, while being easy to evolve as the app grows.
Why? Components often have four files (e.g. *.html, *.css, *.ts, and *.spec.ts) and can clutter a folder quickly.

See the following page for an example of a compliant file and folder structure taken from the John Papa style guide at https://angular.io/guide/styleguide#style-04-06.

```
<project root>
  src
    app
      core
        core.module.ts
        exception.service.ts|spec.ts
        user-profile.service.ts|spec.ts
      heroes
        hero
          hero.component.ts|html|css|spec.ts
        hero-list
          hero-list.component.ts|html|css|spec.ts
        shared
          hero-button.component.ts|html|css|spec.ts
          hero.model.ts
          hero.service.ts|spec.ts
        heroes.component.ts|html|css|spec.ts
        heroes.module.ts
        heroes-routing.module.ts
      shared
        shared.module.ts
        init-caps.pipe.ts|spec.ts
        text-filter.component.ts|spec.ts
        text-filter.service.ts|spec.ts
      villains
```

A sample solution for: app.module.practice.ts

```
import { BrowserModule } from '@angular/platform-browser';
import { NgModule }       from '@angular/core';

import { FooterModule } from './footer/footer.module';
import { HeaderModule } from './header/header.module';
import { MainModule } from './main/main.module';
import { NavModule } from './nav/nav.module';

import { AppComponent }  from './app.component';

@NgModule({
    imports:      [ BrowserModule, FooterModule, HeaderModule, MainModule , NavModule],
    declarations: [ AppComponent ],
    bootstrap:    [ AppComponent ]
})
export class AppModule { }
```

alternatively

```
import { BrowserModule } from '@angular/platform-browser';
import { NgModule }       from '@angular/core';

import { AppComponent }  from './app.component';

@NgModule({
    imports:      [ BrowserModule ],
   declarations: [ AppComponent, FooterComponent, HeaderComponent, MainComponent, NavComponent ],
    bootstrap:    [ AppComponent ]
})
export class AppModule { }
```

5–Guided Exercise: Use the CLI to create app.module.ts

Note This exercise uses the app you've been building with the CLI tool. Be sure to open and start the application.

Step 1 Open a node.js command prompt and change directory to foodPlate-cli. If using WebStorm, open the WebStorm terminal from the main menu bar View → Tool Windows → Terminal or press alt + F12. If using VS Code, you can open a new terminal via the main menu: Terminal → New Terminal or the keyboard command: CONTROL + SHIFT + `. You can rename terminals in both WebStorm and VS Code. In WebStorm, simply double-click the terminal tab and type the new name. In VS Code, activate the terminal and type: CONTROL + SHIFT + P and start typing "terminal: rename" and select that option and rename the active terminal.

Step 2 Delete app.module.ts using your IDE, file system or the command line. If you are using your IDE, right-click the file and choose "delete." Be sure to delete only the file shown below in bold.

foodPlate-cli/src/app/**app.module.ts**

If the app is running, switching back to the browser should now show an error about missing app.module.ts. We now have something to fix and get working again!

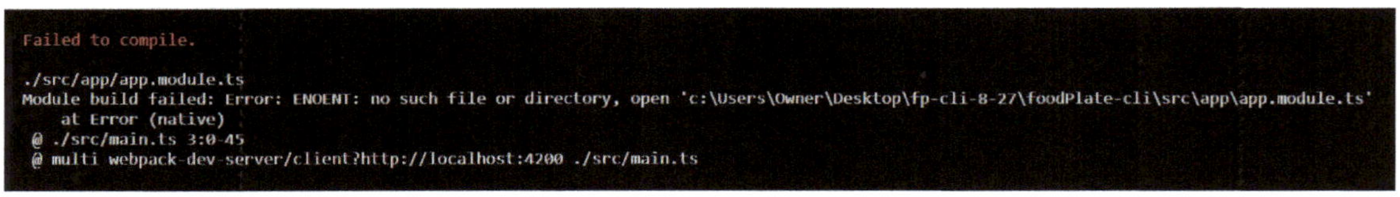

The deleted app.module.ts (shown for reference)

```
import { BrowserModule } from '@angular/platform-browser';
import { NgModule } from '@angular/core';

import { AppComponent } from './app.component';

@NgModule({
  declarations: [
    AppComponent
  ],
  imports: [
    BrowserModule
  ],
  providers: [],
  bootstrap: [AppComponent]
})
export class AppModule { }
```

Note If you would like to see what files the cli will create and/or modify, you can use the - -dry-run flag. This will prevent the command from executing and instead, will list the files that will be created or affected by the command.

Step 3 Using the following command to generate an app module TypeScript file.

```
ng generate module app --flat
```

The `--flat` option will prevent the code from being created in its own directory.

Note The CommonModule is imported and added imports array in the app.module. Be sure to confirm.

Refer to the browser window (keep the DevTools console open) after each remaining step is completed and you should see the application error messages appear and then go away after the issue is resolved.

Step 4 Open the newly generated app.module and confirm the CLI has added the BrowserModule to the imports array.

Step 5 If necessary, in the IDE, add an import statement that imports the BrowserModule (The CLI may add the import statement for you after step 3). The BrowserModule is imported from @angular/platform-browser.

```
import { BrowserModule } from '@angular/platform-browser';
import { CommonModule } from '@angular/common';

@NgModule({
  imports: [
    BrowserModule, CommonModule
  ],
...
```

Step 6 Confirm the CLI has added the AppComponent to the declarations array. You may have to declare this manually.

Step 7 Confirm the CLI has imported the AppComponent. You may have to import this manually.

Step 8 Add the bootstrap property and assign the AppComponent to the bootstrap property.

Note Due to changes in the bootstrap file, you may have to restart the development server via the command `ng serve` to restart the application.

Step 9 Check the browser, to confirm the application runs successfully. Open the DevTools console in Chrome and confirm that there are no error messages.

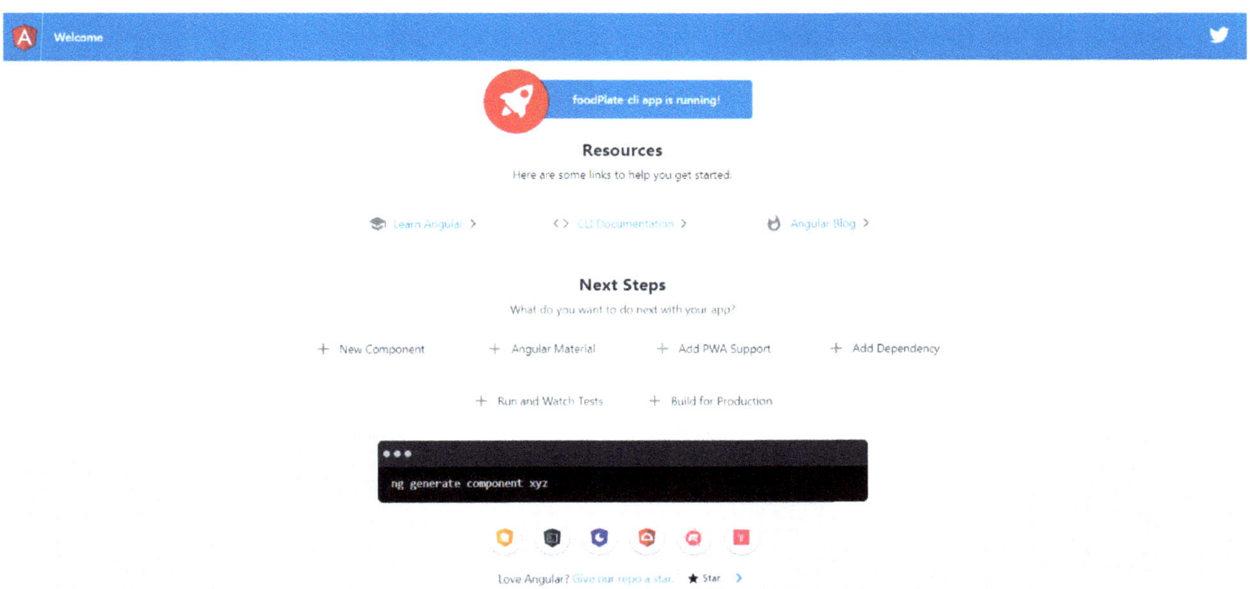

Finished exercise file

```
import { BrowserModule } from '@angular/platform-browser';
import { CommonModule } from '@angular/common';
import { NgModule } from '@angular/core';

import { AppComponent } from './app.component';

@NgModule({
  imports: [
    CommonModule, BrowserModule
  ],
  declarations: [AppComponent],
  bootstrap: [AppComponent]
})

export class AppModule { }
```

Homework Exercise

Step 1 Read the Angular Architecture section of the Angular documentation at https://angular.io/guide/architecture

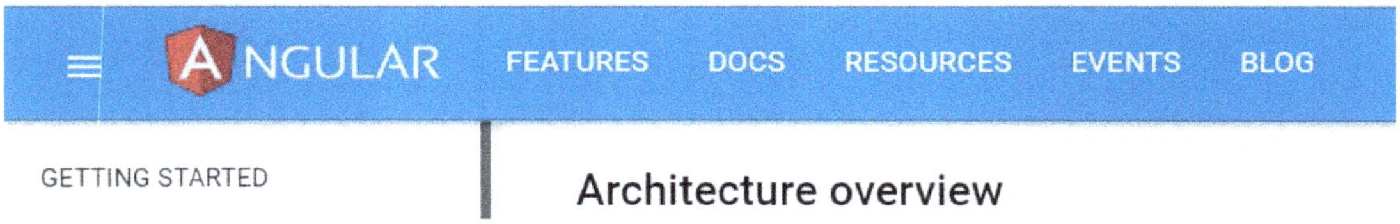

Chapter 4 Quiz

https://tinyurl.com/warjkbn

1) List the seven keys to Angular (try the online quiz at https://quizlet.com/_3kypqv)

   1. ______________________________
   2. ______________________________
   3. ______________________________
   4. ______________________________
   5. ______________________________
   6. ______________________________
   7. ______________________________

2) An Angular application is a tree of ______________________.

3) Angular code is organized in ___________________________.

4) What do developers typically name the root module of their application? ______________________________

5) What is a good name for the login component's template file? ______________________________

Chapter summary

Angular code is organized into cohesive, logical blocks of functionality called modules. Modules are created by class files that use the `@NgModule()` decorator function. All Angular applications have a root module called app.module.ts. that includes a property called "bootstrap" that tells Angular how to compile and run the application.

Modules also reference components. An Angular application is a tree of components. Developers create components by writing class files referenced from modules. The component class has two required properties: selector and template (or templateUrl). The template property's value is the components HTML view and the selector property's value is the custom element that renders the template.

Next Chapter

In the next chapter, components are explored in more depth.

Chapter 5
Understanding Components

Chapter 5: Understanding Components

Objectives

- Define an Angular component
- Describe the files that together, create an Angular Component
- Define a custom element
- Describe an Angular template
- Describe an Angular component
- Create an Angular component
- Define the templateUrl property

Introduction

Components are the building blocks of modern web applications. Components have been a part of the web since the Web Components API was introduced in July of 2014. Web Components were first introduced by Alex Russell at the Fronteers Conference in 2011. Browser implementation has come in the form of various APIs including Custom Elements, Shadow DOM, HTML imports and HTML templates. In 2013 Google introduced a JavaScript library (polyfill) for Web Components called Polymer. Angular uses aspects of all the above-mentioned APIs to construct its unique Component structure.

Recall that an Angular application is a tree of components. Components are the various pieces of our applications such as login screens, navigation, dialog boxes and so on. Components are often comprised of smaller components, such as buttons, links, icons and so on. From a developer's perspective, a component is a class file. In this section, you will understand components and how to build them following the best practices described in John Papa's style guide.

5.0 What is a component?

A component is simply a class file written using TypeScript (as in this course) or JavaScript or Dart. The TypeScript component is composed of two parts: import statements, followed by the component code. The component code is composed of two parts: the @Component decorator or annotation and the exported class.

A Component:

- **Is a class**
- **Imports `{Component}` from @angular/core library**
- **(1) Annotates (or decorates) with `@Component`**
- **(2) Exports a class**
- **Interacts with the view via class properties and methods (API)**

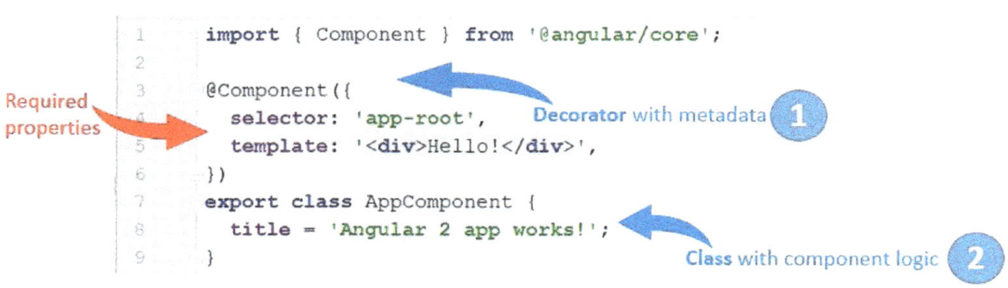

Figure #10: Breakdown of a component.

5.0.1 Component summary

Components:

- are the building blocks of modern web applications
- can render dynamic data
- can respond to user interactions
- can react to events
- are referenced from within modules
- consist of:
- an `@Component()` function (aka annotation or decorator)
- that contains a metadata object that provides:
- the view (html template)
- the html custom element that renders the view
- an exported class

3 – Demo (optional) Components

Step 1 Review the sample app.component code shown below with your instructor.

Step 2 Identify each line and review its purpose.

```
// imports angular Component class from the angular/core barrel
/* in other words: tell the compiler that "@angular/core" defines and
   exports an object that we need called Component; pull it in and
   make it available to this file */
import { Component } from '@angular/core';

/* @Component marks a class as an Angular component and collects
   component configuration metadata.*/
@Component({
  selector: 'my-app', //see custom-elements demo
  template: `<h1>Hello {{name}}</h1>`, //see template-strings demo
})

//export the class for use by the app code
export class AppComponent  {
  //provide properties and methods to the class
  name = 'Angular Components';
}
```

The selector property inside the @Component decorator is typically found in most component metadata. Its value is the name of the HTML custom element that will be used to reference this component. In this case `<my-app></my-app>`.

4 – Demo (optional) Custom Elements

Custom elements allow developers to create new types of HTML elements. It is closely related to the development of Web Components. The specification for writing custom elements includes version 0 and version 1. In this demonstration file, you examine both versions.

Step 1 Open the demo file customElements-v0.html in your IDE and run it in a web browser.

Step 2 Using your web browser, check out the support chart indicating the support for custom elements. The url is http://caniuse.com/#search=custom%20elements.

Step 3 Examine the JavaScript and discuss it with your instructor.

Step 4 Open the demo file custom-elements-v1.html in your IDE and run it in a web browser.

Step 5 Examine the JavaScript and discuss it with your instructor.

Step 6 Close all open files.

5.1 Understanding Angular Components

Modern web applications typically render components with using JavaScript in conjunction with HTML templates. Angular templates are specified via the component metadata using the template property or the templateUrl property. By using HTML templates directly, Angular provides a method (unlike JavaScript) that exposes the HTML so that it is immediately understood by code editors or integrated development environments that make use of code-assist (or intellisense). It can also be immediately understood by web designers and UX designers responsible for writing CSS.

6–Guided Exercise: Create the app component

In this exercise, you create the application component.

Note Begin this exercise by compiling the application in the IDE. Remember, it does not have an application component and therefore, should not compile.

Step 1 Return to the angular-seed project you created earlier and add an application component by creating a TypeScript file in the app directory and name it app.component.ts. You will not use the CLI tool for this exercise.

Step 2 Execute the following steps to create the app component.

- Import the component decorator class
- Call the decorator function @Component()
- Pass the decorator function a configuration option with the settings:
  - selector: 'app',
  - template: `<div><p>The app is working!</p></div>`
- Export the class

The finished file: app.component.ts

```
import { Component } from '@angular/core';

@Component({
    selector: 'app',
    template: `<div><p>The app is working!</p></div>`
})
export class AppComponent {}
```

Step 3 Open index.html and modify the code shown below in bold. This change references the new selector name: app.

```
<app>Loading…</app>
```

Return to the web browser to view the application. It should appear as shown below.

Note If you closed the application earlier, you may need to run the `npm start` command again.

The app is working!

The application shown in the web browser after completing the new app component.

Step 4 In preparations for the next exercise, copy the assets folder from the angular-class-files/foodPlate-cli-files to the foodPlate-cli project's src directory. Notice that there is already an assets folder there, so you will overwrite it. Do the same copy and paste of the assets folder from the angular-class-files/angular-seed folder to the angular-v10-seed project's assets folder which will again be an overwrite of the existing assets folder.

1 –Challenge Exercise: Build a component for the seed application

In this exercise, you build a header component. Be sure to:

- Follow appropriate naming conventions for new files and new directories.
- Follow appropriate scaffolding structure for files and directories.

Simple Instructions

Use **one** of the following methods to create a new component:

1. **Manual approach** (recommended for this exercise only)
2. The **CLI approach**

1. <u>**Manual approach:**</u>
    - Create a folder to store the new component.
    - Create and name the component TypeScript file.
    - Use your IDE's code snippets to generate the file:
        - Webstorm: type `a-component` + tab
        - VS Code:type `a-component` + tab

2. <u>**CLI approach**</u>
    - Use the Angular CLI to create the folder and boilerplate code
    - With this approach you will not need to create a folder or any files; the CLI will handle that for you.

Component Details

- Use the following template content:

```
`<header>
    <h1>Welcome to Angular Seed!</h1>
</header>`
```

- Use the selector: `'app-header'`
- Add an image element to the header html and use the seed-icon.png image as shown below in bold.

```
<header>
    <img src="assets/images/icons/seed-icon.png" alt="">
    <h1>Welcome to Angular Seed!</h1>
</header>
```

- Add the new header component to the app component.
- Add a new title to index.html: `<title>Sample Angular Seed Application</title>`
- Fix any errors that prevent Angular from compiling.

Step by Step Instructions

Hint: If you are using WebStorm or VS Code, use the following shortcuts:

- a-component + TAB (to expand the shortcut)
- You will have to edit the generated code as needed.

Alternatively, you can use the Angular CLI tool.

Step 1 Create a folder in src/app to store the header component files. If you use the Angular CLI tool, this folder will be automatically generated.

Step 2 Write a header component file with the following properties:

```
selector: 'app-header',
template: `<header>
               <h1>Welcome to Angular Seed!</h1>
           </header>`
```

Step 3 Don't forget to declare the header component in the app module.

Step 4 Add the new header component to the app component using the header component's selector property. Format the code on multiple lines and replace the single quote with a back tick as shown below in bold.

```
template: `<div>
                <app-header></app-header>
                <p>The app is working</p>
           </div>`
```

Step 5 To provide a page title, open index.html and modify the existing title element with the code shown below.

```
<title>Sample Angular Seed Application</title>
```

Note Throughout the course you will be working on two projects: the project created with the Angular Seed Project and the FoodPlate project created with the Angular CLI tool. To distinguish between the two, you will add a graphic in the header of each project. For the seed project: a seed graphic that represents the seed project and for the CLI project a CLI icon graphic. In a subsequent exercise, you will add the CLI icon graphic.

Step 6 Add an image element to the header html and use the seed-icon.png image as shown below in bold.

```
<header>
    <img src="assets/images/seed-icon.png" alt="">
    <h1>Welcome to Angular Seed!</h1>
</header>
```

Step 7 When completed, run the page in a web browser. It should match the screenshot below.

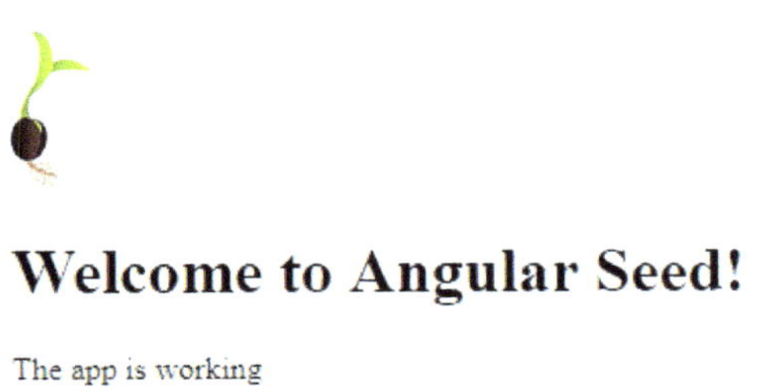

The finished practice exercise as shown in a web browser.

Possible solution code

header.component.ts

```
import { Component } from '@angular/core';

@Component({
    selector: 'app-header',
    template: `<header>
                <img src='assets/images/seed-icon.png'>
                <h1>Welcome to Angular Seed!</h1>
              </header>`
})

export class HeaderComponent {
    constructor() {
    }
}
```

app.component.ts

```
import { Component } from '@angular/core';

@Component({
    selector: 'app',
    template: `<div>
        <app-header></app-header>
        <p>The app is working!</p>
    </div>`
})
export class AppComponent {
}
```

app.module.ts

```
import { NgModule }      from '@angular/core';
import { BrowserModule } from '@angular/platform-browser';

import { AppComponent } from './app.component';
import { HeaderComponent } from './header/header.component';

@NgModule({
    imports:      [ BrowserModule ],
    declarations: [ AppComponent, HeaderComponent ],
    bootstrap:    [ AppComponent ]
})

export class AppModule {
}
```

When building the directory structure for components, consider the following best practices from the official Angular Style Guide by John Papa.

Best Practice 1: from: https://angular.io/guide/styleguide#style-04-06

Do start small but keep in mind where the app is heading down the road.
Do have a near term view of implementation and a long-term vision.
Do put all the app's code in a folder named src.
Consider creating a folder for a component when it has multiple accompanying files (.ts, .html, .css and .spec).
Why? Helps keep the app structure small and easy to maintain in the initial stages, while being easy to evolve as the app grows.
Why? Components often have four files (e.g. *.html, *.css, *.ts, and *.spec.ts) and can clutter a folder quickly.

2 –Challenge Exercise: Using the templateUrl property

In this exercise, you create a separate html file to hold the header component's HTML. You will be working in the Angular seed project.

Step 1 Create an HTML template file in the appropriate directory and name it header.component.html.

Step 2 Cut the HTML template from the header.component.ts file and paste it into the new header.component.html file.

Step 3 Verify header.component.html contains the code shown below.

```
<header>
    <img src="assets/images/seed-icon.png" alt="">
    <h1>Welcome to Angular Seed!</h1>
</header>
```

Step 4 Replace the header components' `template` property with a `templateUrl` property that points to the new header.component.html.

Step 5 Save your work and test it in a web browser.

3 –Challenge Exercise: Create a component with the Angular CLI tool

In this exercise, you create a module and component for the header using commands in the Angular CLI tool. You will be working in the foodPlate-cli project.

Step 1 Return to the foodPlate-cli project and open app.component.ts.

Step 2 First, change the app.component.ts file's selector to match the current naming system `<fp-` by modifying the existing app.component.ts file as shown below in bold. Then remove the code shown below with a strikethrough.

```
import { Component } from '@angular/core';

@Component({
          selector: 'fp-app',
          templateUrl: './app.component.html',
          styleUrls: ['./app.component.css']
          })
export class AppComponent {
          title = 'app';
}
```

Step 3 Modify index.html as shown below in bold and test the application in Chrome.

```
<body>
    <fp-app>Loading…</fp-app>
</body>
```

Step 4 Delete all the code in app.component.html and add the code shown below.

Hint: If you are using the Emmet plugin (https://emmet.io/), you can type:

`div#wrapper>fp-header+p{The app is working}` followed by the tab key.

```
<div id="wrapper">
   <fp-header></fp-header>
   <p>The app is working!</p>
</div>
```

Note Open a node.js command prompt or if you are using WebStorm or VSCode , open the built-in terminal.

Webstorm: from the main menu bar View → Tool Windows → Terminal or press alt + F1

VSCode: from the main menu bar Terminal → New Terminal or press control + shift + `

Step 5 Confirm the terminal directory is the project root directory: foodplate-cli .

Step 6 Use the Angular-cli command to create a component called "`header.component`".

```
ng g c header
```

Hint When writing the `generate` command, you can use the short `g` instead of `generate` and you can shorten `component` to `c`.

Note The generated header.component.ts file will add two methods: a constructor and ngOnInit. These are known as life cycle methods, and they will be addressed in a later chapter.

Step 7 Verify that the new header component has been declared in the app.module.ts file.

Step 8 While in the app.module.ts file, be sure to check your imports include:

```
import { BrowserModule } from '@angular/platform-browser';
import { CommonModule } from '@angular/common';
import { NgModule } from '@angular/core';
...
```

and you're @ngModule decorator includes:

```
@NgModule({
  imports: [
    BrowserModule, CommonModule
  ],
```

Step 9 Confirm your selector property is set in the header.component.ts file.

`selector` is `fp-header`

Hint You can change the default prefix of selectors from "app" to "fp" in the **angular.json** file which is in the application's root folder. To do so, open and modify the file as shown below in bold.

```
  "$schema": "./node_modules/@angular/cli/lib/config/schema.json",
  "version": 1,
  "newProjectRoot": "projects",
  "projects": {
    "foodPlate-cli": {
      "root": "",
      "sourceRoot": "src",
      "projectType": "application",
      "prefix": "fp",
      "schematics": {},
      "architect": {
        "build": {
          "builder": "@angular-devkit/build-angular:browser",
```

Step 10 Change the header.component.html file as shown below.

```
<header>
     <h1>Welcome to Your Food Plate!</h1>
</header>
```

Step 11 Copy the assets folder from the angular-class-files/foodPlate-cli-files to the foodPlate-cli project's src directory. Notice that there is already an assets folder there, so you will overwrite it.

Step 12 Run the application using the command below. If the dev-server is still running, you may need to stop it before running the command below.

```
ng serve
```

Note Throughout the course you will be working on two projects: the project created with the Angular Seed Project and the FoodPlate project created with the Angular CLI tool. To distinguish between the two, you will add a graphic to each project. For the seed project: a seed graphic that represents the seed project and for the CLI project a CLI icon graphic.

Step 13 Add the cli graphic as shown below in bold.

```
<header>
  <img src="assets/images/icons/cli-icon.png" alt="">
  <h1>Welcome to Food Plate!</h1>
</header>
```

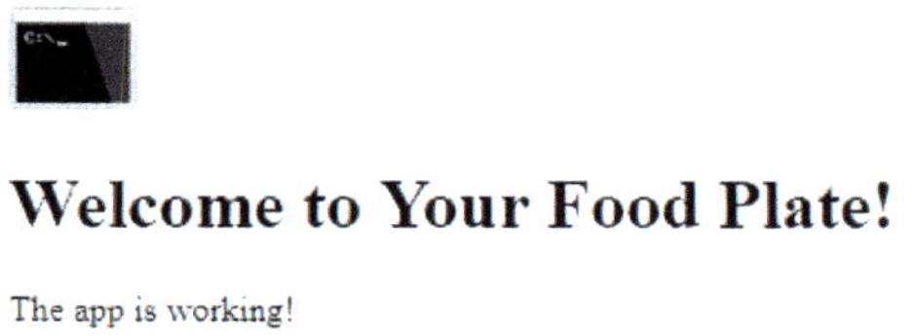

The finished exercise as seen in the browser.

Note Your IDE may display a tslint warning/error: "The selector of the component "AppComponent" should have prefix app." However, we would like to use the prefix "fp" You can remove this warning/error by opening the file called tslint.json and changing the line shown below from "app" to "fp" (changes are shown in bold).

```
    ...
    "extends": "../tslint.json",
    "rules": {
        "directive-selector": [
            true,
            "attribute",
            "fp",
            "camelCase"
        ],
        "component-selector": [
            true,
            "element",
            "fp",
            "kebab-case"
        ]
    }
```

Chapter 5 Quiz

https://tinyurl.com/rxwqwpw

1) Angular application code is organized into logical blocks of functionality called ______________________
2) An Angular application is a tree of _________________________ made from class files.
3) The component class has two commonly used properties: ______________________ and __________________ .
4) All Angular applications have a root module, typically named ____ .

Homework

Step 1 Launch a browser and open the website at https://findadentist.ada.org/ which was built with Angular.

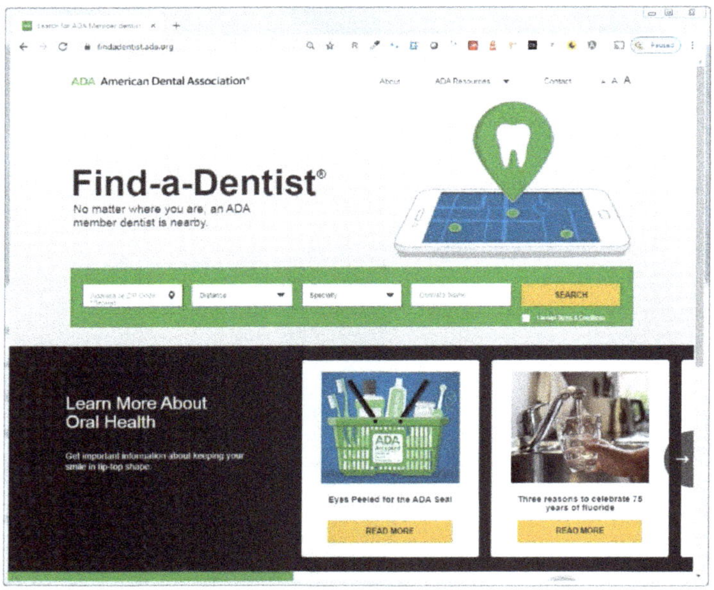

Step 2 Identify the parts of the Application that should be created as components.

Step 3 Identify where modules might be used.

Step 4 Locate opportunities to inject services.

Chapter summary

The component which consists of two parts: the decorator and the exported class is the basic construct upon which Angular applications are built. The reusable logic portion of the component will be addressed later in the chapter on services and dependency injection. Additional topics to be covered in later chapters include data binding to properties declared in the component class as well as further use of the metadata object that is passed to the @Component() decorator function. In this chapter, you learned the importance of Angular components and how to create a component.

Next Chapter

In the next chapter, you will learn how to style components with CSS.

Chapter 6

Styling Components

Chapter 6: Styling Components

Objectives

- Describe Angular's global CSS file: main.css
- Describe the use case for the Component style properties
- Style an Angular Component with a component style block
- Style an Angular Component with an external style sheet
- Explain Angular's CSS Encapsulation rules
- Describe the Shadow DOM's role in Angular's CSS Encapsulation
- Create and style a Component
- Optimize CSS rules within a Component

Introduction

Like all HTML web pages, Angular uses CSS for styling. What makes Angular unique is that it provides a mechanism for removing the cascade or inheritance of styles. The developer can essentially isolate the style rules inside of components, so that they are not visible outside the component. For example, if a component has an `<h1>` element styled in red, this style does not apply to all the other `<h1>` elements on the screen. Styles rules can be encapsulated inside the component class. Styles encapsulated in this way cannot be changed by style sheet changes elsewhere in the application.

Styles are applied in the `@Component()` decorator function. The metadata object passed to the function includes one of the following two properties related to styling the component: `styles` or `styleUrls`. The table on page 76 shows the various methods for styling Angular components.

6.0 Angular's global CSS file

Angular projects may take advantage of a global css file from both seed and cli-generated applications.

6.0.1 Global CSS and Angular CLI

When using the Angular CLI, Angular creates and includes a "styles.css" file as a global CSS file that is linked to index.html. The opening comments on this auto-generated file are:

```
/* You can add global styles to this file, and also import other style files */
```

The styles.css file is added to styles.bundle.js when the `ng build` command is executed. The style files are registered to Angular-CLI in using the .angular-cli.json file (see Figure 11 below) which includes a styles array inside the apps array. It has a single item by default which is styles.css (the path will be relative to the src directory). You may also use SASS for your CSS, but you will need to change the extension of that single item in the styles array to `scss` and change the extension of the src/styles.css. In addition, you can add other stylesheets (including their path) such as Bootstrap CSS.

```
{
  "$schema": "./node modules/@angular/cli/lib/config/schema.json",
  "project": {
    "name": "food-plate-cli"
  },
  "apps": [
    {
      "root": "src",
      "outDir": "dist",
      "assets": [
        "assets",
        "favicon.ico"
      ],
      "index": "index.html",
      "main": "main.ts",
      "polyfills": "polyfills.ts",
      "test": "test.ts",
      "tsconfig": "tsconfig.app.json",
      "testTsconfig": "tsconfig.spec.json",
      "prefix": "app",
      "styles": [
        "styles.css"
```

```
        ],
        "scripts": [],
        "environmentSource": "environments/environment.ts",
        "environments": {
          "dev": "environments/environment.ts",
          "prod": "environments/environment.prod.ts"
        }
      }
    ],
    "e2e": {
      "protractor": {
        "config": "./protractor.conf.js"
      }
    },
    "lint": [
      {
        "project": "src/tsconfig.app.json"
      },
      {
        "project": "src/tsconfig.spec.json"
      },
      {
        "project": "e2e/tsconfig.e2e.json"
      }
    ],
...
```

Figure #11: The angular.json configuration file.

Global CSS is typically added to the styles.css file generated by the angular-cli tool. You can also import CSS into styles.css.

6.1 How does Angular-CLI Apply Global Styles?

The global style rules are packaged and delivered to the client by Webpack. Webpack is a module bundler that takes modules with dependencies and generates static assets that represent those modules. While Webpack's main purpose is to bundle and deliver JavaScript for use in the browser, it takes plug-ins that add to its functionality. The angular-cli tool configures Webpack by providing entry points for the bundles Webpack will create. In addition to these entry points, Webpack uses loaders to load files that are not JavaScript, like CSS. According to the Webpack documentation, "Loaders are transformations that are applied on the source code of a module. They allow you to pre-process files as you import or "load" them... Loaders can transform files from a different language (like TypeScript) to JavaScript, or inline images as data URLs." Angular-cli uses a css-loader to load styles.css. Basically, it exports each CSS module as a string and then uses a style-loader to add the style tag to the page. Finally, Webpack uses the HTML Webpack plugin to add the css to index.html. Angular-cli can also be configured to load SASS, LESS and Stylus and use post-css plugins.

6.1.1 Per angular.io documentation

https://angular.io/guide/component-styles#external-and-global-style-files

External and global style files

When building with the CLI, you must configure the angular.json to include all external assets, including external style files.

Register global style files in the styles section which, by default, is pre-configured with the global styles.css file.

Global styles

The styles.css file allows users to add global styles and supports CSS imports.

If the project is created with the --style=sass option, this will be a .sass file instead, and the same applies to scss/less/style.

You can add more global styles via the styles option inside your project's build target options in angular.json. These will be loaded exactly as if you had added them in a <link> tag inside index.html.

```
"architect": {
  "build": {
    "builder": "@angular-devkit/build-angular:browser",
    "options": {
      "styles": [
        "src/styles.css",
        "src/more-styles.css",
      ],
      ...
```

You can also rename the output and lazy load it by using the object format:

```
"styles": [
  "src/styles.css",
  "src/more-styles.css",
  { "input": "src/lazy-style.scss", "lazy": true },
  { "input": "src/pre-rename-style.scss", "bundleName": "renamed-style" },
],
```

In Sass and Stylus you can also make use of the includePaths functionality for both component and global styles, which allows you to add extra base paths that will be checked for imports.

To add paths, use the stylePreprocessorOptions option:

```
"stylePreprocessorOptions": {
  "includePaths": [
    "src/style-paths"
  ]
},
```

Files in that folder, e.g. src/style-paths/_variables.scss, can be imported from anywhere in your project without the need for a relative path:

```
// src/app/app.component.scss
// A relative path works
@import '../style-paths/variables';
// But now this works as well
@import 'variables';
```

Note: you will also need to add any styles to the test builder if you need them for unit tests.

7—Guided Exercise: Writing global style rules in the seed application

In this exercise, you add global styles to the angular-seed application. The Angular Seed project includes a stylesheet in the src folder called styles.css.

Step 1 Open the stylesheet called styles.css in the src directory.

Step 2 Add the following CSS to styles.css.

```
body {
      font-family: Helvetica, Arial, sans-serif;
      margin: 0;
      padding: 0;
      background: url(/assets/images/seed-icon.png) 10px 10px
                  no-repeat #00b6f1;
}
```

The background-image used in the angular-seed project's css file.

Step 3 Save the file and test it in Chrome.

Note The header component may block the appearance of the seed icon. Check Chrome's DevTools to verify the seed icon is rendered.

Step 4 Verify the image appears when the page is viewed in the web browser.

4 –Challenge Exercise: Add styles to "styles.css" in the CLI project

In this challenge exercise, you use the foodPlate-cli project to add style rules to the global styles.css file.

Note Confirm that you have replaced the assets folder in the angular-cli project with the assets folder from the angular-class-files/foodPlate-cli-files/assets folder.

Step 1 Open the foodPlate-cli project and add the CSS below to the src/styles.css file. You can copy the CSS from the assets/css/foodPlate-cli-global-css.css.

```
@charset "utf-8";
body {
        font-family: Arial, Helvetica, sans-serif;
        padding:0;
        margin:0;
}
#wrapper {
     min-height: 100%;
     width: 100%;
     height: 100%;
     margin-left: auto;
     margin-right: auto;
     position: absolute;
     background: url(assets/images/bgImages/circle1.png) -108px -108px
            repeat, url(assets/images/bgImages/circle2.png) -24px -24px
            repeat #00b6f1;
     text-align: center;
     box-shadow: inset 0 0 95px rgba(0,0,0,.70);
}
```

Step 2 Save the file and verify the styles have been applied when viewed in Chrome.

Step 3 Open index.html and confirm that it does not include a link to styles.css.

Where is the CSS and when was the code circled below generated?

```
<html lang="en">
 ▶<head>…</head>
 ▼<body cz-shortcut-listen="true" style>
   ▼<fp-app _nghost-nep-c0 ng-version="8.2.14">
     ▶<div _ngcontent-nep-c0 id="wrapper">…</div>
    </fp-app>
    <script src="runtime.js" type="module"></script>
    <script src="polyfills.js" type="module"></script>
    <script src="styles.js" type="module"></script>
    <script src="vendor.js" type="module"></script>
    <script src="main.js" type="module"></script>
  </body>
</html>
```

```
<!doctype html>
<html lang="en">
<head>
  <meta charset="utf-8">
  <title>FoodPlateCli</title>
  <base href="/">
  <meta name="viewport"
        content="width=device-width,
                 initial-scale=1">
  <link rel="icon" type="image/x-icon"
        href="favicon.ico">
</head>
<body>
  <fp-app>Loading...</fp-app>
</body>
</html>
```

6.2 Component styling methods

Angular provides several methods for styling both your application and its components. Each method has unique consequences. For example, when styling via the global stylesheet, your style rules are available to the entire application, and they are subject to the cascading rules of CSS. The available methods for styling components result in Angular injecting the CSS in different parts of the compiled application code. For example, some methods allow the CSS to be visible from parent to child component, while other methods encapsulate or scope the CSS to the component only and not its children. The chart below lists the methods Angular provides for styling applications. The guided exercises that follow explain the consequences of using each method.

6.2.1 Component styling methods

Method	Description/Example Code
styles property in the metadata object	Value is an array of CSS styles. styles: ['h1 {color:red}, h2 {color:blue}']
styleUrls property in the metadata object	Style is an array of style sheets. styleUrls: ['styles/header.component.css'] The URL is relative to the application root, not the component file.
Inline in the template	template: '<style> h1 { color: #f00; font-family: Arial; border-bottom: 1px solid #000; } </style> <h1>Title</h1>'
Template link tag	template: ' <link rel="stylesheet" href="app/footer.component.css"> <h1>Title</h1> ... ' The URL is relative to the application root, not the component file.
CSS Imports	Import CSS files into our CSS files by using the CSS @import rule. @import 'dialogBoxes.css' The URL is relative to the CSS file into which we are importing.

Shown below are examples of styling components. The first one uses the styles property and the second one uses the `styleUrls` property. Notice the use of the array syntax with the styleUrls example.

Shown below are examples of styling components. The first one uses the `styles` property and the second one uses the `styleUrls` property. Notice the use of the array syntax with the styleUrls example.

```
import { Component, Input } from '@angular/core';

@Component({
    moduleId: module.id,
    selector: 'fp-header',
    templateUrl: 'header.component.html',
    styles: [`h1 {color: #f00;}`, `p {font-size: 1em}`]
})

export class HeaderComponent {

    @Input() greeting:string;
```

Figure #12: The styles property

```
import { Component, Input } from '@angular/core';

@Component({
    moduleId: module.id,
    selector: 'fp-homeBtn',
    templateUrl: 'homeBtn.component.html',
    styleUrls: ['homeBtn.css']
})

export class HomeBtnComponent {
    private isDisabled: boolean;

    @Input()
    status:boolean;

    constructor() {
        this.isDisabled = false;
    }
}
```

Figure #13: The styleUrls property.

8—Guided Exercise: Styling Angular Components with a component style block

In this exercise, you style a component using both the component style block and template inline style. Be sure to use the angular-seed project for this exercise.

Step 1 Open the file "header.component.ts" and add the CSS shown in bold below. You can find this file in angular-seed-files/code-snippets/style-block-css.txt.

```
@Component({
    selector: 'app-header',
    templateUrl: './header/header.component.html',
    styles: [`header {
                    background-color: #ef952b;
                    display: flex;
                    border-bottom: 3px solid #000;
                    justify-content: center;
                    align-items: flex-start;
                  }
                h1 {
                 text-shadow: 1px 1px #fff;
            }
            header>* {
                          margin: 0 1em;
            }`]
})
```

Step 2 Save and check the file in the web browser. It should look like the screenshot below.

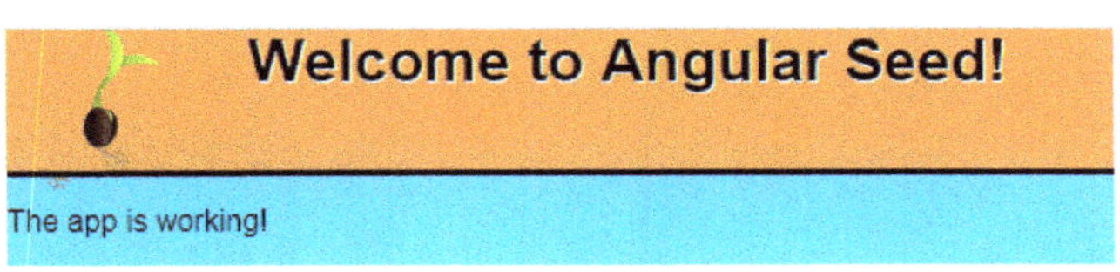

The header component after adding a style block in the component class.

Step 3 In the browser, right-click the header and choose "Inspect" from the menu. Examine where Angular placed the added CSS.

Note The style block can be moved into the template (in header.component.html) as shown below; a technique known as the template inline style.

Step 4 Remove the style block you added in step 1 and add the code below to header.component.html.

```
<style>
    header {
                    background-color: #ef952b;
                    display: flex;
                    border-bottom: 3px solid #000;
                    justify-content: center;
                    align-items: flex-start;
```

```
            }
    h1 {
            text-shadow: 1px 1px #fff;
    }
    header>* {
            margin: 0 1em;
    }
</style>
<header>
  <img src="../../assets/images/icons/seed-icon.png" width="35px" alt="">
  <h1>Welcome to FoodPlate!</h1>
</header>`
})
```

If you move the CSS to the location shown above and run in the browser, the CSS will be placed in the same location in the document. You can verify this by right-clicking the header and choosing "Inspect" from the menu.

Note When you inspect the HTML in the console, you may be wondering about the Angular generated code that was injected into your CSS (see example below). This is how Angular achieves CSS that is encapsulated in the component. You will learn this in more detail in the next session.

```
▼<style>
    header[_ngcontent-wgu-c0] {
            background-color: #ef952b;
            display: flex;
            border-bottom: 3px solid #000;
            justify-content: center;
            align-items: flex-start;
        }
        h1[_ngcontent-wgu-c0] {
            text-shadow: 1px 1px #fff;
        }
        header[_ngcontent-wgu-c0] > *[_ngcontent-wgu-c0] {
            margin: 0 1em;
        }
  </style>
```

3 – Practice Exercise: Styling a component with an external stylesheet

In this practice exercise, you style a component with an external stylesheet. The decision as to when to place both CSS styles and HTML templates into their own files is subjective. Typically, developers move the code to a separate file when it becomes too large or cumbersome to maintain in the component.ts file. It can be helpful to always keep html files in a separate file to facilitate a designer/developer workflow. You will use the Angular seed project for this practice exercise.

Step 1 Using the header.component.ts file or if you completed the previous exercise, then use the header.component.html file, remove the CSS in the component and put it in a separate CSS file to be referenced by the header component class. What should you name the stylesheet and what directory should you save it to?

Step 2 Add a `styleUrls` property that points to the new css file. Be careful with syntax as this property name is plural.

Step 3 Run the file in a web browser. It should look like the image below.

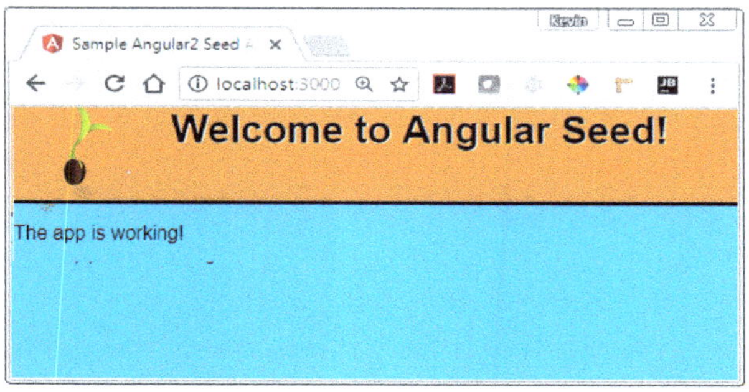

Possible solution code

header.component.ts

```
import { Component, OnInit } from '@angular/core';

@Component({
  selector: 'app-header',
  templateUrl: ' ./header/header.component.html',
  styleUrls: [' ./header.component.css']
})

export class HeaderComponent implements OnInit {
  constructor() {
  }

  ngOnInit() {
  }
}
```

header.component.css

```
header {
    background-color: #ef952b;
    display: flex;
    border-bottom: 3px solid #000;
    justify-content: center;
    align-items: flex-start;
}

h1 {
    text-shadow: 1px 1px #fff;
}

header>* {
    margin: 0 1em;
}
```

header.component.html

```
<header>
  <img src="assets/images/seed-icon.png">
  <h1>Welcome to Angular Seed</h1>
</header>
```

6.3 Where are component styles?

Angular uses Cascading Stylesheets with the added capability of scoping the CSS rules to components thereby isolating components CSS from the rest of the application. This is achieved using Angular's own CSS encapsulation rules.

6.3.1 Angular's CSS Encapsulation Rules

Angular uses its own encapsulation rules for CSS as shown in the table below.

Native	Uses the browsers native ShadowDOM ShadowDOM is a part of the Web Components specification. It provides a subtree of DOM elements that render in the browser but are isolated from the main DOM tree.
Emulated (default)	Emulates the use of the ShadowDOM via preprocessing and then, scopes the CSS to the component.
None	Angular does NOT encapsulate the CSS; it adds the CSS to the global styles. Causes the CSS to behave as if it were pasted into the HTML.

The Emulated method is the default method because not all Browsers implement the Shadow Dom, thus it cannot be relied upon to work universally. In Guided Exercise 2, you examined the Chrome DevTools and located the attribute shown below:

```
header[_ngcontgent-c0]
```

This was added to ensure that the CSS applied to this element is applied only to this element. This Angular implementation of isolated CSS is not fool-proof but is generally effective in most use-cases.

6.3.2 Setting view encapsulation

```
import { Component, Input, ViewEncapsulation } from '@angular/core';

@Component({

    selector: 'fp-header',
    templateUrl: 'header.component.html',
    styleUrls: ['header.component.css'],
    encapsulation: ViewEncapsulation.Emulated
})

export class HeaderComponent {
```

Figure #14: CSS view encapsulation set to Emulated.

Encapsulating CSS inside of components is not new to front-end web development. It is part of a larger scope of functionality known as Web Components. Web Components consists of several separate specifications including Custom Elements, HTML templates, HTML imports and the Shadow DOM. Review the following demo files to gain a better understanding of Web Components.

5 – Demo Understanding CSS encapsulation

This demo file demonstrates encapsulation via the shadow DOM. It is beyond the scope of this course to take a deep dive into the shadow DOM.

For more information, visit https://developer.mozilla.org/en-US/docs/Web/Web_Components and https://www.w3.org/TR/shadow-dom/

Step 1 Open the demo file "shadow-dom.html" in your code editor and run it in Chrome.

Step 2 Open the Chrome Dev Tools and go to the "Elements" tab. Right-click the video in the browser and examine the elements tab.

```
▼<body style>
   <video src="casablanca.mp4" controls></video>
 </body>
```

Step 3 The video shows controls like play button, volume control, seek bar and so on, but the corresponding CSS is hidden. It is in the "shadow dom." Go to the Chrome settings as shown below.

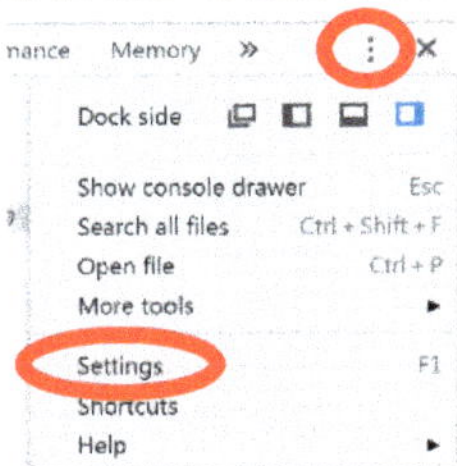

Step 4 Check the "Show user agent shadow DOM" as shown below.

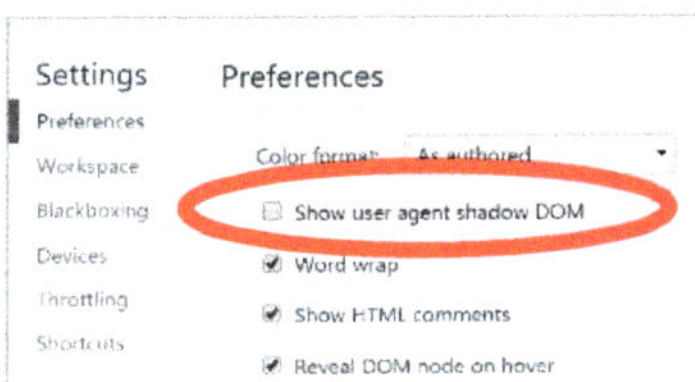

Step 5 Refresh the page in the browser and repeat step 2. You will now see the hidden HTML in the shadow DOM.

Step 6 Open the demo file shadow-dom-demo.html in both a code editor and a web browser.

Step 7 Notice that the page contains an `<h1>` element on line 13 that has been styled via the `<style>` block in the head section shown below.

```
<style>
  h1 {
    font-family: "Helvetica Neue", Helvetica, Arial, sans-serif;
    color: #f00;
  }
</style>
```

Step 8 Notice the `<script>` block on line 16 which creates a shadow DOM on the `<p>` element with the id `hostElement`.

The shadow DOM's inner HTML contains an `<h1>` element that is styled via the shadow DOM. It will be blue.

Step 9 Remove the comment from the additional `<h1>` element on line 46 (at the end of the document). What color do you expect it to be?

Step 10 Close the file in your code editor.

6 – Demo Understanding CSS encapsulation with Shadow DOM and templates

In this file, a template is used in conjunction with the Shadow DOM.

Step 1 Return to the file “shadow-dom-demo.html” in both a code editor and the Chrome web browser.

Step 2 Open the Network tab of the Chrome DevTools and refresh the page. Note the network traffic before and after creating the shadow DOM element.

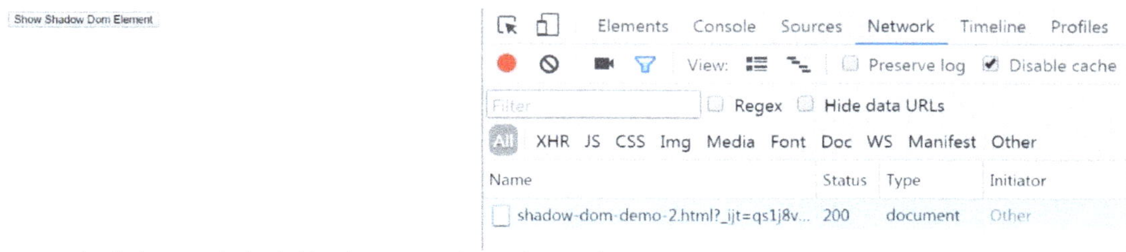

The network tab showing the loaded html prior to rendering the template.

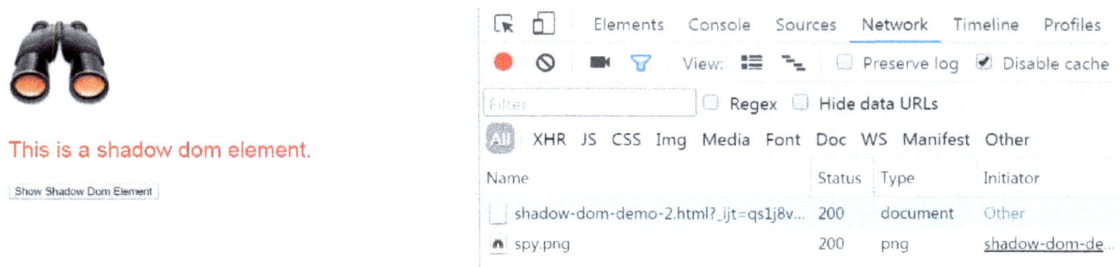

The network tab showing the loaded HTML after the rendering of the template in the shadow DOM.

Note This file’s style block includes a :host selector which represents the host element for the shadow DOM.

Step 4 Remove the comments around the host selector (lines 31-39). Examine the style block and run the file in a web browser. Click the button labeled: “Show Shadow DOM 2 Element.”

Step 5 Close all the demo files.

Another example of scoping CSS can be found in the demo file called “css-scope-demo.html.” At the time of publication, this file will work only in Firefox which currently supports the :scope selector. For more information, see https://developer.mozilla.org/en-US/docs/Web/CSS/:scope.

Web components provide robust capabilities for styling. The above demos provide a peak into using the Shadow DOM, HTML templates and CSS encapsulation. Angular makes use of these capabilities in its framework and will be used throughout the course to style components.

Per the angular.io documentation:

https://angular.io/guide/component-styles#view-encapsulation

ShadowDom view encapsulation only works on browsers that have native support for shadow DOM (see Shadow DOM v1 on the Can I use site). The support is still limited, which is why Emulated view encapsulation is the default mode and recommended in most cases.

9—Guided Exercise: Styling with the CSS cascade

In this exercise, you style a component and allow the CSS to cascade to it's child component. You will work in the angular-seed project for this exercise.

Step 1 Open app.component.ts and add the styleUrls property with a value of 'app.component.css'

```
@Component({
  selector: 'app',
  template: `<div id="wrapper">
    <app-header></app-header>
    <p>The app is working!</p>
  </div>`,
  styleUrls: ['app.component.css']
})
```

Step 2 Create a stylesheet called app.component.css with the following CSS inside

```
p {
  border: 1px solid #000;
  padding: 1em;
  margin: 1em;
  background-color: #fff;
}
```

Step 3 Create a child component to the app component and name it child.component.ts. Use the CLI tool.

```
import { Component, OnInit } from '@angular/core';

@Component({
  selector: 'app-child',
  templateUrl: './child/child.component.html'
})
export class ChildComponent implements OnInit {
  constructor() {
  }
  ngOnInit() {
  }
}
```

Step 4 Edit the child.component.html as shown below.

```
<p>I'm the child.</p>
```

Step 5 Confirm the new component has been declared in the app.module.

Step 6 Confirm the app.component's view is referenced in the component class as app.component.html.

```
@Component({
  selector: 'app',
```

```
  templateUrl: 'app.component.html',
  styleUrls: ['app.component.css']
})
```

Step 7 Use the new component in app.component.html (a separate .html file).

```
<div id="wrapper">
  <app-header></app-header>
  <p>The app is working!</p>
  <app-child></app-child>
</div>
```

Step 8 Save the page and run it in Chrome.

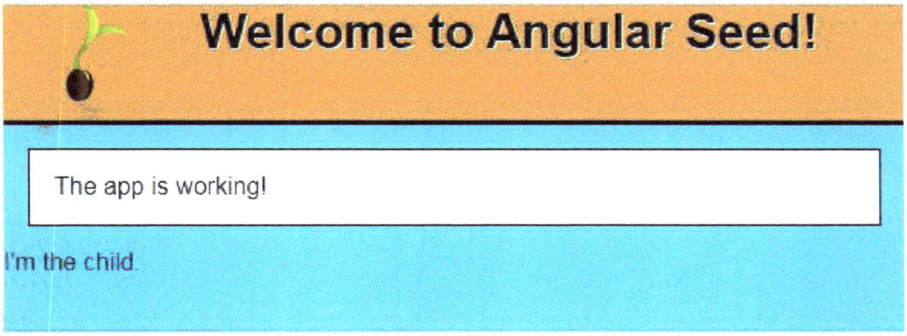

Notice that the parent component's (app.component) CSS does not cascade down to the child.

Step 9 To share the parent CSS with the child, set the app.component's `encapsulation` property to `none`.

```
import { Component, OnInit, ViewEncapsulation } from '@angular/core';

@Component({
  selector: 'app',
  templateUrl: 'app.component.html',
  styleUrls: ['app.component.css'],
  encapsulation: ViewEncapsulation.None
})
```

Step 10 Save the file and view it in Chrome. You should see the CSS cascade from the parent app component to the child component.

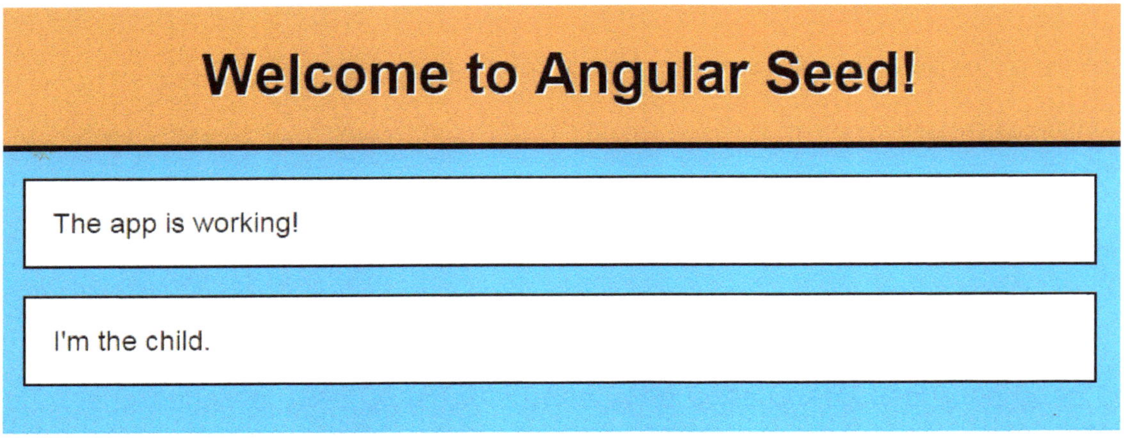

5 –Challenge Exercise: Create and style a footer component using the Angular CLI tool

In this exercise, you style the header component and create a footer module and component for the foodPlate-cli project. Be sure to read all the step instructions before beginning this challenge. When completed, the app should look like the image below.

Simple Instructions

Using the screenshot above for reference, complete the following steps.

- Create a footer component and add it to the application.
- Abstract those CSS properties that are common to both header and footer and create a CSS class for these common properties and assign the CSS class to the proper HTML tags. Name the CSS class `.header-footer`.
- See that the CSS styles that are common to both header and footer such as the orange background color are inherited from the parent component.
- See that the styles unique to header and unique to footer such as the placement of the 3-pixel solid black border that appears on the top of the footer and on the bottom of the header are assigned in the correct file.

Step by step instructions

Step 1 Open the foodPlate-cli project in your IDE or code editor.

Step 2 Using the node.js command prompt or the terminal in your IDE, create a footer component.

Step 3 The footer component's view template looks like this:

```
<footer>
    <p>&copy; 2020 FoodPlate Inc.</p>
</footer>
```

Note Pay attention to where you choose to write your CSS (in the header or footer components vs. in the app.component) as well as your encapsulation strategy.

Step 4 The footer component's CSS looks like this:

```
footer {
    height: 50px;
    position: absolute;
    bottom: 0;
    border-top: 3px solid #000;
}
```

Step 5 The header and footer share some common properties like their background color, width and display properties. Refactor both the header and footer CSS using a class like this:

```
.header-footer {
    background-color: #ef952b;
    width: 100%;
    display: flex;
    justify-content: space-between;
    align-items: center;
}
.header-footer>* {
   margin: 0 1em;
}
```

Step 6 Modify the header component to use the .header-footer class as well as its own CSS shown below.

```
header {
    border-bottom: 3px solid #000;
    margin-bottom: 0;
}
h1 {
    text-shadow: 1px 1px #fff;
}
```

Step 7 Save and run the application in Chrome. It should look like this:

Possible solution code

app.module.ts

```
import { BrowserModule } from '@angular/platform-browser';
import { CommonModule } from '@angular/common';
import { NgModule } from '@angular/core';

import { AppComponent } from './app.component';
import { FooterComponent } from './footer/footer.component';
import { HeaderComponent } from './header/header.component';


@NgModule({
  imports: [
    CommonModule, BrowserModule
  ],
  declarations: [AppComponent, HeaderComponent, FooterComponent],
  bootstrap: [AppComponent]
})
export class AppModule { }
```

app.component.ts

```
import { Component, ViewEncapsulation } from '@angular/core';

@Component({
  selector: 'fp-app',
  templateUrl: 'app.component.html',
  styleUrls: ['app.component.css'],
  encapsulation: ViewEncapsulation.None
})
export class AppComponent {
}
```

app.component.html

```
<div id='wrapper'>
  <fp-header></fp-header>
  <p>The app is working!</p>
  <fp-footer></fp-footer>
</div>
```

app.component.css

```
.header-footer {
    background-color: #ef952b;
    width: 100%;
    display: flex;
    justify-content: space-between;
    align-items:center;
}


.header-footer>* {
    margin: 0 1em;
}
```

header.component.html

```
<header class="header-footer">
    <img src="../../assets/images/icons/cli-icon.png">
    <h1>Welcome to your Food Plate!</h1>
</header>
```

header.component.css

```
header {
    border-bottom:3px solid #000;
    margin-bottom: 0;
}

h1 {
    text-shadow: 1px 1px #fff;
}
```

footer.component.ts

```
import { Component, OnInit } from '@angular/core';

@Component({
  selector: 'fp-footer',
  templateUrl: './footer.component.html',
  styleUrls: ['./footer.component.css']
})
export class FooterComponent implements OnInit {

  constructor() { }

  ngOnInit() {
  }
}
```

footer.component.html

```
<footer class="header-footer">
  <p>&copy; 2020 FoodPlate Inc.</p>
</footer>
```

footer.component.css

```
footer {
  height: 50px;
  position: absolute;
  bottom: 0;
  border-top: 3px solid #000;
}
```

Chapter 6 Advanced: 3rd-Party Libraries and Styling

Objectives

- Install, configure, and use a 3rd-party CSS library
- Use the :host selector to style components
- Define content projection and the problem it solves
- Use Font Awesome to add icons
- Style custom components
- Explain the difference between structural and visual/display
- Describe some aspects of advanced component design
- Create a component that allows developers to add their own content to the component

Introduction

Earlier in this chapter, you learned how Angular implements style isolation which is used to make our CSS more maintainable and to prevent CSS rules from unintentionally leaking into and affecting other components. This also helps us create reusable components with reusable API's. This is a common undertaking in large enterprise applications with many best practices. The ability of a component to be reused lies in how difficult it is for a developer to "break" the component combined with how easy it is for the developer to style the component to fit within their application. In this "Advanced Components" section you will learn how to meet that objective. You will also use a 3rd-party CSS library called Font-Awesome, to add icons to your application. The principles introduced in this section will apply to any 3rd-party CSS you choose for your project.

6.4 Using 3rd Party CSS

There are several ways to add 3rd party libraries to Angular projects including both JavaScript and CSS files.

Here are some of the methods you might deploy:

1. Configure your module loader to use the node require() method to load ES6 modules and then modify the component as shown below.

```
@Component({
  selector: fp-element,
  styles:[require(css-library.css')],
  templateUrl: 'fp-element.component.html'
})
```

2. Import the third-party css in `src/styles.css`

3. Configure the angular.json configuration file by adding file paths to files that will be globally bundled with the application during the build process.

```
"styles": [
        "styles.css",
        "../node_modules/font-awesome/css/font-awesome.min.css"
     ],
```

You will discover additional techniques with a simple Google search, each with its own pros and cons. You will find different techniques depending on which version of Angular you are targeting. Version 5 and higher of the Angular framework provides methods in the Angular-cli tool designed to make it easier to add both JavaScript and CSS 3rd-party libraries. You will see more of these techniques in the chapters ahead.

6.5 Using Font Awesome

Font Awesome is a CSS library of icons that may be used in web applications and Adobe Photoshop documents. The website offers both free and paid services to acquire icons. Font Awesome provides a variety of implementations designed to suit several environments. For example, they provide SVG icons, fonts icons, SVG sprites and more.

The easiest way to acquire and render an icon on a web application using Font Awesome is through the CSS classes the library provides. This is typically accomplished with a CSS style prefix followed by an icon name. The class is accessed via a span element. An example is shown below.

```
<span class="fa fa-comments fa-lg"></span>
```

The fa class ensures the icon displays inline-block with a font of normal, inherited font-size and more. The complete class rules are shown in the next exercise. The fa-comments class selects the comments icon to be rendered and the fa-lg class sets the font-icon's font-size property to .33333333em with a line-height of 0.75em and vertical alignment of -15%.

6.5.1 The Font Icons

The complete set of free and paid icons can be found at https://fontawesome.com/icons?d=gallery.

6.6 Styling custom components

So far, in this chapter, you have styled HTML elements. However, there will be times when you want to style a custom element you have created with Angular. For example, if you want to style the <app-header> component, where would you write the CSS. The header.component.css styles are scoped to the elements inside the template and not the element that hosts the component itself: the outer <app-header> element. Angular provides a pseudo-class selector called :host that targets the host component aka the custom element.

Inside of a component's css, a style like this:

```
:host {
background-color: green;
margin: 1em;
}
```

Looks like this at runtime:

```
<style>
  [_nghost-c0] {
  background-color: green;
  margin: 1em;
 }
</style>
```

The addition of the CSS attribute syntax [_nghost-c0] is used to isolate the CSS to just that component. Angular creates and injects the attribute _nghost-c0 at runtime.

In the following exercise, you will learn more about scoping CSS using the :host pseudo-class selector.

You may encounter the following CSS selectors that are often used with :host:

Selector	Description	Status
`:host`	Selects the host component.	Widely used and recommended method for styling custom elements aka components
`:host h1`	Selects h1 elements inside the template of the host element.	Widely used to style element children of the host element, but not nested children which would contain CSS scoped to their own templates.
`::ng-deep`	Used to penetrate style isolation around a component. It applies CSS to ancestor elements of the component.	Deprecated. Often used with projected content and 3rd party libraries like Material Design and PrimeNG. However, this selector appears to have been deprecated in Angular 5+.
`:host-context`	Used to apply CSS to an element based on CSS found outside the component.	Used in conjunction with themed websites, for example all button component colors may be based on a class set in one of the components ancestors.

10—Guided Exercise: Using 3rd-party CSS Libraries and Advanced Styling

In this exercise, you install and configure a 3rd party CSS library called Font Awesome. It's important to note that this is not necessarily an endorsement of font icons. There are, in fact, numerous methods available for adding icons to web applications. As usual, each project dictates its own set of requirements and therefore the choice of how to implement icons will vary.

Step 1 Return to the Angular-seed project and launch a command prompt/terminal to install the font-awesome library.

Step 2 Install font-awesome with the following command:

```
npm install @fortawesome/fontawesome-svg-core
npm install @fortawesome/free-solid-svg-icons
npm install @fortawesome/angular-fontawesome@0.6
```

Step 3 Create a component called form-input.component. This component will use font icons from Font Awesome.

The component is shown below with relevant code shown in bold.

```
import { Component, Input, OnInit } from '@angular/core';
import { faEnvelope } from '@fortawesome/free-solid-svg-icons';

@Component({
    selector: 'app-form-input',
    templateUrl: './form-input.component.html',
    styleUrls: ['./form-input.component.css']
})
export class FormInputComponent implements OnInit {

    faEnvelope = faEnvelope;

    constructor() { }

    ngOnInit() {
    }
}
```

Step 4 Create the html template for the form-input component.

```
<input type="email" />
```

Step 5 In app.component.html, remove the <p> element with the text "The app is working!" Add a label component and the new form-input component as shown below in bold.

```
<div>
  <app-header></app-header>
  <p>The app is working</p>
  <app-child></app-child>
  <label>Email: </label>
  <app-form-input></app-form-input>
</div>
```

Step 6 Confirm that the new component has been declared in the app module.

Step 7 Import the FontAwesomeModule in app.module.

```
import { FontAwesomeModule } from '@fortawesome/angular-fontawesome';

@NgModule({
    imports:        [ BrowserModule, FontAwesomeModule ],
```

Step 8 Add a font icon in front of the input element as shown below in bold.

Note: To see a gallery of available fonts visit https://fontawesome.com/icons?d=gallery

```
<fa-icon [icon]="faEnvelope"></fa-icon><input type='email' />
```

Step 9 Save the file and run the file in Chrome.

The page should now show the icon. The new component should look like this:

Next step is to style the icon with CSS. Add a class with style rules that will enlarge and add space around the icon.

Step 11 Open the form-input.component.css file and add the style rule below.

```
.icon {
    font-size: 18px;
    padding-left: 15px;
    padding-right: 12px;
}
```

Step 12 Add the new icon class to the icon in the form-input component as shown below in bold.

```
<fa-icon [icon]="faEnvelope" class="icon"></fa-icon><input type="email">
```

Step 13 Check the file in the browser and use the DevTools to verify the styles have been applied.

The next step is to style the component itself, in other words, we are going to style the custom HTML element created by Angular called `<fp-form-input>`.

Step 14 Add CSS to style the host component as shown below. Add this css to form-input.component.css.

```
:host {
    border: 1px solid #333;
    border-radius: 2px;
    padding: 4px;
    background: #fff;
}
```

Step 15 Check the file in Chrome and confirm the styles have been applied. Note the border remains around the inner input element. The custom component has been created to replace the standard HTML input component, but the styling conflict results in a "component inside a component" type look and feel. To make the new input component more cohesive, you will remove the border from the inner HTML input component in the next step.

Step 16 Add the following CSS to remove the border on the input element.

```
input {
    border: none;
    height: 20px;
}
```

Step 17 Add a <small> element to the form-input component as shown below in bold.

```
<fa-icon [icon]="faEnvelope" class="icon"></fa-icon>
<input type="email">
<small>Please enter your business email account.</small>
```

Step 18 Style the small element in the form-input.component.css file as shown below in bold.

```
:host {
  border: 1px solid #333;
  border-radius: 2px;
  padding: 4px;
  background: #fff;
}

:host small {
  color: #f00;
}
```

Step 19 View the file in Chrome. It should look like the screen capture below.

Use the Chrome DevTools to examine how the CSS has been implemented.

```
▼<style>
   [_nghost-yyk-c3] {
       border: 1px solid #333;
       border-radius: 2px;
       padding: 4px;
       background: #fff;
   }

   [_nghost-yyk-c3]   small[_ngcontent-yyk-c3] {
       color: #ff0000;
   }

   input[_ngcontent-yyk-c3] {
       border: none;
       height: 20px;
   }

   .icon[_ngcontent-yyk-c3] {
       font-size: 18px;
       padding-left: 15px;
       padding-right: 12px;
```

This shows how the CSS is isolated to just this component.

We can further exploit the relationship between the host component and its content. In other words, we can set properties on the contents of the component based on properties set on the host. Steps 20 through 26 will demonstrate this concept.

Step 20 Comment the CSS that was added in step 18.

Step 21 To understand the :host-context selector, modify the app.component.html as shown below in bold.

```
<div>
  <app-header></app-header>
  <app-child></app-child>
  <form class="warning">
    <label>Email:</label>
    <app-form-input></app-form-input>
  </form>
</div>
```

Step 22 Add the form element, warning and caution CSS classes to the app.component.css file.

```
form {
    width: 100%;
    height: 3em;
    padding-top: 1.5em;
}
.warning {
    background-color: #f00;
}
.caution {
    background-color: #ffa500;
}
```

The form-input component's new ancestor `<form>` will be used to control the styles applied in the form-input component.

Step 23 First save and test the file in Chrome. The form-input component should look like the image below.

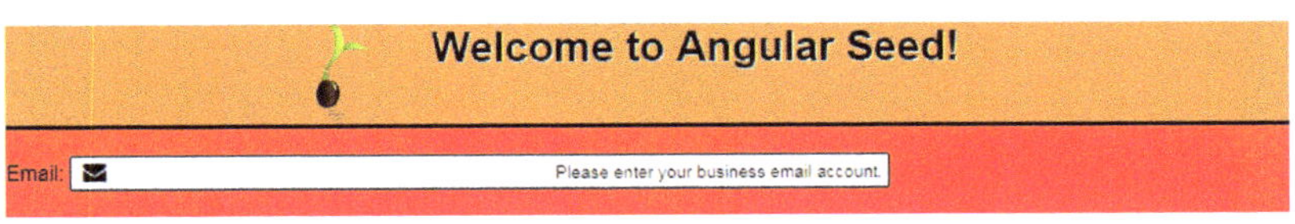

Note The background-color is red, and the small element text content is black.

Step 24 Add the following CSS rule to the form-input component.

```
:host-context(.warning) small {
    color: #f00;
}
:host-context(.caution) small {
    color: #ffa500;
}
```

Step 25 Save and test the file in Chrome.

Step 26 Change the form class to caution and re-test in Chrome.

```
<div>
  <app-header></app-header>
  <p>The app is working</p>
  <app-child></app-child>
  <form class="caution">
    <label>Email:</label>
    <app-form-input></app-form-input>
  </form>
</div>
```

Now that you have learned a little more about styling components via pseudo-selectors, we will continue our look at advanced components and learn about content projection and some best practices around component API design.

First, clean up the current file to prepare for the next exercise.

Step 27 Make the following changes: remove the content shown below with a strikethrough.

form-input-component.html

```
<fa-icon [icon]="faEnvelope" class="icon"></fa-icon>
<input type="email">
<small>Please enter your business email account.</small>
```

app.component.html

```
<div>
    <app-header></app-header>
    <app-child></app-child>
    <form class="caution">
        <label>Email:</label>
        <app-form-input></app-form-input>
    </form>
    <app-child></app-child>
</div>
```

The application as seen in the browser after deleting the code via step 28.

6.7 Advanced Component Design and Content Projection

In this section, we will look at more advanced component features such as the ability to allow a component to contain dynamic content when the component is used. This feature called content projection even lets you project specific content into specific areas of a component.

6.7.1 What is Content Projection?

Because components are composable, it is common to build project components by wrapping simple HTML elements. This is what was done in the previous exercise. The component looked like this:

```
<fa-icon [icon]="faEnvelope" class="icon"></fa-icon>
<input type="email">
```

The custom element is `<form-input>`. Other than the icon, the component simply renders an HTML input element. However, the component itself is missing all the functionality of an input element. Use the DevTools to locate the input element's autocompletion and placeholder properties. As shown in the image below: they are not part of the custom element's API.

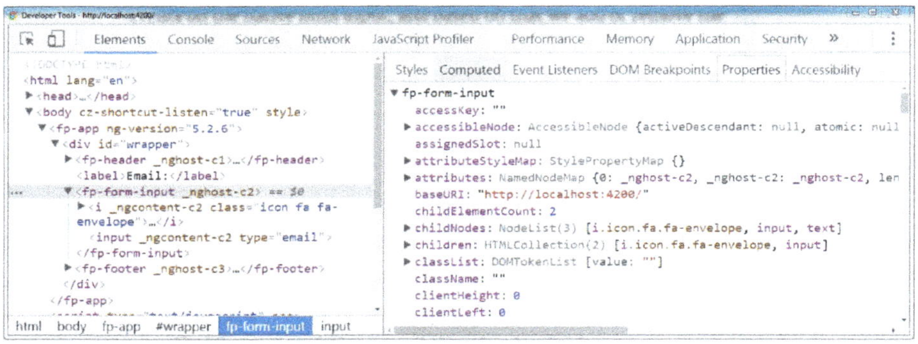

Figure #15: The properties of the custom element <fp-form-input> element. Notably missing are all the HTML input properties.

Compare that screenshot to the properties of the input element inside of the custom component.

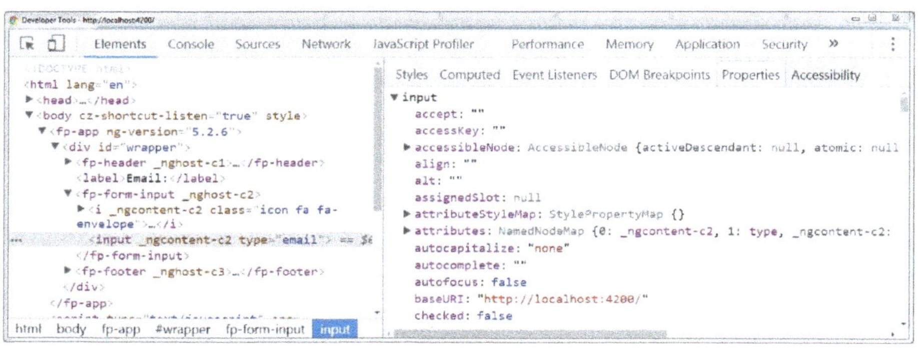

Figure #16: The properties of the native html input element. Here you will find all the HTML input properties including autocomplete and placeholder.

When implementing Component API design, it is unwise to wrap a simple HTML element because of the loss of its properties as shown in the example above. Another problem with wrapping plain HTML elements inside of components is the loss of common DOM events that would be available to the simple element, but not the component the element is wrapped in.

Even when you are not wrapping a plain HTML element inside of a component, it can be helpful if the component were designed in such a way as to allow any content to appear inside the component. Fortunately, we can specify at design-time that a component can accept content at use-time. This is called content projection and it is achieved with an Angular directive called <ng-content>. The following exercise will use content projection.

11–Guided Exercise: Using Content Projection

In this exercise, you learn the limitations of custom components that contain simple HTML content. You overcome these limitations by making components that can have content injected into them making them more reusable and customizable. We will turn our attention to adding content to a specific location in the component.

Step 1 Refactor the app.component.html as shown below in bold.

```
<div>
  <app-header></app-header>
  <app-child></app-child>
  <label>Email:</label>
  <app-form-input icon="envelope">
    <input type="email">
  </app-form-input>
</div>
```

Step 2 Move the label element in the app component's HTML. Add the `for` property to the label and the corresponding `id` property to the input element. Remove the label element as shown below with the strikethrough.

```
<div>
  <app-header></app-header>
  <label>Email:</label>
  <app-form-input icon="envelope">
    <label for="emailAddress">Email:</label>
    <input id="emailAddress" type="email" />
  </app-form-input>
  <app-child></app-child>
</div>
```

Step 3 In the input component's HTML, add an ng-content element with a select attribute above the span element as shown below in bold.

```
<ng-content select="label"></ng-content>
<fa-icon [icon]="faEnvelope" class="icon"></fa-icon>
<ng-content></ng-content>
```

Step 4 Save and run the file in Chrome. Notice the label content appears in the ng-content with the matching select attribute, while the input element appears in the ng-content which is now the default placeholder.

Step 5 Try swapping the ng-content with the select attribute with the existing ng-content as shown below in bold.

```
<ng-content></ng-content>
<fa-icon [icon]="faEnvelope" class="icon"></fa-icon>
<ng-content select="label"></ng-content>
```

Step 6 Save and test the file in Chrome.

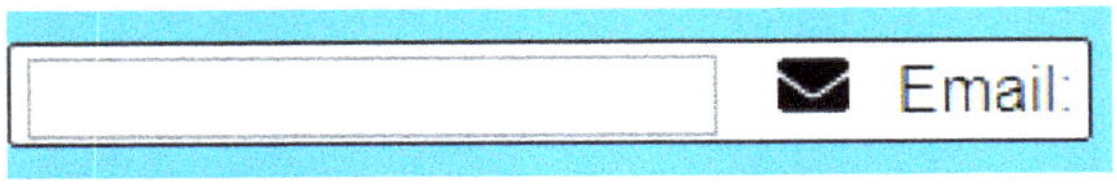

Note To understand how the ng-content serves as a placeholder, you will add additional content and placeholders.

Step 7 Move the content as shown below.

```
<ng-content select="label"></ng-content>
<fa-icon [icon]="faEnvelope" class="icon"></fa-icon>
<ng-content></ng-content>
<ng-content select="small"></ng-content>
```

Step 8 Move the app.component children as shown below.

```
<div>
  <app-header></app-header>
  <app-child></app-child>
  <app-form-input icon="envelope">
    <small>Business email</small>
    <label for="emailAddress">Email:</label>
    <input id="emailAddress" type="email" />
  </app-form-input>
</div>
```

Step 9 Save and view the file in Chrome.

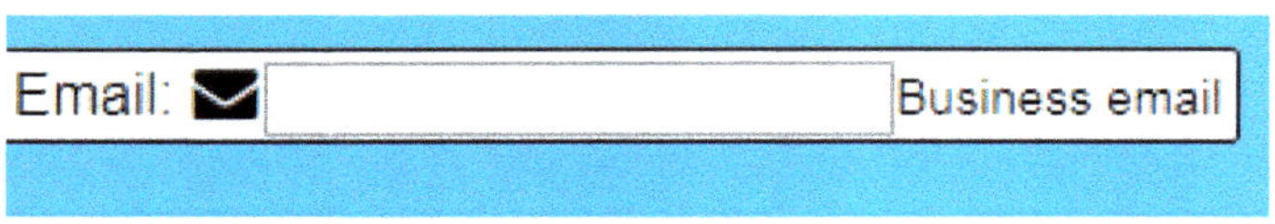

Note **An important note to remember about <ng-content> is that it does not produce content;** it is merely a method for projecting (or rendering) existing content. It's important to keep this in mind because you may want to add life-cycle methods to the rendered content in <ng-content> but you must remember that its' lifecycle begins where it is declared, not where (and when) it is rendered.

Chapter 6 Quiz

https://tinyurl.com/v69m29v

1) Match the CSS style rule with its proper location in the application code.

`background-color` for the entire web app	login.component.css
`background-color` for the login component	styles.css
`background-color` for the admin login only	login.component.css
`background-color` for components A, B,C, all of which have been declared in the ABC.module.ts with view encapsulation set to none	abc.component.css

Chapter Summary

In this chapter, you learned how to style your components with CSS. You also learned how to encapsulate the CSS within the component code to avoid leaking CSS into the global space. You reviewed some of the HTML API's that make CSS encapsulation possible including the Shadow DOM as well as other HTML and CSS concepts such as templates, CSS scoping and the :host selector.

Next Chapter

Now that component styling is out of the way, the next chapter will address how to bind properties in the component classes to the view templates.

Chapter 7
Understanding data binding

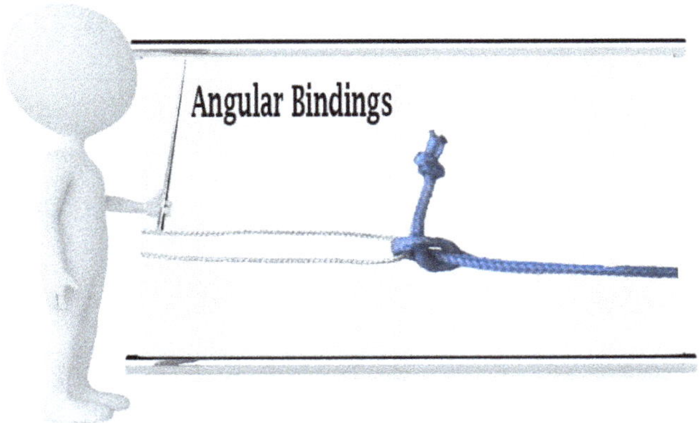

Chapter 7: Data binding

Objectives

- Understand component properties
- Write template expressions
- Use interpolation to display component properties in the view
- Understand property binding
- Know the difference between DOM properties and HTML attributes
- Create a property binding
- Create an attribute binding
- Create a class binding
- Create a style binding

Introduction

Data binding facilitates the communication between a component and its view/template. The Angular framework provides several types of databindings as well as a unique syntax for each type. Some data bindings also have a shortcut syntax. Angular supports binding a data object to the user interface in a one-way binding as well as a one-way binding from the user interface to a data object. Angular also supports a two-way databinding between a data object and the user interface. The target of a data binding is something in the Document Object Model (DOM).

7.0 What is Data Binding?

Angular's data binding capabilities may be broadly categorized into the types shown in the chart below.

Binding Type	Description	Syntax
Interpolation	Properties are defined in the component class and communicated to the template. (one-way)	`{{ property }}`
Property Binding	These are used to set properties and attributes of various HTML elements. (one-way)	`[ attribute ]`
Event Binding	Events that occur in the template (clicks, focus, and so on) are communicated to the component class. (one-way)	`( event )`
Two-way data binding	A combination of one-way data-binding and event binding to bind a component property to an input element. (two-way)	`[( )]`

In this chapter, you will use five kinds of bindings.

- Interpolation
- Property binding
- Attribute binding
- Class binding
- Style binding

7.1 Interpolating Component properties

The Angular component class includes properties that can be bound to the component view.

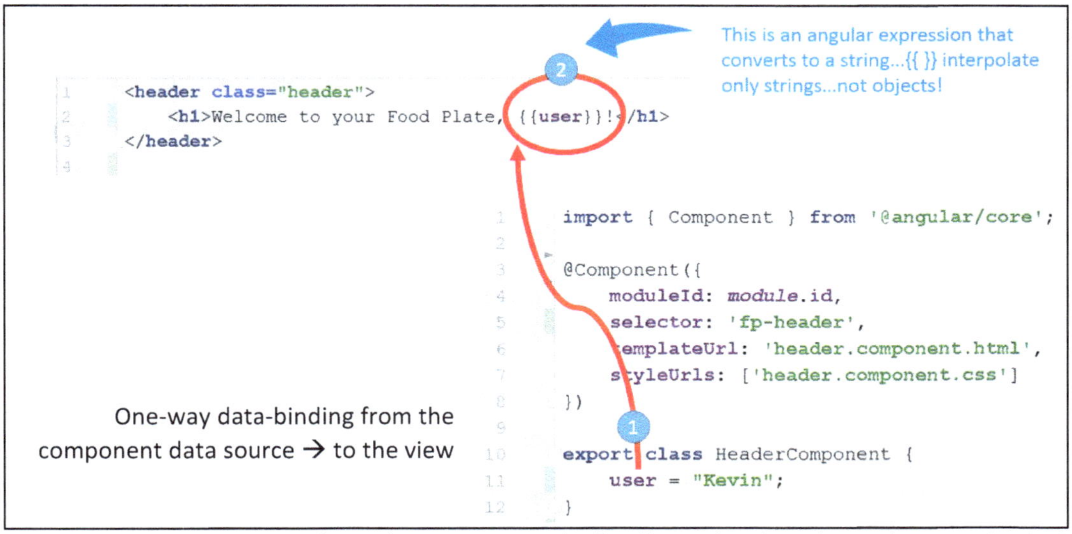

Figure #17: A component exposes data to the view via one-way binding. The template shows the template expression that is evaluated.

7.2 Template expressions

Looking at figure 17 above, locate item #2. In between the curly braces, you find a template expression. Angular evaluates these expressions and converts what it finds to a string which is then displayed when the view template is rendered. Thus, the template expression produces a value.

Template expressions *cannot*:

- use assignments (except in event bindings* more on that later)
- use the new operator
- use bitwise operators: | and &
- refer to anything in the global namespace, including
- Window
- Document
- call console.log()

Template expressions *can*:

- Perform basic math calculations, such as
- Add two values
- Output the value of a component property
- Output the result of a comparison via a
- Ternary operator (e.g. (condition) ? true : false)
- Output the result of a component method
- Complex expressions should be turned into methods on the component

More about template expressions:

- The | and ? have specific Angular meanings
- The safe navigation operator (this will be used later in the course)
  - `{{ user?.firstName }}`
    - Checks for null value for user
    - If `user` is null, Angular
      - Stops processing the path
      - Let's the application continue to run

7.2.1 Rules regarding template expressions

Template expressions should not:

- Change any application state other than the value of the target property.
- This is the job of controller-type code. Template expressions appear in the view template and best practices dictate that keeping the component's presentation logic in the class instead of the template improves testability, maintainability, and reusability.
- Contain complex expressions

Data binding direction chart

From	To	Direction
A data object	The UI	One-way
The UI	A data object	One way
Data object	UI	Two-way

Four types of data binding

- Interpolation
- Property binding uses []
  - a value flows from the model to a target property on screen
  - → one way
- Event binding uses () → one way
  - flow the value from the target property on screen to the model
  - → one way
- Two-way uses [()] *
  - Combination of property and event binding
  - ← → two way

* Banana in a box syntax ☺

Note As you will see in the following exercises, component property values can be interpolated in the view template via the double curly brace syntax: {{ interpolated value }}. This results in the property value placed in between the curly braces being rendered in the browser DOM. You can, however, override the default encapsulation delimiter syntax with your own symbols. You add the symbol to the `@Component` decorator functions supplied config object with the `interpolation` property as shown below with the relevant code in bold.

```
@Component({
    template: `
            <div>
                ((data))
            </div>
            `,
    interpolation: ["((","))"]
})
export class MyComponent {
    data: any = "someValue"
}
```

12—Guided Exercise: Using interpolation with component properties

In this exercise, you store the user's name as a property of the component and then display that property through interpolation.

Step 1 Return to the angular-seed project and open the header.component.ts file.

Step 2 Declare a userName property and assign your first name as the value.

```
export class HeaderComponent {
    userName: string = 'Kevin';
}
```

Step 3 Modify the header.component.html as shown below to use the new property in the view template. This is called a "template expression." It is a simple expression comprised of only a component property.

```
<header>
  <h1>Welcome to Angular Seed, {{ userName }}!</h1>
</header>
```

Angular will replace this property name with the string value of the corresponding component property. Later in the course you will substitute this property name with a template expression that Angular will evaluate and convert to a string.

Step 4 Save the files and view the application in a web browser. It should appear as shown below.

Optional Add-on Exercise

Step 5 A common attack on websites is to inject malicious JavaScript via a rogue `<script>` element which gets interpreted in the Web browser at runtime. Change the interpolation to include a script block as shown below. Let's assume instead of the benign userName property, a malicious script is inserted.

```
<header>
  <h1>Welcome to Angular Seed, {{ <script>userName</script> }}!</h1>
</header>
```

Step 6 Run the file in the web browser. How was the interpolation handled by Angular?

4 – Practice Exercise: Create and use a component property

In this practice exercise, you add a property to the footer component and bind it to the view template.

Simple Instructions

Step 1 Open the footer.component and add a property called versionString. Assign a value of 1.0.0.

Step 2 Using the HTML `<small>` tag, display the version number in the footer after the copyright statement.

The footer component in the finished exercise.

5 – Practice Exercise: Extra Credit

Later in the code, it may become necessary to compare the user's version number to a later version. While it is possible to compare 1.0.0 to 1.0.1, it can be challenging. In this extra credit exercise, you change the value of the versionString property from 1.0.0 to 100. Write a private function that turns the string "1.0.0" to the number 100. Set the property so that when it used as a binding to the view it displays 1.0.0.

Possible solution code

footer.component.ts

```
import { Component } from '@angular/core';

@Component({
    selector: 'fp-footer',
    templateUrl: 'footer.component.html',
    styleUrls: ['footer.component.css']
})

export class FooterComponent {

    versionString: string = '1.0.0';
        versionNumber: number = this.versionStringToNumber(this.versionString);

    private versionStringToNumber(version: string): number {
      return Number(parseFloat(version).toFixed(2));
    }


}
```

footer.component.html

```
<footer class="header-footer">
    <p>&copy; 2018 FoodPlate Inc. <small>Version #{{versionString}}</small></p>
</footer>
```

header.component.ts

```
import { Component, OnInit } from '@angular/core';

@Component({
  selector: 'fp-header',
  templateUrl: './header.component.html',
  styleUrls: ['./header.component.css']
})
export class HeaderComponent implements OnInit {
  title: string = 'Welcome to FoodPlate!';

  constructor() { }

  ngOnInit(): void {
  }
}
```

header.component.html

```
<header class="header-footer">
  <img src="assets/images/icons/cli-icon.png" alt="">
  <h1>{{ title }}</h1>
</header>
```

7.3 Property Binding

Property binding is used to set a property of a view element. Property binding is a one-way binding where a value flows from the model to a target property on the screen. The view element's property is set to the value of the template expression. The example below binds the img element's src property to the component class's icon property.

```
<img [src]="icon">
```

The Angular syntax that signifies a property binding is the square brackets []. The element property between square brackets identifies the target property. The brackets are responsible for evaluating the template expression. If you omit the brackets, Angular treats the string as a constant and initializes the target property with that string. In other words, without the brackets, Angular does not evaluate the string. You cannot use property binding to pull values out of the target element. Nor can you bind to a property of the target element to read it. You can only set it. In addition, you cannot use property binding to call a method on the target element. Notice in the code example that the square brackets eliminate the need for interpolation of the 'icon' value with curly braces.

7.3.1 Binding to DOM properties vs. HTML attributes

It is important to understand that Angular's binding mechanism works with properties of DOM elements (and components and directives). So, you may think you are setting HTML attributes like `id` because `id` is both an HTML attribute and a DOM property. You must remember that attributes are defined by HTML and properties are defined by the Document Object Model (DOM). The main distinction regarding Angular is that HTML attributes initialize DOM properties and then they are set and done. DOM property values can change while HTML attribute values cannot change. Figure 3 below, shows the input element's value attribute on the console with the original value of "Angular" while the same element's DOM property value has changed to "Kevin" which was typed into the input element after the page loaded.

Figure #18: The input tag's value attribute shows the original value of "Angular" while the DOM value property has been changed to "Kevin."

To try this yourself, open angular-class-files/demos/attr-vs-property.html.

13—Guided Exercise: Setting a property binding

In this exercise, you will bind an `<img>` element's src property to a property from the component class.

Step 1 Open the footer.component.ts file from the foodplate project.

Step 2 Add an icon property to the class as shown below in bold.

```
...
export class FooterComponent {
    versionString: string = '1.0.0';
    icon: string = 'assets/images/icons/icons-29.png';
}
```

Step 3 Open the footer.component.html file and modify it by adding an image tag. Use the new icon property to supply the src attribute to the new image tag. The target property in the following code is the image element's src property.

```
<footer class="header-footer">
    <img [src]="icon">
    <p>&copy; 2018 KRA Inc. <small>Version #{{versionString}}</small></p>
</footer>
```

Step 4 Open footer.component.css and confirm the style rules match those shown below.

```
footer {
    height: 50px;
    position: absolute;
    bottom: 0;
    border-top: 3px solid #000;
    justify-content: space-between;
}

footer>* {
    padding: 0 1em;
}
```

Step 5 Run the file in a web browser. It should match the screenshot below.

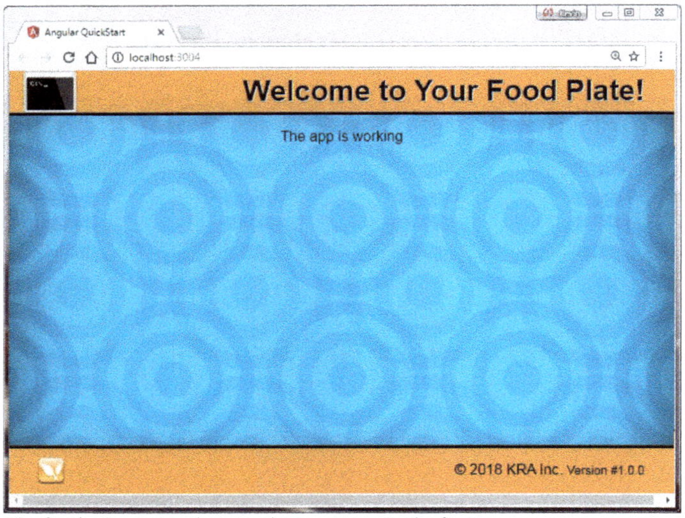

The finished exercise showing the image tag in the footer.

Note An alternative binding method to the above technique is shown below.

```
<img bind-src="icon">
```

7.3.2 Property binding vs. Interpolation

As shown in the Angular documentation, the following lines of code do the same thing:

```
<p><img src="{{heroImageUrl}}"> is the <i>interpolated</i> image.</p>
<p><img [src]="heroImageUrl"> is the <i>property bound</i> image.</p>
```

"When rendering data values as strings, there is no technical reason to prefer one form to the other. You lean toward readability, which tends to favor interpolation. You suggest establishing coding style rules and choosing the form that both conforms to the rules and feels most natural for the task at hand. When setting an element property to a non-string data value, you must use property binding."[1]

[1] https://angular.io/docs/ts/latest/guide/template-syntax.html

6 – Practice Exercise: Create property bindings

In this practice exercise, you add another property and binding.

Step 1 Add an alt attribute to the img tag in the footer component and use a component property called "logoAlt" to assign a value of "FoodPlate logo."

Step 2 Test your code in Chrome. The elements tab should show your `alt` attribute as shown below.

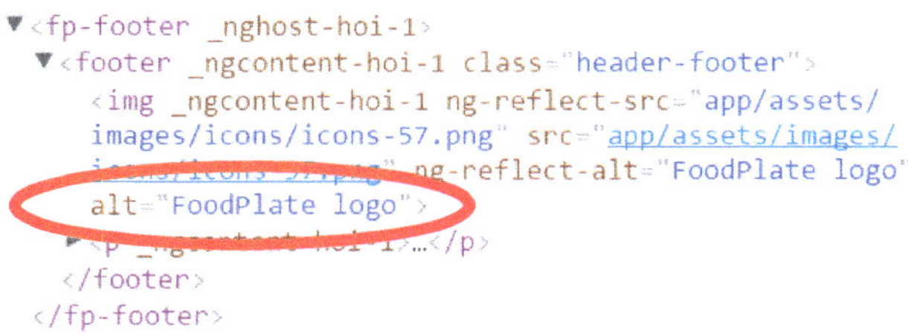

```
▼<fp-footer _nghost-hoi-1>
  ▼<footer _ngcontent-hoi-1 class="header-footer">
     <img _ngcontent-hoi-1 ng-reflect-src="app/assets/
     images/icons/icons-57.png" src="app/assets/images/
     icons/icons-57.png" ng-reflect-alt="FoodPlate logo"
     alt="FoodPlate logo">
   ▶<p _ngcontent-hoi-1>…</p>
   </footer>
  </fp-footer>
```

Step 3 Create a title property in the header component and use the string "Welcome to FoodPlate!" as the value.

Step 4 Modify the existing text in the header component's H1 element to use interpolation to display the title property.

Possible solution code

footer.component.ts

```
import { Component } from '@angular/core';

@Component({
    selector: 'fp-footer',
    templateUrl: 'footer.component.html',
    styleUrls: ['footer.component.css']
})

export class FooterComponent {
    versionString: string = '1.0.0';
    icon: string = 'assets/images/icons/icons-29.png';
    logoAlt: string = 'FoodPlate logo';
}
...
```

footer.component.html

```
<footer class="header-footer main-footer">
    <img [src]="icon" [alt]="logoAlt">
    <p>&copy; 2018 KRA Inc. <small>Version#{{versionString}}</small></p>
</footer>
```

header.component.ts

```
import { Component } from '@angular/core';

@Component({
    selector: 'fp-header',
    templateUrl: './header.component.html',
    styleUrls:: ['./header.component.css']
})

export class HeaderComponent {
    title: string = 'Welcome to FoodPlate!';
}
```

header.component.html

```
<header class="header-footer">
    <img src="../../assets/images/icons/cli-icon.png">
    <h1>{{ title }}</h1>
</header>
```

7.4 Attribute binding

Remember that Angular's databinding mechanisms are used to bind to properties. However, you may encounter situations where there is an HTML attribute, but not a DOM property to bind to. See the section above titled "Binding to DOM properties vs. HTML attributes" for a refresher. In cases like this, you need attribute bindings. An example of an attribute binding is shown below.

```
[attr.colspan]=newData
```

Attribute binding syntax looks like property bindings. Instead of placing the element property between brackets, you start with the prefix `attr`, followed by a dot (.) and the name of the attribute you are binding to. The attribute value is set using an expression that resolves to a string.

7.5 Class binding

Class bindings add and remove CSS class names from an element's class attribute. It should be noted, however, that this is not the only nor the best way to add CSS classes to DOM elements. Later you will be introduced to the structural directives: `NgIf` and `NgSwitch` which may be used to assign CSS classes as well. Below is a code example that assumes a class property called `inStock` will be used to render the section if the property `isOutOfStock` is false.

```
<section [class.inStock]="!isOutOfStock
```

Class binding syntax is like property binding syntax. Instead of placing an element property between brackets, you start with the prefix `class`, which may be followed by a dot (.) and the name of a CSS class as in:

```
[class.class-name]
```

7.5.1 Data-attributes

Many web applications benefit from the use of metadata within HTML elements. For example, a list of employees is returned via AJAX from a server-side database; the application logic depends on knowing whether employees on the list are part-time or full-time. Perhaps a table or unordered list will be created from this data. In a case like this, the following form might be helpful: `<li data-emp-status="part-time">`. Now, the `<li>` element has metadata associated with its contents. HTML elements can carry custom data attributes in the following form: `<element data-customname = "value">`. The data- attribute is used to associate proprietary information with a particular DOM element.

HTML5 provides a custom data attribute used to store custom data that is private to the page or application. The attribute begins with "data-"which must be followed by more than one character after the hyphen. Multiple `data-` attributes may be used on any HTML element and assigned any value.

You can read more about data- attributes at https://www.w3.org/TR/2014/REC-html5-20141028/dom.html#embedding-custom-non-visible-data-with-the-data-*-attributes.

7.5.2 data-* syntax rules

These custom attributes, also known as the data-* attributes, allow developers to associate data with HTML attributes. The data-* attribute must follow certain rules.

data-* attribute rule	Example
Must begin with data-	`<h1 data-`
Must contain only letters, numbers	`<h1 data-status>` `<p data-rule-1>`

May contain these symbols: dash (-), dot (.), colon (:), underscore (_)	`<li data-account-number>`
	`<li data-code.rule>`
	`<li data-employee:code>`
	`<li data-employee_record>`

Should not contain ASCII capital letters (A–Z).	

The data- attribute name is transformed into a `DOMStringMap` object. A `DOMstringmap` is defined by the W3C HTML specification (at http://www.w3.org/TR/html5/infrastructure.html#domstringmap-0) as follows:

The `DOMStringMap` interface represents a set of name-value pairs. It exposes these using the scripting language's native mechanisms for property access.

When a `DOMStringMap` object is instantiated, it is associated with three algorithms, one for getting the list of name-value pairs, one for setting names to certain values, and one for deleting names.

The transformed data- attribute name (the `DOMStringMap`) follows the rules shown below.

Attribute to DOMStringMap rules	
1	The data- prefix is removed (including the dash (-).
2	For any dash in the attribute that is followed by an ASCII lowercase letter (**a–z**), the dash is removed, and the letter is changed to uppercase.
3	All other characters, including dashes are left unchanged.

The transformed data- attribute name (the `DOMStringMap`) follows the rules shown below.

DOMStringMap key to attribute rules	
1	A data- prefix is added (including the dash [-]). RESTRICTION: A dash must not be immediately followed by an ASCII lowercase letter (`a-z`) before the transformation.
2	Any ASCII uppercase letter (`A-Z`) is changed into a dash followed by its lowercase equivalent.
3	All other characters are left unchanged.

Here is an example transformation (from data-attribute to DOMString):

<li data-employee-status> becomes the key employeeStatus.

7.5.3 The dataset API

The dataset API provides access to data- attributes. It does so by providing an HTML attribute called "`dataset`." The dataset attribute contains the `DOMStringMap` object. The `DOMStringMap`'s key contains the name of the data attribute without the data- prefix (and subject to the rules in the "Attribute to DOMStringMap" rules table above).

Without the dataset API, the dataset attribute could be accessed via the standard HTML getters and setters for attributes, including `setAttribute(),getAttribute(),` and `removeAttibute()`.

You can compare the performance with and without the dataset API at jsperf.com using the test found at http://jsperf.com/dataset-vs-attributes-loop/3.

The dataset API can be used any time metadata needs to be added to DOM elements. However, you may get better performance when accessing the data- attributes with standard DOM scripting.

Dataset API	
To set values	`document.getElementById("tag").dataset.status="fulltime";`
To get values	`var data=document.getElementById("tag").dataset.status`
To remove values	`delete document.getElementById("tag").dataset.status;`

7 – Demo (optional) Data-attributes

In this demonstration, the dataset API is used to get the values associated with data- attributes. The data-attribute exercises looked at the need to add metadata to DOM elements. The dataset API provides that capability through the creation of data- custom attributes, and the API provides access to these attribute values. The details of getting and setting data- attributes were examined, and the rules governing the use of the HTML dataset property were explained.

Step 1 Open the file data-attributes-demo.html from the angular-class-files/demos/data-attributes folder in a code editor and a web browser.

Step 2 Click the two buttons on the page. The results should look like the screenshots below.

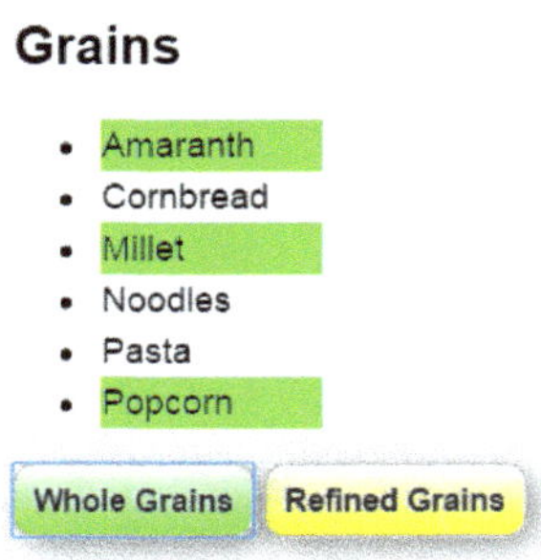

After clicking the Whole Grains button:

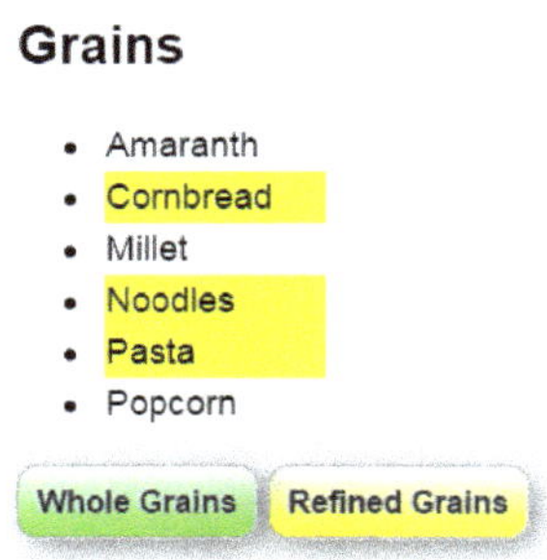

After clicking the Refined Grains button

Step 3 Examine and discuss the code with your instructor.

14—Guided Exercise: Adding a class and attribute binding

In this exercise, you change the style of the "Version: 1.0.0" in the footer using a class binding.

Step 1 Open the footer.component.ts and add a property called isCurrent, typed as a boolean and set to true. The relevant code is shown below in bold.

```
export class FooterComponent {
    versionNumber: number = 100;
    icon: string = 'app/assets/images/icons/icons-57.png';
    logoAlt: string = 'FoodPlate logo';
    isCurrent: boolean = true;
}
```

Step 2 Add two new CSS classes to the footer component's CSS file with the following class names and properties. Modify the footer>* as shown below in bold. You can find this file in foodPlate-cli-files/code-snippets/class-binding.txt.

```
footer>* {
    padding: 0 .25em;
}
.footer--update {
    color: #F00;
    font-weight: bold;
    font-size: .65em;
    border: 1px solid #000;
    border-radius: .20em;
    padding: .35em;
    background-color: #fff;
}

.footer--update::after {
    content: " Update Needed!";
}
```

Step 3 Open the view template footer.component.html and use a class binding to bind the new styles rules to the <small> tag. Then add an attribute binding to the data- attribute.

```
<footer class="header-footer">
    <img [src]="icon" [alt]="logoAlt">
    <p>&copy; 2018 FoodPlate Inc. <small [attr.data-version]="versionString"
[class.footer--update]="!isCurrent">Version {{versionString}}</small></p>
</footer>
```

The [attr.data-version] creates and binds a data-version attribute to the small element. The data-attributes are described in the section following this exercise along with a demonstration file that you can open to better understand the use-case for the data- attributes.

Step 4 Test the file in a web browser. The footer element will be rendered regardless of the isCurrent variable's value. The CSS used to render the element will be determined by the isCurrent variable's value. If it is false the --footer-update class will be used.

Step 5 Try setting the `isCurrent` variable to false and retest the file in the browser. It should match the screenshot below.

Step 6 Reset the isCurrent variable back to “true” and save the file.

Note When managing multiple classes, the `NgClass` directive is the preferred method. This method will be examined in the structural directives section of this course.

Debugging Tip

Angular 9 provides additional debugging capabilities in the browser console using a new global called window.ng.

Window.ng allows developers to access Angular components, directives and view containers for debugging.

To use this new feature, you need:

- Angular Version 9
- An Ivy enabled project
- To be in development mode

Open the console and type the following.

```
let el = $('fp-footer');
let comp = ng.getComponent(el);
```

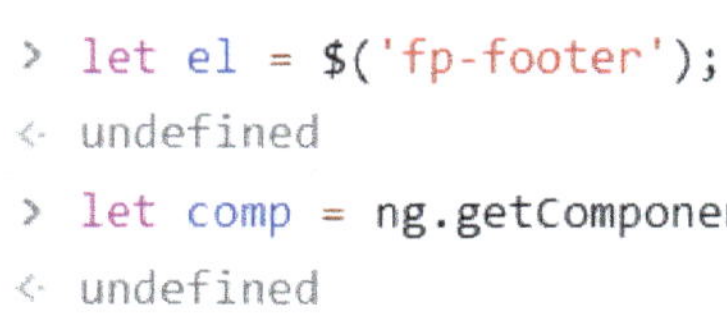

Now, type `comp.` and view the code assist which recognizes your component properties.

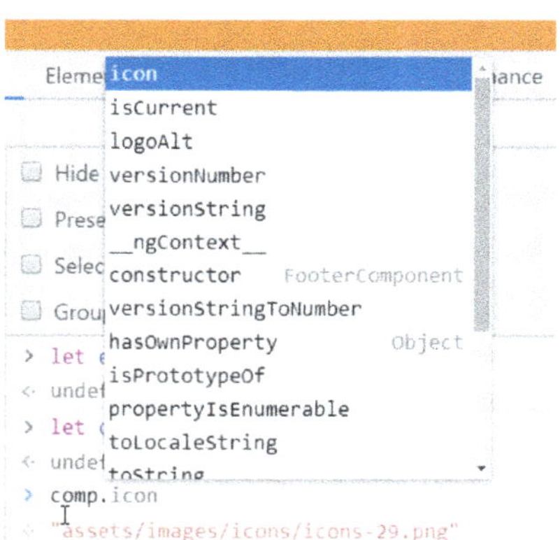

7.6 Style binding

Style bindings are used to set inline CSS style rules. Style binding syntax is like property binding syntax. Instead of an element property between brackets, you set the prefix `style`, followed by a dot (.) and the name of a CSS style property as in:

```
[style.style-property]
```

Because of their similarity to class bindings, there will be no guided or practice exercise using style bindings.

It is important to understand when to use style bindings as well as the other bindings you have learned. Style bindings are different from class bindings in that class bindings assign a CSS class which can contain multiple CSS properties and values. Style bindings are used when you need to dynamically set specific individual CSS properties like font-family or font-size. Unlike a class these CSS properties can be set individually based on data in the component class.

7.7 Event binding

Event bindings allow Angular to respond to DOM events typically triggered by user input such as mouse-clicking, typing in text input fields and so on. The idea is to capture user-initiated events from the view and tie them to logic found in the component. As you can derive from that explanation, an event binding is a one-way binding. Some developers think of the event binding as the opposite of the property binding where data is sent from the component to the view. You will make many event bindings throughout the course.

7.7.1 Creating an event binding

To bind to a DOM event, surround the DOM event name in parentheses and then assign a template statement that invokes a method of the component. Angular can bind to standard event categories like mouse events, media events, progress events, storage events, and more.

15—Guided Exercise: Create an Event binding

In this exercise, you add the code to pop-up an alert box when the user clicks the icon in the footer.

Step 1 Open footer.component.ts.

Step 2 Add a method (called `moreInfo`) to the footer component class that pops up an alert box with the following message: "For more information about the Food Plate, visit https://www.choosemyplate.gov/"

```
export class FooterComponent {
    icon:string = 'assets/images/icons/icons-29.png';
     ...
    moreInfo():void {
        alert('For more information about the Food Plate, visit
https://www.choosemyplate.gov/');
    }
}
```

Step 3 Bind the click event of the footer icon to the new method. The event binding syntax uses parentheses instead of square brackets.

```
<footer class="header-footer">
  <img [src]="icon" (click)="moreInfo()" [alt]="logoAlt">
```

Step 4 Modify the CSS for the footer so that the cursor changes to a pointing finger when the user hovers their mouse over the icon image. To do this, create a CSS utility class called "pointer" that can be used on any element in the application. Where should you write this CSS class?

Step 5 Examine the CSS below which was placed in the footer.component.css file. It provides feedback to the user that the image is "clickable" by changing the standard cursor to a pointing finger.

```
...
img {
    cursor: pointer;
}
```

Step 6 Save the file and test the application in Chrome. Be sure to mouseover and click the image in the footer to test the alert box and the CSS pointer icon.

7 – Practice Exercise: Create the bindings

Given the following files, add the bindings to the proper file to achieve the result shown below. You may write your answer in the spaces on the following page.

Current Customers

- Customer Name: Widgets, Inc.
  Customer Balance: $12,435.00
- Customer Name: Thingamabobs Enterprises
  Customer Balance: $1,435.00

The finished file as seen in Chrome.

main.component.ts

```
import { Component, OnInit } from '@angular/core';


@Component({
  selector: 'app-main',
  templateUrl: './main.component.html',
  styleUrls: ['./main.component.css']
})
export class MainComponent implements OnInit {

  customers:Array<any>;
  constructor() { }

  ngOnInit() {
    this.customers = [
        {
          name: 'Widgets, Inc.',
          id: 123,
          balance: '$12,435.00',
          status: 'pastDue'
        },
          {
          name: 'Thingamabobs Enterprises',
          id: 124,
          balance: '$1,435.00',
          status: 'current'
      }
    ]
  };
}
```

main.component.css

```
.current {
    color: green;
}

.pastDue {
    color: red;
}

p, li {
    font-family: Arial, Helvetica, sans-serif;
    font-size: .75em;
    font-weight: 300;
    line-height: 1.3em;
    padding: 0;
    margin: 0;
}
```

main.component.html

```
<div>
  <h1>
   Current Customers
  </h1>
  <ul>
    <li *ngFor="let customer of customers">
      <p>Customer Name: ________________________________________</p>
      <p>Customer Balance: <span ____________________________>
        _______________________________________________________</span></p>
    </li>
  </ul>
</div>
```

The `*ngFor` code in the `<li>` element is an Angular directive that will essentially create a loop iterating through the number of customers and create a new `<li>` element for each customer.

Homework Exercise

Step 1 Read the event binding section of the Angular documentation at https://angular.io/guide/template-syntax#event-binding

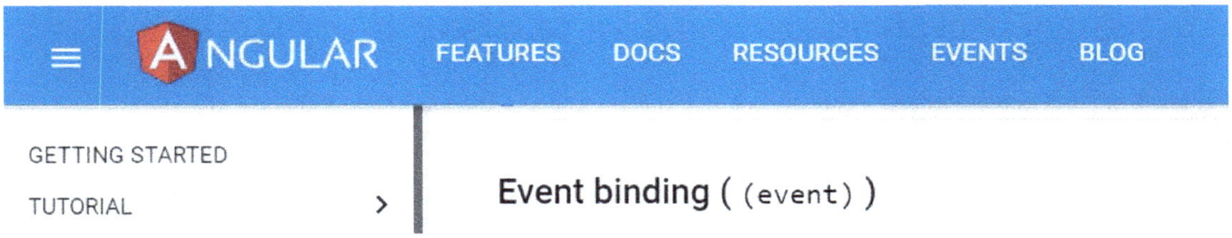

Chapter 7 Quiz

https://tinyurl.com/t2629ka

1) Given the following scenarios choose the correct binding type.
   A. Property binding
   B. Attribute binding
   C. Class binding
   D. Style binding
   E. Event binding
2) You need to style a DOM element based on the boolean value of a property in the component class. ____________
3) You need to bind an `href` attribute to a component class property. ____
4) You need to bind a DOM element to a CSS class based on data found in the component class.

   ____
5) You need to bind a `click` event to component class method. ____
6) You need to set the `className` property for an H1 element. ____
7) You need to bind the `colspan` attribute of a <td> element to a component property.______________________
8) You need to set multiple specific CSS properties based on data found in the component class.

   ____

Chapter Summary

In this chapter, you learned how to set properties in your component classes that can be used dynamically in your component views by way of Angular's data binding approaches.

Next Chapter

In the next chapter, you are introduced to how components pass data. Specifically, how a parent component can share data with its' children.

Chapter 8
Data Models and Services

Chapter 8: Services

Objectives

- Define data modeling
- Define Domain Models
- Describe an Angular Service and a typical use-case
- Write and use a service
- Explain how dependency injection works in Angular

Introduction

A service is a TypeScript (or JavaScript) file that contains functionality that you need to share between components. Keeping this type of logic separate from the rest of application keeps your code organized and easier to unit test and maintain over time. The Angular documentation states that "Almost anything can be a service. A service is typically a class with a narrow, well-defined purpose. It should do something specific and do it well." The documentation further states "Component classes should be lean. They don't fetch data from the server, validate user input, or log directly to the console. They delegate such tasks to services."

Angular services are simply classes that contain properties and methods. Angular provides services for sharing logic between components. Think of services as the location for your application and business logic. Services are typically created as singletons. Therefore, a single service instance may be shared among the applications components and its children. A common service would be code that fetches data from a database or a JSON file on the server. In this chapter, you create a simple service, but don't worry if it is too simple, you will be creating more complex services as the course continues.

8.0 How do services fit in Angular architecture?

Figure 19 below shows how Angular's services fit into the overall architecture of Angular. The figure is taken from the Angular documentation at https://angular.io/guide/architecture. The injector holds the services and are shown on the lower left corner of figure 1.

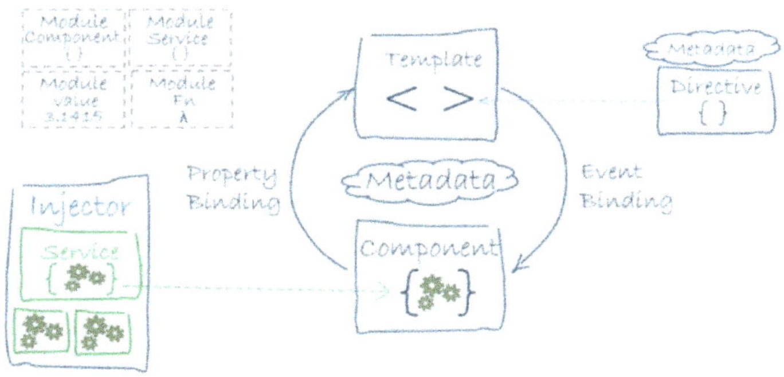

Figure #19: Angular services as defined in the Angular documentation.

8.1 When should you create a service?

Any functionality your application needs can be a service. There is nothing specific in the file that makes it an Angular service. This is because Angular doesn't specifically define a service through a base class of any kind. One common use case for services is to acquire data from the server. Once that data becomes part of the application, it is helpful to take advantage of the datatyping features of TypeScript. This typically requires data modeling and the use of domain models.

8.2 Domain Models

Most developers agree that it is a best practice to isolate the data structures from the rest of your application code. When using the Angular framework, that means keeping data structurs out of components. Instead we create a plain class that stores the data known as a domain model. This serves as the conceptual model of the domain that incorporates both behavior and data.[i]

8.2.1 The FoodPlate application's user model

The FoodPlate application's main function is to track the users' consumption of the five major food groups. After the user registers (Chapter 12 Forms), the application code will consider the users' age and gender to determine how much food from each food group should be consumed daily.

You will create a data model to explicitly describe the structure of the data. You may also use this file, when appropriate as a domain model.

Our user data model will need to keep track of the following:

- User name (as a string)
- User age (as a string)
- User gender (as a string)
- A code to use with lookup tables that determine their daily requirement of fruit, vegetables, protein and grains. (as a string)
- Their daily food group requirements (as an array of numbers)
- Their status regarding daily food group consumption (as an array of numbers)
- Their registration status (as a Boolean)

16—Guided Exercise: Create a data model

In this exercise, you create a typescript file that exports a User class. When the user logs into the application, a user object will be instantiated from this class. That user object will store basic information about the user as well as how much food from each food group has been consumed.

Step 1 Create a folder inside of the app folder called "models." The first model our application will need is the user model.

Step 2 Inside of the new "models" directory, create a TypeScript class called User.ts You may copy and paste this file from the assets/code-snippets/User.ts file.

```
export class User {
  id: number;
  firstName: string;
  gender: string;
  ageGroup: string;
  userCode: string;
  reqs: {
    fruitReqs: number,
    vegReqs: number,
    proteinReqs: number,
    grainReqs: number
  };
  reqsStatus: {
    fruitMet: boolean,
    vegMet: boolean,
    proteinMet: boolean,
    grainMet: boolean
  };
  registered: boolean;
  email: string;
  constructor(id, firstName, gender, ageGroup, userCode, reqs, reqsStatus,
registered, email) {
    this.id = id;
    this.firstName = firstName;
    this.gender = gender;
    this.ageGroup = ageGroup;
    this.userCode = userCode;
    this.reqs = reqs;
    this.reqsStatus = reqsStatus;
    this.registered = registered;
    this.email = email;
  }
}
```

In this exercise, you created a class to serve as the user data model when instantiating the user at login time. The user will also hold information about the user, such as if he/she has registered, their age group and the number of food items they have consumed from each food group.

8.3 What is a service?

Services provide components with business logic, shared functionality and just about any code used in the application. As stated previously, according to the Angular docs: "Service is a broad category encompassing any value, function, or feature that an app needs. A service is typically a class with a narrow, well-defined purpose. It should do something specific and do it well."

Components are typically the consumers of services; thus services are injected into components allowing the component access to the injected service class. This process creates a dependency between the component and the service which is resolved via Angular's dependency injection. It is important to remember, however, that a dependency does not have to be a service. A dependency and an injection can, in fact, be simply a function or a value.

8.4 What is dependency injection?

Dependency injection provides a means to make parts of our application code accessible to other parts of our application. Angular's implementation of dependency injection provides several benefits. One benefit, common to all dependency injection patterns, is the fact that the component does not need to be aware of how to create dependencies. It simply interacts with the dependencies. For example, if we access data via a service and that service calls a database to get the data, our components have no knowledge of this; they simply act on the data they received. This makes it very easy to change the service later without affecting the component code. For example, we can change the service to look at localStorage or cookies to retrieve the data, instead of a database. Simply put (by the Angular docs), "dependency injection (DI) is a way to create objects that depend on other objects (called the dependencies) when it create ds an instance of an object."

8.4.1 Angular's Dependency Injection

Angular's dependency injection is composed of three parts:

- The **Provider** that tells Angular how to create an object
  Note: the provider maps a token (a string, object, class, and so on) to a list of dependencies.
  A token is a key that is used to reference a provider. This tells Angular to create the object, given that token.
- The **Injector** that resolves dependencies and injects them when creating objects
- The **dependency** which is what is being injected

Together, these three parts tell Angular what is being injected and how the injection will be resolved.

Getting data, (or any other type of business logic that is required by multiple parts of an application), is one of many compelling reasons to use dependency injection. We don't want each component to create objects for what it needs via a factory. Ultimately this leads to tightly coupled application code, where each component takes on too much responsibility. Instead, we'd like to register classes with an injector that can be used by components. Components, then simply ask for what they need, and the injector delivers it, with no need for the component to create or even understand what it receives.

Fortunately, you do not have to create an injector because it comes with the angular framework and is created during the bootstrap process. The @Injectable() decorator marks the class as available to an injector for instantiation.

8.5 The hierarchical nature of Angular's dependency injection

When making architecture decisions, it is important to know that angular does not use one single injector. In the Angular Architecture chapter, you learned that an Angular application is a tree of components. Each component has its own injector, thus there is an injector tree that mimics the tree of components. When a component requests a dependency, Angular looks up this tree of component injectors to find the dependency. If it can't find it in the parent component, it continues to bubble up, stopping only when it reaches the component that has declared itself to be the "host" component.

By providing a service at the component level (as opposed to app.component), you can essentially control where that service is accessible. In this chapter, you will provide all services in the app component, making application-wide services as singletons. In some applications, this could cause the overwriting of data, due to a single service providing the "write" privileges, perhaps in areas of the application where it shouldn't. Moving the service provider to the component that requires that services limits its reach from other component that shouldn't have access to the service.

8.5.1 Angular 9 Services and services Injection

For any dependency that your application needs, you must register a provider with Angular's application injector. This allows the injector to use the provider to create new instances of the dependency. For most services, the provider is the service class itself.

When a service is created via the Angular 9 CLI tool, the service is provided in the app module via the code below.

```
@Injectable({
  providedIn: 'root',
})
```

When provided this way (at the root level), Angular creates a single shared instance of the service class and injects it into any class that asks for it.

You can also register a provider with a specific module, in which case the same instance of the service class is made available to all components in that ngModule. This is done with the code below.

```
@NgModule({
  providers: [
      DataService,
      LoggerService
 ],
 ...
})
```

Finally, services can also be provided at the component level, in which case, Angular creates a new instance of the service with each new instance of that component. This is done with the code below.

```
@Component({
  selector:    'app-product-list',
  templateUrl: './product-list.component.html',
  providers:  [ ProductService ]
})
```

In Angular 6 and higher Services Injection services can be provided at the root level via:

```
@Injectable({
  providedIn: 'root',
})
```

In Angular 9, you can change the providedIn property to 'any' or 'platform'. The 'any' property creates a separate service instance for each lazy-loaded module (more on lazy loading in the Advanced Routing chapter) as well as one for the "root" module. Choosing 'any' creates a new isolated instance of a service for every child injector, thus not a singleton.

When lazy-loading modules, you typically want a new service instance to be creation when the module is loaded. This is what we get when using "any" as the providedIn property. The 'any' value works when providing services in NgModules (not the root or app module).

Choosing 'platform' results in a singleton injector that would be shared by all applications, thus making a service available between multiples applications.

8.5.2 Angular 6 and higher Services Injection

Angular version 6 changes the method for providing services. A service file from an Angular 6 project will use the format shown below from the documentation at https://angular.io/guide/dependency-injection. The line shown below in bold declares that the service should be created by the root application injector. "root" can be replaced with any module. This change was made due to JavaScript bundling that resulted in a module ending up in the final bundle even if it was not used in the application. This approach results in better tree shaking to remove unused modules from the final bundle.

```
import { Injectable } from '@angular/core';

@Injectable({
  providedIn: 'root',
})
export class HeroService {
  constructor() { }
}
```

8.5.3 Angular 5 or lower

In Angular 5 and lower, services need to be declared as providers (of a service) to the module. This is done via the providers property. See the example with the provider shown in bold below.

```
@NgModule({
  imports: [
    CommonModule, BrowserModule
  ],
  declarations: [ AppComponent, MainComponent ],
  bootstrap: [ AppComponent ],
  providers: [ UserService ]
})
```

This tells TypeScript to emit the metadata about your service. Because type definitions are specific to Typescript, the compiled JavaScript would not know anything about the parameter passed to the providers property shown above in bold. See the tsconfig.json snippet below that demonstrates how the compiler will emit metadata about the type of the parameter passed to @Injectable. In Angular 6 the method of providing services has changed. See the section "Angular 6 Services Injection" below for more details.

```
..."compilerOptions": {
  "outDir": "./dist/out-tsc",
  "sourceMap": true,
  "declaration": false,
  "moduleResolution": "node",
  "emitDecoratorMetadata": true,
  "experimentalDecorators": true,
  "target": "es5",
  "typeRoots": [
    "node_modules/@types"
  ],...
```

Figure #20: Tsconfig.json showing the emitDecoratorMetadata property set to true.

This allows Angular to inject other dependencies into the service. You will also need to import the Injectable decorator from the @angular/core package.

Angular and dependency injection summary

- Collaborating Components need to:
- Know which components to communicate with
- Where to locate them
- How to communicate with them
- i.e.: Services (access can be changed)
- Solution: Injectable dependencies!
- Components embed the logic for locating and/or instantiating services as part of their own logic

Using dependency injection summary

- Have the application declare the components dependencies
- Have external code assume the responsibility of locating and/or instantiating the objects or services required
- Supply these service references to the components when needed

8.6 How to use a service with dependency injection

Services are injected into the components that need them. This is done with the steps, shown below.

1. Create the service, typically with the name structured as name.service.ts (example: user.service.ts)
2. Provide the service to the module that uses it, through the providers property as shown in the example below.

```
@NgModule({
  imports: [
    CommonModule, BrowserModule
  ],
  declarations: [ AppComponent, MainComponent ],
  bootstrap: [ AppComponent ],
  providers: [ UserService ]
})
```

3. Inject the service into the component's constructor function as shown in the example below. Notice the use of the keyword "private" which creates a class property (called userService) that is private. It is the JavaScript engine that calls our classes' constructor function, making it out of the control of the Angular framework. To control when our code is executed, Angular provided the ngOnInit lifecycle hook. By passing the UserService in the constructor, we can tell Angular what dependencies the component requires and map them to a specific property in the class.

```
constructor(private userService: UserService) {}
```

4. Use the service as needed. In the example below the service returns a user object. A user property is created, and the service supplies the value when the component is initialized. Component initialization is a life-cycle hook (you will learn more about life cycle hooks throughout the course). `ngOnInit` is a life cycle hook that is called right after the component's properties have been checked for the first time, but before any of its children have been checked. ngOnInit is used here because it guarantees that the class binding will be readily available. This is because ngOnInit is called after initializing the component, thus the framework has run a Change Detection phase against all the classes properties that are bound to the component.

```
ngOnInit() {
    this.user = this.userService.getUser();
  }
```

5. Bind to the service as needed. In the example below, the user service provides a user object with a reqsStatus.fruitMet property. The user service supplied property is interpolated in the view template.

```
<p>{{(user.reqsStatus.fruitMet) ? 'You ate all your fruit today!' : 'You still
have more fruit to eat.'}}</p>
```

17–Guided Exercise: Using an Angular built-in service

In this exercise, you use a built-in Angular service which provides a title for the index.html page. Because the Angular framework uses a single-page architecture, you will often need to change the page title so that it corresponds to the components loaded into the page. For example, you might want the home page to be titled "Welcome to FoodPlate" but you might want the register page to be titled "FoodPlate: Register Page."

This could not be accomplished with a binding because the <title> element is inside of the <head> section which is not accessible via Angular data-binding. Fortunately, the Angular browser platform framework provides a service that will allow us to set the index page's title. It is appropriately named the Title service and you will use it in this exercise.

Step 1 Open the FoodPlate-cli project. Refresh the page in the browser and confirm the current title on the browser window or tab that currently reads: FoodPlateCli.

Note Because the Title class is already registered as a service by the Angular dependency injection system, it does not need to be imported or added to the app module's providers array.

Step 2 Modify the app.component.ts as follows:

- Import the Title class from the Angular platform-browser
- Implement the OnInit interface so that you can use the ngOnInit() lifecycle method to call the service Remember that ngOnInit is called to initialize the component after Angular first displays the data-bound properties and sets the component's input properties.
- Inject the Title service into the component constructor so that it can be used in the component
- Call the `setTitle()` method of the Title service at initialization of the component

The relevant changes are shown below in bold.

```
import { Component, OnInit, ViewEncapsulation } from '@angular/core';
import { Title } from '@angular/platform-browser';

@Component({
  selector: 'fp-app',
  templateUrl: './app.component.html',
  styleUrls: ['./app.component.css'],
  encapsulation: ViewEncapsulation.None
})

export class AppComponent implements OnInit {
  constructor(private titleService: Title) {
  }
  ngOnInit(): void {
    this.titleService.setTitle('Welcome to FoodPlate!');
  }
}
```

Step 3 Save and run the file in Chrome to confirm the new Title. The new title tab is shown below.

18—Guided Exercise: Creating and using a service

In this exercise, you create and use a simple service in the angular-seed project. The service will simply provide a title for any component that needs it. The title will be the string "Welcome to Angular Seed" and it will be used by the header component.

Step 1 In the app folder, create a service called title via the CLI command:
`ng g s services/headerTitle`

Note This will create a folder call services with a service file called "title.service.ts."

Step 2 Our title.service will follow the best practice mentioned and include @Injectable().

```
import { Injectable } from '@angular/core';

@Injectable({
  providedIn: 'root'
})
export class HeaderTitleService {
}
```

Step 3 Now add the service method `getTitle()`.

```
import { Injectable } from '@angular/core';

@Injectable({
  providedIn: 'root'
})
export class HeaderTitleService {
    getTitle(): string {
        return 'Welcome to Angular Seed';
    }
}
```

Step 4 Open header.component.ts and prepare the file to use the service. The relevant code is shown in bold.

```
import { Component, OnInit } from '@angular/core';
import { HeaderTitleService } from '../services/header-title.service';
@Component({
    selector:       'app-header',
    templateUrl:    './header/header.component.html',
    styleUrls:      ['./header/header.component.css']
})
export class HeaderComponent implements OnInit {
     userName: string = "Kevin";
     title: string;
     constructor(private headerTitleService: HeaderTitleService) {
    }
    ngOnInit(): void {
        this.title = this.headerTitleService.getTitle();
    }
}
```

Step 5 Use of the title property in header.component.html.

```
<header class="header-footer">
    <img src="assets/images/seed-icon.png">
    <h1>{{ title }}, {{ userName }}!</h1>
</header>
```

Step 6 Run the application in the browser and you should see the title property of the header component rendered as shown below.

6 –Challenge Exercise: Create and use a service

In this exercise, you add a simple service to the FoodPlate cli application.

Simple Instructions

- Create a service that returns a user object. Call the service user.service
- The user you create should look like this (substitute the sample code below with your own information):
  - `private user: User = new User(1, 'Kevin', 'M', '51+', 'M51+', {}, {fruitMet: false, vegMet: false, proteinMet: false, grainMet: false}, false, 'kevin@kevinruse.com');`
- Create a method to return the user called `getUser`.
- Use the service in app.component by injecting it and calling `getUser()` onInit to store the user in a app.component property called `user`.
- View the file in Chrome using Augury to confirm the existence of the user object as shown below.
  - Launch the DevTools in Chrome
  - Access the Augury extension tab
  - Click on the AppComponent in the Component tree.
  - Expand the user object on the left.

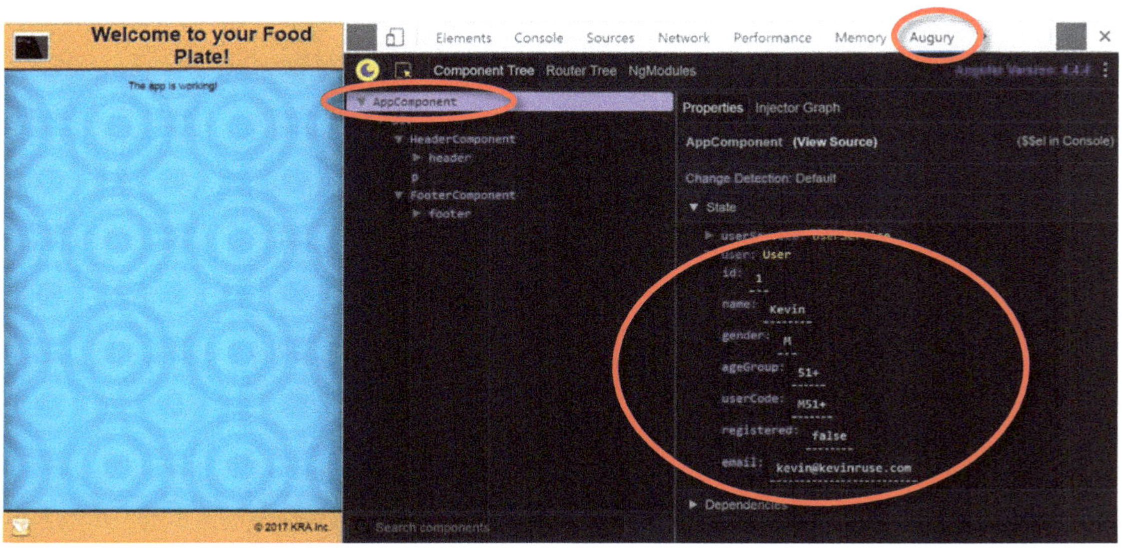

Step by Step Instructions

Create the service

Step 1 Create a file called user.service.ts.

```
ng g s services/user
```

Step 2 Open services/user.service.ts and note the `@Injectable()` function.

```
@Injectable({
      providedIn: 'root'
    })
export class UserService {
}
```

We add @Injectable() when our service injects providers. It simply tells Angular to store the metadata it needs. Our user service does not inject any providers itself. By passing in the object with the providedIn property, our service is provided to the application at root level.

Step 3 Inside of the new service file, create a private property called user, so that we can test our service.

```
private user: User = new User(1, 'Kevin', 'M', '51+', 'M51+', {}, {fruitMet:
false, vegMet: false, proteinMet: false, grainMet: false}, false,
'kevin@kevinruse.com');
```

Note This code is temporary because typically you will not use the new keyword to construct a data model. This code will be refactored later. Ultimately, in the FoodPlate application, a form will collect data about the user and create the user object from that data.

Step 4 Create a `getUser` method that returns the `testUser`.

```
getUser(): User {
  return this.user;
}
```

Step 5 Import the User data model. The finished code is shown below.

```
import { Injectable } from '@angular/core';

import { User } from '../models/User';

@Injectable({
  providedIn: 'root'
})

export class UserService {

  private user: User = new User(1, 'Kevin', 'M', '51+', 'M51+', {}, {fruitMet:
false, vegMet: false, proteinMet: false, grainMet: false}, false,
'kevin@kevinruse.com');
```

```
  getUser(): User {
    return this.user;
  }
}
```

Use the service

To use the new service, refactor the existing code that utilizes the User data model. First, we must "inject" the user into the component that needs it.

Step 6 Open app.component.ts and add the following code shown in bold.

```
...
import { User } from './models/User';
import { UserService } from './services/user.service';
...
export class AppComponent implements OnInit {

  user: User;

  constructor(private userService: UserService,
          private titleService: Title) {
    }
    ngOnInit() {
          this.titleService.setTitle('Welcome to FoodPlate! ');
          this.user = this.userService.getUser();
    }
}
```

Notice the constructor function. This function is part of the life cycle of components. In a subsequent chapter, you will take a deep dive into component life cycle. For now, it's sufficient to understand that the constructor function is invoked after Angular creates a component or directive. The constructor method is used as a hook that provides access to this point in time in the component's life.

Note Save and run the file in Chrome. If you are using Angular 4 or 5, you will get the error message shown below.

```
▶ERROR Error: No provider for UserService!                    AppComponent_Host.html:1
    at injectionError (core.es5.js:1169)
    at noProviderError (core.es5.js:1207)
    at ReflectiveInjector_.webpackJsonp.../../../core/@angular/core.es5.js.ReflectiveInjector_._throwOrNull
  (core.es5.js:2649)
```

Error message due to not providing the UserService in the module.

To correct the error, add the providers property to the app.module as shown below in bold. Notice that the user previously created in the constructor function has now been removed as well as the import of the user class.

```
import { NgModule } from '@angular/core';
import { CommonModule } from '@angular/common';
import { BrowserModule } from '@angular/platform-browser';

import { AppComponent } from './app.component';
import { HeaderComponent } from './header/header.component';
import { FooterComponent } from './footer/footer.component';
```

```
import { UserService } from './services/user.service';
@NgModule({
  imports: [
    CommonModule, BrowserModule
  ],
  declarations: [AppComponent, HeaderComponent, FooterComponent],
  bootstrap: [AppComponent],
  providers: [UserService]
})
export class AppModule { }
```

The providers property is used to register a service in a module, so that Angular knows about it. The provider above is shorthand for:

```
providers: [
    provide: UserService,
    useClass: UserService
]
```

The provide property is the token for the provider that is being registered and the useClass property is used to look up what is stored under the token. This allows two provides to have the same class. Likewise, we can override a provide while still using the same token. You will have more opportunities to explore dependency injection throughout the course.

When using Angular 6 or higher, the Angular CLI tool uses Services Injection. Therefore, the service will automatically be provided in the root module via code in the service TypeScript file.

Step 7 Return to Chrome and use the Augury extension to see the userService and user object.

Debugging Tip

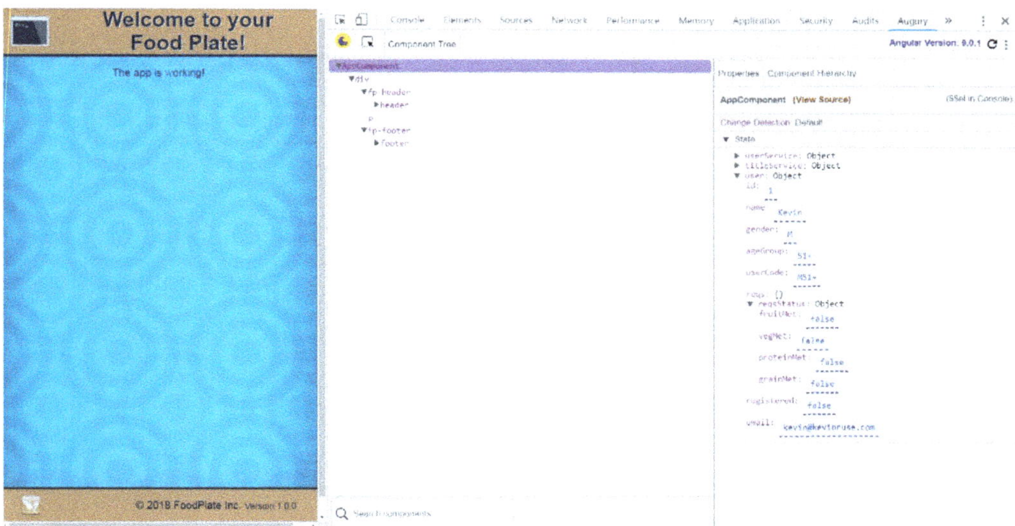

Use the Augury extension to see your component tree, component properties, and more.

Chapter 8 Advanced: Optional Services and Dependency Injection

Objectives

- How to make service dependencies optional

Introduction

Earlier in this chapter, you learned how to use services provided by the Angular framework. After that, you learned how to create your own services, and in both cases, you learned how to use dependency injection to use services. In this section, you will explore more advanced aspects of dependency injection.

8.6 Optional Dependencies

When using dependency injection in Angular, it is possible to mark some services as optional. You indicate to Angular that a dependency is optional by annotating the argument passed into the constructor with a decorator as shown in the example code below.

```
constructor(@Optional() private optionalServiceDependency: Type) {
}
```

Because it is an optional dependency, it is now possible that there is no registered class for the service, making it null when it is used by another service. In the next exercise, you will make a service, set is use in another service as optional and lastly, write code that is ready for a null value for the dependent service.

19—Guided Exercise: Make a service intended for optional use in other services

In this exercise, you will make a service that is used to log the status of users.

Step 1 Create a service inside of the services folder called `userStatus`.

```
ng g s services/userStatus
```

Step 2 Write the service with a registered property as a boolean type, a user property as a User type and two methods: getRegisterStatus and getUserStatus.

Note The code below uses Angular 6 and higher Services Injection (shown in bold @Injectable()).

```
import { Injectable } from '@angular/core';
import { User } from '../models/User';

@Injectable({
  providedIn: 'root'
})
export class UserStatusService {
  registered: boolean;
  user: User;

   getRegisterStatus(currentUser): void {
    if (currentUser.registered === true) {
        console.log(`User Registered is: ${currentUser.registered}`);
    }
  }

   getUserStatus(currentUser): void {
    console.table(currentUser);
  }

  constructor() { }
}
```

Step 3 Inject the new service into the user.service.ts file and annotate it as an optional dependency.

```
constructor(@Optional() private userStatusService: UserStatusService) {
     this.userStatusService.getUserStatus(this.user);
}
```

Step 4 Import the Optional, User and UserStatusService classes in the user.service.ts file as shown below in bold.

```
import { Injectable, Optional } from '@angular/core';
import { User } from '../models/User';
import { UserStatusService } from './user-status.service';
```

Step 5 Save and run the file in Chrome. Open the DevTools to see the result of the service call.

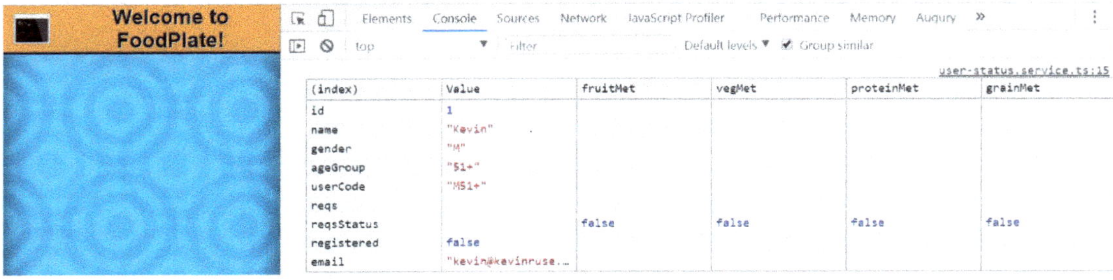

Step 6 Now, let's see what happens if this optional service is not injected. Open user-status.service.ts and remove the provider in user-status.service.ts as shown below.

```
@Injectable()
```

Step 7 Refresh the file in Chrome and examine the DevTools.

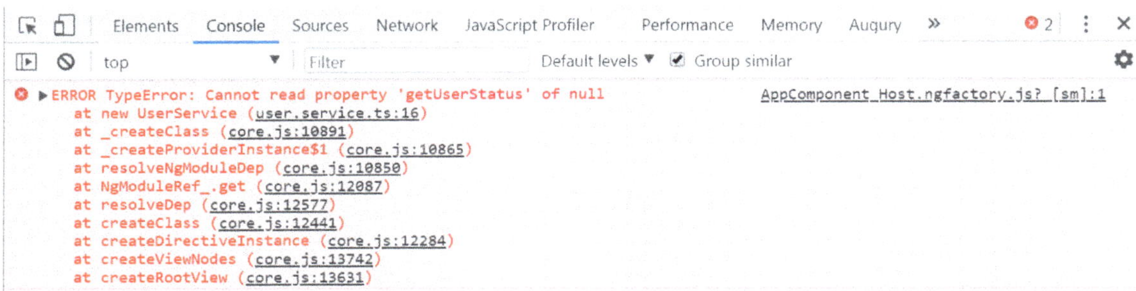

Step 8 To allow for a null value, modify the user.service.ts as shown below.

```
constructor(@Optional() private userStatusService: UserStatusService) {
    if (this.userStatusService) {
            this.userStatusService.getUserStatus(this.user);
    }
}
```

Step 9 Save and refresh the file in Chrome to confirm there is no longer an error. Be sure to add back the `providedIn: 'root'` that you removed in the step 6 instruction before moving on to the next chapter.

Chapter 8 Quiz

https://tinyurl.com/vulur5u

1) True or False Any sort of business logic may be placed in a service file.

2) Below are the steps needed for using a service. Which step is missing?
   a. Create the service file.
   b. Inject the service in the constructor function of the component that requires the service.
   c. Use the service methods and properties as needed.
   d. From the component's view template, bind to the service as needed.

Homework

Step 1 Create a data model using the fm-sm.json as the data source. A snippet is shown below.

```
{
    "FMID": "1011871",
    "MarketName": " Stearns Homestead Farmers' Market",
    "Website": "http://Stearnshomestead.com",
    "street": "6975 Ridge Road",
    "city": "Parma ",
    "County": "Cuyahoga",
    "State": "Ohio",
    "zip": "44130",
    "x": "-81.7285969",
    "y": "41.3751180",
    "Credit": true,
    "Bakedgoods": true,
    "Cheese": "N",
    "Crafts": "N",
    "Flowers": true,
    "Eggs": true,
    "Seafood": "N",
    "Herbs": true,
    "Vegetables": true,
    "Honey": true,
    "Jams": true,
    "Maple": true,
    "Meat": true,
    "Nursery": "N",
    "Nuts": "N",
    "Plants": true,
    "Poultry": "N",
    "Soap": "N",
    "Trees": "N",
    "Wine": "N",
    "Coffee": "N",
    "Beans": "N",
    "Fruits": true,
    "Grains": "N",
    "Juices": "N",
    "Mushrooms": "N",
    "PetFood": true,
    "updateTime": "4/9/2016 8:05:17 PM"
}
```

Chapter summary

In this chapter, you learned what services are and when you should use them. You created a simple service and learned about dependency injection as a means of using the service.

Next Chapter

In the next chapter, you learn how to share information from a parent to a child component.

Chapter 9
Understanding Component Communication

Chapter 9: Component Communication

Objectives

- Describe how parent components share their data with child components
- Use Angular's `@Input` decorator to share data from a parent to a child component
- Use Angular's `@Output` decorator to share data from a child to a parent component

Introduction

This chapter is about understanding how components communicate. Specifically, it is about how a parent component can communicate and share data with its children.

Components communicate through various means, including using services, input and output decorators and local variables. This chapter will focus on the `@Input()` and `@Output()` decorator methods.

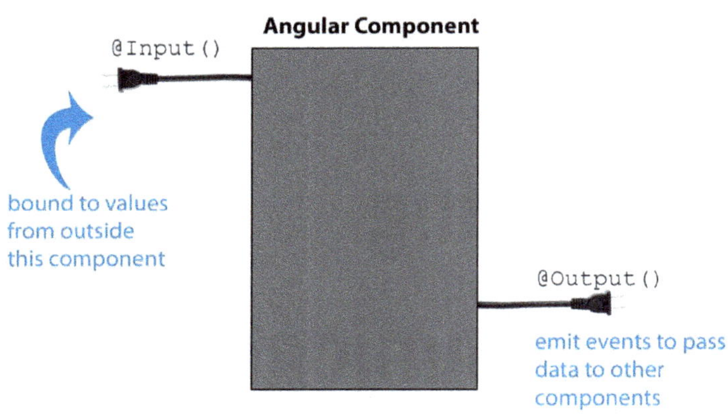

Figure #21: Components share data through Input and Output decorators.

9.0 Nesting components

Because components are composable, it is common to place components inside of other components, as shown below.

```
    selector: 'fp-welcome',
    template: `
            <fp-static-plate></fp-static-plate>
            <fp-plate></fp-plate>
            `
})
```

Figure #22: welcome.component.ts with the template showing the child components: fp-static-plate and fp-plate.

Part of Angular's component communication is sharing data between the parent and child components. Passing data from the parent component to the child component is done using the `@Input()` decorator function.

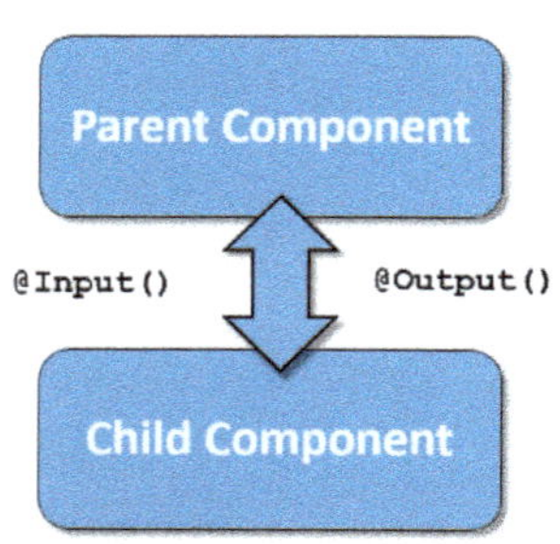

Figure #23: Parent to child communication takes place via @Input() and @Output()

9.0.1 An app module showing parent and child

The parent component

Child component

```
import { NgModule }       from '@angular/core';
import { BrowserModule } from '@angular/platform-browser';

import { AppComponent }  from './app.component';

import { ChildComponent } from './child.component/child.component'

@NgModule({
  imports:      [ BrowserModule ],

  declarations: [ AppComponent, ChildComponent ],

  bootstrap:    [ AppComponent ]
})
export class AppModule {

}
```

Figure #24: The app module showing the relevant code for a parent and child component.

Child components' template

```
import { Component } from '@angular/core';

@Component({
  selector: 'my-app',
  template: `<h1>Hello </h1>

            <child-component [something]="nameProperty"></child-component>`,
})
export class AppComponent  {

  //something I want to share with other components
  nameProperty:string;

  constructor() {
    this.nameProperty = "Kevin"
  }
}
```

Figure #25: The parent component with a property injected from the parent.

Showing the @Input

```
import { Component,Input } from '@angular/core';

@Component({
    selector: 'child-component',
    template: `<h2>{{something}}</h2>`,
})
export class ChildComponent  {
    @Input()
    something:string;
}
```

Figure #26: The @Input decorator in the child component.

The @Input property can be renamed via an alias by passing the alias name to the @Input decorator as shown below.

```
@input('aliasName')
propertyName: string
```

Best Practice 1: from: https://angular.io/guide/styleguide#style-05-13
Avoid input and output aliases except when it serves an important purpose.
Why? Two names for the same property (one private, one public) is inherently confusing. You should use an alias when the directive name is also an input property, and the directive name doesn't describe the property.

20–Guided Exercise: Use @Input to share data from parent to child component

In this exercise, you change the greeting in the header based on whether the user has registered. If the user has registered the header will read: "Welcome to Food Plate!" If the user has already registered, the header will read "Welcome back to FoodPlate." In addition, the header should greet the user by name: "Welcome back to FoodPlate, Kevin!" You will use the FoodPlate seed project for this exercise.

Step 1 For this exercise, instead of building a user service, you will create a user object property inside of app.component.ts with the values shown below. You can copy and paste this file from code snippets/user-object.txt.

```
user = {id: 1, name: 'Kevin', gender: 'M', ageGroup: '51+', userCode: 'M51+',
reqs: {}, reqsStatus: {fruitMet: false, vegMet: false, proteinMet: false,
grainMet: false}, registered: false, email: 'kevin@kevinruse.com'};
```

Step 2 You will need to modify the header.component.ts with @Input decorators for a user as shown below in bold.

```
import { Component, Input, OnInit } from '@angular/core';
import { TitleService } from '../services/title.service';
@Component({
    selector:        'app-header',
    templateUrl:     './header/header.component.html',
    styleUrls:       ['./header/header.component.css']
})
export class HeaderComponent implements OnInit {
    @Input()
    user;
```

Step 3 You will need to modify the header.component.html to use the new input.

```
<header>
  <img src="assets/images/seed-icon.png"app.c>
  <h1>Welcome {{(user.registered) ? 'back' : ''}} to Angular
Seed{{(user.registered) ? ", " + user.name : ''}}!</h1>
</header>
```

Step 4 You will need to modify the app.component.html template to input the user so that it generates the correct message: "Welcome " or "Welcome back ".

```
<div>
  <app-header [user]="user"></app-header>
  <p>The app is working!</p>
  <app-child></app-child>
  ...
</div>
```

Step 5 Check your code by changing the users' registered property from 'true' to 'false.'

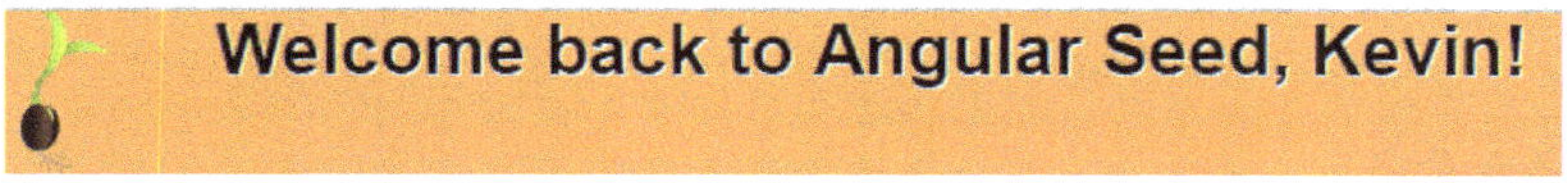

The header component when the user.registered is true.

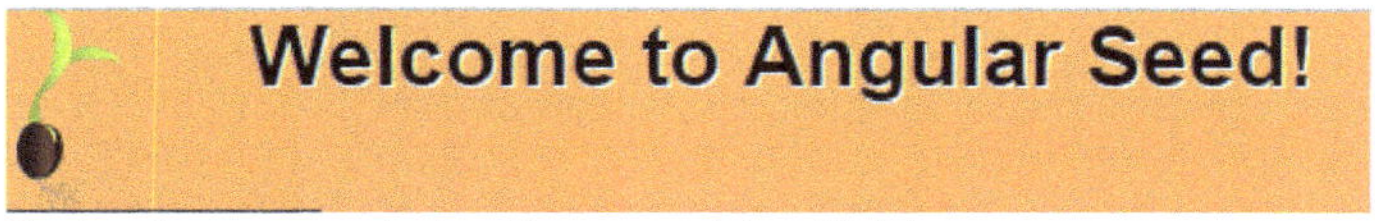

The header component when the user.registered is false.

7 –Challenge Exercise: Create parent/child relationships between components

In this exercise, you create a component that is placed in between the header and footer components. This component called main.component will have one child, a button component called home-btn.component.

Simple Instructions

- Create a component called "main".
- Add an html `<main>` element to the foodPlate-cli's main component view template.
- Add the following CSS to the main component:

```
main {
    display: flex;
    align-items: center;
    flex-direction:column;
}
```

- Create a component called "homeBtn"
- Add the following HTML to the homeBtn's view template:

```
<input type="button" class="fpButton">
```

  - Add the homeBtn component inside the HTML `<main>` element in the foodPlate-cli's main component.
- Copy the contents of the src/assets/css/button-styles.css into the global css file for the app.
- Add the new component to app.component's HTML between the fp-header and the fp-footer

Step by Step Instructions

Step 1 Create a new component called "main."

```
ng g c main
```

Step 2 Open main.component.html and replace the generated code with the HTML shown below.

```
<main>
    <fp-home-btn></fp-home-btn>
</main>
```

This creates the relationship between the parent component (main.component.ts) and the child component (home-btn.component.ts)

Step 3 Open main.component.css and add the CSS below for the view template.

```
main {
    display: flex;
    align-items:center;
    flex-direction:column;
}
```

Step 4 Create a new component called "HomeBtn".

```
ng g c homeBtn
```

Step 5 Replace the home-btn.component.html file's generated HTML with the code shown below.

```
<input type="button" class="fpButton">
```

Step 6 The home-btn component style rules should apply to all buttons on the application, so its CSS should be written in styles.css. Copy the contents of the src/assets/css/button-styles.css file and paste it into src/styles.css below the existing CSS.

Step 7 Declare the new components in app.module.ts and then add the main component to app.component.html.

```
<div id="wrapper">
  <fp-header></fp-header>
  <fp-main></fp-main>
  <fp-footer></fp-footer>
</div>
```

You have now built a component with a child. Run the file in Chrome. *The button will not have a label.*

Step 8 Use the Angular extension in Chrome to examine the new parent/child relationship.

```
⌄ fp-app
    fp-header
  ⌄ fp-main
      fp-home-btn
    fp-footer
```

8 –Challenge Exercise: Parent to child component communication

In this exercise, you share the user data from the parent app.component to the child components.

The button's value (the label the button displays) will come from the parent component and will change based on the data found in the parent component.

Simple Instructions

Create a property that identifies the user. Share this property with the main and homeBtn components' so that the homeBtn's label can be either "Check In" (if the user has already registered) or "Register" if the user has not registered.

- Add an `@Input()` decorator to the main component class file and name the input property `user`. Set the datatype of the input property as a User object.
- Bind the input property from the homeBtn component to the main component.
- Add an `@Input()` decorator to the homeBtn component class file and name the input property `user`.
- Bind the value property of the homeBtn's input to a conditional value based on the value of the `user.registered` property (true/false).
- Make any necessary bindings in the templates to the Input `user` property.
- The end result is shown below.

user.registered = true

User.registered = false

Step by Step Instructions

Step 1 Modify the main.component.ts file by adding the @Input decorator function and importing the Input class as shown below in bold.

```
import {Component, Input, OnInit} from '@angular/core';
import {User} from '../models/User';

@Component({
  selector: 'fp-main',
  templateUrl: './main.component.html',
  styleUrls: ['./main.component.css']
})
export class MainComponent implements OnInit {
  @Input()
  user: User;

  constructor() { }
  ngOnInit() {
  }
}
```

In this exercise, remember that the app.component is the parent component that includes the child component: `<fp-homeBtn>`. The `@Input` decorator or input properties are used to pass data from the parent to the child component.

Step 2 Modify the main.component.html template by adding the databinding to the child component. Note the use of square brackets to bind to the user property.

```
<main>
    <fp-home-btn [user]="user"></fp-home-btn>
</main>
```

To pass a value to the child component, pass the child component property inside of square brackets. Then set its value to a property of parent component; in this case the user property. We are passing the value of the user property from the parent component (app.component) to the `user` property of the child component.

Step 3 Add the @Input decorator to the home-btn.component.ts and add the necessary imports.

```
import {Component, Input, OnInit} from '@angular/core';
import {User} from '../models/User';
...
export class HomeBtnComponent implements OnInit {

  @Input()
  user: User;

  constructor() {
...
```

Step 4 Add the databinding that uses the @Input() user property. It will bind the value property of the button to a ternary operator with a condition that evaluates the value of the user property.

```
<input type="button"
       id="home_btn"
       class="fpButton"
       [value]="(user.registered) ? 'Check In' : 'Register'">
```

Step 5 In the app component's template, bind the user object. Use the line shown below in bold.

```
<div id="wrapper">
   <fp-header></fp-header>
   <fp-main [user]="user"> </fp-main>
   <fp-footer></fp-footer>
</div>
```

Step 6 In user.service.ts, change the user's registered property to true and run the file in a web browser. The button values are shown below.

user.registered = true

User.registered = false

Debugging Tip

You can use the Angular extension to change user's registered property from true to false as shown below.

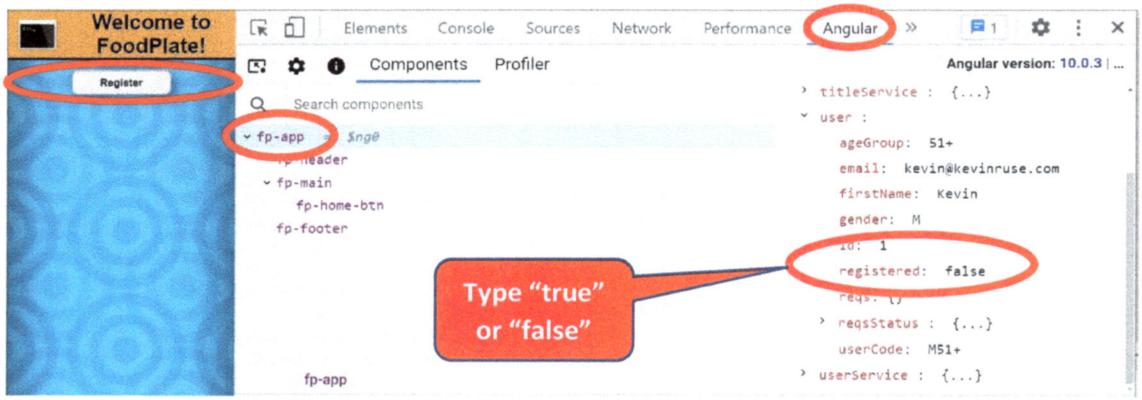

1. Using the component tree, select the HomeBtnComponent.
2. Expand the user object by clicking the triangle next to the User object.
3. Double-click the "false" value in the registered property and change it to "true."
4. In the browser window. The button label should now read "Check In."

9 –Challenge Exercise: Use parent/child communication

In this exercise, you create the initial view the user sees at startup (a component called main). This component will contain the html 5.2 `<main>` element used to host the main pieces of the application. The main component will have a child plate component and a child component called message. The message component will be used to display feedback to the user as they keep track of the foods they eat. The goal of the exercise is to have the plate component parent communication with its child component message. You will use the FoodPlate cli project for this challenge exercise.

The plate component contains four boolean properties called fruitMet, vegMet, proteinMet and grainMet, all initialized to false. When the user has eaten their daily requirement of fruit, the property fruitMet property will become true. That property change should trigger two results: first, the color of the plate changes to red and second, a message appears alerting the user they have met their daily fruit requirement. The images below demonstrate the view changes.

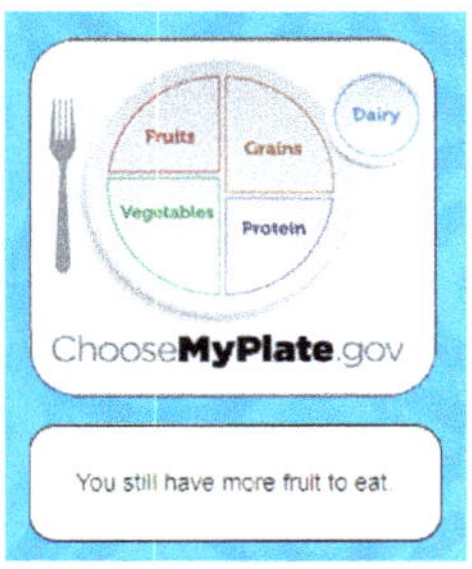

fruitMet = false

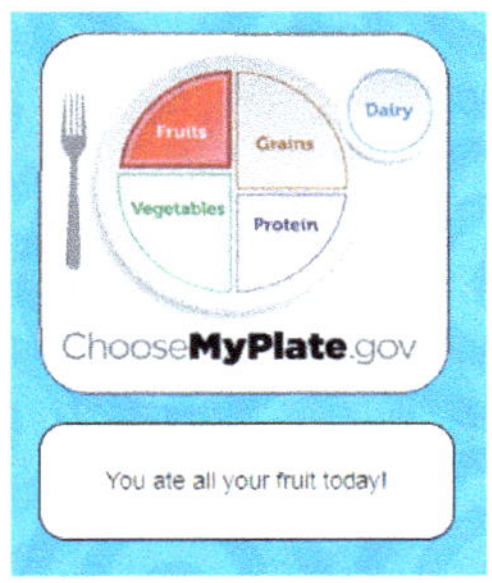

fruitMet= true

Simple Instructions

- Create a new component called "plate".
- Copy and paste the plate component class properties from assets/code-snippets/plate-component-ts.txt.
- Copy the CSS for the plate component from assets/css/plate.css.
- Display the white plate if the user has not met their food group requirement as shown in the Grains, Protein and Vegetable images above. Display a colored plate if the user has met their food group requirement as shown in the fruit portion of the image above..
    - Create a conditional in the plate component html that binds the src property of the plate to the `user.reqsStatus` property for each food group. Example:
        - `user.reqsStatus.fruitMet`; if the `fruitMet` is true bind to `fruitFull` and if false bind to `fruitEmpty`
- Add the plate component to the main component (above the home-btn).
- Create a message component (you will use it in a subsequent exercise) and place it below the plate graphics in the plate component.

<u>Code snippets used in this exercise:</u>

Plate CSS	assets/css/plate.css
Plate HTML	assets/code-snippets/plate-component-html.html
Plate Component properties	assets/code-snippets/plate-component-ts.txt
Message Component CSS	assets/css/message-component-css.css

- Check your work in the browser.

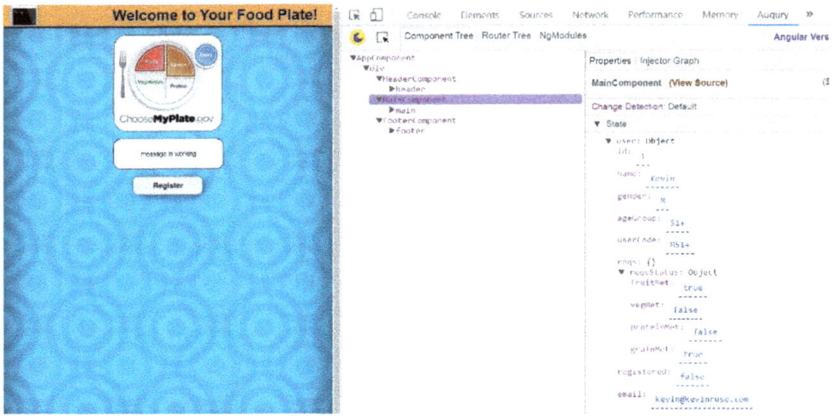

Step by Step Instructions

Step 1 Create a plate component.

```
ng g c plate
```

Step 2 Modify the plate.component.ts so that the exported class declares the properties shown below. You can copy and paste this content from assets/code-snippets/plate-component-ts.txt.

```
  plateImgPath: string = '../../assets/images/plateImages/';
  fruitEmpty: string = `${this.plateImgPath}fruit-empty.png`;
  grainDairyEmpty: string = `${this.plateImgPath}graindairy-empty.png`;
  proteinEmpty: string = `${this.plateImgPath}protein-empty.png`;
  vegEmpty: string = `${this.plateImgPath}veg-empty.png`;
  fruitFull: string = `${this.plateImgPath}fruit-full.png`;
  grainDairyFull: string = `${this.plateImgPath}graindairy-full.png`;
  proteinFull: string = `${this.plateImgPath}protein-full.jpg`;
  vegFull: string = `${this.plateImgPath}veg-full.jpg`;
```

Step 3 Copy the CSS from assets/css/plate.css to the plate.component.css

Step 4 Add the following HTML to the plate component. You can copy and paste this file from assets/code-snippets/plate-component-html.html, **then add the bindings shown below in bold**.

```
<section id="plate">
  <div id="foodPlateWrapper">
    <div id="colwrap1">
      <img [src]="(user.reqsStatus.fruitMet) ? fruitFull : fruitEmpty"
id="fruit"/>
      <img [src]="(user.reqsStatus.vegMet) ? vegFull : vegEmpty"
id="veg"/></div>
    <div id="colwrap2">
      <img [src]="(user.reqsStatus.grainMet) ? grainDairyFull :
grainDairyEmpty" id="grain"/>
      <div id="logoContainer" class="clearFloat"></div>
      <img [src]="(user.reqsStatus.proteinMet) ? proteinFull : proteinEmpty"
id="protein" />
```

```
      <div class="clearFloat"></div>
    </div>
    <img src="assets/images/plateImages/text.png" id="text" alt=""/>
  </div>
</section>
```

The single plate graphic is composed of five different images: four images make up the plate and one image contain the text ChooseMyPlate.gov. When the user first registers the plate is "empty" as in each graphic is white. When the user eats the required quantity of a food group, the graphic will become colorized. Notice the bindings in the HTML to the different images that make up the foodplate graphic. Consider the first image element.

```
<img [src]="(fruitMet) ? fruitFull : fruitEmpty" id="fruit"/>
```

If the `fruitMet` property is true, the image used will be the one called fruitFull.png with the red color. If the `fruitMet` property is false the image with white plate will be used (fruitEmpty.png).

Step 5 Add the plate component to the main component, placing it above the `<fp-home-btn>`.

Step 6 Create a message component.

Step 7 Replace the generated HTML in message.component.html to the code shown below.

```
<section>
  <p>message is working</p>
</section>
```

Step 8 Create the message.component.css shown below. You can copy this from assets/css/ message-component-css.css/

```
section {
    width: 90%;
    padding: .75em;
    border: 1px solid #000;
    border-radius: 1em;
    background-color: #fff;
}
p {
    text-align: center;
    font-size: .85em;
}
```

Step 9 Add the message component before the closing </section> element in the plate component.

Step 10 Add the code required to achieve the results shown in the screenshots below.

Step 11 Don't forget to add your new components to the app.module and add the new components to the app.

Hint Use the plate.component.html as a guide.

Step 12 Test the file by changing the fruitMet and proteinMet value from false to true. The graphic representing the fruit portion of the plate should turn red and the protein portion of the plate should turn purple.

Possible solution code

app.module.ts

```
import { NgModule } from '@angular/core';
import { CommonModule } from '@angular/common';
import { BrowserModule } from '@angular/platform-browser';

import { AppComponent } from './app.component';
import { HeaderComponent } from './header/header.component';
import { FooterComponent } from './footer/footer.component';
import { UserService } from './services/user.service';
import { MainComponent } from './main/main.component';
import { HomeBtnComponent } from './home-btn/home-btn.component';
import { PlateComponent } from './plate/plate.component';
import { MessageComponent } from './message/message.component';

@NgModule({
  imports: [
    CommonModule, BrowserModule
  ],
  declarations: [AppComponent, HeaderComponent, FooterComponent, MainComponent,
HomeBtnComponent, PlateComponent, MessageComponent],
  bootstrap: [AppComponent],
})
export class AppModule { }
```

app.component.ts

```
import { Component, Input, OnInit, ViewEncapsulation } from '@angular/core';
import { Title } from '@angular/platform-browser';
import { User } from './models/User';
import { UserService } from './services/user.service';

@Component({
  selector: 'fp-app',
  templateUrl: './app.component.html',
  styleUrls: ['./app.component.css'],
  encapsulation: ViewEncapsulation.None
})
export class AppComponent implements OnInit{

  @Input()
  user:User;

constructor(private userService: UserService, private titleService: Title)  {
}

ngOnInit() {
  this.titleService.setTitle('Welcome to FoodPlate!');
  this.user = this.userService.getUser();
   }
}
```

app.component.html

```
<div id="wrapper">
    <fp-header></fp-header>
    <fp-main [user]="user"> </fp-main>
    <fp-footer></fp-footer>
</div>
```

main.component.ts

```
import { Component, Input, OnInit } from '@angular/core';

import { User } from '../models/User';

@Component({
  selector: 'fp-main',
  templateUrl: './main.component.html',
  styleUrls: ['./main.component.css']
})
export class MainComponent implements OnInit {

  @Input()
  user:User;

  constructor() { }

  ngOnInit() {
  }
}
```

main.component.html

```
<main>
  <fp-plate [user]="user"></fp-plate>
  <fp-home-btn [user]="user"></fp-home-btn>
</main>
```

main.component.css

```
main {
    display: flex;
    align-items: center;
    flex-direction: column;
    section {
    width: 90%;
    padding: .75em;
    border: 1px solid #000;
    border-radius: 1em;
    background-color: #fff;
}
p {
  text-align: center;
  font-size: .85em;
}

}
```

plate.component.ts

```
import { Component, Input, OnInit } from '@angular/core';
import { User } from '../models/User';

@Component({
    selector: 'fp-plate',
    templateUrl: './plate.component.html',
    styleUrls: ['./plate.component.css']
})
export class PlateComponent implements OnInit {

    @Input()
    user: User;

    plateImgPath = '../../assets/images/plateImages/';
    fruitEmpty = `${this.plateImgPath}fruit-empty.png`;
    grainDairyEmpty = `${this.plateImgPath}graindairy-empty.png`;
    proteinEmpty = `${this.plateImgPath}protein-empty.png`;
```

```
    vegEmpty = `${this.plateImgPath}veg-empty.png`;
    fruitFull = `${this.plateImgPath}fruit-full.png`;
    grainDairyFull = `${this.plateImgPath}graindairy-full.png`;
    proteinFull = `${this.plateImgPath}protein-full.jpg`;
    vegFull = `${this.plateImgPath}veg-full.jpg`;

    constructor() { }

    ngOnInit() {
    }
}
```

plate.component.html

```
<section id="plate">
  <div id="foodPlateWrapper">
    <div id="colwrap1">
      <img [src]="(user.reqsStatus.fruitMet) ? fruitFull : fruitEmpty" id="fruit"/>
      <img [src]="(user.reqsStatus.vegMet) ? vegFull : vegEmpty" id="veg"/></div>
    <div id="colwrap2">
      <img [src]="(user.reqsStatus.grainMet) ? grainDairyFull : grainDairyEmpty" id="grain"/>
      <div id="logoContainer" class="clearFloat"></div>
      <img [src]="(user.reqsStatus.proteinMet) ? proteinFull : proteinEmpty" id="protein"/>
      <div class="clearFloat"></div>
    </div>
    <img src="../../assets/images/plateImages/text.png" id="text" alt=""/>
  </div>
  <fp-message [user]="user"></fp-message>
</section>
```

plate.component.css

```
/* ******************************the food plate ************ */
section {
    display: flex;
    flex-direction: column;
}

#colwrap1 {
    float: left;
    margin-left: 0;
    margin-top: 0;
    width: 112px;
}
#fruit {
    margin-left: 0;
    margin-top: 0;
    display: inline;
    float: left;
    height: 81px;
    margin-bottom: 0;
    width: 112px;
}
#veg {
    margin-left: 0;
    margin-top: 0;
    display: inline;
    float: left;
    height: 93px;
    margin-bottom: 0;
    width: 112px;
}
#colwrap2 {
    float: left;
    margin-left: 0;
    margin-top: 0;
```

```
    width: 122px;
}
#grain {
    margin-left: 0;
    margin-top: 0;
    display: inline;
    float: left;
    height: 93px;
    margin-bottom: 0;
    width: 122px;
}
#protein {
    margin-left: 0;
    margin-top: 0;
    display: inline;
    float: left;
    height: 81px;
    margin-bottom: 0;
    width: 122px;
}
#text {
    margin-left: 0;
    margin-top: -1px;
    display: inline;
    float: left;
    height: 40px;
    margin-bottom: 0;
    width: 234px;
}
#iconList li {
    list-style-image:none;
    display:inline;
}
#content {
    margin-left:10%;
    margin-right:10%;
}
#foodPlateWrapper {
    width: 235px;
    margin: 1em auto;
}
```

message.component.ts

```
import { Component, Input, OnInit } from '@angular/core';
import { User } from '../models/User';

@Component({
  selector: 'fp-message',
  templateUrl: 'message.component.html',
  styleUrls: ['message.component.css']
})
export class MessageComponent implements OnInit {

  @Input()
  user: User;

  constructor() { }

  ngOnInit() {
  }

}
```

message.component.css

```
section {
    width: 90%;
    padding: .75em;
    border: 1px solid #000;
    border-radius: 1em;
    background-color: #fff;
}
p {
    text-align: center;
    font-size: .85em;
}
```

21–Guided Exercise: Use @Output to share data from child to parent component

In this guided exercise, you pass the log-in status of the user from a child component to a parent component.

Step 1 Open child.component.ts and add an output decorator to the exported class.

```
@Output()
login;
```

Step 2 Set the value of the onLogin property to a new event emitter that will emit a boolean value.

```
login = new EventEmitter<boolean>();
```

Step 3 Confirm that the EventEmitter and Output classes have been imported as shown below.

```
import {Component, EventEmitter, OnInit, Output} from '@angular/core';
```

Step 4 Open child.component.html and add an event binding that binds a `<p>` element's click event to a component method called `loginOuput()` and pass a single boolean argument of `true`. Add the text "Output Login Status" to the `<p>` element as shown below.

```
<p (click)="loginOutput(true)">Output Login Status</p>
```

Step 5 Return to the child.component.ts and add the method.

```
loginOutput(login: boolean): void {
    this.login.emit(login);
    console.log(login);
}
```

Step 6 Open app.component.html and add an event binding that listens to the `onLogin` event that was emitted from the child. Bind the event to a component method called `logIn()` and pass the event object as shown below in bold.

```
<div>
    <app-header [user]="user"></app-header>
    <app-child (login)="logIn($event)"></app-child>
     <app-form-input icon="envelope">
         <small>Business email</small>
         <label for="emailAddress">Email:</label>
         <input id="emailAddress" type="email">
     </app-form-input>
    <app-child></app-child>
</div>
```

Note The `$event` parameter is analogous to HTML inline event handlers like `onclick= "clickHandler(event)"` where `event` represents the event object itself. However, for `EventEmitter` events, the emitted value is available as $event. Thus, $event is the event itself which carries the value (true, in this case).

Step 7 Add a `<p>` element so that is displays the data emitted from the child component as shown below in bold.

```
<div>
  <app-header [user]=""></app-header>
  <p>Logged In: {{ loggedIn }}</p>
  <app-child (onLogin)="logIn($event)"></app-child>
</div>
```

Step 8 Open the app.component.ts and add a `loggedIn` property and a `logIn()` method as shown below.

```
...
loggedIn: boolean;
logIn(evt): void {
   console.log(evt);
   this.loggedIn = evt;
}
```

Step 9 Add a child component css file that changes the cursor when hovered over the <p> element to a pointer

```
p {
      cursor: pointer;
}
```

Step 10 Test the file in Chrome. After clicking the text "Output Login Status," it should match the image shown below.

Chapter 9 Advanced: Component Communication with view children decorators

Objectives

- Define the decorators: `@ViewChild`, `@ViewChildren`, `@ContentChild` and `@ContentChildren`
- Use the decorators above to communicate between components

Introduction

In this section, you learn more about component communication using the @ViewChild decorator. When a component template has children, the children elements are called view children. It is possible to reference view children from the component class. Consider the example below. The view children are shown in bold.

```
@Component({
      selector: 'app-parent-component'
      template: '<section>
                     <app-child-one></app-child-one>
                     <app-child-two></app-child-two>
                  </section>
                  <ng-content select="app-content"></ng-content>
```

Elements that are used inside of a host element are called content children. Consider the example below. The content children are shown in bold.

```
<app-parent-component>
   <app-content>
      <h1>Welcome</h1>
   </app-content>
</app-parent-component>
```

If you need to access the component and/or the content children, the Angular framework provides decorators to help. The @angular/core package makes available the following decorators:

```
@ViewChild
@ViewChildren
@ContentChild
@ContentChildren
```

If you need to select the first element (or directive) from the view DOM, use create a reference using `ViewChild` as shown:

```
@ViewChild('app-child-one') child: AppChildOne
```

In this example above, `@ViewChild` returns the first element (or directive) that matches the selector. The selector is the argument passed into the decoration function `@ViewChild`, which in this case is 'app-child-one.' Now, the parent component can access the methods and properties of that component. Thus, we have another method of component communication.

`@ViewChildren` works in a similar way but returns multiple view children.

When using view children, it's important to understand the lifecycle of a component. See the chart below for a list of Angular's lifecycle hook methods that are used to interject code at certain points in the life a component. The chart below is from the Angular documentation at https://angular.io/guide/lifecycle-hooks#lifecycle-sequence.

9.1 Component Lifecycle sequence

Hook	Purpose and Timing
`ngOnChanges()`	Respond when Angular (re)sets data-bound input properties. The method receives a SimpleChanges object of current and previous property values. Called before ngOnInit() and whenever one or more data-bound input properties change.
`ngOnInit()`	Initialize the directive/component after Angular first displays the data-bound properties and sets the directive/component's input properties. Called once, after the first `ngOnChanges()`.
`ngDoCheck()`	Detect and act upon changes that Angular can't or won't detect on its own. Called during every change detection run, immediately after `ngOnChanges()` and `ngOnInit()`.
`ngAfterContentInit()`	Respond after Angular projects external content into the component's view / the view that a directive is in. Called once after the first ngDoCheck().
`ngAfterContentChecked()`	Respond after Angular checks the content projected into the directive/component. Called after the ngAfterContentInit() and every subsequent ngDoCheck().
`ngAfterViewInit()`	Respond after Angular initializes the component's views and child views / the view that a directive is in. Called once after the first ngAfterContentChecked().
`ngOnDestroy()`	Cleanup just before Angular destroys the directive/component. Unsubscribe Observables and detach event handlers to avoid memory leaks. Called just before Angular destroys the directive/component.

You must understand a bit about the lifecycle of a component to be able to access the `viewChild`. The `viewChild` component will not be available until after the component is initialized because prior to that its children will not have been created. Therefore, to access `viewChildren` you must wait until the lifecycle hook: `ngAfterViewInit` has been called.

Component Lifecycle Sequence

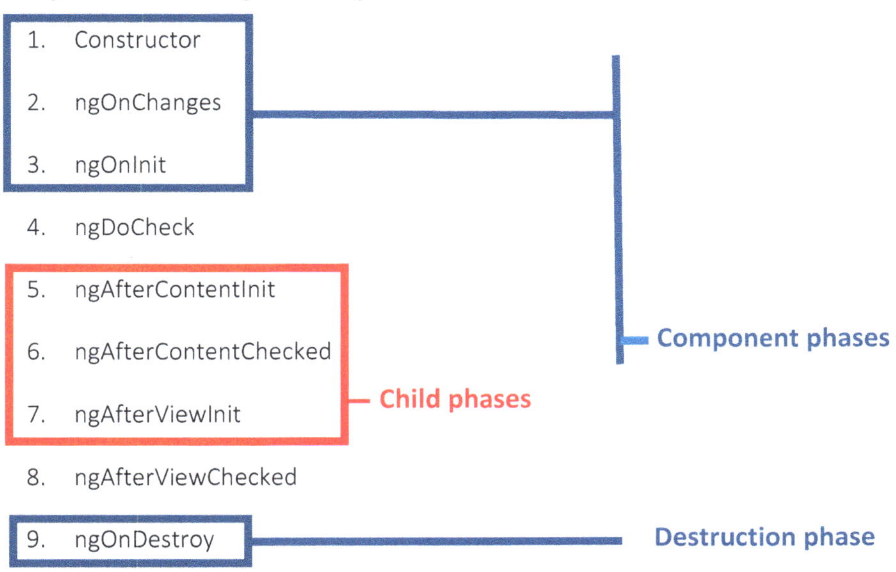

22–Guided Exercise: Understanding the @ViewChild decorator

In this guided exercise, you use the @ViewChild decorator function.

Step 1 Open app.component.ts and add an `@ViewChild()` decorator to the exported class that will be used to communicate with the child component. To use @ViewChild, you need to import the ViewChild class from '@angular/core'. The second argument: static, is set to true to resolve query results before change detection occurs. Setting static to false will ensure query matches that are dependent on binding resolution like `*ngIf` and other structure directives will be found.(See: https://stackoverflow.com/questions/56359504/how-should-i-use-the-new-static-option-for-viewchild-in-angular-8) for more information.

Note As of Angular 9, the `static` property is set to "false" by default. Therefore, the only reason to pass the argument is to set it to "true."

```
@ViewChild(ChildComponent, {static: false}) childView: ChildComponent;
```

Step 2 Log the view child to the console from the constructor function.

```
constructor() {
   console.log(this.childView);
}
```

Note When a component's constructor function is called, the component's children have not yet been initialized, so this will return undefined.

```
undefined                app.component.ts:16
```

Step 3 Save and test the file to confirm the note above. See the chart on the previous page for more information about lifecycle hook functions.

Step 4 Comment the code added in step 2 and log the view child to the console in the ngAfterViewInit method. Implement the `AfterViewInit` in the exported class.

```
ngAfterViewInit() {
      console.log(this.childView);
}
```

Step 5 Save and refresh the page in Chrome with the DevTools console running.

```
▶ ChildComponent {login: EventEmitter}
```

Now that you've seen how to access a single view child, you will add more view children and access them with @ViewChildren.

Step 6 Open app.component.html and add more children as shown below in bold. You can comment the app-form-input element.

```
<app-child (onLogin)="logIn($event)"></app-child>
<app-child></app-child>
<app-child></app-child>
<app-child></app-child>
```

Step 7 Save the file and refresh the page in Chrome. It should look like the image below.

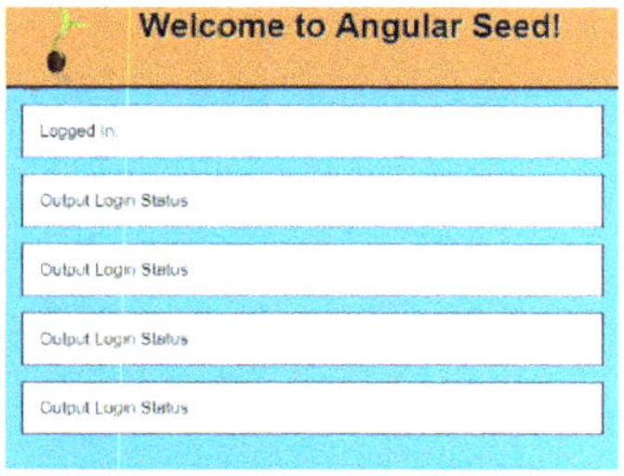

Step 8 To access all the view children, add the @ViewChildren decorator function to app.component.ts as shown below.

```
@ViewChildren(ChildComponent) childrenView: QueryList<any>;
```

Note The Angular documentation describes the `QueryList` as follows:

- An unmodifiable list of items that Angular keeps up to date when the state of the application changes.
- The type of object that `ViewChildren`, `ContentChildren`, and `QueryList` provide.
- Implements an iterable interface, therefore it can be used in both ES6 javascript for (`var i of items`) loops as well as in Angular templates with `*ngFor="let i of myList"`.
- Changes can be observed by subscribing to the changes Observable.

In the future this class will implement an Observable interface.

Step 9 Add additional code to the `ngAfterViewInit` method to:

a. Convert the childrenView from a QueryList to an array
b. Log the new array of view children to the console

```
ngAfterViewInit(): void {
    console.log(this.childrenView);
    const children: ChildComponent[] = this.childrenView.toArray();
    console.log(children);
    console.log(this.childView);
}
```

Step 10 Save and refresh the page in Chrome. Open the console to view the results of the log statement. The console should match the screenshot below.

```
                                                   app.component.ts:23
▼QueryList {_dirty: false, _results: Array(4), _emitter: EventEmitter}
    changes: (...)
    dirty: (...)
    first: (...)
    last: (...)
    length: (...)
    _dirty: false
  ▶_emitter: EventEmitter {_isScalar: false, observers: Array(0), closed:
  ▶_results: (4) [ChildComponent, ChildComponent, ChildComponent, ChildCom
  ▶__proto__: Object
                                                   app.component.ts:25
▼(4) [ChildComponent, ChildComponent, ChildComponent, ChildComponent]
  ▶0: ChildComponent {}
  ▶1: ChildComponent {}
  ▶2: ChildComponent {}
  ▶3: ChildComponent {}
    length: 4
  ▶__proto__: Array(0)
```

Step 11 Delete the added `<app-child>` component view children from app.component.html.

Before we begin communication between the parent and child via the new viewChild, let's look at one more way to access a view child — through a template variable.

Template variables are written in component view templates and provide access to a DOM element, an instance of a component or a directive in the template. You create template variable with the hash # symbol as in:

```
<h1 #headerTitle>
```

Step 12 To see a template variable in action add the following code to the child.component.html (shown in bold).

```
<p (click)="loginOutput(true)">Output Login Status</p>
<input type="text" (change)="true" #templateVar>
{{templateVar.value}}
```

Note Template variables may be accessed via @ViewChild.

Step 13 Save and refresh in Chrome. Type a value in the input field and then change focus by either pressing the tab key or moving the cursor outside of the input field. Notice the update from the binding `{{ templateVar.value}}`.

Step 14 Delete or comment the code added in step 12.

Note The goal of this component communication exercise is to create a button on the app component that when clicked will add a serving of fruit to a fruit serving counter placed below the button.

To setup this functionality you create a template variable that holds a reference to an empty span element that will serve as the counter. Next, you will add the button that calls a method on the child component that will increment the number of fruit servings.

Step 15 Add the following code to the app.component.html file.

```
<div>
    <app-header [user]= "user"></app-header>
    <button (click)="addFruit()">Add a serving of fruit</button>
    <h2>Fruit Counter: <span #fruit></span></h2>
    <p>Logged In: {{ loggedIn }}</p>
    <app-child (onLogin)="logIn($event)">
    </app-child>
...
```

Step 16 Create the view child reference to the template variable as shown below in app.component.ts.

```
@ViewChild('fruit', {static: false}) fruit: ElementRef;
```

Notice that the viewChild reference is datatyped as an ElementRef. The Angular documentation warns about using ElementRef as it presents a security risk because "permitting direct access to the DOM can make your application more vulnerable to XSS attacks. Carefully review any use of ElementRef in your code. For more detail, see the Security Guide"[2] at https://angular.io/guide/security.

[2] https://angular.io/api/core/ElementRef

Step 17 Modify the ngAfterViewInit method to log the fruit view child to the console as shown below in bold.

```
  ngAfterViewInit() {
        const children: ChildComponent[] = this.childrenView.toArray();
        console.log(children);
        console.log(this.fruit);
        console.table(this.childView);
    }
}
```

Step 18 Save and refresh the file in Chrome with the console open. The console should show the screenshot below.

```
▼ ElementRef {nativeElement: span}
  ▶ nativeElement: span
  ▶ __proto__: Object
```

Step 19 Add the code to the child.component.ts file that provides the fruit counter functionality as shown below in bold.

```
import {Component, EventEmitter, OnInit, Output} from '@angular/core';

@Component({
    selector: 'app-child',
    templateUrl: './child/child.component.html',
    styleUrls: ['./child/child.component.css']
})

export class ChildComponent implements OnInit {
    fruitStatus: number = 0;

    @Output()
    onLogin = new EventEmitter<boolean>();

    loginOutput(login: boolean) {
        this.onLogin.emit(login);
    }

    fruitCounter(): number {
        return this.fruitStatus++;
    }

    constructor() {
    }

    ngOnInit() {
    }
}
```

Step 20 Activate the button in the app.component by calling the methods in the child component. The code is below.

```
addFruit(): void {
        this.childView.fruitCounter();
        this.fruit.nativeElement.innerText = this.childView.fruitStatus;
        console.log(this.childView.fruitStatus);
}
```

Step 21 Save and refresh the file in Chrome. Click the "Add a serving of fruit" button. The span element should populate with a number that represents the number of fruit servings tallied as shown in the screenshot below which represents 3 button clicks.

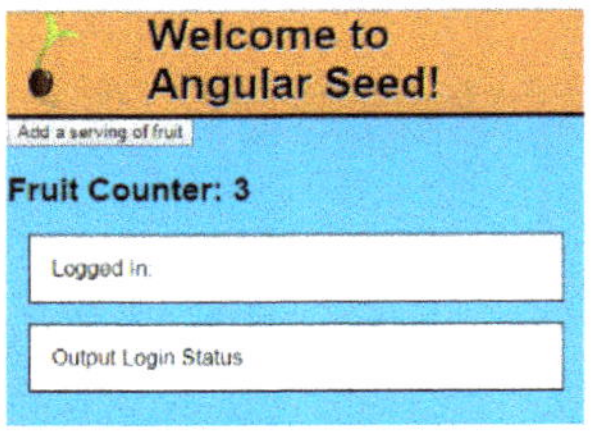

23–Guided Exercise: Using @Child() to access a native element

Angular's `@ViewChild()` decorator provides a method to query a plain old DOM element. In this exercise, you use the `@Child()` decorator to query and access a child component's native element. This is done in order to gain access to the native child element from the parent. For this exercise, you will change the background color of the element.

Step 1 Open message.component.html and add the code shown below in bold.

```
<section>
    <p>message is working</p>
    <label for="firstnameElement">First Name:</label>
    <input type="text" id="firstnameElement">
</section>
```

Step 2 Provide a template variable for the text input field as shown below in bold.

```
<input type="text" id="firstnameElement" #firstnameElement>
```

Step 3 Add the following CSS to message.component.css.

```
input:focus {
    background-color: lightblue;
}
```

Step 4 Open the message.component.ts and add a reference called an ElementRef type to the firstname template variable in the text input element. Import the necessary classes.

```
@ViewChild('firstnameRef') firstnameElementRef: ElementRef;
```

Step 7 Access the elementRef afterViewInit and set the background color. Be sure to implement the AfterViewInit lifecycle method. Log the firstnameElementRef to the console.

```
ngAfterViewInit(): void {
  this.firstnameElementRef.nativeElement.style.backgroundColor = 'lightblue';
  console.log(this.firstnameElementRef);
}
```

Step 8 Test the file in the web browser.

24–Guided Exercise: Using @Child() to access a native element

Angular's @ViewChild() decorate can be used to query a custom component. In this exercise, you use @Child() to reference, query and call a method of a child component from the parent.

Step 1 Open the header component and a message string property.

```
message: string = 'Welcome to your Food Plate';
```

Step 2 Add a method that gets the message string.

```
getMessageString() {
    return this.message;
}
```

Step 3 Add a template variable to the fp-header element in app.component.html. The additional code is shown below in bold.

```
<div id='wrapper'>
  <fp-header #fpHeader></fp-header>
  <fp-main [user]="user"></fp-main>
  <fp-footer></fp-footer>
</div>
```

Step 4 Open app.component and query the child header component.

```
@ViewChild('fpHeader') headerComponent: HeaderComponent;
```

Step 5 Implement the AfterViewInit and access the header child component's `getMessageString()` method via the lifecycle hook `ngAfterViewInit`.

```
ngAfterViewInit() {
    console.log(`messageString: ${this.headerComponent.getMessageString()}`);
}
```

Step 6 Check the web browser's DevTools console for the message.

```
▸ ElementRef {nativeElement: input#firstnameElement}                                message.component.ts:19
messageString: Welcome to your Food Plate                                            app.component.ts:29
Angular is running in the development mode. Call enableProdMode() to enable the production mode.   core.js:39988
[WDS] Live Reloading enabled.                                                          client:52
```

Chapter 9 Quiz

https://tinyurl.com/rh9t9mt

1. The app component needs to share data (invoice object) with its child component, details. The code below will not work. See if you can spot the errors.

Details child:

```
import {Component, Input} from '@angular/core';

@Component({
    selector: 'fp-details,
    templateUrl: 'details.component.html',
    styleUrls: ['details.component.css']
})

export class DetailsComponent {
    @Input()
    invoice: Invoice;

}
```

Details HTML

```
<div>
    <h1>Invoice # {invoice.number} </h1>
</div>
```

app.component parent

```
import {Component, Input, ViewEncapsulation} from '@angular/core';

@Component({
    selector: 'fp-app',
    template: `<div>
                   <fp-details></fp-details>
               </div>`,
    styleUrls: ['app.component.css'],
    encapsulation: ViewEncapsulation.None
})
export class AppComponent {

    invoice = {
        number:1,
        client:'KRA Inc.',
        amount:$1,500.00};
}
```

Chapter Summary

In this chapter, you added data to components and then displayed that data in the view template. In doing so, you learned the role of the `@Input` and `@Output` decorators.

Next Chapter

In the next chapter, you learn another one of the seven keys of Angular: Directives.

Chapter 10

Angular Directives

Chapter 10: Angular Directives

Objectives

- Understand the role of directives in Angular
- Describe the different type of directives in the Angular framework
- Write and use a structural directive called `ngIf`
- Write and use a structural directive called `ngFor`
- Describe the role of HTML5 templates in Angular structural directives
- Describe an attribute directive
- Write an attribute directive called `ngStyle`
- Write an attribute directive called `ngClass`
- Describe component directives

Introduction

When Angular first came on the scene, it was often said that the framework taught HTML new tricks. Angular directives do this in several ways: they can manipulate the DOM, change the look and behavior of an element, create an encapsulated behavior in a UI widget or control. Syntactically, directives are attributes that give dynamic behavior to the HTML elements in which they appear. Like most of Angular, a directive is a JavaScript class. It is decorated with @directive to provide its basic functionality. Angular 4 has three distinct types of directives, as shown below.

10.0 Angular's Directive Types

- Structural directives
  - They manipulate the DOM by adding or removing elements.
- Attribute directives
  - They change the look or behavior of a DOM element.
- Component directives
  - They encapsulate visual behavior by using the shadow DOM.

10.1 Structural Directives

Structural directives manipulate the document object model (DOM) and they are largely responsible for the applications' HTML layout. They are called "structural directives" because they affect the DOM's structure by adding, removing or manipulating elements in the DOM.

A structural directive is applied to an element called the "host element" where it works on that element and its descendants. The directive is preceded by an asterisk (*). A detailed explanation of the asterisk is provided on the next page.

10.1.1 Common structural directives

- `ngIf` to conditionally add or remove an element from the DOM
- `ngFor` to repeat a template for each item in a list
- `ngSwitch` to switch among alternative views

When the directive is spelled with a capital letter as in: NgIf, it is referencing the Angular class file. When the directive is spelled like this: ngIf, it is referencing the directive itself (as used in the code like this: <div *ngIf=...

10.1.2 ngIf directive

The ngIf directive takes a boolean expression and uses it to remove or insert content into the DOM. If the expression is true the element is added to the DOM; if the expression is false the element is not added to the DOM In the code example below, the first paragraph will be added to the DOM and rendered by the browser, but the second paragraph will not.

```
<p *ngIf="true">
```

```
  Expression is true and ngIf is true.
  This paragraph is in the DOM.
</p>
<p *ngIf="false">
  Expression is false and ngIf is false.
  This paragraph is not in the DOM.
</p>
```

It is important to understand that `ngIf` does not hide content with CSS but removes elements from the DOM. Be sure to check your browser's dev tools to confirm that you are getting the result you want.

The asterisk(*) before the ngIf plays a key role within the Angular framework. All structural directives support either the asterisk(*) or the use of the template syntax shown below. Refer to the code below to understand the role of the asterisk. For more information see https://netbasal.com/the-power-of-structural-directives-in-angular-bfe4d8c44fb1.

```
<p *ngIf="clientStatus.active">
  Client Status: {{client.name}}
</p>
```

Angular turns the host element <p> into a template as shown below. The ngIf is transformed into a property binding.

```
<template [ngIf]="clientStatus.active">
  Client Status: {{client.name}}
</template>
```

The `<template>` element is used to declare fragments of HTML that can be copied and injected into a webpage by a JavaScript. These HTML fragments may be unused by the document when loaded, but still parsed as HTML and available for use by the page at runtime. Each `<template>` element has an associated DocumentFragment object that holds the templates contents.

The <template> element provides true client-side templating. Basically, a template is a fragment of HTML that can be used and reused at will. It will not load at startup (it is hidden in the DOM, not rendered and cannot be queried), but it will load when called upon.

10.1.2.1 Angular 5 added an optional else to ngIf

Angular 5 allows an else statement as shown below.

```
<p *ngIf="clientStatus.active else nonActive">
  Client Status: {{client.name}}
</p>
<ng-template #nonActive>
      <p>Client is not active</p>
</ng-template>
```

Alternatively, you can use the binding syntax shown below.

```
<ng-template [ngIf]="client.active"; [ngIfElse]="nonActive">
        <section>
              … content
         </section>
        </ng-template>
<ng-template #nonActive>
        <section>… alternative content</section>
</ng-template>
```

8 – Demo (optional) HTML5 Template Demo

To see a template example, in action, open the demo file and follow the instructions below.

Step 1 In your IDE, open the file template-starter.html from the angular-class-files/demos folder.

Step 2 Run the file in the Chrome web browser. Launch the Chrome DevTools and active the "Network" tab.

Step 3 Refresh the page and notice the network traffic as shown below.

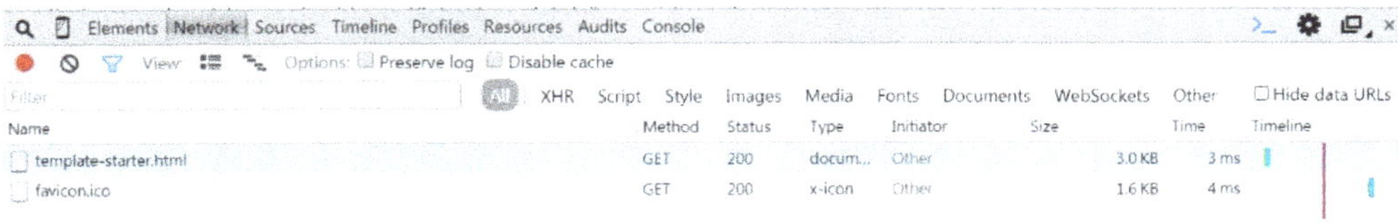

Step 4 The Network panel shows the GET request for the template-starter.html page and the favicon.ico file.

Step 5 Return to the IDE and add the template element under the comment on line 28.

```
<template id="tpl">
    Hi <span class="name"></span>!<img src="../images/glad.png"
            width="42" height="42">
</template>
```

The JavaScript on line 52 exceeds the scope of this course, but it is briefly explained in the comments and on the web page itself.

Step 6 Save the page and re-load it in the Chrome browser. Again, pay attention to the Network tab.

Step 7 Click the "Show the Template" button and look at the Network tab again. It should match the image below.

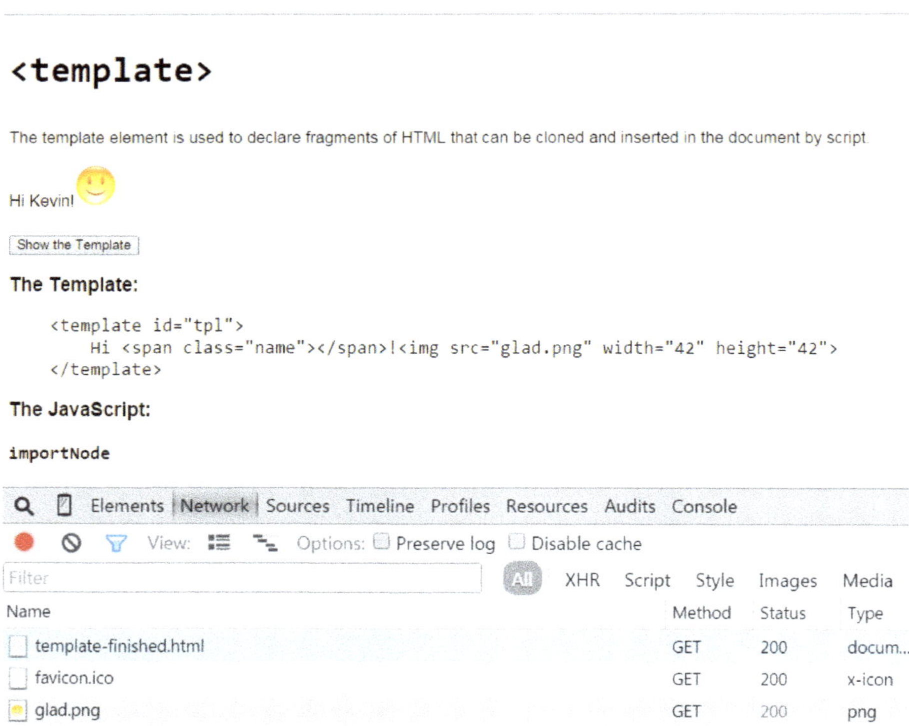

The "glad.png" image is not downloaded until the template element is parsed.

25—Guided Exercise: Using the ngIf structural directive

In this guided exercise, you hide or show a DOM element using the `ngIf` structural directive. If the user has registered they will see an image of a FoodPlate from the U.S. government website. If they have not, they will see a generic image of the food plate. You will use the angular-seed project for this guided exercise.

Step 1 Open the app.component.html in the angular-seed project.

Step 2 Comment the code from the previous exercise and add the following HTML below the <app-header> element using the *ngIf directive shown below.

```
<app-header [user]="user"></app-header>
   <section *ngIf="!user.registered">
     <img src="../assets/images/chooseMyPlate.gov.png">
   </section>
   <section *ngIf="user.registered">
      <img src="../assets/images/generic-plate.png">
   </section>
  <p>Logged In: {{ loggedIn }}</p>
  <app-child (login)="login($event)"></app-child>
  <!-- <app-form-input icon="envelope">
      <small>Business email</small>
      <label for="emailAddress">Email:</label>
      <input id="emailAddress" type="email" />
  </app-form-input> -->
```

Step 3 Change the app.component user's registration status from true to false and vice-versa and verify the results..

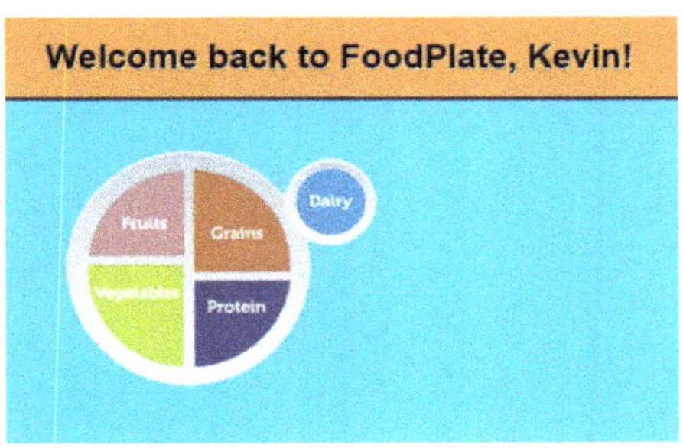

Result when the user has registered

Result when the user has not registered.

Step 4 Try using the (Angular-5 added) alternative else statement.

See the following page for a possible solution.

Alternative solution to step 4:

```
<div *ngIf="!user.registered; then notRegistered else isRegistered">
    <ng-template #notRegistered>
        <section>
            <img src="../assets/images/chooseMyPlate.gov.png">
        </section>
    </ng-template>
    <ng-template #isRegistered>
        <section>
            <img src="../assets/images/generic-plate.png">
        </section>
    </ng-template>
</div>
```

10.2 Change Detection

Angular maintains the UI and state of an application by combining state information with view templates. In the simple example below, username is the data in state and the binding displays that data in the template.

```
<span>User Name: {{ userName }} </span>
```

Change detection is the process of updating the view (or DOM) when the data has changed. Property changes are an ongoing process throughout the life of any typical web application. Code in the application updates a data model and then Angular syncs the updated data model with the view by re-rendering the component template. For this process to work, Angular must detect any changes in the data. Angular does this by checking every component in the tree of components (from top to bottom) to determine if any components data models have changed. If a data value has changed Angular updates the component's view template. Technically, Angular does this by marking the component's data model via setting the `isChanged` property to true. Be aware that Angular does not perform a deep object comparison during its change detection cycles; it compares only the previous and current value of properties in the view template. Below are some of the triggers for change detection.

- Browser events like click's, keyup's and so on
- HTTP requests using the `XMLHttpRequest` object
- JavaScript timing functions like `setInterval` and `setTimeout`

10.2.1 How does Angular Change Detection work?

Because JavaScript is inherently overridable, Angular can utilize and alter browser API's. This is exactly what it does when it comes to listening to events, so that it can respond by detecting changes. Angular overrides JavaScript's `addEventListener` method so that after responding the event it can call its `runChangeDetection` method and ultimately re-render the user interface as needed. Within the Angular framework is a library called Zone.js. This library allows Angular to use zones or execution contexts to trigger the change detection process. Thus, Angular patches the browser API's in the bulleted list in section 10.2 above to trigger change detection.

10.2.3 Angular's Default Change Detection

Change detection (by Angular's default) checks for all components from to bottom of the component tree if any template value has changed. Despite Angular being very fast at change detection, this can have an effect on performance. The framework provides to the developer two change detection strategies: the `default` and `onPush` shown below.

```
changeDetection: ChangeDetectionStrategy.OnPush
```

or

```
changeDetection: ChangeDetectionStrategy.Default
```

Default is, of course, the framework's default change detection strategy and it checks every component in the tree after a trigger action takes place.

10.2.1 Angular's onPush Change Detection

It is often the case (and some argue it is always the case) that components should update themselves and only themselves when data within them change. This can be accomplished by changing the `changeDetection` property to `OnPush`. In order for this strategy to work, Angular must detect a reference change in its input. For example, if your code directly mutates an element in the UI, but not a component property, Angular will not detect the change. Components using the OnPush strategy will cause Angular to check the component when any of its properties change or when it fires an event or when an Observable fires an event.

Sometimes, you might trigger a callback that changes one of the bindings as shown in the example below with the relevant code shown in bold.

```
<p *ngIf="getFoodGroupsMet()">You have eaten all your {{ groupsMet }}</p>

getFoodGroupsMet(): string {
let messageString = `You have eaten all your `;

if (this.user.reqsStatus.fruitMet === true) {
   this.groupsMet.push('fruit');
}
if (this.user.reqsStatus.vegMet === true) {
   this.groupsMet.push(' vegetables');
}
if (this.user.reqsStatus.proteinMet === true) {
   this.groupsMet.push(' protein');
}
if (this.user.reqsStatus.grainMet === true) {
   this.groupsMet.push(' grains');
}
messageString += this.groupsMet.toString();
return messageString;
}
```

In this case, an error message will appear indicating that an expression (messageString) has changed after it was checked, followed by the previous and current values of that expression. This can be due to the default change detection and may be resolved by changing the detection strategy to OnPush as shown in the component class snippet below.

```
@Component({
  selector: 'fp-message',
  templateUrl: './message.component.html',
  styleUrls: ['./message.component.css'],
  changeDetection: ChangeDetectionStrategy.OnPush
})
export class …
```

10 –Challenge Exercise: Add an ngIf to the Foodplate-cli application

In this challenge exercise, you write a simple expression to notify the user when they have met both their fruit and protein requirements.

Step 1 In the message component's view template, comment the code for the label and input and delete the paragraph as shown below.

```
<section>
    <!-- <label for="firstnameElement">First Name:</label>
    <input type="text" id="firstnameElement" #firstnameElement> -->
</section>
```

Step 2 Add a new paragraph that results in the image shown below when viewed in a web browser.

With no requirements met:

With fruit and protein met:

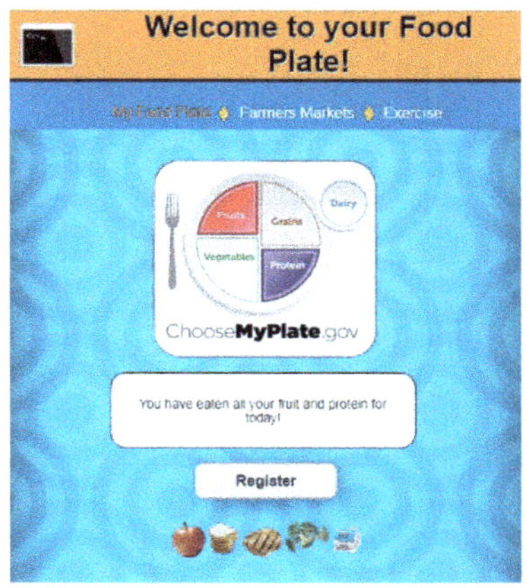

Note Hard-code the fruit and protein met in user.service.ts as shown below to test your code or use the AngularDevTools. Warning: The AngularDevTools will not affect the message component's verbiage. You can try using it to compare the difference between changing properties in the DevTools vs. changing the code as shown below.!

```
private user: User = new User(1, 'Kevin', 'M', '51+', 'M51+', {}, {fruitMet:
true, vegMet: false, proteinMet: true, grainMet: false}, false,
'user@foodplate.com');
```

Extra Credit

Step 1 Add any code necessary to message.component.html and message.component.ts to generate an automatic message like the one shown here.

Possible Solution

Message.component.ts

```
import { AfterViewInit, Component, ElementRef, Input, OnInit, ViewChild } from '@angular/core';
import { User } from '../../models/User';

@Component({
  selector: 'fp-message',
  templateUrl: './message.component.html',
  styleUrls: ['./message.component.css']
})
export class MessageComponent implements OnInit, AfterViewInit {

  @ViewChild('firstnameElement') firstnameElementRef: ElementRef;

  @Input()
  user: User;

  groupsMet = [];

  constructor() { }

  ngOnInit(): void {
  }

  ngAfterViewInit(): void {
    // this.firstnameElementRef.nativeElement.style.backgroundColor = 'lightblue';
    // console.log(this.firstnameElementRef);
  }

  getFoodGroupsMet(): string {
    let messageString = `You have eaten all your `;

    if (this.user.reqsStatus.fruitMet === true) {
      this.groupsMet.push('fruit');
    }
    if (this.user.reqsStatus.vegMet === true) {
      this.groupsMet.push(' vegetables');
    }
    if (this.user.reqsStatus.proteinMet === true) {
      this.groupsMet.push(' protein');
    }
    if (this.user.reqsStatus.grainMet === true) {
      this.groupsMet.push(' grains');
    }
    messageString += this.groupsMet.toString();
    return messageString;
  }
```

message.component.html

```
<section>
  <!-- <label for="firstnameElement">First Name:</label>
  <input type="text" id="firstnameElement" #firstnameElement>-->
  <p *ngIf="user.reqsStatus.fruitMet === false && user.reqsStatus.grainMet === false && user.reqsStatus.proteinMet === false &&
user.reqsStatus.vegMet === false">You have not met any requirements. </p>
  <!-- <p *ngIf="user.reqsStatus.fruitMet === true && user.reqsStatus.proteinMet === true">You have eaten all your fruit and protein for
today!</p>-->
  <p *ngIf="getFoodGroupsMet()">You have eaten all your {{ groupsMet }}</p>
</section>
```

10.1.3 The ngFor directive

The *ngFor directive produces an output for a JavaScript iterable like an array, by iterating across each of its elements and applying a template. Use the code sample below to understand the ngFor syntax.

```
<tr *ngFor="let client of clients">
    <td>{{client.name}}</td>
</tr>
```

The *ngFor directives is given an iteration expression wherein a loop variable is created called "client" (via the JavaScript "let" keyword). The iteration expression takes the form "var i of items." The "client" variable is visible only inside the loop. The value of the index is derived from the let keyword and can be accessed by adding the code shown below in bold.

```
<tr *ngFor="let client of clients; let i=index">
    <td>{{client.name}}</td>
</tr>
```

10.1.4 ngFor local variables

*ngFor also supports helpful exported values that can be aliased to local variables in the view template. Below is a list of exported values recognized by Angular

Value	Data Type	Description
$implicit	<T>	The value of the individual items in the iterable (ngForOf).
ngForOf	<T>	The value of the iterable expression. Useful when the expression is more complex than a property access, for example when using the async pipe (userStreams | async). *
index	number	The index of the current item in the iterable.
first	boolean	True when the item is the first item in the iterable.
last	boolean	True when the item is the last item in the iterable.
even	boolean	True when the item has an even index in the iterable.
odd	boolean	True when the item has an odd index in the iterable.

<T> allows capturing whatever type the user provides so that it can be used later.

* When the contents of the iterator changes, `NgForOf` makes the corresponding changes to the DOM:

- When an item is added, a new instance of the template is added to the DOM.
- When an item is removed, its template instance is removed from the DOM.
- When items are reordered, their respective templates are reordered in the DOM.

.

26–Guided Exercise: Using the ngFor structural directive

In this guided exercise, you create a component view by iterating through an array of objects using the ngFor directive.

A foodGroups object will store the name of the foodgroup and a graphical icon that represents the food group. The component shown below will be created by iterating through the foodGroups object to create the image elements.

The food-groups component.

Step 1 Add a file called food-groups.service.ts to the services folder.

```
ng g s services/food-groups
```

The finished file is shown below. You may also copy this file from code-snippets/food-groups.service.txt.

```
import { Injectable } from '@angular/core';

@Injectable({
    providedIn: 'root'
})

export class FoodGroupsService {
    private foodIconsPath = "assets/images/foodImages/";
    private foodGroups = [
        {   "name" : "fruit",
        "icon" : this.foodIconsPath + 'apple.png'},
        {   "name" : "grains",
            "icon" : this.foodIconsPath + 'bread.png'},
        {   "name" : "protein",
            "icon" : this.foodIconsPath + 'chicken.png'},
        {   "name" : "vegetables",
            "icon" : this.foodIconsPath + 'broccoli.png'},
        {   "name" : "dairy",
            "icon" : this.foodIconsPath + 'milk.png'},
    ];
    getFoodGroups(): Array<object> {
        return this.foodGroups;
    }

    constructor() { }
}
```

Step 2 Create a new module and component called food-groups.

```
ng g m food-groups
```

```
ng g c food-groups
```

Step 3 To access the new food-groups component in modules that import it, you must export the component from the module that declares it (food-groups-module.ts – shown below in bold with the added export property).

```
@NgModule({
  declarations: [FoodGroupsComponent],
  exports: [
    FoodGroupsComponent
  ],
  imports: [
    CommonModule
  ]
})
export class FoodGroupsModule { }
```

Step 4 Import the FoodGroupsModule in the app.module. The relevant code is shown below in bold.

```
import {MessageComponent} from "./message/message.component";
import {FoodGroupsModule} from "./food-groups/food-groups.module";

@NgModule({
    imports:       [ CommonModule, BrowserModule, FoodGroupsModule ],
    declarations: [ AppComponent, HeaderComponent, FooterComponent,
MainComponent, HomeBtnComponent, PlateComponent, MessageComponent ],
    bootstrap:     [ AppComponent ],
    providers:     [Title, UserService]
})
```

Step 5 Add the code below to the food-groups.component.ts.

```
import { Component, OnInit } from '@angular/core';

import {FoodGroupsService} from '../services/food-groups.service';

@Component({
  selector: 'fp-food-groups',
  templateUrl: './food-groups.component.html',
  styleUrls: ['./food-groups.component.css']
})
export class FoodGroupsComponent implements OnInit {

  foodGroups;
  constructor(private foodGroupsSvce: FoodGroupsService) { }

  ngOnInit(): void {
    this.foodGroups = this.foodGroupsSvce.getFoodGroups();
  }
}
```

Step 6 Add the food-groups.component.html as shown below, including the *ngFor directive.

```
<section>
<img *ngFor="let group of foodGroups"
        src="{{ group.icon}}" alt="{{ group.name}}">
</section>
```

Step 7 Add the food-groups.component.css as shown below.

```
img {
    display: inline;
}
```

Step 8 Add the new component to the app.component file. Place it above the `<fp-footer>` element.

```
  <fp-food-groups></fp-food-groups>
  <fp-footer></fp-footer>
</div>
```

Step 9 Test the file in Chrome. It should match the screen shot below.

*The new food-groups.component created with the *ngFor directive.*

Step 10 To examine some of the additional variables of ngFor, add the following CSS.

```
.isFirst {
    background-color: #FFBC2F;
    border: 1px solid #000;
    border-radius: 50%;
    padding: .15em;
}

.isLast {
    background-color: #008000;
    border: 1px solid #000;
    border-radius: 55%;
    padding: .20em;
}
```

Step 11 Add the first property shown below in bold.

```
<section>
    <img *ngFor="let group of foodGroups; first as isFirst"
         src="{{ group.icon}}" alt="{{ group.name}}">
</section>
```

"`first`" is an exported value that has been aliased to a local variable called "`isFirst`."

Step 12 Bind the `isFirst` css class to the `isFirst` local variable.

```
<section>
    <img *ngFor="let group of foodGroups; first as isFirst"
         src="{{ group.icon}}" alt="{{ group.name}}"
         [class.isFirst]="isFirst">
</section>
```

Step 13 Save and test the file in Chrome. It should match the image below.

Step 14 Swap the value first for the value last. Then try using some of the other values from the chart in section 10.1.4 ngFor local variables.

Step 15 Steps 12 through 16 were for demonstration purposes only. Remove the code shown below with a strikethrough, because that is not how the finished product should look.

```
<section>
    <img *ngFor="let group of foodGroups; last as isLast; first as isFirst"
         src="{{ group.icon}}" alt="{{ group.name}}"
         [class.isLast]="isLast" [class.isFirst]="isFirst">
</section>
```

10.1.5 The ngSwitch directive

This structural directive add or removes templates, thus displaying or hiding views. The `ngSwitch` directive is analogous to a standard switch/case in JavaScript. The `*ngSwitch` directives specifies an expression that matches an `ngSwitchCase` directive. Every view that matches the ngSwitch expression is rendered. If there are no matches, a view with a provided `ngSwitchDefault` directive is rendered. Additional elements can be added within an ngSwitch statement (but outside of any `ngSwitchCase` or `ngSwitchDefault`) will be rendered at their current location. See the sample below from the Angular documentation.

```
<container-element [ngSwitch]="switch_expression">
    <!-- the same view can be shown in more than one case -->
    <some-element *ngSwitchCase="match_expression_1">...</some-element>
    <some-element *ngSwitchCase="match_expression_2">...</some-element>
    <some-other-element *ngSwitchCase="match_expression_3">...</some-other-element>
    <!--default case when there are no matches -->
    <some-element *ngSwitchDefault>...</some-element>
</container-element>
```

27—Guided Exercise: Using the ngSwitch structural directive

In this guided exercise, you hide or show a DOM element using the `ngSwitch` structural directive. If the user has registered the child component displays true as shown below. After adding the ngSwitch directive the boolean value will display in a normal font-weight if it's true and it will display in bold and red if it is false. You will use the angular-seed project for this guided exercise.

Step 1 Open the app.component.ts file and assign a value of "false" to the loggedIn property as shown below in bold.

```
loggedIn: boolean = false;
```

Step 2 Add a CSS utility class that makes text bold and red. Using the app.component.css file, write the code shown below in bold.

```
.notRegistered {
    font-weight: bold;
    color: #f00;
}
```

Step 3 Refactor the paragraph in app.component.html using the ngSwitch directive that provides the code that will be evaluated just once to determine the correct case to apply. You will apply the switch case in step 4.

```
<div [ngSwitch]="loggedIn">
     <p>Logged In:
        <span>{{ loggedIn }}</span>
     </p>
</div>
```

Step 4 Add the two *ngSwitchCase directives for each case: true and false.

```
<div [ngSwitch]="loggedIn">
   <p>Logged In:
     <span *ngSwitchCase="false" class="notRegistered">{{ loggedIn }}</span>
     <span *ngSwitchCase="true">{{ loggedIn }}</span>
   </p>
</div>
```

Note With just two cases here, an ngIf might be sufficient, however, throughout the course as well as in your own projects, you will see that if/else can not only be tedious to maintain, but it results in each if condition being evaluated as opposed to the ngSwitch which results in one evaluation of one condition.

Step 5 Save and refresh the file in Chrome. The results should match the screenshots below.

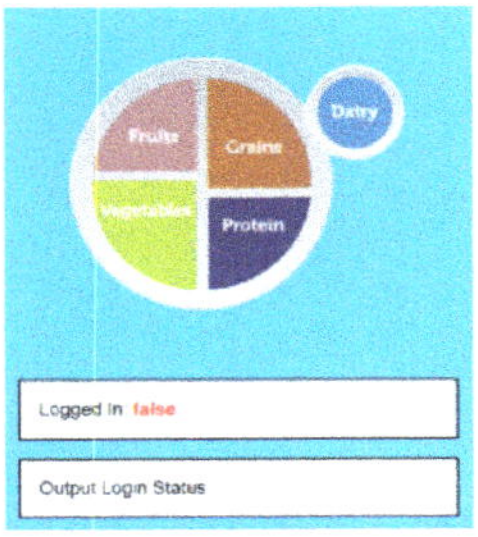

The page at startup.

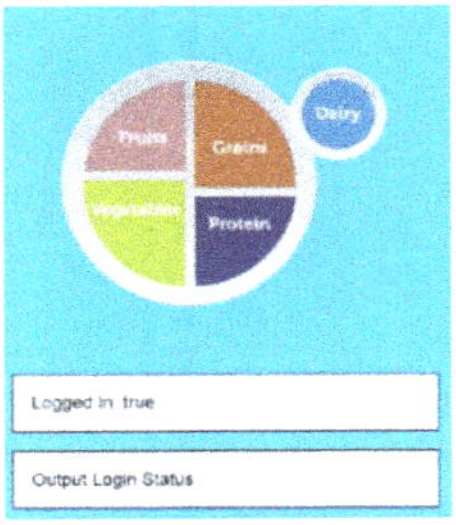

The page after clicking "Output Login Status"

Note Remember that clicking the "Output Login Status" invokes the function shown below in bold which sets the loggedIn property to true.

```
<p (click)="loginOutput(true)">Output Login Status</p>
```

Clicking the paragraph will not change the image because it does not change the user's registered property.

Step 6 To see the image respond to the paragraph click (and to see change detection as well), add the following line to the login method in app.component.ts. The additional code is shown below in bold.

```
login(evt) {
    console.log(evt);
    this.loggedIn = evt;
    this.user.registered = !this.user.registered;
}
```

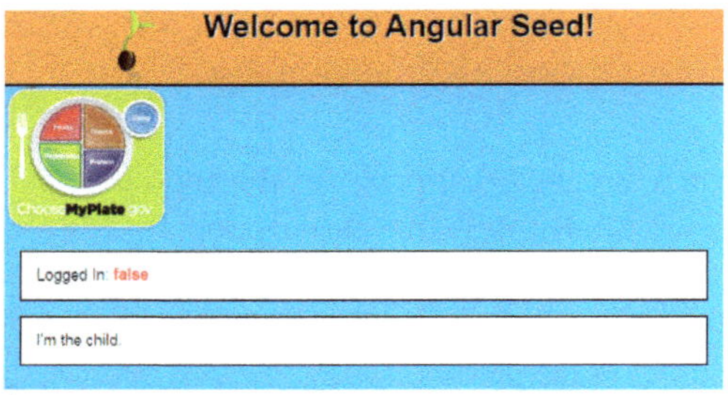

The page at startup.

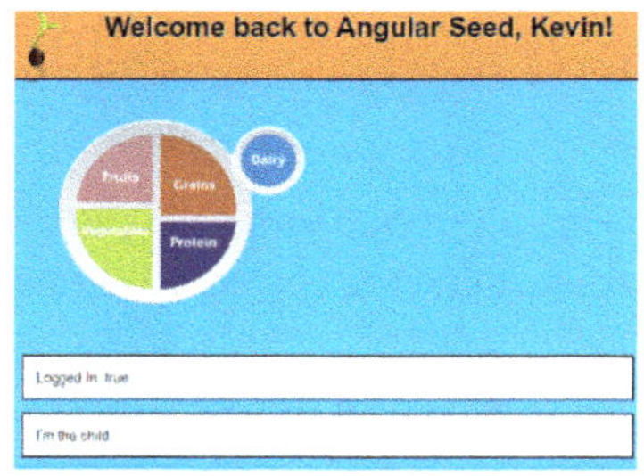

The page after clicking "Output Login Status"

Step 7 Finally, add a default condition to the switchCase as shown below in bold.

```
<div [ngSwitch]="loggedIn">
   <p>Logged In:
      <span *ngSwitchCase="false" class="notRegistered">{{ loggedIn }}</span>
      <span *ngSwitchCase="true">{{ loggedIn }}</span>
      <span *ngSwitchDefault>Default Text Goes Here</span>
   </p>
</div>
```

Step 8 You can test the default text by changing the [ngSwitch] value to an undefined value as shown below in bold.

```
<div [ngSwitch]="noSuchProperty">
```

Step 9 View the page in the web browser. It should match the image below.

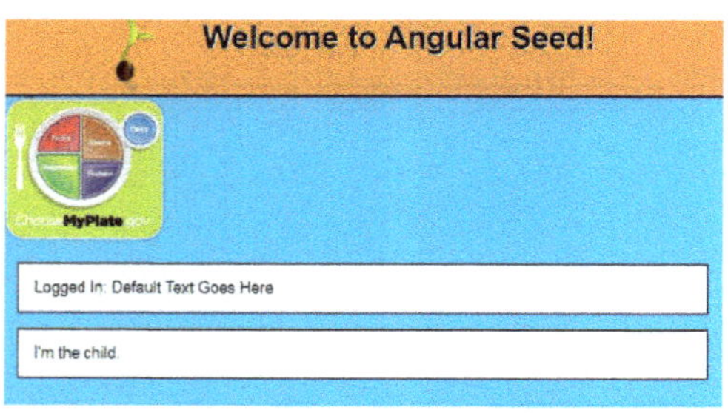

Step 10 Return the [ngSwitch] value to loggedIn.

```
<div [ngSwitch]="loggedIn">
```

10.2 Attribute Directives

Attribute directives change the appearance or behavior of a DOM element. They are used as attributes of elements. Some of these attributes include the style and class attributes which can be changed via ngStyle and ngClass. Recall however, that you can also bind to the style and class attributes via [class] and [style] as opposed to [ngStyle] and [ngClass].

10.2.1 The ngStyle directive

Typically, CSS styles are added with either a style attribute or a class attribute. Both HTML attributes will do the job, but they are not dynamic. There are times when an element should be styled different based on some state of the application. For example, in a listing of products, you might want to highlight those products that are out of stock with a yellow background.

As explained in previous chapters, you can keep track of the status of a product with component properties. Then, you can use bindings to tie the state of the component to an element. The property could be a boolean called outOfStock and the binding might look like this:

```
<table>…
<td [style.background-color]= "outOfStock">
```

You can also use data-binding to conditionally change the style via a ternary operator, like this;

```
<table>
…
<td [style.background-color]= "outOfStock ? 'yellow' : '#fff'">
```

This technique works well for simple one-rule CSS styles. This is because you are simply binding to the HTML style property which is designed to bind one CSS value after another. However, you may want to apply multiple styles rules like a yellow background, bold text and a border, making the code verbose and, therefore, harder to read. In addition, you may need the same set of style rules on other elements. That's where ngStyle comes in. ngStyle lets you set multiple inline styles simultaneously, which is more efficient than using multiple style bindings. The ngStyle directive sets inline styles dynamically, based on the state of the component in which they are used. Here is an example using ngStyle.

```
<tr data-status= "outOfStock" [ngStyle]= "outOfStockStyle">
      <td …
```

The corresponding component code would look like this:

```
this.outOfStockStyle = {
      'backgroundColor' : 'yellow',
      'font-weight' : 'bold',
      'border' : '1px solid red'
}
```

10.2.1.1 ngStyle summary

- ngStyle applies styles and not classes.
- ngStyle can accept a key-value pair as input, where the key is a valid CSS Style
- ngStyle can be passed input via inline or a Typescript property or method
- ngStyle under the hood utilizes Angular's Renderer2 to invoke `setStyle()` and `removeStyle()`
- ngStyle will overwrite existing styles on the element.
- ngStyle is reserved for only those occasions when you have a dynamically calculated embedded style

28–Guided Exercise: Add an ngStyle directive

In this guided exercise, you set a class in your view template based on a binding using the `ngStyle` directive. You create a CSS style rule dynamically based on user interaction with the app component.

Step 1 Open app.component.ts and add the following property shown below in bold.

```
export class AppComponent {

    loggedIn: boolean = false;
    stylePreference: string;
```

Step 2 Open app.component.html and add two radio buttons as shown below.

```
<input type="radio" name="preference"
       id="importantHighlight"
       style="transform:scale(1.5)"
       (click)="setStylePreference('hilite')">
    <label for="importantHighlight">Highlight</label>
<input type="radio" name="preference"
       id="importantCaps"
       style="transform:scale(1.5)"
       (click)="setStylePreference('caps')">
    <label for="importantCaps">Caps</label>
```

Step 3 Add the setStylePreference() method in the app component class.

```
setStylePreference(value): void {
        this.stylePreference = value;
}
```

Step 4 Above the radio buttons add the paragraph shown below. Notice the `ngStyle` binding.

```
<p>This text is <span [ngStyle]="setImportance()">very</span> important!</p>
```

Step 5 In the component class, add the method called `setImportance` that is bound to the ngStyle directive.

```
setImportance(): object {
if (this.stylePreference === 'hilite') {
    return { 'background-color' : 'yellow' };
    } else if (this.stylePreference === 'caps') {
        return { 'text-transform' : 'uppercase' };
    }
}
```

Step 6 Save and test the file by clicking the radio buttons.

10.2.2 The ngClass directive

The ngClass directive adds and removes CSS classes on HTML elements. The classes can be set dynamically. The Angular directive is called `ngClass` and it is used as a binding as shown below.

```
<h1 [ngClass]={'class-name' : true}>
```

In the example above the h1 element will receive a class called 'class-name' because the value that follows is true. The true value can be replaced with an expression as shown below.

```
<h1 [ngClass]={'class-name' : user.status === 'active'}>
```

ngClass can take any of the following as input:

- String
- Array
- Object
- Ternary if it returns a string, array or object
- Property or a method that returns a string, array or object

You should use the ngClass directive when you are applying classes conditionally or dynamically as opposed to statically. In addition, ngClass is helpful when applying more than one class.

Behind the scenes, the ngClass directive is adding and removing classes by way of Renderer2's `addClass()` and `removeClass()` methods.

11 –Challenge Exercise: Add an NgClass directive

In this challenge exercise, you create a new navigation component that consists of three links. You'll wire up these links to display different components after you learn about routing. The `ngClass` directive will be used (for demonstration purposes) to activate a CSS class that will change the color the link that represents the current view/page. In the next chapter on Routing, you will learn some router properties that better address the active component.

Simple Instructions

- Create a new component called "nav."
- Copy and paste the CSS for the nav component from assets/css/nav.css. Note the class called `.active`.
- Copy and paste the HTML for the nav component from assets/code-snippets/nav.component.html
- Trigger the `.active` CSS class from nav.css so that if the link on the nav component's "My Food Plate" link `isActive` property is true, the CSS class called `active` will be used.

Note In a subsequent chapter, you will use the Angular router module to create a more elegant and maintainable solution to styling the active link.

Step by Step Instructions

Step 1 Create a new component called nav.

Step 2 Use the code below for the nav component's HTML.

```
<nav>
  <ul>
    <li>My Food Plate</li>
    <li>Farmers Markets</li>
    <li>Exercise</li>
  </ul>
</nav>
```

Step 3 Add the CSS below to the nav.component.css file. You can copy and paste the finished file from assets/css/nav.css.

```
ul {
    list-style-type: none;
    background-color: #0071BC;
    height: 2.25em;
    margin-top: 0;
    padding-top: 1em;
    display:flex;
    flex-direction:row;
    align-items:center;
    justify-content:center;
}
li {
    color: #fff;
    display:inline;
    background-image: url(../../assets/images/icons/diamond.svg);
    background-position:right center;
    background-repeat: no-repeat;
    padding-right: 1.45em;
    padding-left: .45em;
    cursor: pointer;
}
.active {
    color: #ef952b;
}
li:last-child {
    background: none;
}
@media (max-width: 444px) {
    ul {
        height: auto;
        flex-direction:column;
```

```
        margin: 0;
        padding: 0;
    }
    li {
        background: none;
        margin: .15em;
        margin-top: .75em;
        padding-bottom: .25em;
        border-bottom: 1px solid #FFBC2F;
        width: 100%;
        text-align: center;
    }
}
```

Step 4 Add a property called `isActive`, datatyped as a Boolean to the nav.component.ts file.

```
...
export class NavComponent implements OnInit {

  isActive: boolean = true;

  constructor() { }

  ngOnInit() {
  }
}
```

Step 5 Add the ngClass directive to the nav.component. html file as shown below in bold.

```
<nav>
  <ul>
    <li [ngClass]="{active: isActive}">My Food Plate</li>
    <li>Farmers Markets</li>
    <li>Exercise</li>
  </ul>
</nav>
```

Step 6 Add the nav component to the app.component.html under the `<fp-header>` element.

Step 7 Declare the nav component in the app module.

Step 8 Save the files and test in the web browser. The page should look like the screenshot below.

The nav component

Possible solution code

nav.component.ts

```
import { Component, OnInit } from '@angular/core';

@Component({
  selector: 'fp-nav',
  templateUrl: './nav.component.html',
  styleUrls: ['./nav.component.css']
})
export class NavComponent implements OnInit {

  isActive:Boolean = true;

  constructor() { }

  ngOnInit() {
  }
}
```

nav.component.html

```
<nav>
  <ul>
    <li [ngClass]="{active: isActive}">My Food Plate</li>
    <li>Farmers Markets</li>
    <li>Exercise</li>
  </ul>
</nav>
```

nav.component.css

```
ul {
  list-style-type: none;
  background-color: #0071BC;
  height: 2.25em;
  margin-top: 0;
  padding-top: 1em;
  display: flex;
  flex-direction: row;
  align-items: center;
  justify-content: center;
}
li {
  color: #fff;
  text-decoration: none;
  display: inline;
  /*border-right: 1px solid #fff;*/
  background-image: url(../../assets/images/icons/diamond.svg);
  background-position: right center;
  background-repeat: no-repeat;
  padding-right: 1.45em;
  padding-left: .45em;
  cursor: pointer;
}


.active {
  color: #ef952b;
}

li:last-child {
  /*border-right: none;*/
  background: none;
}
@media (max-width: 444px) {
  ul {
```

```
    height: auto;
    flex-direction: column;
    margin: 0;
    padding: 0;
  }
  li {
    background: none;
    margin: .15em;
    margin-top: .75em;
    padding-bottom: .25em;
    border-bottom: 1px solid #FFBC2F;
    width: 100%;
    text-align: center;
  }
}
```

app.component.html

```
<div id="wrapper">
  <fp-header></fp-header>
  <fp-nav></fp-nav>
  <fp-main [user]="user">Main is working</fp-main>
  <fp-food-groups></fp-food-groups>
  <fp-footer></fp-footer>
</div>
```

app.module.ts

```
import { NgModule } from '@angular/core';
import { CommonModule } from '@angular/common';
import {BrowserModule} from '@angular/platform-browser';

import {AppComponent} from "./app.component";
import {HeaderComponent} from "./header/header.component";
import {FooterComponent} from "./footer/footer.component";
import {UserService} from "./services/user.service";
import {MainComponent} from "./main/main.component";
import {HomeBtnComponent} from "./home-btn/home-btn.component";
import {PlateComponent} from "./plate/plate.component";
import {MessageComponent} from "./message/message.component";
import {FoodGroupsModule} from "./food-groups/food-groups.module";
import {FoodGroupsComponent} from "./food-groups/food-groups.component";
import {NavComponent} from "./nav/nav.component";

@NgModule({
  imports: [
    CommonModule, BrowserModule, FoodGroupsModule
  ],
  declarations: [AppComponent, HeaderComponent, FooterComponent, MainComponent,
HomeBtnComponent, PlateComponent, MessageComponent, NavComponent],
  bootstrap: [AppComponent],
  providers: [UserService]
})
export class AppModule { }
```

10.2.3 [class] vs. [ngClass]

Recall in a previous chapter, you learned the class binding shown below.

```
<footer class="header-footer">
    <img [src]="icon" (click)="moreInfo()" [alt]="logoAlt">
    <p>&copy; 2018 KRA Inc. <small [attr.data-version]="versionString" [class.footer-
-update]="!isCurrent">Version #{{versionString}}</small></p>
</footer>
```

In the bolded code above the CSS class called `footer-update` will be applied to the small tag if the `isCurrent` class property is false. You might be wondering what the main difference is between this approach and the ngClass directive you just learned. As is typical among development teams, consistencie rules. However, the two methods do differ with the ngClass being the more robust choice. This is because with an [ngClass] binding you can apply multiple classes.

The differences are summarized below.

Class	Description
`[class]`	Applies a single style per binding Removes all the existing classes on the element
`[ngClass]`	Applies multiple styles Can apply a style with a function that returns an object of classes Can apply a style to an array of strings
other options	There are numerous ways to apply styles with [class] such that they mimic the features of [ngClass]. It is , however, best to stick to one context or use case for consistency within your code.

Chapter 10 Advanced Directives

Objectives

- Implement your own logic for any element with a custom directive
- Describe the role of the ComponentFactory in Angular
- Use Angular's ComponentFactoryResolver

Introduction

In this section, in you not only build a custom directive, but you use it to dynamically load a component at runtime.

10.3 Dynamic Component Loading

Not all your components will be creating at startup time. There are many reasons an application may need to load a component at runtime including:

- User is not authenticated making a particular component unnecessary
- A component may only load upon completion of a form
- A component may load only after a call to the server for more data
- And so on...

Angular provide a `ComponentFactoryResolver` class to add dynamic components. To understand this class, it's helpful to know a few things about how Angular deals with components. All components are built internally with factories. You can think of Angular's component factories as a conveyer belt of components. The conveyor belt takes the components raw data (including its view template broken down into smaller components like text nodes, element nodes, properties and so forth) as input and delivers as output, components.

As developers that want to dynamically create components, we need access to a factory, so that we can create component instances and add them to the DOM. Fortunately, each module in Angular provides a service for its components to get a factory. This is the `ComponentFactoryResolver`.

Before using the ComponentFactoryResolver to add a component to the DOM, you must define an "anchor point" indicating where Angular should insert the new component. This is done with a `ViewContainerRef` class which represents a container where one or more views can be attached. An example anchor point is shown below.

```
<div anchorPoint></div>
```

anchorPoint is a directive that injects a ViewContainerReference.

So, how does the dynamically created component come to life? The ComponentFactoryResolver has a method called `resolveComponentFactory` that has a component factory. The component name of the dynamically created component is passed to the resolveComponentFactory method. To insert the new component into the DOM, the ViewContainerRef class has several methods including `createEmbeddedView` and `createComponent`. The `createComponent` method accepts as an argument the component factory.

29—Guided Exercise: Create a custom directive and dynamically insert a component

In this guided exercise, you control the display of a DOM element using a custom directive. You will create a directive that creates a "popup-like" tooltip that will display a dynamically created component. The result is shown below.

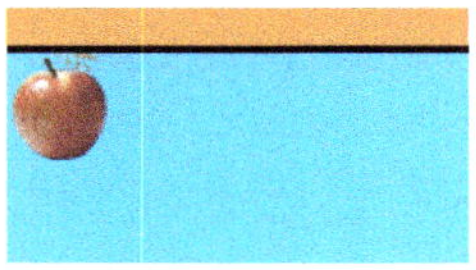

Before clicking the apple

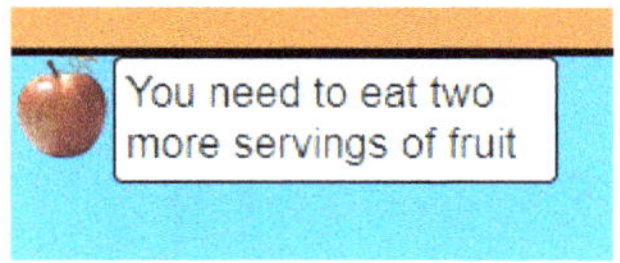

After clicking the apple

The directive you create in this exercise will dynamically create a component. So, before creating the directive, the first step will be to create the component called status component.

Step 1 Create a component called status.component. The file is shown below. Use the command: `ng g c status`

```
import {Component} from '@angular/core';

@Component({
    selector: 'app-status',
    template: `{{content}}`,
})
export class StatusComponent {
    content: string = '';
}
```

Note Notice in the code above that the view template consists of only a binding to the property called `content`.

Angular components can style the element that serves as the component host. In other words, Angular lets us style the custom component HTML element itself as opposed to styling an element inside the template. This is done with the :host pseudo-selector.

Step 2 Add the CSS style rules to the component class via the pseudo-selector :host as shown below in bold.

```
@Component({
    selector: 'app-status',
    template: `{{content}}`,
    styles: [`
    :host {
        background: white;
        padding: 0.25em;
        border: solid 1px #000;
        border-radius: .25em;
        position: absolute;
        font-family: Arial, Helvetica, sans-serif;
        font-size: 16px;
        line-height: 20px;
        width: 10em;
    }
  `]
})
```

The component that will be created dynamically is now finished. It's time to make the custom directive.

For clarity and simplicity in the seed project, create a folder called "directives" that will hold the new custom directive. In a real-world project the folder would follow the Angular style guide and use a more descriptive name.

Step 3 Create a folder called "directives" and add a new file into the folder called `status.directive.ts`. Begin the custom directive class with the `@Directive` decorator.

Use the CLI command: `ng g d directives/status`

Note In the file below, the selector indicates that our directive is accessed via an attribute. This is denoted by the square brackets (CSS selector matching pattern that matches attributes with the name in the brackets). It is considered a best practice to namespace directives to avoid naming collisions. In this code there is no namespace, however, if you were inside the FoodPlate cli project, you would name the selector `fp-status` to avoid any conflicts with other attributes.

```
import { Directive } from '@angular/core';
@Directive({
    selector: '[status]',
})

export class StatusDirective {
}
```

Note The custom directive's decorator is using a property called host which is used to map class properties to host element bindings for events, properties and attributes. In this case, it is mapping the `click` and `mouseleave` events to event handlers. You can accomplish the same thing by importing the `HostBinding` class and using the code sample below.

```
import { HostBinding } from '@angular/core';

@HostBinding({
  hostPropertyName?: string
})

@HostListener('event') onEvent {}
```

The Angular style guide recommends the @HostBinding. See Style 06-03 at https://angular.io/guide/styleguide#style-06-03. However, projects that use the Angular Material Library (https://material.angular.io/) recommends host bindings. See below.

"Prefer using the host object in the directive configuration instead of @HostBinding and @HostListener. We do this because TypeScript preserves the type information of methods with decorators, and when one of the arguments for the method is a native Event type, this preserved type information can lead to runtime errors in non-browser environments (e.g., server-side pre-rendering)." [3]

Because the hide and show status methods remove an element from the DOM, they both refer to the element via a class property called `statusRef`. Create two properties: the first one called `element` will reference a specific element later in the code. The second one, called `statusRef` will reference that `StatusComponent` element that you created in steps 1 and 2.

Step 4 Add the @HostListener as shown below.

```
@HostListener('click') onclick(): void {
    this.showStatus();
```

[3] https://github.com/angular/material2/blob/master/CODING_STANDARDS.md#host-bindings

```
}

@HostListener('mouseleave') onmouseleave(): void {
    this.hideStatus();
}
```

At the top of the exported directive class add the two properties shown below in bold.

```
...
export class StatusDirective {
     private element: HTMLElement;
     private statusRef: ComponentRef<StatusComponent>;
}
...
```

Step 5 Add the two event handlers to the exported directive class.

```
hideStatus(): void {
    if (this.statusRef) {
        this.statusRef.destroy();
        this.statusRef = null;
    }
}
showStatus(): void {
    this.statusRef = this.createStatus(this.status);
    const statusEl = this.statusRef.location.nativeElement;
    console.log(this.status);
}
```

The `hideStatus` methods' first line of code verifies the existence of the Status component. It then invokes the destroy method which destroys the component instance and all the data structures associated with it. The last line of code sets the status components reference to null.

The `showStatus` method assigns a value to the statusRef property by invoking a method called `createStatus` which you will write in the next step.

Step 6 Add the constructor function that injects the ElementRef, the ViewContainerRef and the ComponentFactoryResolver which will be required by the createStatus function added in step 7..

```
constructor(private elementRef: ElementRef, private viewContainer:
ViewContainerRef, private componentFactoryResolver:
ComponentFactoryResolver){
}
```

Step 7 Write the `createStatus` method which does the following:

- Accepts the string property passed in that will serve as the popup message text
- Clears the container that will serve as the placeholder of the StatusComponent that is being created
- Note: The container has not been created yet; it will be created in a view template later
- Create a component factory
- Use the component factories resolveComponentFactory

- Create the component using the factory
- Insert content from the content property into the newly created component
- Return the component

```
private createStatus(content: string): ComponentRef<StatusComponent> {
        this.viewContainer.clear();
        const statusComponentFactory =
this.componentFactoryResolver.resolveComponentFactory(StatusComponent);
        const statusComponentRef =
this.viewContainer.createComponent(statusComponentFactory);
        statusComponentRef.instance.content = content;
        return statusComponentRef;
}
```

Step 8 To use the ElementRef, ComponentFactoryResolver, ComponentRef and ViewContainerRef introduced in step 6, you need to import them using the code shown below in bold.

```
import { ComponentFactoryResolver, ComponentRef, Directive, ElementRef,
ViewContainerRef} from '@angular/core';

import {StatusComponent} from '../status/status.component';
```

Note When the component initializes, the element property can be set to the `ElementRef`. Specifically, however, it is the native element of the `ElementRef` that is needed. The Angular documentation suggest we use the `nativeElement` property as a last resort when direct access to the DOM is needed as it is considered a security risk. It is suggested that Rendered2 class is used instead. You will learn more about renderers later in the course.

Step 9 Add the ngOnInit() method to assign a value to the element property as shown below in bold.

```
ngOnInit(): void {
   this.element = this.elementRef.nativeElement;
}
```

Note You will receive error messages due to missing content in the class file. Subsequent steps will fix these errors as additional code is added.

Step 10 Add the ngOnDestroy() lifecycle method that invokes the hideStatus() method to remove the component.

```
ngOnDestroy(): void {
        this.hideStatus();
}
```

Step 11 The last step to completing the directive is to add the property that will hold the message used in the popup component. The code to add is shown below in bold.

```
import {ComponentFactoryResolver, ComponentRef, Directive, ElementRef, Input,
ViewContainerRef} from '@angular/core';
...
export class StatusDirective {
     ...
   @Input()
```

```
    status: string ='';
...
```

The completed directive code is shown below.

```
import {
  ComponentFactoryResolver,
  ComponentRef,
  Directive,
  ElementRef,
  HostBinding, HostListener,
  Input,
  OnDestroy,
  OnInit,
  ViewContainerRef
} from '@angular/core';

import { StatusComponent } from '../status/status.component';

@Directive({
  selector: '[status]',
})

export class StatusDirective implements OnInit, OnDestroy {

  private element: HTMLElement;
  private statusRef: ComponentRef<StatusComponent>;

  @Input()
  status: string = '';

  @HostListener('click') onclick(): void {
    this.showStatus();
  }

  @HostListener('mouseleave') onmouseleave(): void {
    this.hideStatus();
  }


constructor(private elementRef: ElementRef,
            private viewContainer: ViewContainerRef,
            private componentFactoryResolver: ComponentFactoryResolver){
  }

  ngOnInit(): void {
    this.element = this.elementRef.nativeElement;
  }

  ngOnDestroy(): void {
    this.hideStatus();
```

```
  }

  hideStatus(): void {
    if (this.statusRef) {
      this.statusRef.destroy();
      this.statusRef = null;
    }
  }
  showStatus(): void {
    this.statusRef = this.createStatus(this.status);
    const statusEl = this.statusRef.location.nativeElement;
    console.log(this.status);
  }

  private createStatus(content: string): ComponentRef<StatusComponent> {
    this.viewContainer.clear();
    const statusComponentFactory =
this.componentFactoryResolver.resolveComponentFactory(StatusComponent);
    const statusComponentRef =
this.viewContainer.createComponent(statusComponentFactory);
    statusComponentRef.instance.content = content;
    return statusComponentRef;
  }
}
```

Step 12 Now it's time to add the placeholder that will hold the new component. The status directive is added to inject the `ViewContentRef`. An image of the apple will invoke the creation of the component. Open app.component.html and add the bolded code shown below.

```
<app-header [user]="user"><app-header>
<img status="You need to eat two more servings of fruit" src="assets/images
/apple.png">
```

Throughout the course, you have added components to the app.module by declaring them. So far, in this exercise, we have not declared either the new status component or the new directive.

Note Angular 8 and lower:

Save and test the file in Chrome. Be sure to click the apple image to see the popup. The popup will NOT work. If you open the console in the DevTools, you should see an error message like the one below.

```
▶ERROR Error: No component factory found for StatusComponent. Did you add it to
@NgModule.entryComponents?
```

To understand this error message, it is helpful to know that there are two distinct kinds of components in Angular.

1. Components included in a template
    a. Known as "declarative" components
    b. These components are declared inside the template of other components as shown below

```
<fp-main>
   <fp-nav> </fp-nav>
</fp-main>
```

2. Components not included in a template
    a. Known as "imperative" components
    b. These components are loaded 'imperatively'
        i. The app or root component, for example, is not declared inside of a template, but loaded via the bootstrap method:

```
bootstrap: [ AppComponent ],
```

        ii. Components specified in a route definition are not loaded declaratively

```
const fallbackRoute:Route = {
   path: '**',
   component: DefaultComponent
};
```

Components that are loaded "imperatively" must be declared in a module via an `entryComponents` property.

Open app.module.ts and add the `entryComponents` as shown below in bold.

```
    imports:       [ BrowserModule ],
    declarations: [ AppComponent, HeaderComponent, ChildComponent,
WarningDirective, StatusComponent, StatusDirective ],
    entryComponents: [ StatusComponent ],
    bootstrap:     [ AppComponent ],
```

Step 13 Save and refresh the file in Chrome. Click the apple to see the dynamically created component that was created via the ViewContainerRef injected into the custom directive.

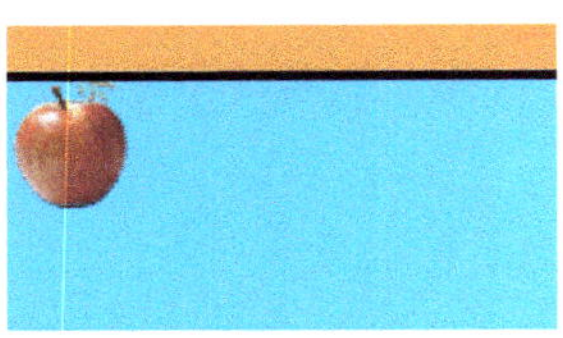

Before clicking the apple

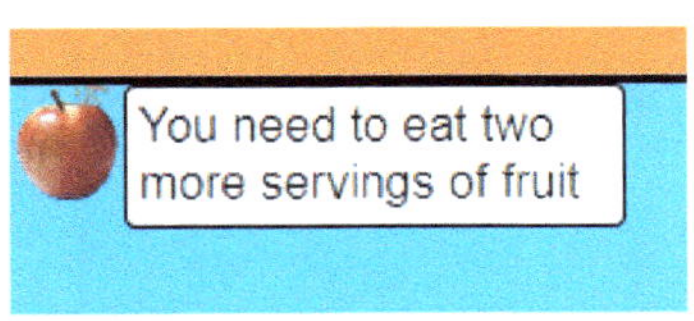

After clicking the apple

Homework Exercise

Step 1 Try using this directive on another element.

Chapter 10 Quiz

https://tinyurl.com/wyftqep

1) Match the terms with their definitions.

Structural directives	They encapsulate visual behavior by using the shadow dom
NgIf	Use to switch among alternative views
Attribute directives	They manipulate the DOM by adding/removing elements
NgFor	Can repeat a template for each item in the loop
Component directives	They change the look or behavior of a DOM element
NgSwitch	Use to conditionally add or remove an element from the DOM

2) Which element is created by the asterisk(*) in *ngIf:

   a. <shadow-dom>
   b. <template>
   c. <section>

Chapter summary

In this chapter, you learned some of Angular's built-in directives and identified some use cases. You learned what a directive is as well as when and where to place directive code.

Next Chapter

In the next chapter, you will learn how to make "links" to move the user from screen to screen. Remember, that Angular creates a single page application, which means you don't make hypertext links to move from page to page. Instead of links, you make routes that load and unload components views.

Chapter 11
Angular Routing

Chapter 11: Angular Routing

Objectives

- Define routing
- Understand the need for routing in single page applications
- Create a route in an Angular application

Introduction

Routing is what makes single page applications behave as if they were multi-page apps. In a single page application, the user is delivered a single HTML page (index.html) throughout the lifetime of the application. In component-based frameworks like Angular, components are loaded as "pages" into index.html. Components can make up an entire page or as in the food plate application, the header and footer remain in place and the component in the middle is replaced. Routes configure what "pages" or components will load as well as when and where they will load. For example, a route might specify that when the user visits foodplate.com/myplate, the plate component will display between the header and footer components. Routes allow us to refresh the page and maintain our current location. They also allow us to bookmark pages in our application and come back to them later. Without routes, you would not be able to share the URL of a specific "page" in the application. Routes also help us maintain state in our applications. In other words, routes allow to define a URL like foodplate.com/register that specifies what part of the application the user should see; in this case the register page.

Routing is often done on the server, such as in a node.js application using the express framework. In that case the server accepts a request from the client and routes to a controller that runs the route depending on the path and parameters passed in with the request. Angular provides client-side routing. As you might guess, with client-side routing the client is not making a request of the server. The first client-side routing technique was called "hash-based routing" because it makes use of the HTML anchor syntax (#). A typical route might look like this:

```
http://foodplate.com/#/myplate
```

Since that time, HTML5 introduced the history API which provided the ability to programmatically create browser history that changed the URL without having to request a new page. This part of the API is the `history.pushState()` method. Angular provides two mechanisms for routing, largely because not all browsers support HTML5 based routing. Therefore, with Angular, you may choose the older hash-based routing (for broader support on older browsers) or the newer HTML5 based routing.

So far, in the FoodPlate application, the user sees the header, the footer, and a main section that currently holds a graphic and a button to register. When the user clicks the "Register" button they should be routed to the register form. Throughout the remainder of the course, you will continue to make routes as needed, to navigate to various parts of the application.

11.0 Understanding Angular routing

Angular routing uses three main classes, shown below. There are other routing classes (see the documentation for a complete list), some of which will be introduced in Chapter 16: Advanced Routing.

`Routes` – they describe the routes the application understands and supports

`RouterOutlet` – this is the "place in the application" that the route's component will occupy

`RouterLink` – this is a directive that will link to a route

To begin using routes, you will need an Angular package called router. As usual, you import this package into the module that needs it as shown below.

```
import { RouterModule, Routes } from '@angular/router';
```

The next step is defining the routes for your application. This can be done in a separate file or inside of app.module.ts. Typically, a constant called routes is created and typed as a Routes object and set to a configuration of routes.

```
const routes:Routes = [
```

```
{ path: 'home', component: HomeComponent },
{ path: 'about', component: AboutComponent }
```

In the example above, two routes are being configured. The first route will display the Home Component when the user goes to www.foodplate.com/home via the browser's URL location field. The second route will be invoked when the user goes to www.foodplate.com/about, loading the AboutComponent. What happens when the user passes a bad path into the browser? You can redirect them to another path via the code below.

```
{ path: '', redirectTo: 'home', pathMatch: 'full' },
```

This route states that when the user visits the path location, the browser should redirect the user to the 'home' path instead. A redirect route requires a `pathMatch` property that tells the router how to match a URL to the path of a route. The router throws an error if you don't add this property to a redirect. In the example above, the router should select the route to the HomeComponent only when the entire URL matches '. Thus, the pathMatch value is set to 'full'.

For more information, visit https://angular.io/guide/router and http://vsavkin.tumblr.com/post/146722301646/angular-router-empty-paths-componentless-routes

In addition to the redirect path, you will need a path for bad URLs that originate with the domain path. For example, in the FoodPlate application, going to http://localhost:4200/register (in development) or http://foodplate.com/register (in production) should direct us to the registration page, but going to http://localhost:4200/bogus-page (in development) or http://www.foodplate.com/bogus-page (in production) should take us to a default page. To redirect the user in this type of scenario, you configure a fallback path like the example below.

```
{ path: '**', component: MainComponent}
```

The path value of `'**'` matches all URLs.

It is important to remember that routes are searched in the order in which they are supplied in the routing configuration file. Therefore, the fallback route should be the last route in the configuration. If it is first, the problem is that the path value `'**'` matches all URLs, thus all site navigation will lead to the fallback route component being invoked.

11.0.1 Route Summary

The `path` identifies the URL that the route will handle.

`component` is what ties the component to the path the route handles.

`redirectTo` is used to redirect certain paths to a previously defined route.

11.1 The RouterModule

Angular uses its `RouterModule` to invoke routes. `RouterModule.forRoot()` is a method that routes the route module of the application. The `forRoot()` method is passed a list of route configurations.

11.2 The base href

A <base> element in the head section of index.html tells the router how to compose its navigational URLs. Typically, when the app folder is the application root folder the base is set with an href attribute as shown below.

```
<base href="/">
```

Name	Construct	Description
Router	Object	Object that represents the router Contains the methods to navigate to a route: navigate() navigateByUrl()
RouterOutlet	Directive	Placeholder in the web page where the router should render the component: <router-outlet></router-outlet>
Routes	Array	An array of routes that map URLs to components to rendered inside of the routerOutlet
RouterLink	Directive	Declares a link to a route when using HTML anchor tags <a [routerLink]=['/FoodPlate']>Food Plate</a>
ActivatedRoute	Object	Represents the route or routes that are currently active constructor(route:ActivatedRoute) { this.foodGroup = route.snapshot.params['foodGroup']; }
Location	Class	Used to navigate URLs outside of the Angular router with the methods: go() forward() back()

30—Guided Exercise: Create routes

In this guided exercise, you add the necessary code so that users can navigate between screens in your application. To do this, you create a routing configuration file and add routes to the foodPlate-cli application.

Step 1 Create a routing configuration file inside of src/app and name it `app.routing.module.ts`.

Note Angular CLI tool will create an app-routing.module.ts file for you when you first create the project. The latest version of the CLI will prompt the question do you want to add routing. If you are using an older version of the CLI, the key is to use the following command when creating a project (with the ng new command).

```
ng new projectName --routing
```

Step 2 As usual, when creating a module, you must import the `NgModule` package from the angular core package.

```
import { NgModule } from '@angular/core';
```

Step 3 Now import the necessary routing packages.

```
import { RouterModule, Routes } from '@angular/router';
```

Step 4 Create the routes constant, beginning with the default route (`path: ''`).

```
const routes: Routes = [
  { path: '', component: DefaultComponent },
  { path: 'register', component: RegisterComponent },
  { path: '**', component: PlateComponent},
];
```

Note The first route is for the Default component and the second route will load the RegisterComponent, but you haven't yet created either of these components. You will create the RegisterComponent in step 9 and the default route in step 10. The last route is the fallback route invoked whenever the user invokes a non-existent route, for example, if you try to navigate to http://localhost:4200/nosuchpage.

Step 5 In the app.routing.module.ts file, add the `@NgModule()` decorator.

```
@NgModule()
```

Step 6 Pass the decorator a configuration object that declares the modules imports and exports, shown below in bold.

```
@NgModule({
  imports: [
    RouterModule.forRoot(
      routes)
  ],
  exports: [
    RouterModule
  ]
})
```

Step 7 Export the `AppRoutingModule` class.

```
export class AppRoutingModule { }
```

Step 8 Because the routing configuration is routing the Register, Default and Plate components, they must be imported.

```
c
```

Note Your IDE may warn you that the RegisterComponent and the DefaultComponent can't be found. That's because we haven't created them yet!

Step 9 Create a simple `Register` component. Add the `--skip-import` command in the CLI. You will manually declare the component in the app module in step 11.

```
ng g c register --skip-import
```

The default HTML is shown below.

```
<p>register works!</p>
```

Step 10 Build a simple component that will hold a placeholder image for the default route. To automatically declare the new component in the app module, add the `-m app` to the end as shown below in bold.

```
ng g c components/default -m app
```

Step 11 Declare the RegisterComponent in the app.module.

Note Now that you have a register and default component, be sure they have been imported in app.routing.module.ts.

Step 12 Add the HTML to the default.component.html as shown below.

```
<img src="assets/images/plateImages/choose-my-plate-gov.png" alt="">
```

Step 13 As per the usual order of operations, you must now import the app.routing.module.ts to the app.module file as shown in bold in the code snippet below. You also have to declare the RegisterComponent (also shown in bold).

```
...
import { DefaultComponent } from './components/default/default.component';
import { RegisterComponent } from './register/register.component';

@NgModule({
  declarations: [ AppComponent,
                  DefaultComponent,
                  FooterComponent,
                  HeaderComponent,
                  HomeBtnComponent,
                  MainComponent,
                  MessageComponent,
                  NavComponent,
                  PlateComponent,
                  RegisterComponent
                ],
  imports: [
      AppRoutingModule,
      BrowserModule,
      CommonModule,
      FoodGroupsModule
```

Step 14 The register component will need a place to load. That's where the `<router-outlet>` comes in. Add the `<router-outlet>` to the main.component.html as shown below in bold.

```
<main>
  <router-outlet></router-outlet>
  <fp-plate [user]="user"></fp-plate>
  <fp-home-btn [user]="user"><fp-home-btn>
</main>
```

Step 15 Comment out the <fp-plate> component (shown above with a strikethough).

Step 16 The Register button (<fp-home-btn>) component will serve as the trigger to activate the route to the register component. Add an HTML <a> element to invoke the route. The component's routerLink property is bound to the '/register/ path.

```
<main>
<router-outlet></router-outlet>
<a routerLink="register">
  <fp-home-btn [user]= "user" ></fp-home-btn>
</a>
</main>
```

Step 17 When the register route is visited, the user should no longer see the register button. To hide them, add the code shown below in bold.

```
<main>
  <router-outlet></router-outlet>
  <a routerLink="register">
    <fp-home-btn [user]= "user" [hidden]="this.router.url ===
'/register'"></fp-home-btn>
  </a>
</main>
```

Step 18 To reference the router object and its properties from the main component add the following code to main.component.ts

```
import { Router } from '@angular/router';
...
export class MainComponent implements OnInit {

  @Input()
  user:User;

constructor(private _router: Router) {
}
  ngOnInit(): void {
  }
}
```

Step 19 Add a router property to the main component class and assign the injected router as its value in the constructor.

```
router: Router;

  constructor(private _router: Router) {
    this.router = _router;
  }
```

Step 20 If necessary, change the user object's registered property to false (in user.service.ts).

Step 21 Run the app in Chrome and confirm that clicking the register button loads the register component as shown below.

Before the Register button click.

After the Register button click, route is activated.

Step 22 Prior to the creation of the Angular DevTools chrome extension, an extension called Augury was commonly used.

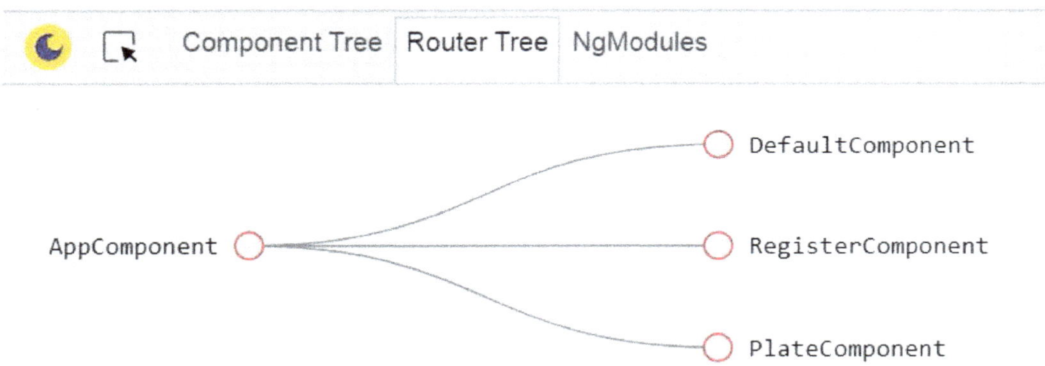

It is still available at https://chrome.google.com/webstore/detail/augury-extension/nakmndgaejmkmbhmmfjmlidbolcoiidi?hl=en-US. The screenshot above is from Augury's Router Tree Tool. Your version of Augury may not support the "Router Tree" view tab.

12 –Challenge Exercise: Add routes to the nav component

In this challenge, you add functionality to the nav component you created earlier. When the user clicks one of the navigation "links" a new component will display. You will build the routes for these components.

Note You will be making routes for the links in the nav component. The Plate component exists, but there is currently nothing to route to for the Farmers Markets and the Exercises links.

Simple Instructions

- Create two new components:
  - "exercises" Component
  - "farmers-markets" Component
- Add routes to the two new components and the plate component.

Note All the routes should work, but the PlateComponent is broken. Don't worry, it will be fixed shortly (in chapter 13)! See the screenshots below showing the broken images in the PlateComponent.

Step by Step Instructions

Step 1 Create a component for Farmers Markets and Exercises. Name the first one farmers-markets and the second one exercises. The default view templates the CLI creates will be sufficient (as shown below).

```
<p>
  exercises works!
</p>
```

```
<p>
  farmers-markets works!
</p>
```

Step 2 Open the app.routing.module.ts file and add routes for the following components:

- farmersMarkets route should load FarmersMarketComponent
- exercises route should load ExerciseComponent
- myPlate route should load PlateComponent

Step 3 Open the nav component's view template and add the routerLink's via the HTML <a> element

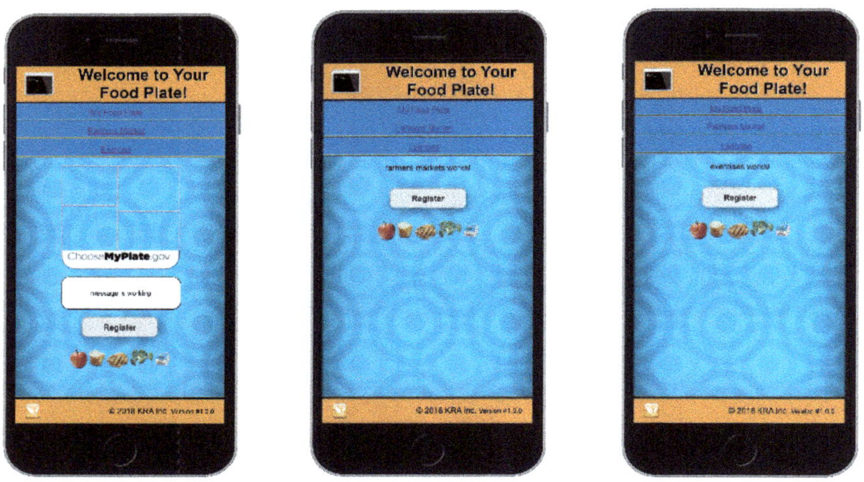

Note All the routes should work, but the PlateComponent is broken. Don't worry, it will be fixed shortly (in chapter 13)!

Step 4 Try moving the routerLink directive to the `<li>` element instead of the <a> element. What are the consequences? Which location is best?

Possible solution code

app.routing.module.ts

```
import { NgModule } from '@angular/core';
import { RouterModule, Routes} from '@angular/router';

import {RegisterComponent} from './register/register.component';
import {PlateComponent} from './plate/plate.component';
import {ExercisesComponent} from './exercises/exercises.component';
import {FarmersMarketsComponent} from './farmers-markets/farmers-markets.component';

const routes: Routes = [
    { path: '', component: PlateComponent },
    { path: 'register', component: RegisterComponent },
    { path: 'farmersMarkets', component: FarmersMarketsComponent },
    { path: 'exercises', component: ExercisesComponent },
    { path: 'myPlate', component: PlateComponent },
    { path: '**', component: PlateComponent},
];

@NgModule({
    imports: [RouterModule.forRoot(routes)],
    exports: [ RouterModule ]
})

export class AppRoutingModule {}
```

nav.component.html

```
<nav>
  <ul>
    <li [ngClass]="{active: isActive}">
      <a routerLink="myPlate">My Food Plate</a>
    </li>
    <li>
      <a routerLink="farmersMarkets">Farmers Market</a>
    </li>
    <li>
      <a routerLink="exercises">Exercise</a>
    </li>
  </ul>
</nav>
```

11.3 Styling Router Links

In the Angular Directives chapter, the following code was created in the nav component (shown in bold):

```
<nav>
    <ul>
        <li [ngClass]="{active: isActive}"><a routerLink="myPlate">My Food
Plate</a></li>
        <li><a routerLink="farmersMarkets">Farmers Market</a></li>
        <li><a routerLink="exercises">Exercise</a></li>
    </ul>
</nav>
```

It was noted in that chapter, that the Angular router provides a means for adding styles to routes. It is also a directive and it's called the `routerLinkActive` directive. This directive tells the router which CSS class to use in conjunction with an active route. The directive is part of the @angular/router package and it lets you add a CSS class to an element when the link's route becomes active.

11.3.1 Example

```
<a routerLink="/invoices/1234" routerLinkActive="active-invoice">1234</a>
```

In the example code above, when the URL /invoices/1234 is the active route, the CSS class called active-invoice will be applied to the <a> element. If the user moves away from that route via a different URL, the CSS class will be removed.

It is possible to set more than one class with the routerLinkActive directive. The code would look like this:

```
<a routerLink="/invoices/1234" routerLinkActive="['invoice', 'active-
invoice']">1234</a>
```

31—Guided Exercise: Add style to the active route in the nav component

In this exercise, you refactor the [ngClass] directive in the "My Food Plate" link by using the activeRouterLink directive for this and the remaining links.

Step 1 Open the nav.component.css file and refactor the `li` and the `li:last-child` CSS rules as shown below in bold, so that the selector for the links takes the newly inserted <a> element into consideration.

```
li>a {
    color: #fff;
    text-decoration: none;
    display: inline;
    background-image: url(../../assets/images/icons/diamond.svg);
    background-position: right center;
    background-repeat: no-repeat;
    padding-right: 1.65em;
    padding-left: .45em;
    cursor: pointer;
}
li:last-child>a {
    background-image: none;
}
```

Step 2 While still in the nav.component.css, refactor the .active class to increase its specificity as shown below in bold.

```
nav ul li a.active {
    color: #ef952b;
}
```

Step 3 Open nav.component.html and add the routerLinkActive directive as shown below in bold.

```
<nav>
    <ul>
        <li><a routerLink="myPlate" routerLinkActive="active">My Food
Plate</a></li>
        <li><a routerLink="farmersMarkets" routerLinkActive="active">Farmers
Market</a></li>
        <li><a routerLink="exercises"
routerLinkActive="active">Exercise</a></li>
    </ul>
</nav>
```

Step 4 Check the file in Chrome and click the links in the nav component.

myPlate route active

FarmersMarkets route active

Exercises route active

11.4 Breaking up routes

Any route that might change or standout for its role, such as the entry point at index.html route or the fallback route may be broken out into a variable.

For example, you could refactor the existing routes in the FoodPlate cli project from the existing code (shown below)

```
const routes: Routes = [
    { path: '', component: PlateComponent },
    { path: 'myPlate', component: PlateComponent},
    { path: 'register', component: RegisterComponent },
    { path: 'farmersMarkets', component: FarmersMarketsComponent },
    { path: 'exercises', component: ExercisesComponent },
    { path: '**', component: PlateComponent},
];
```

into this code (relevant changes are shown in bold):

```
const indexRoute:Route = {
    path: "",
    component: PlateComponent
};

const fallbackRoute:Route = {
    path: '**',
    component: PlateComponent
};

const routes: Routes = [
    indexRoute,
    { path: 'myPlate', component: PlateComponent},
    { path: 'register', component: RegisterComponent },
    { path: 'farmersMarkets', component: FarmersMarketsComponent },
    { path: 'exercises', component: ExercisesComponent },
    fallbackRoute
];
```

11.5 Child Routes

You can also configure your routes with child routes. In this case, you might have one main entry point route such as the indexRoute shown above and the remaining routes are defined as children of that route. It is important to remember that only one route may be activated at a time.

Below is an example of the foodplate application routes defined with one main entry route and child routes.

```
const fallbackRoute:Route = {
    path: '**',
    component: PlateComponent
};
```

```
const routes: Routes = [
    {
        path: '',
        children: [
            { path: 'myPlate', component: PlateComponent},
            { path: 'register', component: RegisterComponent },
            { path: 'farmersMarkets', component: FarmersMarketsComponent },
            { path: 'exercises', component: ExercisesComponent },
            fallbackRoute
        ]
    }
];
```

32—Guided Exercise: Use child routes

In this exercise, you refactor the existing routing config (to break up the routes) and use child routes in a new component – food-groups.component.ts, shown below.

When the user clicks a food icon, a details component is loaded. For example, the screenshot below shows the results of the fruit icon being clicked.

To complete this guided exercise, you will need to:

- Add the new nav link for "Food Groups"
- Refactor the current app.routing.module.ts by adding the new route
- Create a second routing configuration file for the food-groups.component and its routes
- Create the details components for fruit, vegetable, protein and grains

Step 1 Open the app.routing.module.ts and refactor the code to use child routes as shown below.

```
import { NgModule } from '@angular/core';
import {Route, RouterModule, Routes} from '@angular/router';

import { DefaultComponent } from './components/default/default.component';
import { ExercisesComponent } from './exercises/exercises.component';
import { FarmersMarketsComponent } from './farmers-markets/farmers-
markets.component';
import { PlateComponent } from './plate/plate.component';
import { RegisterComponent } from './register/register.component';

const fallbackRoute: Route = {
  path: '**',
  component: DefaultComponent
};
```

```
const routes: Routes = [
  {
    path: '',
    children: [
      { path: 'myPlate', component: PlateComponent},
      { path: 'register', component: RegisterComponent },
      { path: 'farmersMarkets', component: FarmersMarketsComponent },
      { path: 'exercises', component: ExercisesComponent },
      fallbackRoute
    ]
  }
];

@NgModule({
  imports: [RouterModule.forRoot(routes)],
  exports: [ RouterModule ]
})

export class AppRoutingModule {}
```

Step 2 Run the app in Chrome and make sure all the links still work.

Note It is considered a best practice to break down lengthy and/or complex routing configuration into multiple configuration files. You may use your discretion, however, for this exercise, you will move the food-group.components routing to a separate configuration file.

Step 3 Create a new routing configuration file for the food-groups.component's routes and name it food-groups.routing.ts. The code is shown and explained below. Create the file in the food-groups folder. You can copy and paste the file from assets/code-snippets/food-groups-routing-ts.txt.

```
import {FoodGroupsComponent} from './food-groups/food-groups.component';
import {ProteinDetailComponent} from './food-detail/protein-detail/protein-
detail.component';
import {VegetableDetailComponent} from './food-detail/vegetable-
detail/vegetable-detail.component';
import {FruitDetailComponent} from './food-detail/fruit-detail/fruit-
detail.component';
import {GrainsDetailComponent} from './food-detail/grains-detail/grains-
detail.component';

export const foodGroupsRoutes = [
  {
    path: 'foodGroups',
    children: [
      {
        path: '',
        component: FoodGroupsComponent,
        outlet: 'foodGroupOutlet'
```

```
        },
        {
          path: 'protein',
          component: ProteinDetailComponent,
        },
        {
          path: 'fruit',
          component: FruitDetailComponent
        },
        {
          path: 'vegetables',
          component: VegetableDetailComponent
        },
        {
          path: 'grains',
          component: GrainsDetailComponent
        },
      ]}
];
```

In this routing configuration, a default path is set for the foodGroup path and it loads the FoodGroupsComponent. It uses the outlet property to ensure that the component loads in a <router-outlet> element with a name of "foodGroupOutlet." It then sets the remaining child paths for: foodGroups/protein, foodGroups/fruits, foodGroups/vegetables and foodGroups/grains, with each pointing to a detail component.

Note Alternatively, you could create a child routing module instead of the constant used below (from routing.module.ts).

The food-groups.component generates the images of the food icons with an @ngFor directive. Each image should respond to a mouse click by invoking the appropriate child route.

Step 4 Add the path constant to app.routing.module.ts and import the foodGroupsRoutes as shown below.

```
const routes: Routes = [
    {
        path: '',
        children: [
            { path: 'myPlate', component: PlateComponent},
            { path: 'register', component: RegisterComponent },
            { path: 'farmersMarkets', component: FarmersMarketsComponent },
            { path: 'exercises', component: ExercisesComponent },
            ...foodGroupsRoutes,
            fallbackRoute
        ]
    }
];
```

Step 5 Modify the food-groups.component.ts to add the following:

- a showGroup() method that will be called on the click event of the image
- A reference to the currently active route

The modified code is shown below in bold.

```
import {Component, OnInit} from '@angular/core';
import {ActivatedRoute, Router} from '@angular/router';

import {FoodGroupsService} from '../services/food-groups.service';

@Component({
    selector: 'fp-food-groups',
    templateUrl: 'food-groups.component.html',
    styleUrls: ['./food-groups.component.css']
})

export class FoodGroupsComponent implements OnInit {
    foodGroups;
    iconStyles = {
        'cursor' : 'pointer',
        'display' : 'inline'
    };
    constructor(private foodGroupsSvce:FoodGroupsService,
                private router: Router,
                private route: ActivatedRoute) {
    }

    ngOnInit():void {
        this.foodGroups = this.foodGroupsSvce.getFoodGroups();
    }

    showGroup(group): void {
       console.log(group.name);
       this.router.navigate([group.name], {relativeTo: this.route
});
    }
}
```

The `showGroup()` method will be passed the group the image belongs to as a parameter. Log that group's name property to the console to ensure it's getting the right group. The router objects `navigate()` method is used to invoke the route. The route can be passed in as an absolute path like this:

```
this.router.navigate([`foodGroups/${group.name}`]);
```

or a relative path like this:

```
this.router.navigate([group.name],{relativeTo: this.route});
```

When using the relative, path you need to add the relativeTo property and provide the value of the current route, as shown below in bold.

For this reason, the ActivatedRoute must be imported and injected into the constructor function.

Now it's time to invoke the click event listener from the template.

Step 6 Open food-groups.component.html and add the click event listener shown below in bold.

```
<section>
    <img *ngFor="let group of foodGroups;"
         src="{{group.icon}}"
         alt="{{group.name}}"
         (click)="showGroup(group)">
</section>
```

We need <router-outlet> elements to hold the food-group component and the detail components (the detail components have not been created).

Step 7 Open main.component.html and add the named router outlet as shown below in bold.

```
<main>
  <router-outlet name="foodGroupOutlet"></router-outlet>
  <router-outlet></router-outlet>
  <a routerLink="register">
    <fp-home-btn [hidden]="this.router.url === '/register'">
    </fp-home-btn>
  </a>
</main>
```

Step 8 Add the "Food Groups" link to the nav bar by editing nav.component.html as shown below in bold. Add a new route to the app.routing.module to foodGroups.

```
<nav>
    <ul>
        <li><a routerLink="myPlate" routerLinkActive="active">My Food
Plate</a></li>
        <li><a routerLink="foodGroups" routerLinkActive="active">Food
Groups</a></li>
        <li><a routerLink="farmersMarkets" routerLinkActive="active">Farmers
Market</a></li>
        <li><a routerLink="exercises"
routerLinkActive="active">Exercise</a></li>
    </ul>
</nav>
```

Step 9 Make a new module called food-detail.module.ts and a component called fruit-detail. Import the new food-detail.module in app.module.ts.

```
ng g m food-groups/food-detail
ng g c food-groups/food-detail/fruit-detail -m food-detail
```

The fruit-detail component should be created it its own folder called "fruit-detail" inside the food-detail folder. The fruit-detail's HTML template is shown below and can be copied and pasted from assets/code-snippets/fruit-detail-html.html.

```
<section>
<h1>What foods are in the fruit group?</h1>
```

```
<p>Any fruit or 100% fruit juice counts as part of the Fruit Group. Fruits may
be fresh, canned, frozen, or dried, and may be whole, cut-up, or pureed.
</p>
<h2>What counts as one cup of fruit?</h2>
     <ul>
           <li>1 small apple (2 1/4" diameter)</li>
           <li>1 large banana (8" to 9" long)</li>
           <li>1 cup melon balls</li>
           <li>1 cup of fruit juice</li>
           <li>1/2 cup of dried fruit</li>
           <li>1 medium pear</li>
           <li>2 halves canned peach</li>
     </ul>
</section>
```

Step 10 Add the following CSS to fruit-detail.component.css. You can copy the code from assets/css/fruit-detail-component-css.css.

```
section {
    background-color: #fff;
    border: 1px solid #000;
    border-radius: 1em;
    width: 70%;
    margin: auto;
    display: flex;
    flex-direction: column;
    align-items: center;
    justify-content: space-around;
}
section>h1, section>h2 {
    margin-top: 1em;
    margin-bottom: 0;
    padding: .25em;
}
section>p {
    width: 80%;
    font-size: 1em;
    line-height: 1.4em;
    text-align: left;
}
ul>li {
    text-align: left;
    line-height:1.35em;
}
```

Step 11 Use the cli to make the components listed below. Each component should be made in its own directory in the food-detail folder.

- grains-detail
- protein-detail
- vegetable-detail

Example command: `ng g c food-groups/food-detail/grains-detail -m food-detail`

The default HTML templates will be sufficient to complete the exercise.

Step 12 Remove the food-groups component from the app.component.html file as shown below with a strikethrough.

```
<div id= "wrapper">
  <fp-header></fp-header>
  <fp-nav></fp-nav>
  <fp-main [user]="user">Main is working</fp-main>
  <fp-food-groups></fp-food-groups>
  <fp-footer></fp-footer>
</div>
```

Step 13 Confirm that all new components have been imported in food-groups.routing.module.ts.

Step 14 Confirm that app.module imports FoodGroupsModule and FoodGroupsModule imports FoodDetailModule.

Step 15 Confirm that all components have been declared in their respective modules.

Step 16 Test the file in Chrome by using the following steps:

a. Launch the application.
b. Click the "Food Groups" link in the main navigation bar beneath the header.
c. Click the fruit icon.
d. Click the remaining icons.

Homework

The goal of this exercise is to refactor code to make a more reusable component. Rather than four detail components (FruitDetail, ProteinDetail, VegetableDetail and GrainsDetail), you make one component and called FoodGroupDetails. Use properties to make each instance unique.

Remove the FruitDetailComponent, ProteinDetailComponent, VegetableDetailComponent and GrainsDetailComponent and replace them with a single FoodGroupDetails component.

Hints Add properties to the food-groups.service.ts to hold the contents of the component such as:
foods:string: "Any fruit or 100% fruit juice counts as part of the Fruit Group. Fruits may be fresh, canned, frozen, or dried, and may be whole, cut-up, or pureed."

foodList:array:

1 small apple (2 1/4" diameter)
1 large banana (8" to 9" long)
1 cup melon balls
1 cup of fruit juice
1/2 cup of dried fruit
1 medium pear
2 halves canned peach

Chapter 11 Quiz

https://tinyurl.com/yx84dgpb

1) Routing can be *completely* configured by the Angular CLI tool. true false
2) Correct the error in this route: `{ path: 'home', module: 'Home' }`
3) Define the following routing-related objects and their purpose:
   a. Router
   b. RouterOutlet
   c. Routes
   d. RouterLink
   e. ActivatedRoute
   f. Location

Chapter summary

In this chapter, you learned how to create a single page Angular application by using routes and child routes to navigate as though it were a multi-page application. You learned some of the classes used in routing including:

- Router
- RouterModule
- Routes

Common routes:

- Default route
- Index route
- Fallback route

Next Chapter

In the next chapter, you learn all about Angular forms.

Chapter 12

Angular Forms

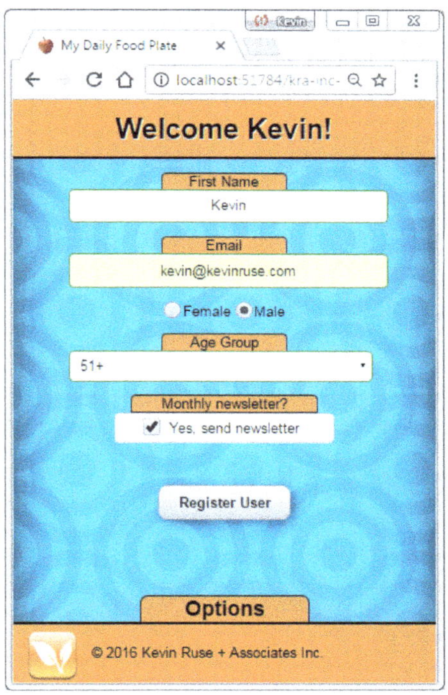

Chapter 12: Angular Forms

Objectives

- List the main classes used by the Angular framework to make forms
- Describe the properties and methods of Angular's form classes
- Describe the two main approaches to making forms in Angular
- Build a template-driven form
- Build a Reactive form
- Describe the use case for Angular's FormBuilder class
- Use Angular's built-in form validation

Introduction

Most applications require feedback from the user and that's where forms come in. Forms provide ample opportunity to get critical data input as well as modify data on the server. Angular provides a good deal of functionality in the framework to deal with typical form issues such as validating data, modifying component properties via form fields and maintaining state within the application. In the chapter, you will create a form and use some of Angular's built-in form features. Forms will be used again later in the course in conjunction with topics like HTTP (AJAX requests) and filtering data.

12.0 About Angular Forms

Angular provides two techniques for creating forms:

- Template-driven forms
- Reactive forms

Although they live in two different modules, both belong to the library '@angular/forms' and they share form classes for common properties and behaviors. The modules are:

- ReactiveFormsModule
- Provides form directives including:
  - formControl
  - ngFormGroup
  - FormsModule
- Provides form directives including:
  - NgModel
  - NgForm

12.1 Angular Form classes

Angular forms have many features. In this section we will examine the main features that provide the robust functionality of Angular forms. Angular forms can:

- use controls (user inputs, buttons, sliders, etc.)
- bind data to the form controls
- specify validation rules for the data entered into the form controls
- enable and disable form controls based on certain conditions
- show or hide form controls based on certain conditions
- provide visual feedback based on user inputs

The fundamental form classes include:

- FormControl
  - A single input field that encapsulate the input in our forms and provide a way to work with them
- FormGroup
  - A wrapper interface composed of a collection of inputs
- FormArray
  - Aggregates the values of each child FormControl into an array

12.1.1 Form Controls

A form control is one of the three main building blocks of Angular forms. The FormControl object inherits from the AbstractControl class. The AbstractControl class has properties that make it easier to access the parts of the form we need.

12.2 Some AbstractForm properties

Property	Description/Example Code
`value`	The value entered in the control. `let userName = nameControl.value;`
`errors`	Errors in the form control. `emailControl.errors`
`dirty`	Indicates that the value of the element has been changed by the user.
`valid`	Indicates that the value of the element is valid.
`pristine`	The form has not been touched.
`touched`	The form has been touched.

For complete coverage of the AbstractControl class see the source code at: https://github.com/angular/angular/blob/24db1ed9384827989fea1100dc4b2173d70cac32/packages/forms/src/model.ts#L79

12.2.1 FormGroup

`FormGroups` provide a wrapper interface around a collection of FormControls. The `FormGroup` also inherits from the `AbstractControl` making it just as easy to access form control properties.

12.2.2 FormArray

A `FormArray` aggregates the values of each child `FormControl` into an array. It is important to remember, that if one of the controls in a `FormArray` is invalid, the entire array becomes invalid. Like `FormGroup` and `FormControl`, the `FormArray` inherits from the `AbstractControl` class. You can change the controls in the array, by using the `push()`, `insert()`, or `removeAt()` methods in the `FormArray` itself. These methods ensure the controls are tracked and maintained in the form's hierarchy.

12.3 Building Angular Forms

Recall Angular's two approaches for building forms:

- Template driven forms
- Reactive Forms

We'll begin with template-driven forms.

12.4 Template-driven forms

Template driven forms require importing a package called FormsModule located in '@angular/forms.' Template driven forms provide the following useful directives (not a complete list):

- NgModel
- NgForm

Template-driven forms use the `ngForm` directive. Using this directive results in the `NgForm` class being added to our `<form>` tags. The two primary consequences of adding this `NgForm` class to our forms include the addition of a `FormGroup` and an output of the form values.

We can create a local variable that points to this form as follows:

```
<form #myForm = "ngForm"> ...
```

The `ngForm` that serves as the value of this local variable that was created with the `ngForm` directive and is a `FormGroup`. Remember the forms output is also a result of the `ngForm`, so we can use it with the submit button as shown below in bold.

```
<form #myForm = "ngForm" (ngSubmit)="onSubmit(myForm.value)"> ...
```

Here we use event binding syntax () to bind the `ngSubmit` (which comes from `NgForm`) to the `onSubmit()` method that would be defined in our component class and pass the form's key-value pairs.

33—Guided Exercise: Understanding template-driven forms and FormControls

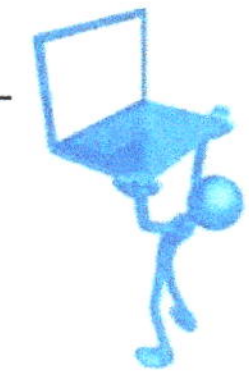

In this exercise, you learn about the FormControl object by creating a simple template-driven form.

Step 1 Open app.module.ts and import the necessary form module as shown below in bold.

```
import { NgModule } from '@angular/core';
import { BrowserModule } from "@angular/platform-browser";
import { FormsModule } from '@angular/forms';
… more imports here
@NgModule({
    imports:[ BrowserModule, FontAwesomeModule, FormsModule ],
… more properties here
```

Step 2 Create a login folder inside of the app folder and create a login component. Be sure to add the component to the app.module.

```
ng g c login -m app
```

Step 3 Confirm the component's selector value is `app-login`.

Step 4 Add the following HTML to the login.component.html file to create the basic form structure.

```
<form>
        <label for="userName">User Name</label>
        <input type="text"
               id="userName"
               name="userName">
        <button type="submit">Submit</button>
        <button type="button" (click)="log(userNameForm)">Access Form
Properties with ngForm</button>
</form>
<h1>Hi {{ userName }}</h1>
```

Step 5 Next, add the Angular specific code to the form.

```
<form #userNameForm="ngForm"
      (ngSubmit)="onSubmit(userNameForm.value)">
        <label for="userName">User Name</label>
        <input type="text"
               id="userName"
               name="userName"
               [(ngModel)]="userName">
        <button type="submit">Submit</button>
        <button type="button" (click)="log(userNameForm)">Access Form
Properties with ngForm</button>
</form>
<h1>Hi {{ userName }}</h1>
```

Creates a local variable/is a formgroup

Creates a form control class

This template variables makes the userNameForm a reference to the NgForm directive that will govern the form and its contents.

(ngSubmit)="onSubmit(userNameForm.value)"

This binds the forms ngSubmit event property to the component's onSubmit method.

[(ngModel)]="userName"

Notice the ngModel and its binding syntax.

The ngModel directive creates a new FormControl that is added to form. It binds a DOM element to that new FormControl. In other words, it creates an association between the input tag (named userName) in the view and the FormControl object.

The binding syntax (called the banana in the box) creates a two-way binding. You have seen input bindings with square brackets [] and you've seen output bindings with parenthesis (). The [( )] binding is a combination of the two resulting in a two-way binding. You will be writing many bindings like this throughout the course.

Finally, notice the interpolation in the <h1> element. We are interpolating the value of the userName data model that was created by ngModel.

Step 6 Open the app.component.html file and comment out the code shown below in bold.

```
<div>
  <app-header [user]="user"></app-header>
  <app-login></app-login>
  <!-- <img status="You need to eat two more servings of fruit"
src="assets/images/apple.png">
    <div status></div>
    <section>
        <img *ngIf="!user.registered"
             src="../assets/images/chooseMyPlate.gov.png">
    </section>
    <section *ngIf="user.registered">
        <img src="../assets/images/generic-plate.png">
    </section>
   <p [ngSwitch]="loggedIn">Logged In:
        <span *ngSwitchCase="false" class="notRegistered">{{ loggedIn
}}</span>
        <span *ngSwitchCase="true">{{ loggedIn }}</span>
    </p>
    <app-child (onLogin)="logIn($event)"></app-child> ...-->
</div>
```

Step 7 Add the login component to the app.component's html template as shown below in bold.

```
<div>
  <app-header [user]="user"></app-header>
  <app-login></app-login>
```

```
  <!-- <img status="You need to eat two more servings of fruit"
src="assets/images/apple.png">
    <div status></div>
    <section>
...
```

Step 8 Add the onSubmit() method inside the exported class of the login.component.ts as shown below.

```
onSubmit(form: any): void {
     console.log('you submitted value: ', form);
}
```

Step 9 Add the `log()` method that will demonstrate the `ngForm's` role in accessing form properties exported to the local template variable `#nameForm`.

```
log(val):void {
   console.log(val);
}
```

Step 10 Add a username property to the login component.

```
export class LoginComponent implements OnInit {
  userName: string;
```

Step 11 Save the file and run it Chrome, but do not fill out the form yet. First, open the DevTools and examine the input element. Notice the properties that Angular has injected. Watch the values of these properties change as you fill out the form field and remove focus.

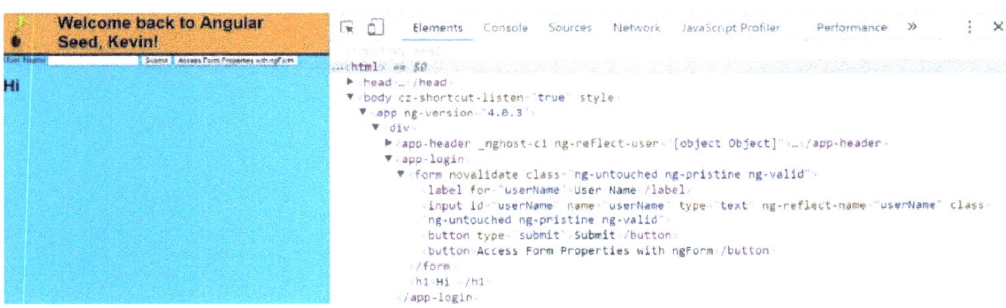

The Angular form before any user interaction.

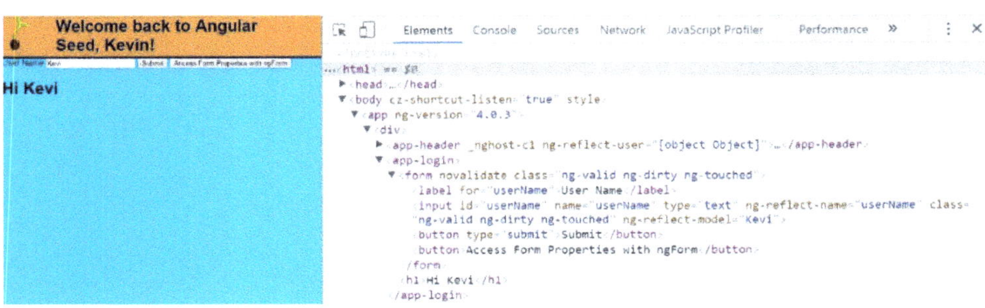

Angular form after user interaction.

Notice the classes that Angular has added to the form element and input fields, including:

- ng-valid

- ng-pristine
- ng-dirty
- ng-touched

These classes used in form validation and will be used later in this chapter. They are injected because of the ngModel directive.

Step 12 Remove the binding to ngModel and run the file in the browser. The validation classes should still be there.

```
<input id="userName" name="userName" [(ngModel)]="userName">
```

Step 13 Now remove the ngModel entirely and run the file in the browser.

```
<input id="userName" name="userName">
```

The validation classes should be gone.

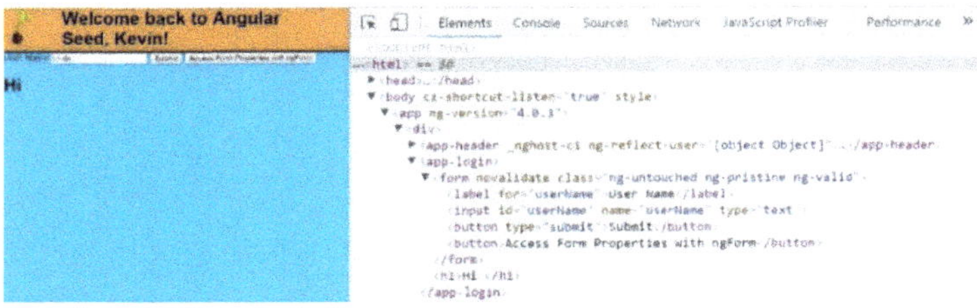

Angular form without the ngModel directive.

Step 14 Return the ngModel directive to its original state.

```
<input type="text"
       id="userName"
       name="userName"
       [(ngModel)]="userName">
```

12.5 Reactive forms with Angular FormBuilder

Now that you have seen template-driven forms, let's look at Reactive forms.

Reactive forms provide these useful directives (not a complete list):

- FormControl
- FormGroup

And these classes (not a complete list)

- FormBuilder

Angular provides a helper class called `FormBuilder` that configures your Forms. `FormBuilder` behaves like a "factory" object that builds your `FormControls` and `FormGroup` objects. Like `FormModule`, and `ReactiveFormModule`, this helper class must be imported in your module as shown below.

```
import { FormBuilder } from '@angular/forms';
```

To use the FormBuilder, you must inject it into your exported class file, typically through the constructor function as shown below.

```
export class EmployeeFormComponent implements OnInit {
...
employeeForm:FormGroup;

constructor(fb: FormBuilder) {
this.employeeForm = fb.group({
...
})
```

Now you have an instance of `FormBuilder,` and you can start using it to configure your form. The `FormBuilder` method `group()` creates a `FormGroup` which will take an object of key-value pairs that specify the `FormControls` in the `FormGroup`.

FormControls are then created and passed to the `FormGroup's group()` method as shown below in bold.

```
this.employeeForm = fb.group({
      'firstName' : [null],
      'lastName' : [null],
      'department' : [null],
      'status' : [null]
});
```

The object passed to the `group()` method provides a ControlForm name (firstName) and an initial value: null. Additional arguments include:

- An array of form field validators
- An array of asynchronous validators

To bind the form (employeeForm) to the form element in the view template, use the code below.

```
<form [formGroup]="employeeForm">
```

Now Angular knows that we'd like to use the employee form as the `FormGroup` for this form. In addition to this, Angular needs to know how to submit the form using the ngSubmit event binding (shown below).

```
<form [formGroup]="employeeForm"
      (ngSubmit)="onSubmit(employeeForm.value)">
```

12.6 Getting form and form control values

The data entered by the user can be retrieved via the `FormGroup.value` property.

```
FormGroup.value
```

Individual form fields can be obtained via [FormGroupName].controls.[FormControlName].value

```
this.form.controls.firstName.value
```

12.6.1 Setting form and form control values

The FormControl values can be set from the component class (e.g. onInit) via the following methods:

```
FormGroup.setValue()
FormGroup.patchValue()
FormControl.setValue()
```

All of the methods shown above will pull and push data synchronously.

34–Guided Exercise: Create a reactive form with FormBuilder

In this guided exercise, you create a register form for the FoodPlate cli project.

Step 1 Open the app.module.ts file and import the `FormsModule` and the `ReactiveFormsModule` as shown below.

```
...
import {FormsModule, ReactiveFormsModule} from '@angular/forms';
...
@NgModule({
  imports: [
    CommonModule, BrowserModule, FoodGroupsModule, AppRoutingModule,
FormsModule, ReactiveFormsModule
  ],
```

Step 2 Open the register.component.ts file and import the FormBuilder and FormGroup packages.

```
import { FormBuilder, FormGroup } from '@angular/forms';
```

Step 3 Declare the following properties (they will be needed to register a user object):

- `currentUser` typed as a User data model object
  - Import the `User` class
- `ageGroups` (you will use this to create a drop-down menu in the view template).
- `regForm` property datatyped as a `formGroup` (used by the FormBuilder)

```
currentUser: User;
ageGroups = ['select your age group', '2-3', '4-8', '9-13', '14-18', '19-30',
'31-50', '51+'];
regForm: FormGroup;
```

Step 4 The register class will need the user service to create a new user as well as the form builder class and router. Import these classes. Inject these classes in the constructor function as shown below in bold.

```
constructor(private userService: UserService, private fb: FormBuilder,
private router: Router) {
}
```

Step 5 Inside the constructor function, set the `regForm` equal to the `FormBuilder's group()` method and pass in the following properties (as shown below in bold):

```
constructor(private userService:UserService, private fb: FormBuilder, private
router: Router) {
    this.regForm = fb.group({
      'firstname' : [null],
      'email' : [null],
      'gender' : [null],
      'ageGroup' : [null]
    });
}
```

Step 6 Confirm that the `UserService`, `FormBuilder` and `Router` have been imported.

Step 7 Add the onSubmit method with the following specifications:

- Let `currentUser` equal the form's value property
- Set the `currentUser` component property equal to the currentUser holding the form values
- Set the `currentUser's` id property to `1`
- Set the `currentUser's` registered property to `true`
- Set the currentUser's reqsStatus property to {fruitMet: false, vegMet:false, proteinMet:false, grainMet: false}
- Call the `UserService's setUser()` method and pass it the currentUser
- Log the `currentUser` to the console.
- Optional: In the `onSubmit()` method, push the user object into the browser's local storage. Later we will store it server-side as well.

```
onSubmit(formValues): void {
    const currentUser = this.regForm.value;
    this.currentUser = currentUser;
    console.log(this.regForm.value);
    this.currentUser.id = 1;
    this.currentUser.registered = true;
    this.currentUser.reqsStatus = {fruitMet: false, vegMet: false, proteinMet:
false, grainMet: false};
    localStorage.setItem('user', JSON.stringify(currentUser));
}
```

Step 8 Create the view template in `register.component.html`. You can copy and paste it from angular-class-files/foodPlate-files/code-snippets/register-form-component-html.html

```
<form [formGroup]="regForm" class="box" id="registerForm">
  <label for="firstname" class="block labelTop">First Name</label>
  <input type="text" id="firstname"
         formControlName="firstname" tabindex="1"
         placeholder="Enter your first name here.">
  <label for="email" class="block labelTop">Email</label>
  <input type="email" id="email" formControlName="email"
         placeholder="Enter your email address here."
         minlength="5" tabindex="2">
  <section id="genderFields">
  <label for="sexF">
    <input type="radio" name="gender" id="sexF" value="F" class="radioLg"
formControlName="gender" tabindex="3">Female</label>
  <label for="sexM">
    <input type="radio" name="gender" id="sexM" formControlName="gender"
tabindex="4" value="M" class="radioLg"/>Male
  </label>
  </section>
  <label for="ageGroup" class="block labelTop">Age Group</label>
  <select id="ageGroup" size="1" formControlName="ageGroup" tabindex="5">
```

```
    <option *ngFor="let group of ageGroups; let i = index"
value="{{this.ageGroups[i]}}">{{this.ageGroups[i]}}</option>
  </select>
  <input type="submit" tabindex="7"
         id="register-user"
         value="Register"
         class="fpButton box-extra">
</form>
```

Step 9 Add a binding to the form for the ngSubmit event as shown in bold below.

```
<form [formGroup]="regForm" (ngSubmit)="onSubmit(regForm.value)" class="box"
id="registerForm">
```

Step 10 To view the `regForm’s` value and status properties, add the following lines below the closing form element. The `| json` formats the properties values to JSON format. You will learn more about pipes in a subsequent chapter.

```
<p>Form value: {{ regForm.value | json }}</p>
<p>Form status: {{ regForm.status | json }}</p>
```

Step 11 Add the styles for the register-form.component.css file. They can be copied and pasted from the assets /css folder. The file is called register-form-component-css.css.

Step 12 Trying running the application in Chrome. If it does not compile or displays with errors, check the error messages and try fixing the issues.

The application should look and behave as shown in the screenshots below.

The form at startup.

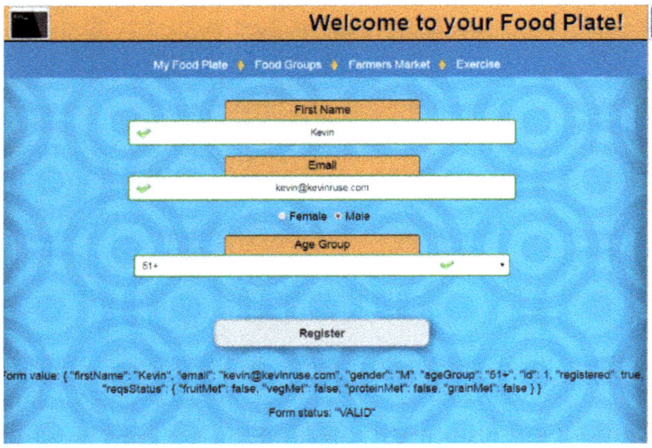

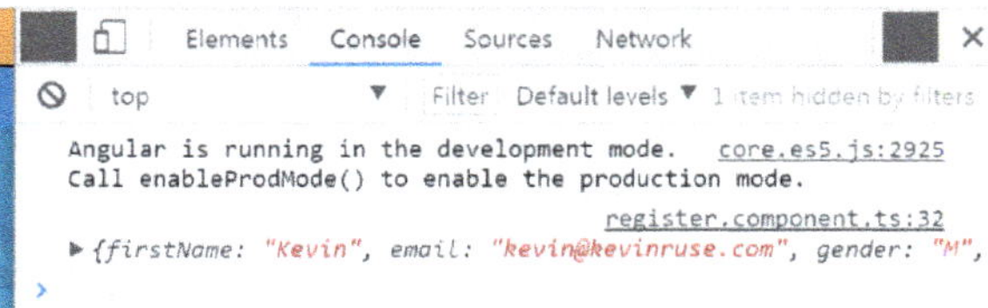

The form after its' been filled out. The Console after completing the form and clicking the "Register".

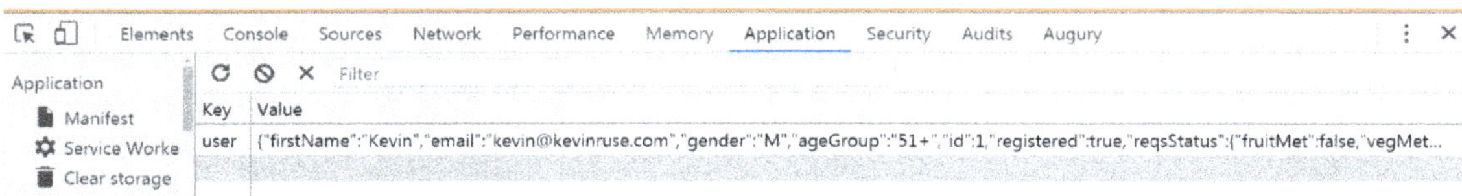

The Chrome DevTools showing the user in local storage.

8 – Practice Exercise: Convert the template-driven form to a reactive form

In this practice exercise, you convert the template-driven form to a reactive form. You will use the FoodPlate seed project for this practice exercise.

Step 1 Before beginning this practice exercise, refactor the existing form as shown below (in bold).

```
<form #userNameForm="ngForm"
      (ngSubmit)="onSubmit(userNameForm.value)">
    <label for="userName">User Name</label>
    <input type="text"
           id="userName"
           name="userName"
           [(ngModel)]="userName">
    <button type="submit">Submit Template-Driven Form</button>
    <button (click)="log(userNameForm)">Log Template Form Properties with
ngForm</button>
</form>
<h1>Hi {{ userName }}</h1>
```

Step 2 Copy and paste the template driven form, then comment out the original template-driven form.

Step 3 Refactor the copied template-driven form as shown below in bold.

```
<form #userNameForm="ngForm"
      (ngSubmit)="onSubmit(userNameForm.value)">
    <label for="userName">User Name</label>
    <input type="text"
           id="userName"
           name="userName"
           [(ngModel)]="userName">
    <button type="submit">Submit Reactive Form</button>
    <button (click)="log(userNameForm)">Log Reactive Form Properties with
ngForm</button>
</form>
<h1>Hi {{ userName }}</h1>
```

Step 4 Now work through the exercise using the copied template-driven form (now a reactive form).

Step 5 Refactor the login-form.component.html so that it is a reactive form.

Step 6 Have the form simply log its output to the console on ngSubmit event.

Step 7 Make sure you have refactored the login-form.component.ts as needed.

Step 8 Don't forget the changes you need to make to app.module.

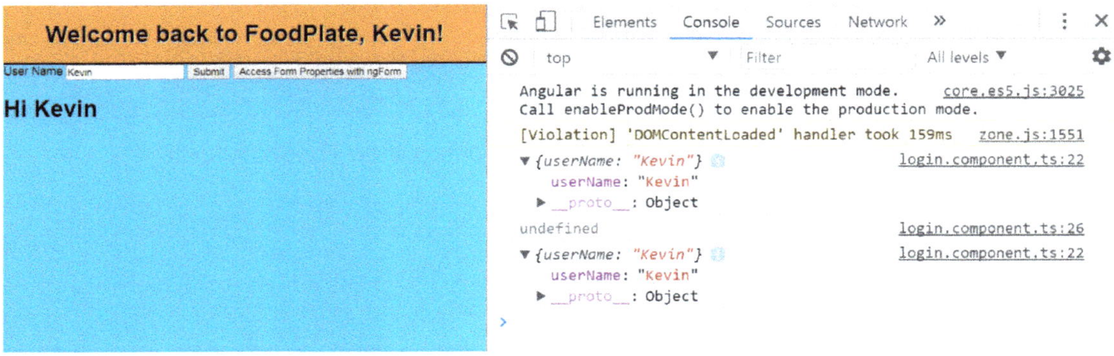

Finished file in the browser with the following console.log statements:

```
onSubmit(formValues):void {
    console.log(formValues);
}

log(val) {
    console.log(val);
}
```

Possible solution code

login.component.ts

```
import { Component, OnInit } from '@angular/core';
import { FormBuilder, FormGroup} from '@angular/forms';

@Component({
  selector: 'app-login',
  templateUrl: './login.component.html'
})

export class LoginComponent implements OnInit {

  nameForm: FormGroup;
  userName: any;

  constructor(private formBuilder: FormBuilder) {
    this.nameForm = formBuilder.group({
      'userName' : [null]
    });
    this.userName = this.nameForm.controls['userName'];
  }

  onSubmit(formValues): void {
    console.log(formValues);
  }

  log(val): void {
    console.log(val);
  }

  ngOnInit(): void {
  }
}
```

login.component.html

```
<!--Reactive Form-->
<form [formGroup]="nameForm"
      (ngSubmit)="onSubmit(nameForm.value)">
    <label for="userName">User Name</label>
    <input type="text"
           id="userName"
           name="userName"
           formControlName="userName">
    <button type="submit">Submit Reactive Form</button>

    <button (click)="log(nameForm)">Access Reactive Form Properties with ngForm</button>
</form>
<h1>Hi {{ userName.value }}</h1>


<!--template-driven form-->
<!--<form #userNameForm="ngForm"
      (ngSubmit)="onSubmit(userNameForm.value)">
    <label for="userName">User Name</label>
    <input type="text"
           id="userName"
           name="userName"
           [(ngModel)]="userName">
    <button type="submit">Submit</button>
    <button (click)="log(userNameForm)">Access Form Properties with ngForm</button>
</form>
<h1>Hi {{ userName }}</h1>-->
```

app.module.ts

```
import { NgModule } from '@angular/core';
import { BrowserModule } from '@angular/platform-browser';
import { FormsModule, ReactiveFormsModule } from '@angular/forms';

import { AppComponent } from './app.component';
import { ChildComponent } from './child/child.component';
import { FormInputComponent } from './form-input/form-input.component';
import { HeaderComponent } from './header/header.component';
import { LoginComponent } from './login/login.component';
import { StatusComponent } from './status/status.component';
import { StatusDirective } from './directives/status.directive';

import { FontAwesomeModule } from '@fortawesome/angular-fontawesome';

@NgModule({
    imports:       [ BrowserModule,
                     FontAwesomeModule,
                     FormsModule,
                     ReactiveFormsModule],
    declarations: [ AppComponent,
                     ChildComponent,
                     FormInputComponent,
                     HeaderComponent,
                     StatusComponent,
                     StatusDirective,
                     LoginComponent ],
    bootstrap:     [ AppComponent ]
})

export class AppModule {}
```

12.7 Binding to Form Controls

ngModel assigned to a template reference variable

- Reference variable assigned to the ngModel directive on a form control
  - <input #userName="ngModel" type="text" name="userName">
- Any element with an ngModel directive requires a name attribute.
- The template reference variable is now the NgModel directive on the input element.
  - NgModel gives us a FormControl instance that provides:
    - Value
    - User interaction
    - Validation status
  - And keep the view synced with the model

12.7.1 Binding to a select menu

```
<label for="ageGroup" class="block labelTop">Age Group</label>
<select name="ageGroup" id="ageGroup" size="1"
       required [(ngModel)]="user.ageGroup" #selectedAge="ngModel">
    <option *ngFor="let age of ageGroups" [value]="age">{{age}}</option>
</select>
```

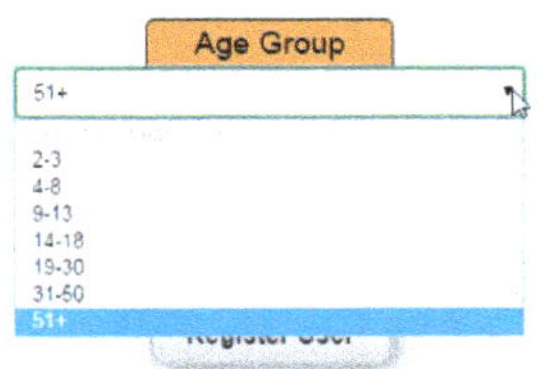


```
export class RegisterFormComponent {
   ageGroups = ['select your age group', '2-3', '4-8', '9-13', '14-18', '19-30','31-50', '51+'];
   user = new User('Kevin', 'kevin@kevinruse.com', 'M', '51+', true);
   submitted = false;
    onSubmit() {
        this.submitted = true;
    }
}
```

12.7.2 Binding to a checkbox

```
<label for="sexF">
    <input [(ngModel)]="user.gender" type="radio" name="gender" id="sexF"
           value="F" class="radioLg">Female</label>
<label for="sexM">
    <input [(ngModel)]="user.gender" type="radio" name="gender" id="sexM"
           value="M" class="radioLg"/>Male
</label>
```

```
export class User {
    constructor(
        public firstName: string,
        public email: string,
        public gender: string,
        public ageGroup: string,
        public newsletter: boolean
    ) {
    }
}
```

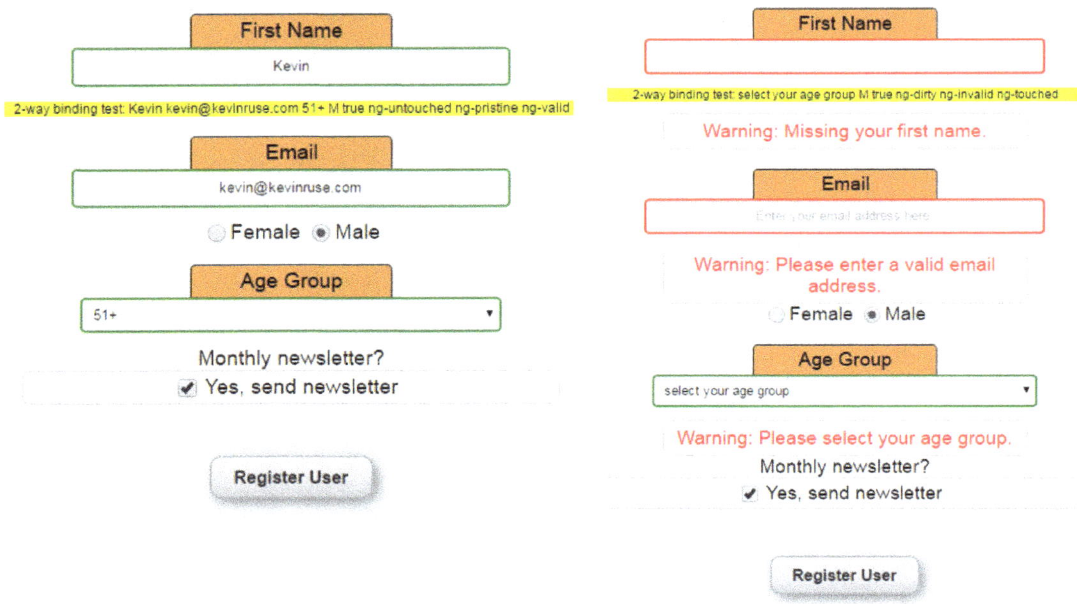

12.8 Angular Form Validation

Form validation ensures the values that users enter are of the correct type and format. For example, some form fields require numbers only while other controls may hold strings or even specifically formatted strings such as an email address. In addition, many forms have fields that are required and fields that are optional. To assist in form validation, Angular provides a helpful class called Validators. Below is a common validator.

```
Validators.required
```

This indicates that the field is required. If left untouched by the user, the FormControl will be considered invalid.

12.8.1 What makes a form field valid?

- Minimal amount of characters
- Maximum amount of characters
- Required vs. optional data
- Valid email address
- Number field vs. text field
- Patterns like zip codes or credit card numbers
- And so on...

12.8.2 How to use Validators

Using validators is a two-step process. First, you assign a validator to a FormControl object in your form. Second, you check the status of the validator from the view template and take any necessary actions if the field is invalid.

12.8.2.1 First Step: Assigning Validators

Below are two different approaches to assigning validators. The first approach is for a template-driven form and the second approach is for a ReactiveForm using FormBuilder.

12.8.2.2 Template-driven form example

To assign a validator to a FormControl, you pass it as the second argument in the constructor as shown below.

```
let nameControl = new FormControl('name', Validators.required);
```

12.8.2.3 Reactive form example

If you are building a ReactiveForm using FormBuilder, you can pass the Validator as shown below.

```
this.employeeForm = formbuilder.group({
      'firstName' : [null, Validators.required],
      'email' : [null, Validators.compose([Validators.required, Validators.email])],
});
```

12.8.2.4 Second Step: Use Validation in the view

You must be able to access the validation values in the view to respond accordingly to validation errors. There are two ways to do this:

1. Assign all the FormControls to instance variables in the component class.

   Example: this.firstName = this.employeeForm.controls['firstName'];

   Now to respond to an error, you add code to the view. This can be done a variety of ways including one or more approaches from the following list.

   - Show error messages
   - Change the color of the control
   - Disable the submit button

   To show an error message you could use the following code example:

   ```
   <label for="employeeId">Employee ID:</label>
   <input type="text"
        id="employeeId"
        placeholder="Employee Identification Number"
        [formControl]="empId">
    <div *ngIf="!empId.valid"
        class="errorMessage">Employee ID is invalid</div>
   ```

2. Lookup the FormControl from the form in the view.

   Here is an example of showing an error message by looking up the FormControl from the form.

   ```
   <input type="text"
        id="employeeId"
        placeholder="Employee Identification Number"
        [formControl]="employeeForm.controls[empId]">
   <div *ngIf="! employeeForm.controls[empId].valid"
        class="errorMessage">Employee ID is invalid
   </div>
   ```

12.9 Angular Form Validation

State classes applied to form fields include:

- `ng-pristine`
    - The form field was touched, but not edited by the user
- `ng-touched`
    - The form field was touched by the user (set on the onBlur event)
- `ng-dirty`
    - The user touched and edited the form field
- `ng-valid`
    - The form field is in a valid state
- `ng-invalid`
    - The form field is not in a valid state

Hooks to add your own CSS

Outline in red if form field is invalid

```
.ng-dirty.ng-invalid {
    border: 2px solid red;
}
```

35—Guided Exercise: Add validation to the registration form

In this exercise, you add validation to the register-form component in the foodplate cli project.

Step 1 Refactor register.component.ts to add the following validation rules:

`firstName` is required.
`email` is required and must be of type email.
`gender` is required
`ageGroup` is required

Note You can use `Validators.compose([rule1, rule2])` to add more than one validation rule.

```
constructor(private userService: UserService, private fb: FormBuilder, private
router: Router) {
    this.regForm = fb.group({
      'firstname' : [null,[Validators.required]],
      'email' : [null, Validators.compose([Validators.required,
Validators.email])],
      'gender' : [null, [Validators.required]],
      'ageGroup' : [null, [Validators.required]]
    });
}
```

Step 2 Import the Validator class.

```
import {FormBuilder, FormGroup, Validators} from '@angular/forms';
```

Step 3 Refactor the register-form.html to display a message when fields are invalid.

```
<form [formGroup]="regForm" (ngSubmit)="onSubmit(regForm.value)"
name="registerForm" class="box" id="registerForm">
  <label for="firstname" class="block labelTop">First Name</label>
  <input type="text" id="firstname" name="firstname" autocomplete="name"
         formControlName="firstname" tabindex="1"
         placeholder="Enter your first name here.">
  <p *ngIf="!regForm.controls['firstname'].valid &&
regForm.controls['firstname'].touched" class="formMessage">Please enter a
first name.</p>
  <label for="email" class="block labelTop">Email</label>
  <input type="email" name="email" id="email" formControlName="email"
         placeholder="Enter your email address here."
         minlength="5" tabindex="2" autocomplete="email">
  <p *ngIf="!regForm.controls['email'].valid &&
regForm.controls['email'].touched" class="formMessage">Please enter a valid
email address.</p>
  <section id="genderFields">
    <label for="sexF">
```

```
            <input type="radio" name="gender" id="sexF" value="F"
                   class="radioLg" formControlName="gender"
                   tabindex="3">Female</label>
        <label for="sexM">
            <input type="radio" name="gender" id="sexM" formControlName="gender"
                   tabindex="4" value="M" class="radioLg"/>Male</label>
    </section>
    <p *ngIf="!regForm.controls['gender'].valid &&
regForm.controls['gender'].touched" class="formMessage">Please enter your
gender.</p>
    <label for="ageGroup" class="block labelTop">Age Group</label>
    <select name="ageGroup" id="ageGroup" size="1" formControlName="ageGroup"
tabindex="5">
        <option *ngFor="let group of ageGroups; let i = index"
value="{{this.ageGroups[i]}}">
            {{this.ageGroups[i]}}
        </option>
    </select>
    <p *ngIf="!regForm.controls['ageGroup'].valid &&
regForm.controls['ageGroup'].touched" class="formMessage">Please enter your
age group.</p>
    <input type="submit" tabindex="7"
           id="register-user"
           class="fpButton box-extra">
</form>
```

Notice the `formMessage` class that is applied to the message. This class is part of the register-form.component.css The remaining messages are:

Please enter a valid email address.
Please select your gender.
Please select your age group.

Step 4 Save your work and test it in the browser by adding invalid input.

Step 5 Compare your results to the screenshot below.

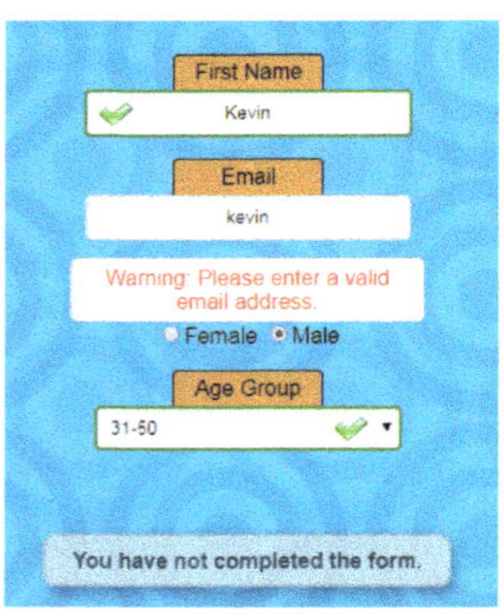

The form with a valid firstName and ageGroup and an invalid email.

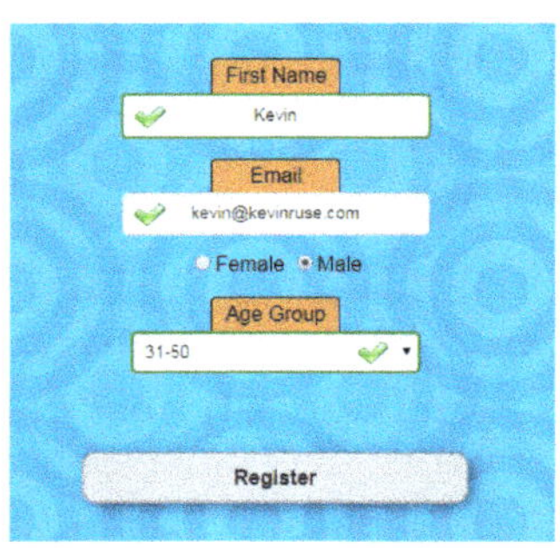

The form with all the controls in a valid state.

Extra Credit Challenge

Step 1 Disable the submit button and change its label to: "You have not completed the form correctly" when the form is in an invalid state.

Step 2 Make sure the button label is "Register" when the form is in a valid state.

Step 3 Notice that choosing "select your age group" from the Age Group dropdown results in a valid form. Correct this, so that the user must select an age group.

Possible solution code

register.component.ts

```
import { Component, OnInit } from '@angular/core';
import {FormBuilder, FormGroup, Validators} from '@angular/forms';
import {Router} from '@angular/router';


import {User} from '../models/User';
import {UserService} from '../services/user.service';

@Component({
  selector: 'fp-register',
  templateUrl: './register.component.html',
  styleUrls: ['./register.component.css']
})
export class RegisterComponent implements OnInit {
  currentUser:User;
  regForm:FormGroup;
  ageGroups = ['2-3', '4-8', '9-13', '14-18', '19-30','31-50', '51+'];

  constructor(private userService:UserService, private fb: FormBuilder, private router: 
Router) {
    this.regForm = fb.group({
      'firstname' : [null,[Validators.required]],
      'email' : [null, Validators.compose([Validators.required, Validators.email])],
      'gender' : [null, [Validators.required]],
      'ageGroup' : [null, [Validators.required]]
    });
  }

  ngOnInit() {
  }

  onSubmit(): void {
    const currentUser = this.regForm.value;
    this.currentUser = currentUser;
    console.log(this.regForm.value);
    this.currentUser.id = 1;
    this.currentUser.registered = true;
    this.currentUser.reqsStatus = {fruitMet: false, vegMet:false, proteinMet:false, grainMet: 
false};
    localStorage.setItem('user', JSON.stringify(currentUser));
  }
}
```

register.component.html

```
<form [formGroup]="regForm" (ngSubmit)="onSubmit(regForm.value)" name="registerForm" 
class="box" id="registerForm">
  <label for="firstname" class="block labelTop">First Name</label>
  <input type="text" id="firstname" name="firstname"
         formControlName="firstname" tabindex="1"
         placeholder="Enter your first name here.">
  <p *ngIf="!regForm.controls['firstName'].valid && regForm.controls['firstName'].touched" 
class="formMessage">Please enter a first name.</p>
  <label for="email" class="block labelTop">Email</label>
  <input type="email" name="email" id="email" formControlName="email"
         placeholder="Enter your email address here."
         minlength="5" tabindex="2">
  <p *ngIf="!regForm.controls['email'].valid && regForm.controls['email'].touched" 
class="formMessage">Please enter a valid email address.</p>
  <section id="genderFields">
    <label for="sexF">
```

```
      <input type="radio" name="gender" id="sexF"
             value="F" class="radioLg" formControlName="gender" tabindex="3">Female</label>
    <label for="sexM">
      <input type="radio" name="gender" id="sexM" formControlName="gender" tabindex="4"
             value="M" class="radioLg"/>Male
    </label>
  </section>
  <p *ngIf="!regForm.controls['gender'].valid && regForm.controls['gender'].touched"
class="formMessage">Please enter your gender.</p>
  <label for="ageGroup" class="block labelTop">Age Group</label>
  <select name="ageGroup" id="ageGroup" size="1" formControlName="ageGroup" tabindex="5">
    <option [value]="null">Select your age group</option>
    <option *ngFor="let group of ageGroups; let i = index" value="{{this.ageGroups[i]}}">
      {{this.ageGroups[i]}}
    </option>
  </select>
  <p *ngIf="!regForm.controls['ageGroup'].valid && regForm.controls['ageGroup'].touched"
class="formMessage">Please enter your age group.</p>
  <input type="submit" tabindex="7"
         id="register-user"
         [value]="regForm.valid ? 'Register' : 'You have not completed the form.'"
         class="fpButton box-extra"
         [disabled]="!regForm.valid">
</form>

<p>Form value: {{ regForm.value | json }}</p>
<p>Form status: {{ regForm.status | json }}</p>
```

9 – Practice Exercise: Validate a simple form

In this practice exercise, you add validation to the simple form you created earlier.

Step 1 Add the code to validate the simple form.

The validation specifications are:

The `userName` is required

The `userName` cannot exceed five (5) characters.

Step 2 Add a paragraph that reads "You must enter a name and it cannot exceed five characters" and show the paragraph whenever the form is in an invalid state.

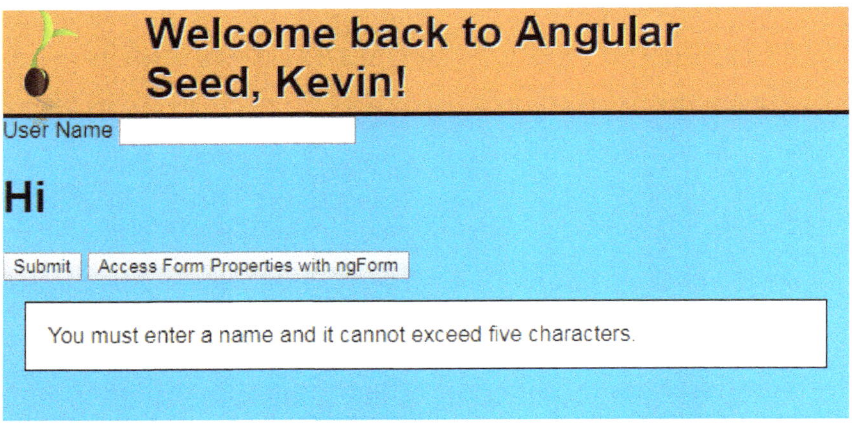

Possible solution code

login.component.ts

```
import { Component, OnInit } from '@angular/core';
import { FormBuilder, FormGroup, Validators} from '@angular/forms'

@Component({
  selector: 'app-login',
  templateUrl: './login/login.component.html'
})

export class LoginComponent implements OnInit {

  nameForm: FormGroup;
  userName;

  constructor(private formBuilder: FormBuilder) {
    this.nameForm = formBuilder.group({
      'userName' : [null, [Validators.required, Validators.maxLength(5)]]
    });
    this.userName = this.nameForm.controls['userName'];
  }

  onSubmit(): void {
    console.log(this.nameForm.value);
  }

 log(val) {
    console.log(val);
  }

  ngOnInit() {
  }
}
```

login.component.html

```
<form [formGroup]="nameForm"
      (ngSubmit)="onSubmit(nameForm.value)">
  <label for="userName">User Name</label>
  <input type="text"
          id="userName"
         name="userName"
         formControlName="userName">
  <button type="submit">Submit</button>
  <button (click)="log(userNameForm)">Access Form Properties with ngForm</button>
  <p *ngIf="!nameForm.controls['userName'].valid && nameForm.controls['userName'].touched">You
must enter a name and it cannot exceed five characters.</p>
</form>
<h1>Hi {{ userName.value }}</h1>
```

36–Guided Exercise: Update form data onBlur and onSubmit

Angular 5: Updating form data onBlur and onSubmit

Angular 5.0 and higher provide a new method for form validation that my show an increase in performance. In the last exercise, you saw form validations instantly, and you may or may not have noticed that the form model data also updates instantly. You might want to wait on updating the form data until the form has been validated in the view and the user can fix it. In this exercise, you take a closer look at form data model updates and change the behavior of the form controls so that the data updates either onBlur or onSubmit.

Step 1 Return to Chrome and navigate to the Register form. Fill out the form slowly, by first adding your first name. Notice that the data model is updated as you type.

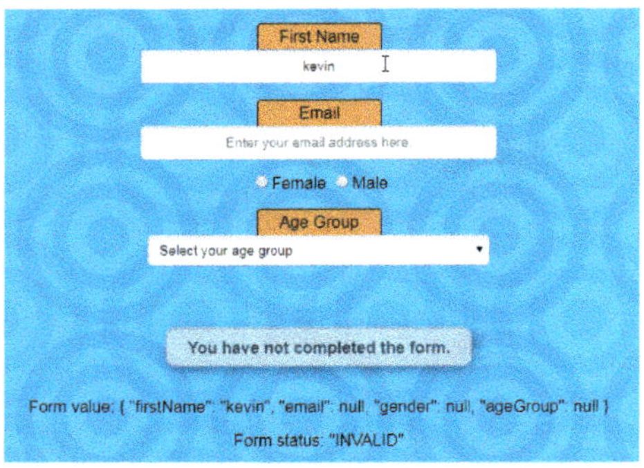

Angular 5 and higher allows the data model update to occur `onBlur` or `onSubmit`.

Step 2 Open the register.component.ts file and comment the existing constructor function and replace it with the one below. The file can be cut and pasted from assets/code-snippets/register-component-ts-upate-on-blur.txt.

```
constructor() {
        this.regForm = new FormGroup({
            firstname: new FormControl(null, {validators:
Validators.required}),
            email: new FormControl(null, [Validators.required,
Validators.email]),
            gender: new FormControl(null, [Validators.required]),
            ageGroup: new FormControl(null, [Validators.required])
        }, {updateOn: 'blur'});
}
```

Note You may have to import the FormControl class as shown below.

```
import {FormBuilder, FormGroup, Validators, FormControl } from
'@angular/forms';
```

Code Review

Note: There may be a bug related to this feature in Angular 8 when using onBlur.

The regForm now calls a new FormGroup as opposed to group. This is due to an active issue as of the publication date of this course (see https://github.com/angular/angular/issues/20176 for more information).

The FormControls are then instantiated for firstName, email, gender and ageGroup much like they were before with the `group()` method.

The main difference is the last argument passed to FormGroup: the object with the property `updateOn` set to the string `'blur'`. This property will make the value of every Form Control subject to change with the blur event of the input element associated with it.

Step 3 Save and refresh the page in the browser. Test the file the way you did in step 2. The data model will not update until the blur event on the input element.

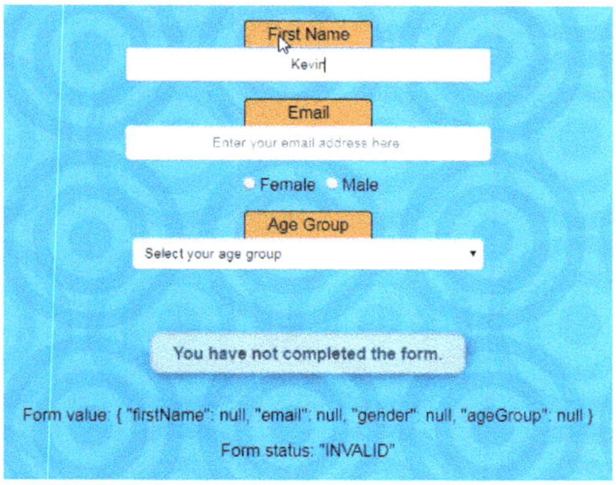

Step 4 Try changing the updateOn property to "submit" and test the file.

This presents a problem. First, we can no longer disable the button until the form is validated because the form is not validated until the onSubmit. Here is how it works now:

1. The FormGroup directive calls onSubmit as shown below.

```
@Directive({
  selector: '[formGroup]',
  providers: [formDirectiveProvider],
  host: {'(submit)': 'onSubmit($event)', '(reset)': 'onReset()'},
  exportAs: 'ngForm'
})
```

2. OnSubmit calls syncPendingControls

```
onSubmit($event: Event): boolean {
   (this as{submitted: boolean}).submitted = true;
   syncPendingControls(this.form, this.directives);
   this.ngSubmit.emit($event);
   return false;
   }
```

3. syncPendingControls updates the data model

```
export function syncPendingControls(form: FormGroup, directives:
        NgControl[]): void {
  form._syncPendingControls();
  directives.forEach(dir => {
    const control = dir.control as FormControl;
    if (control.updateOn === 'submit' && control._pendingChange) {
      dir.viewToModelUpdate(control._pendingValue);
      control._pendingChange = false;
      }
      });
}
```

Step 5 Refactor the submit button in register.component.html to hard code the value to "Register" and remove the disabled binding.

```
<input type="submit" tabindex="7"
       id="register-user"
       value="Register"
       class="fpButton box-extra">
```

Step 6 Save the file and refresh it in Chrome. Test the form controls in the browser.

Step 7 Return the updateOn to 'onBlur'.

Forms summary

In this chapter, you learned Angular's basic form classes and how to use them. You built a simple template-driven form as well as a ReactiveForm with the FormBuilder helper class. You learned how to validate form fields and display messages in the view templates when form fields are invalid.

Chapter summary

In this chapter, you learned two ways to approach building forms in your applications: template-driven forms and reactive forms. You learned how to tap into Angular's built-in validation classes and properties and used them to validate a simple form. You worked with the data the form submits and used CSS classes to increase the forms usability.

Chapter 12 Quiz

https://tinyurl.com/udaca9q

1) Describe the fundamental difference between template-driven and reactive forms.

____

____

____

2) Which Angular module is necessary to build a template-driven form? ____________________

3) Which Angular modules are necessary to build a reactive form? ____________________

4) What specific class properties are bound by the directive [(ngModel)]

____

5) Where is form validation code found in a reactive form? Name the file and location.

Next Chapter

In the next chapter, you prepare to work with back-end data as well as used more robust techniques in general when working with events. The next chapter is all about streaming data and responding to those data streams with observables.

Chapter 13
Observables

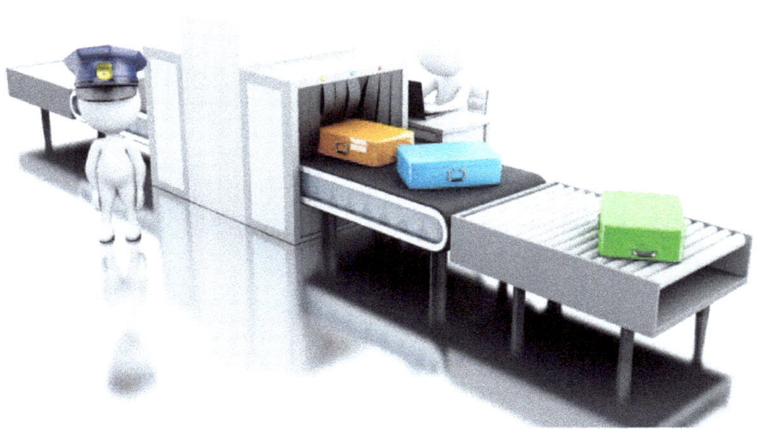

Chapter 13: Observables

Objectives

- Describe how we currently handle asynchronous tasks in JavaScript
- Understand the role of RxJS in Angular
- Define an observable
- Describe how observables work
- Define Subjects
- Define BehaviorSubjects

Introduction

In this chapter, you learn a new way to respond to asynchronous events and communicate between components called Observables. This chapter will also address the current methods for handling asynchronous code. In addition to observables, this chapter will also introduce:

- Observable object and methods
- Subject
- BehaviorSubject

13.0 Current methods of handling asynchronicity

Today's web applications typically deal with asynchronous operations using one or more of the following methods.

1. Callbacks
   - Can be complex and do not scale well in terms of code readability
2. XMLHttpRequest Object (XHR)
   - Can be complicated to handle cross-domain requests
   - Needs a fair amount of boilerplate code to get started
3. Promises API
   - More readable than XHR, but promises cannot be cancelled
   - Handle single responses well, but can be complicated when handling multiple values
4. Fetch API
   - Uses promises

13.1 Observables vs. Promises

Most Angular developers quickly realize that they can interchange promises for observables in many cases such as delivering values to an application asynchronously. This chapter will serve as an introduction to observables. Because Angular allows for the use of both promises and observables, we will first look at the difference between observables and promises.

1. When storing data with observables, the data is not accessible until we subscribe to the observable. This is different from promises which execute immediately upon creation.

2. Observables can provide multiple values, whereas promises supply only one. This fact, alone, should help developers determine appropriate uses cases for each. For example, if you expect a stream of values from the server (like stock quotes or real-time inventory updates) then use observables that can get multiple values over time. If you expect a single value back from the server (like user authentication: true or false), then use promises.

3. Promises are said to be in one of three states: pending, fulfilled or rejected. When a promise is fulfilled or rejected , the promise can be handled with a function passed to the promises' then() method. Chaining then methods is possible but can be tedious to write and reason about. Observables use a publish/subscribe pattern allowing greater efficiency.

4. Promises push errors to child promises and therefore are handled per promise. Observables subscribe method is responsible for handling errors which allow for a centralized location for error handling.

5. Observables can be cancelled, while promises cannot.

6. Observables have built-in methods to retry. Promises do not have this capability built-in to their API.

The Angular documentation provides this excellent cheat sheet at https://angular.io/guide/comparing-observables#cheat-sheet comparing promises to observables.

Operation	Observable	Promise
Creation	`new Observable((observer) => { observer.next(123); });`	`new Promise((resolve, reject) => { resolve(123); });`
Transform	`obs.map((value) => value * 2 );`	`promise.then((value) => value * 2);`
Subscribe	`sub = obs.subscribe((value) => { console.log(value) });`	`promise.then((value) => { console.log(value); });`
Unsubscribe	`sub.unsubscribe();`	Implied by promise resolution.

Figure #27: The Angular Cheat Sheet comparing Promises to Observables

For more detail information see https://angular.io/guide/comparing-observables#observables-compared-to-other-techniques

13.2 Introduction to Promises

This section will provide a brief overview of promises with a simple guided exercise to help demonstrate the promise API.

13.2.1 What is a Promise?

A promise is a representation of a value that is not known when the promise is created. Promises allow developers to add logic to respond to data that may or may not be available when the code executes, making it ideal for asynchronous operations like calls to the server to fetch data. Instead of responding immediately to a value as in synchronous operations, a function can return a promise that will supply the value at a later point in time. Promises can also handle the success or failure of an operation when they are created. Ultimately, a promise is an object that returns a single value.

13.2.2 How do promises work?

A promise is created to serve as a placeholder for data that is unknown when the promise is make. In addition, the promise may never return a value and throw an error. Therefore, the promise is designed to handle both success and failure of the promise. See the code below and the explanation below the code. The handling of the promise is through a callback function provided to the promise and executed when the promise is resolved.

```
const aPromise = new Promise((resolve, reject) => {
  //   resolve(someValue); // method to execute when the promise is fulfilled
  // or
  //   reject("failure reason"); // method to execute when the promise is rejected
});
```

A promise is evaluated and set to one of three states.

`pending` – this is the initial state when the promise is neither fulfilled nor rejected
`fulfilled` – the promise is fulfilled when the operation has successfully completed

`rejected` – the promise is rejected when the operation fails.

Once a promise is fulfilled or rejected, an associated function (via a `then()` method which accepts a function argument) is executed. The promises' then method can itself return a promise, thus they can be chained. The Promise method also has a `catch()` method to handle errors. The following diagram from https://developer.mozilla.org/en-US/docs/Web/JavaScript/Reference/Global_Objects/Promise explains the promise flow.

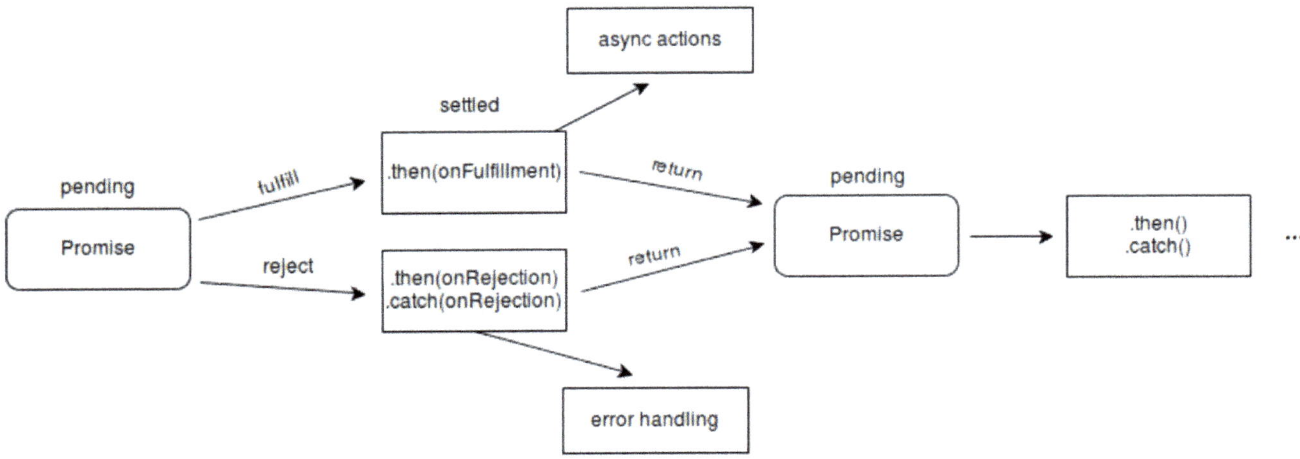

Figure #28: The promise flow from the Mozilla Developer Network Reference at from https://developer.mozilla.org/en-US/docs/Web/JavaScript/Reference/Global_Objects/Promise

The complete promise specification can be found at ECMA-international at http://www.ecma-international.org/ecma-262/6.0/#sec-promise-objects

9 – Demo (optional) Understanding Promises

In this exercise, you create three promises using the promise API.

Step 1 Using your code editor, open promise-demo-starter.html from the demos folder.

Step 2 Run the file in Chrome. It contains three buttons, each of which will call a function that makes a promise.

Step 3 Return to your editor and locate the script block. Under the comment "Write promise one here", add the code below.

```
let promiseOneTest = function() {
    let promiseOne = new Promise(function(resolve, reject) {
        setTimeout(function() {
           console.log('promiseOneTest called');
           document.querySelector('#promiseOne').innerText = "promiseOneTest
promise fulfilled";
           console.log('promiseOneTest promise fulfilled');
        }, 2000);
    });
    console.log('promiseOne:');
    console.log(promiseOne);
};
```

Step 4 Save the file and refresh it in Chrome with the console open. Click the "Call Promise One" button to see the results. To mimic an asynchronous operation, there will be a two-second delay before the code executes (due to the setTimeout() method in the code).

Step 5 Return to your editor and add the code for the second promise beneath the comment "Write promise two - make the promise"

```
let trigger = true;
let promiseTwo;
function promiseTwoTest() {
    promiseTwo = new Promise(
       function (resolve, reject) {
          if (trigger) {
                let promiseMessage = 'promiseTwoTest is fulfilled';
                resolve(promiseMessage);
             } else {
               let promiseMessage = new Error('second promise is rejected with
error');
               reject(promiseMessage);
          }
    });
    console.log('promiseTwo:');
    console.log(promiseTwo);
}
```

Step 6 Before you can test the file in Chrome, you need to call the promise. Beneath the comment "Call the promise" add the following code.

```
let callPromiseTwo = function() {
promiseTwoTest();
console.log('promiseTwoTest called');
promiseTwo
    .then(function(fulfilled) {
        console.log('promiseTwo promise is fulfilled');
        document.querySelector('#promiseTwo').innerText = 'second promise is
fulfilled'
    })
    .catch(function(error) {
         console.log(`promiseTwo ${error.message}`);
         document.querySelector('#promiseTwo').innerText = 'second promise is
rejected with error';
    })
};
```

Notice the call to the `then()` method of the promise. The then method appends success and error handlers to the promise and returns a new promise that resolves to the return value of the called handler, or to is original status if the promise was unfulfilled or rejected.

Step 7 Save and test the file in Chrome. Click the first button, followed by the second button. Your results should match the console image below.

```
▸ Promise {<pending>}                promise-demo-starter…pbkgv8dgohhh8p7i:29
promiseTwo called                    promise-demo-starter…pbkgv8dgohhh8p7i:38
                                     promise-demo-starter…pbkgv8dgohhh8p7i:48
▸ Promise {<resolved>: "twoPromise is fulfilled"}
first promise called                 promise-demo-starter…pbkgv8dgohhh8p7i:24
first promise fulfilled              promise-demo-starter…pbkgv8dgohhh8p7i:26
```

Step 8 Change the trigger variable to false as shown below in bold.

```
//Write promise two - make the promise
let trigger = false;
```

Step 9 Save the file and refresh it in Chrome with the console open. Test the first and second promise buttons. Your results should match the console shown below.

```
▸ Promise {<pending>}                promise-demo-starter…pbkgv8dgohhh8p7i:29
promiseTwo called                    promise-demo-starter…pbkgv8dgohhh8p7i:38
                                     promise-demo-starter…pbkgv8dgohhh8p7i:48
▸ Promise {<rejected>: Error: second promise is rejected with error
     at http://localhost:49337/2019-angular-courseware-…}
promiseTwo second promise is         promise-demo-starter…pbkgv8dgohhh8p7i:59
rejected with error
first promise called                 promise-demo-starter…pbkgv8dgohhh8p7i:24
first promise fulfilled              promise-demo-starter…pbkgv8dgohhh8p7i:26
```

Step 10 Return the trigger variable to a value of true.

Step 11 Add the third promise as shown below.

```
let promiseThree = function(info) {
    let promiseThree = new Promise(function (resolve, reject) {
        setTimeout(function () {
           console.log('third promise called');
             resolve({data: '123'})
        }, 2000);
    })
    .then(function (result) {
           console.log('promise three fulfilled with data');
           document.querySelector('#promiseThree').innerText = `second promise
with data: ${result.data}`
             });
        return promiseThree;
};
```

In this promise, the resolve method is used to return the promise with a given value. If the value is "thenable" meaning it has a `then` method, the returned promise is available in the then method. See the simple example shown below.

```
var promise = Promise.resolve([1, 2, 3]);

promise.then(function(value) {
  console.log(value);
  // expected output: Array [1, 2, 3]
});
```

Step 12 Save the file and refresh it in Chrome with the console open. Test all the promise buttons.

Step 13 Use the `promise.all()` method as shown below.

```
let promiseA = Promise.resolve(2);
let promiseB = Promise.resolve(7);
let promiseC = new Promise(function(resolve, reject) {
     setTimeout(function() {
                console.log('promiseC called');
                resolve('PromiseC resolved')
     }, 6000);
});

Promise.all([promiseA, promiseB, promiseC]).then(function(values) {
       console.log(values);
});
```

The Promise.all (iterable) method returns a single Promise that resolves when all the promises in the iterable argument have resolved or when the iterable argument contains no promises. It rejects with the reason of the first promise that rejects.[4]

Step 14 Save the file and refresh it in Chrome with the console open.

[4] https://developer.mozilla.org/en-US/docs/Web/JavaScript/Reference/Global_Objects/Promise/all

13.3 Introduction to Observables

Observables are not a current feature of ECMAScript 10 (ECMAScript 2019), but they are used in Angular via a popular library called RxJS. The RxJS API can be found at http://reactivex.io/rxjs/. The RxJS library defines itself as "a library for reactive programming using Observables, to make it easier to compose asynchronous or callback-based code." It is a JavaScript implementation of the Reactive Extensions (Rx) which was originally developed by Microsoft and is largely an observer pattern operation (albeit complex). In an observer pattern, a publisher object emits values and a subscriber receives the values. Observers are analogous to promises, but they are more robust in that they can be cancelled and unlike promises, they can return multiple values.

13.4 What is an Observable?

An observable is a collection of values over time. Almost anything can be made into an observable. Observables can be created from built-in functions in RXJS. An observable definition is often accompanied by a marble diagram. Below is an example of a marble diagram.

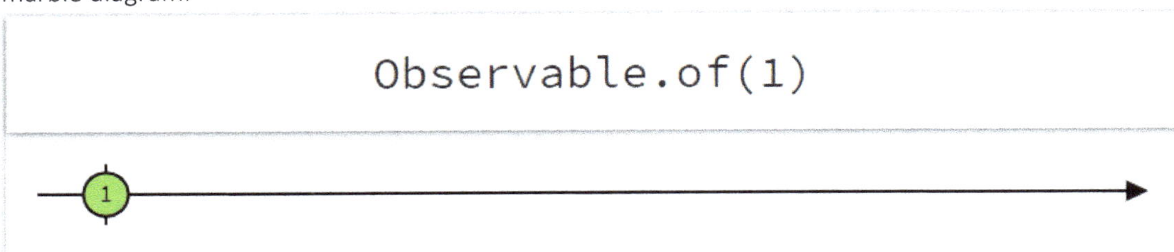

Figure #29: A marble diagram showing the Observable object's of() method creating an observable with one piece of data.

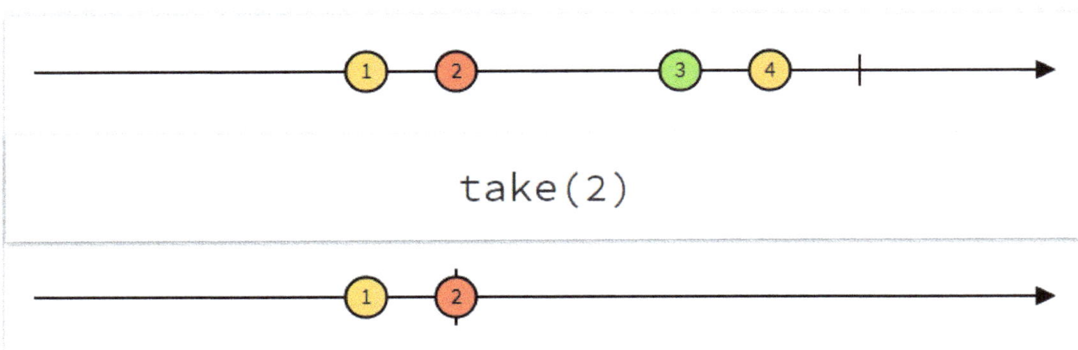

Figure #30: A more complex marble diagram, showing the take operator which takes only the first 2 emitted values from the observable.

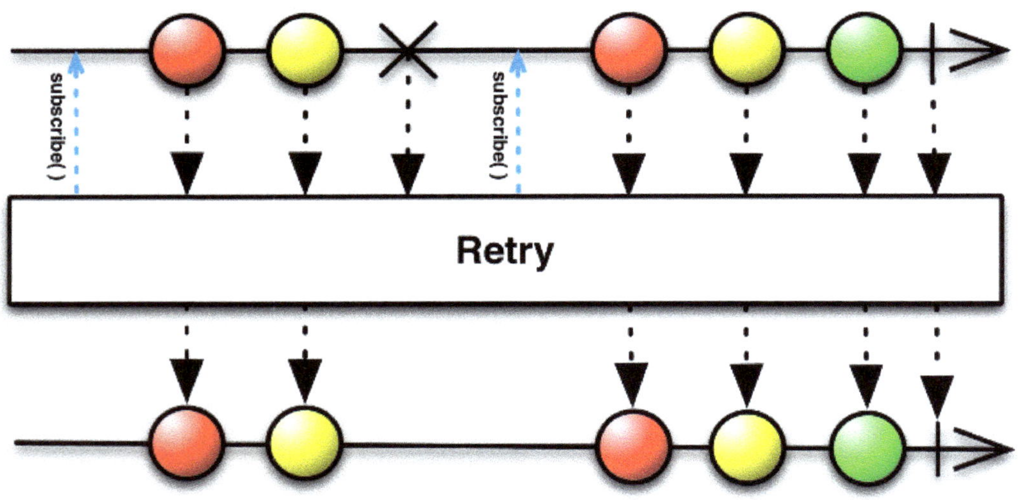

Figure #31: A marble diagram showing an error with a retry operator. Image from: http://reactivex.io/documentation/operators/retry.html

Marble diagrams show time flowing from left to right representing the execution of the input Observable. The "marbles" represent the values that are emitted over time. The vertical line indicates the "complete" notification which indicates the observable has completed successfully and the last of the data stream has been delivered. An X on the line indicates an error has been emitted by the output Observable and nothing will be delivered after that point.

Once you have an observable, interested components can subscribe to it. Individual components can subscribe to the observable and handle the data stream uniquely. The data stream can be cancelled, errors can be handled, and the data stream can be passed on to other functions.

13.4.1 Observables:

- are a collection of values over time that may or may not arrive *and* you don't know when they will arrive
  - Examples include: data from a websocket or on-screen mousemove data
  - Some data streams are in fact only one piece of data such as an http get request, or a single mouse click
  - Thus, the "collection of values" may in fact be only one value; either way the observable is handled in the same manner
- help you manage asynchronous data, such as data coming from a backend service
- are used within Angular itself, including:
  - Angular's event system
  - Http client service
- are implemented by Angular via the Reactive Extensions (RxJS) library
- are a proposed feature for ES2016 and ES2017, but they did make it into the final draft and are still be evaluated by TC39, the technical committee responsible for Ecma updates.

13.5 What is an Observer?

An observer consumes the values delivered by the Observable. Observers consist of a set of callbacks based on the notifications delivered by the observable. Consider the (mock) Observer interface below indicating the observable's three notifications:

- `next()` what to do upon receipt of the next data point in the observable stream of data
- `error()` what to do if the observable throws an error
- `complete()` what to do when the data stream is completed

```
interface Observer<T> {
      next(value: T): void;
      error(err: any): void;
      complete() : void
}
```

13.5.1 Code example for an Observer

```
const observer = {
  next: x => console.log('Observer got a next value: ' + x),
  error: err => console.error('Observer got an error: ' + err),
  complete: () => console.log('Observer got a complete notification'),
};
```

Here, `x` is the next data point and `err` is the error message.

RXJS refers to "Observers" as "Subscribers." An RXJS Observer is an interface that a Subscriber implements.

13.6 What is a subscription?

A subscription starts the data stream and manages the observation of that stream of synchronous values. Observables are inert in that they do not stream data until the observable's subscribe method is called. Thus, a subscription is created when the observable calls the subscribe() method. Ultimately calling the subscribe method will set up event listeners for the data stream. Upon creation of a subscription, communication is established (by default) between the observable and the observer.

To create a subscription, you call the subscribe method and supply a function (or object) known as an observer. This is somewhat analogous to an event handler that receives the event object.

Consider the (mock) interface of a subscription below.

```
interface Subscription {
      unsubscribe(): void;
}
```

Unsubscribe would contain any clean up logic such as removing the appropriate event listeners.

The subscribe method accepts an object to handle both error (`error()`) and completion (`complete()`) as well as the behavior upon receipt of the next data point (`next()`). These methods are optional.

Each subscription creates a new execution context for the observable. Therefore, calling subscribe a second time will create a new event listener.

13.7 How do Observables work?

Let's return to the first marble diagram and break down the observable created by the RXJS of() operator which creates an observable by emitting variable amount of values in a sequence and then emits a complete notification.

The `of()` method is an observable creation method that is part o the RXJS library of operators which are helper functions for creating and working with observables. It is a convenience method however, an understanding of what it does "under the good" will be helpful in understanding observables in general.

The `of()` method returns an observable that iterates through all the values provided as arguments. In this simple example, we have a single value (1). The observable is passed an observe() factory function for observing the asynchronous stream of values. The factory function is passed an observer designed to interact with the stream of values. The factory function wires up the observer to its underlying stream of data.

Worth noting again is that an Observable's observe() method is not called until you invoke the subscribe() method.

13.8 What is RxJS?

RxJS is the library used by Angular to implement a functional approach to event handling. It has a very large API as well as a high learning curve. The library is used for asynchronous event-based programming. It uses Observable sequences as demonstrated in the marble diagrams above (think of them as asynchronous data streams).

The RxJS website (http://reactivex.io/rxjs/manual/overview.html) defines the library as:

"RxJS is a library for composing asynchronous and event-based programs by using observable sequences. It provides one core type, the Observable, satellite types (Observer, Schedulers, Subjects) and operators inspired by Array#extras (map, filter, reduce, every, etc.) to allow handling asynchronous events as collections."

13.8.1 The RxJS library consists of:

- One core type called an Observable
  - An invokable collection of future values or events
- Satellite types
  - Observers
    - A collection of callbacks that listens to values delivered by the Observable
  - Schedulers
    - Centralized dispatchers that control when data is emitted from an observable, such as when subscriptions could start receiving values
  - Subjects
    - Equivalent to an EventEmitter; it is the only way of multicasting a value or event to multiple observers
- Operators
  - Pure functions that provide a way of dealing with collections of data
    - map()
    - filter()
    - reduce()
    - concat()
    - And over 100 more

13.8.2 Simple RxJS Example for events

Typical JavaScript event handling

```
var button = document.querySelector('button');
button.addEventListener('click', () => console.log('You clicked me!'));
```

Event Handling with RxJS

```
var button = document.querySelector('button');
Rx.Observable.fromEvent(button, 'click')
  .subscribe(() => console.log('You clicked me!'));
```

The value added by the observable includes:

- Add functions to deal with the incoming event without altering the state of the data or incoming event
- Control how the events flow through your observables
- Transform the values that flow through your observables
- Cancel the event or data stream

37—Guided Exercise: Creating Observables

There are several ways to create observables, such as invoking a constructor function as well as creation operators like `of()`, `from()`, `interval()` and more.

Step 1 Open Chrome and visit jsBin.com or using your IDE open the file below:

angular-class-files/demos-exercises/observables/**guided-exercise-creating-observables.html**

If using jsBin:

Step A: Click inside the HTML panel and place your cursor after the <title> tag.

Step B: Click the Add Library menu and start typing RxJS5.0.3; select the RXJS option from the drop-down menu.

Step C: Make sure the JavaScript, Console and Output tabs are open and the HTML and CSS tabs are closed.

Step D: Type the JavaScript in the JavaScript section

Step E: Click the "Run with JS" button to execute the code and see the results.

Note: It may be necessary to add `//jshint esnext:true` before writing any JavaScript.

The jsbin website used to test JavaScript using libraries and frameworks with little setup.

If using your IDE and opening the file locally

The `create()` operator

RxJS provides a `create()` method which is an alias for the Observable constructor function. It takes one argument that is the subscribe function.

Step 1 Remove the comments from the code block shown below.

```
// the create method
      const yo = rxjs.Observable.create(function(observer) {
       const fn = setInterval(() => {
           observer.next(`Hello from the observable`);}, 1000);
      });
      console.log(`observable's subscribe: `);
      yo.subscribe(data => console.log(data));
      const subscribe = yo.subscribe(val => console.log(`this is from the
subscriber: \n ${val}`));
```

Step 2 Run the file in Chrome.

This code would result in no console log statements.

Step 3 Remove the comment from the first subscribe.

```
// the create method
const yo = rxjs.Observable.create(function(observer) {
    const fn = setInterval(() => {
        observer.next(`Hello from the observable`);}, 1000);
});
console.log(`observable's subscribe: `);
yo.subscribe(data => console.log(data));
// const subscribe = yo.subscribe(val => console.log(`this is from the subscriber: \n
${val}`));
```

The result of this code would be like this:

```
observable's subscribe:
6 Hello from the observable
```

Step 4 Comment the first subscribe and remove the comment before the second subscribe as shown below.

```
// yo.subscribe(data => console.log(data));
const subscribe = yo.subscribe(val => console.log(`this is from the subscriber: \n
${val}`));
```

The result of this code in the console would look like this:

```
observable's subscribe:
7 this is from the subscriber:
  Hello from the observable
```

Step 5 Remove the comments from the first subscribe. What should happen now?

The `of()` creation operator

Used for a single value as an Observable. The result parameter in the example below will contain the result of the data stream.

Step 1 Remove the comments from the second script block in guided-exercise-creating-observables.html.

```
rxjs.of(`Hello World`)
        .subscribe(result => console.log(result));
```

The result of this code in the console would look like this:

```
Hello World
```

Step 2 Run the file in Chrome.

The result of this code will look like this:

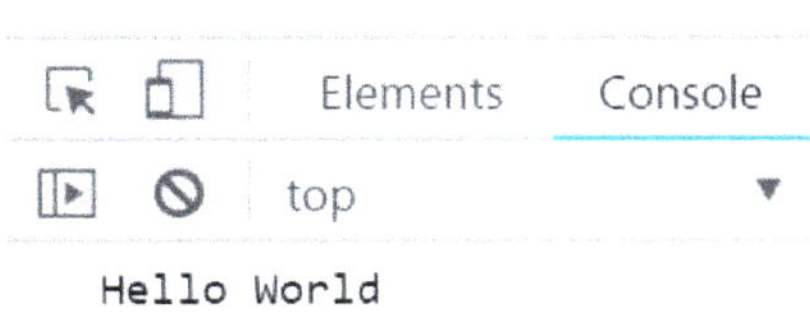

Step 3 Return the comments around the script block from step 1.

The `from` creation operator

Creates an Observable sequence from arrays or array-like objects such as iterables like Map, Set and String.

Step 1 Remove the comments around the next script block.

```
const src = rxjs.from([1,2,3]);
                src.subscribe(x => {
                        console.log(x * 2);
                        },                                    // next
                        error => console.error(error),        // error
                        () => console.log('done')             // complete
              );
```

In this example, the subscribe method is passed three functions. The first is the next function that passes the data (x) on. The second function is the error handler and the last function is the complete function which is run when the data stream ends. The result of this code in the console would look like this:

```
2
4
6
done
```

Step 2 Run the file in Chrome.

The results of this code will look like this:

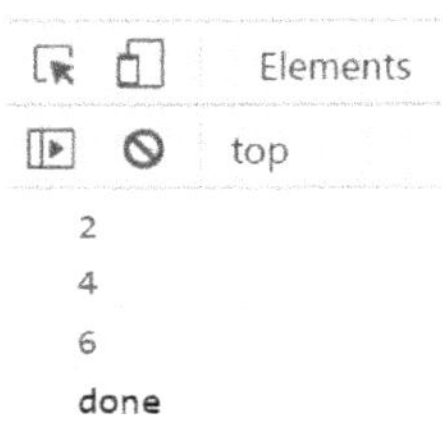

Step 3 Re-comment the code block.

The `fromEvent` creation operator

Creates an Observable from an event listener.

Step 1 Remove the comments from the following code block.

```
rxjs.fromEvent(document, 'mousemove')
        .subscribe(event => console.log(event.clientX, event.clientY),
             (error)=> console.log(error),
             () => console.log('done')
        );
```

Step 2 Run the file in Chrome and move the mouse around the browser.

The results of this code should be the x and y coordinate of your mouse moves. Example code is shown below (your numbers will be different and will continue to display as you move your mouse).

```
194 167
193 161
```

It should be noted here that observables can be used to create new Observables.

NOTE: This chapter is an introduction to Observables and their features. Not all topics introduced in this chapter will play a role in the subsequent exercises, however, you will be using Observables throughout the remainder of the course and it is important that you understand how Observables work.

13.9 Subjects

The subject is the most basic implementation of the Observable interface. Later in this chapter, you will learn `ReplaySubject` and `BehaviorSubject`. For now, we'll stick to the Subject! You can think of the Observer as the reader of the data and the Observable as the consumer of the data. While the Observable is ideal for wrapping functionality that produces values over time (like a web socket connection), the Subject can do more. This is because it implements both the Observable and Observer APIs. Recall that the Observer subscribes to an Observable and an Observable is what produces the sequences that the Observer receives The Subject can trigger new events which makes it equivalent to an EventEmitter. You can also connect existing observables to Subjects. Perhaps the most important aspect of Subjects is that they are the only way of multicasting a value to multiple observers.

Step 1 Try the following code examples at jsbin.com or you can return to the file guided-exercise-creating-observables.html.

Step 2 Remove the comments for the subject example shown below.

Note This demo file uses the older version 5.0.3 of RXJS.

13.9.1 Example Subject

```
const subject = new Rx.Subject();
const dataSource = Rx.Observable.interval(100)
            .map(x => `interval message ${x}`)
            .take(5);
dataSource.subscribe(subject);
subject.subscribe(x => console.log(x),
                  error => console.error(error),
                  () => console.log('done'));

subject.next(`message #1`)
subject.next(`message #2`)

setTimeout(() => subject.complete(), 300);
```

this should output:

```
message #1
message #2
interval message 0
interval message 1
interval message 2
done
```

Step 3 Run the file in Chrome. Your output should look like:

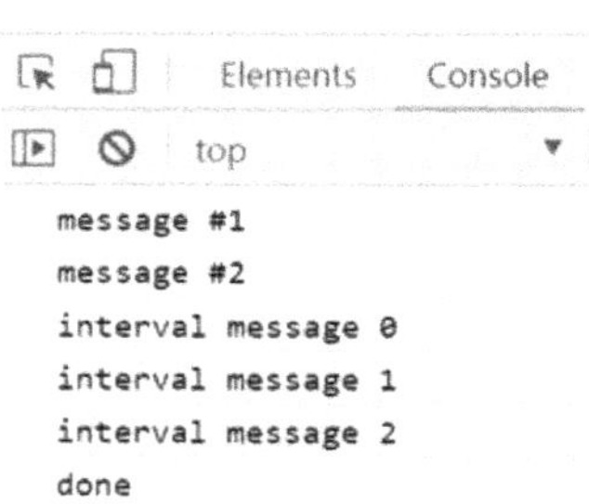

Notes regarding the example code:

- The dataSource sequence will not begin until there is a subscription on the subject
- After the dataSource is complete, subscribers will no longer be actively subscribed
- The `map()` operator will pass each dataSource value through a transformation function and return new output. In this code, the map function takes each data source and returns it in a string: interval message #
- The `take()` operator is a filtering operator the emits only the first five values emitted by the dataSource

For more information about RxJS and operators see http://reactivex.io/rxjs/manual/overview.html. In its simplest form, the Subject class is used to subscribe just like an observable, with the biggest difference being that the subject cal also emit values to its subscribers.

```
subject.next(newValue)
```

38–Guided Exercise: Examining Observables, Observers and Subjects

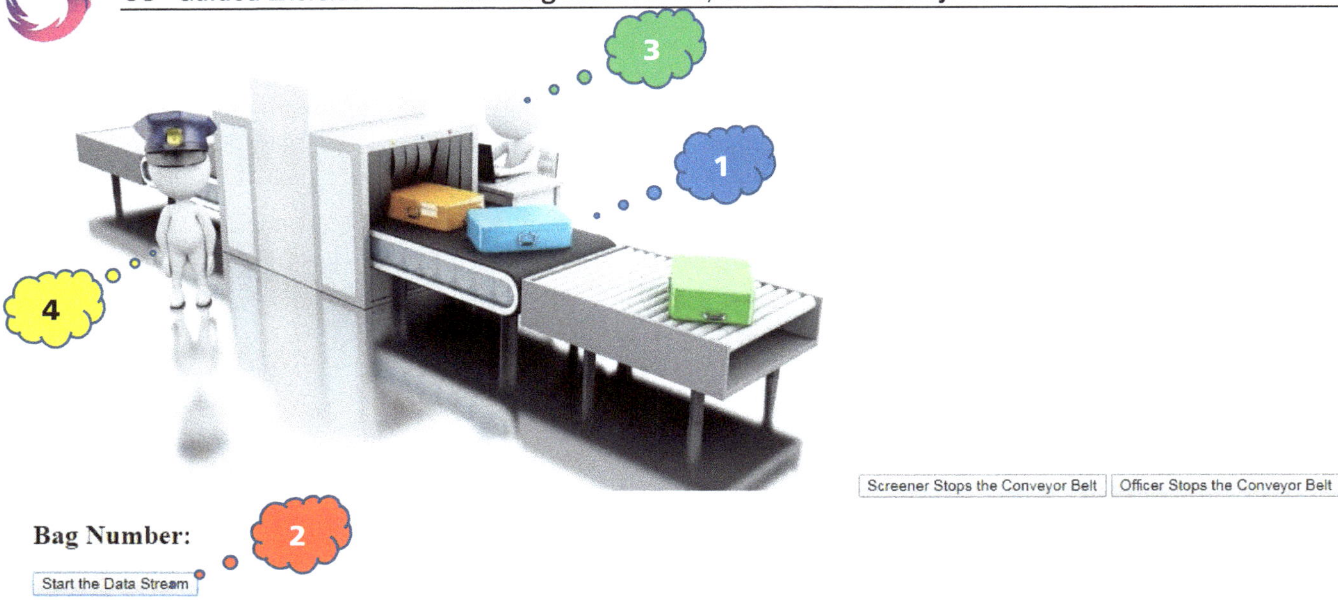

Step 1 Open observable-examples.html in your editor and run it in Chrome.

Step 2 The conveyor belt represents the observable stream of data over time. Click on the luggage to show a popup that describes the observable. Remove the comments beginning at approximately line 54(per the pop-up) around the creation of the observable. Discuss the uncommented code with your instructor.

Step 3 Refresh the file in Chrome and open the console. Click the "Start the Data Stream" button and follow the instructions on the popup to start the data stream.

Step 4 Save and refresh the file in Chrome. You should see the Bag Number counter incrementing because you have subscribed to the data stream.

Step 5 The screener behind the conveyor belt represents an observer object. Clicking on the screener presents a popup that describes the observer. Follow the instructions on the pop-up.

Step 6 The officer with the hat represents a subject. Clicking on the officer presents a popup that describes the subject. Follow the instructions on the pop-up.

Step 7 What should happen when the screener stops the conveyor belt? Click the "Screener Stops the Conveyor Belt" button.

Step 8 What should happen when the officer stops the conveyor belt? Click the "Officer Stops the Conveyor Belt" button.

Step 9 Discuss any questions or concerns with the code with your instructor.

39—Guided Exercise: Create and use an Observable

In this exercise, you create an observable that dispatches a message. You create a new component that allows the user to select a specific goal for the day, such as eating more fruit. That component uses a new service that makes the goal an observable. The footer component then subscribes to the observable and reminds the user of their goal throughout their session.

The new todays-goals.component before the user selects a goal.

The new todays-goals.component after the user selects a goal.

Step 1 Create a new service in the services directory called todays-goal.service.ts via the command:

`ng g s services/todays-goal`. Add the code shown in bold.

```
import { Injectable } from '@angular/core';
import { Observable, Subject } from 'rxjs/index';


@Injectable({
  providedIn: 'root'
})

export class TodaysGoalService {
    private subject = new Subject<any>();

    sendGoal(goal: string): void {
        this.subject.next(goal);
        console.log(goal);
    }

    clearGoal(): void {
        this.subject.next();
    }

    getGoal(): Observable<any> {
        return this.subject.asObservable();
    }
}
```

Notice the use of the Subject. The Subject implements both Observable and Observer APIs .

Step 2 Create a new component called todays-goal.component.ts. This is the component that will send the goals. Modify the generated code as shown below in bold.

```
import { Component, OnInit } from '@angular/core';
import {TodaysGoalService} from '../services/todays-goal.service';

@Component({
```

```
  selector: 'fp-todays-goals',
  templateUrl: './todays-goal.component.html',
  styleUrls: ['./todays-goal.component.css']
})
export class TodaysGoalsComponent implements OnInit {

  goals: Array<string> = [
    'Eat more Fruits',
    'Eat more Vegetables',
    'Eat more Protein',
    'Eat more Grains',
    'Exercise',
  ];

  constructor(private todaysGoalSvce: TodaysGoalService) {
  }

  ngOnInit():void {
  }

  sendGoal(goal): void {
    this.todaysGoalSvce.sendGoal(goal);
  }

  clearGoal(): void {
    this.todaysGoalSvce.clearGoal();
  }
}
```

Step 3 Create the todays-goal.component.html view template.

```
<h1>Today's Goal</h1>
<ul>
    <span *ngFor="let goal of goals">
        <input type="radio" name="goal" (click)="sendGoal(goal)">
        <li >{{ goal }}</li>
    </span>
</ul>
```

Step 4 Create the todays-goals.component.css stylesheet. You can copy and paste this file from assets/css/todays-goals-component-css.css.

```
li, input {
    margin: 0;
    padding: 0;
}

span {
    display: block;
    text-align: left;
    margin: 4px 0;
}
```

```
ul li {
    text-align: left;
    display:inline;
}
ul {
    list-style-type: none;
}

input[type=radio] {
    width:24px;
    height:24px;
    display: inline;
}
```

Step 5 The component that will "listen" or subscribe to the observable subject is the footer. Modify the footer.component.ts to subscribe to the subject by making the following changes:

- Import the necessary classes: Subscription and TodaysGoalService
- Create a goal property to store the goal received from the observable subject
- Create a subscription property
- Inject TodaysGoalService into the constructor function
- Subscribe to the observer subject
- Write a clearGoal function using the services clearGoal method.
- Respond to the lifecycle event `OnDestroy` that is called when a directive, pipe or service is destroyed.

```
import { Component } from '@angular/core';

import { Subscription } from 'rxjs/index';

import { TodaysGoalService } from '../services/todays-goal.service';

@Component({
  selector: 'fp-footer',
  templateUrl: './footer.component.html',
  styleUrls: ['./footer.component.css']
})
export class FooterComponent implements OnInit, OnDestroy {
  goal: any;
  subscription: Subscription;
  versionString: string = "1.0.0";
  icon: string = 'assets/images/icons/icons-29.png';
  logoAlt: string = 'FoodPlate logo';
  isCurrent: Boolean = true;

  moreInfo(): void {
    alert("For more information about the food plate, visit
https://www.choosemyplate.gov/");
  }

  constructor(private todaysGoalSvce: TodaysGoalService) {
    this.subscription = this.todaysGoalSvce.getGoal()
      .subscribe(goal   => this.goal = goal);
```

```
  }

  ngOnInit(): void {
  }

  clearGoal(): void {
    this.todaysGoalSvce.clearGoal();
  }

  ngOnDestroy(): void {
    this.subscription.unsubscribe();
  }
}
```

Step 6 Now modify the footer's view template to display todays goal. The modifications are shown in bold.

```
<footer class="header-footer">
    <img [src]="icon" (click)="moreInfo()" [alt]="logoAlt">
    <p *ngIf="goal" (click)="clearGoal()">Don't forget today's goal! -
{{goal}}</p>
    <p>&copy; 2019 KRA Inc.
        <small [attr.data-version]="versionString"
        [class.footer--
update]="!isCurrent">Version#{{versionString}}</small></p>
</footer>
```

Step 7 Confirm the new todays-goal component has been added to the app module's declarations property.

Step 8 Open app.component.html and comment `<fp-main>`. The main.component.html is no longer displaying the food plate images, but this will be fixed with an observable in this chapter. Without the main component in place, the nav links will no longer work.

Step 9 Add the todays-goal component to the application via app.component.html. The finished app.component.html is shown below.

```
<div id="wrapper">
  <fp-header></fp-header>
  <fp-nav></fp-nav>
  <fp-todays-goal></fp-todays-goal>
  <!--<fp-main [user]="user"> </fp-main>-->
  <fp-footer></fp-footer>
</div>
```

Step 10 Save and all the files and test the application in a web browser.

Step 11 Choose a goal from one of the radio buttons and you should see the goal in the footer component.

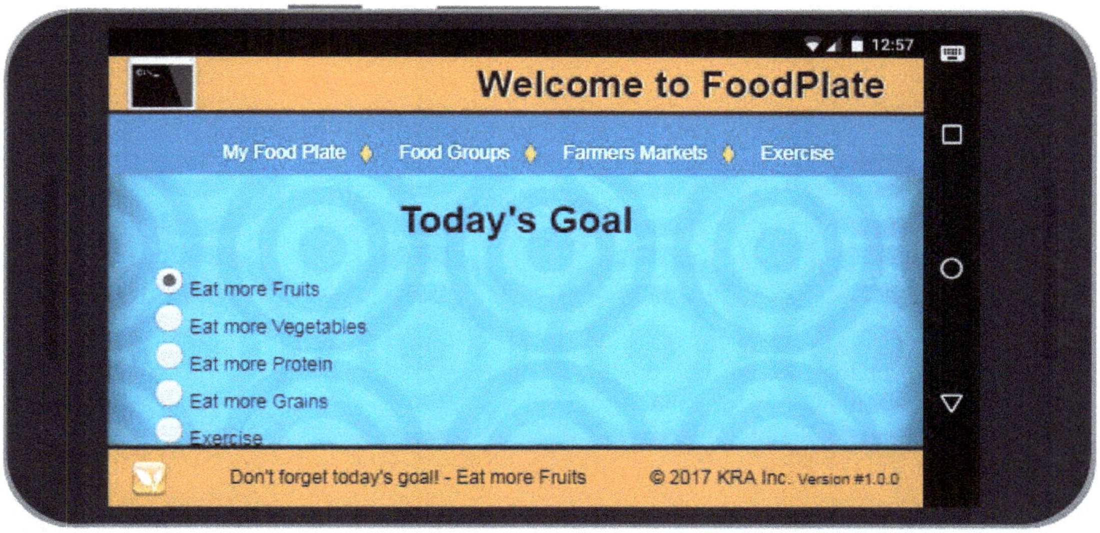

40—Guided Exercise: AsyncSubject, ReplaySubject and BehaviorSubject

In addition to Subject, RxJS provides AsyncSubject, RetrySubject and BehaviorSubject all of which are leveraged within Angular applications. Here are more details about each Subject class.

AsyncSubject

This subject emits the last value of a sequence if the sequence is completed. The last value is cached. If there is an error, the AsyncSubject will return and cache the error.

Step 1 Open Chrome and go to http://jsbin.com.

Note If you do not have access to jsbin, you can open the file "guided-exercise-async-replay-behavior-subjects.html" from the demos-exercises folder.

Step 2 Add the RxJS library and type the code below in the JavaScript panel, then press the "Run" button. If you are working locally, simply remove the comments around the first script block.

```
// AsynchSubject
    const rangeOfNumbers = rxjs.range(0, 5);
    const subject = new rxjs.AsyncSubject();

    rangeOfNumbers.subscribe(subject);
    subject.subscribe(x => console.log(x),
        error => console.error(error),
        () => console.log('done'));
```

The range operator emits numbers in the provided range. The first argument is the start number and the second argument is the count. In the example above, the range would include: 0, 1, 2, 3, 4. Due to the AsyncSubject this code will output:

```
4
done
```

ReplaySubject

This subject re-emits values that have already been emitted before any Observer has subscribed to it. It can store only a maximum number of previously emitted values based on a buffer-size limit that is passed in as the first argument. The second argument determines how many values you can retrieve based on time.

Step 3 Delete or comment the code from step 3 and add the code below.

```
const subject = new rxjs.Subject();

subject.next('emitted before a subscribe');
subject.next('also emitted before a subscribe');
subject.next('one more time');
subject.subscribe(x => console.log(x),
                  error => console.error(error),
                  () => console.log('done'))
```

```
subject.next('emitted after subscribe');
subject.next('also emitted after subscribe');
subject.complete();
```

outputs nothing emitted prior to the subscription

```
"emitted after subscribe"
"also emitted after subscribe"
"done"
```

Step 4 Now change the Subject into a ReplaySubject and you get the following output:

```
"emitted before a subscribe"
"also emitted before a subscribe"
"one more time"
"emitted after subscribe"
"also emitted after subscribe"
"done"
```

Step 5 Now add a buffer size.

```
const subject = new Rx.ReplaySubject(1);
```

and the output is:

```
"one more time"
"emitted after subscribe"
"also emitted after subscribe"
"done"
```

How many values you receive based on time.

Step 6 Now add a window size.

```
const subject = new Rx.ReplaySubject(5, 100);
setTimeout(() => subject.next('emitted before a subscribe'), 100)
setTimeout(() => subject.next('also emitted before a subscribe'), 200)
setTimeout(() => subject.next('one more time'), 300)
     setTimeout(() => {
          subject.subscribe(x => console.log(x),
                error => console.error(error),
                () => console.log('done'))
  subject.next('emitted after subscribe');
  subject.next('also emitted after subscribe');
  subject.complete();
}, 350);
```

and the output is:

```
"one more time"
"emitted after subscribe"
"also emitted after subscribe"
"done"
```

BehaviorSubject

This subject represents a value that changes over time, where Observers receive the last emitted value as well all subsequent values. It is the only subject that guarantees at least one value will be emitted. This is because the BehaviorSubject will always get the initial or the last value that the subject emits. Upon completion of the data stream, the BehaviorSubject will no longer emit any values.

In the FoodPlate application we need to store the user object which stores the minimum required servings of fruit, protein, grains and vegetables. The application will keep track of each serving consumed and let the user know if they have met their requirements. Therefore, the user object will be storing properties such as fruitMet, proteinMet and so on. The application needs to allow these properties to be updated and accessed at any given time. The behavior object is ideally suited for this. This is because the Subject class will not return the last value when you subscribe to it; that will only happen when some application code somewhere calls the next() method. On the other hand, the BehaviorSubject, when subscribed to, will return the last value of the data stream or the initial value if no value was emitted. For this reason, it is important to remember the BehaviorSubject needs an initial value set. In addition, the BehaviorSubject can return the current value of the stream at any time, by calling its' `getValue()` method.

Step 7 Delete or comment the code from step 3-6 and the code below.

```
const behaviorSubject = new Rx.BehaviorSubject(0); // 0 is the initial value
behaviorSubject.subscribe({
        next: (value) => console.log('observer-A: ' + value)
});

behaviorSubject.next(1);
behaviorSubject.next(2);

behaviorSubject.subscribe({
        next: (value) => console.log('observer-B: ' + value)
});
behaviorSubject.next(3);
```

In this example the behavior subject is initialized with a value of 0. This is the value the first subscriber (observer-A) receives after it subscribes. The BehaviorSubject's `next()` method then dispatches the values 1 and 2. The second observer (observer-B) receives the value 2 (the second dispatch) even though it subscribed after the value 2 was sent. This is because the BehaviorSubject stores the latest value emitted to its consumers and when a new observer subscribes it immediately receives the "current value" (2 in this case) as well as subsequent values emitted.

Thus, the output is:

```
observer-A: 0
observer-A: 1
observer-A: 2
observer-B: 2
observer-A: 3
observer-B: 3
```

41–Guided Exercise: Refactor the user.service as an Observable with a BehaviorSubject

In this exercise, you refactor the user.service and its related code to use an Observable with a BehaviorSubject. We need to keep track of the user's name, there registration status, how much food they have eaten from each food group. We also need to access this information at any time and any place in the application. Using the BehaviorSubject with observables will make it far easier to share the user object and its properties.

Step 1 Open and refactor the user.service.ts file to use Observables. The relevant changes are shown in bold. The deletions are shown with a strikethrough.

```
import { Injectable, Optional } from '@angular/core';
import { BehaviorSubject } from 'rxjs/index';

import {User} from "../models/User";
import {UserStatusService} from './user-status.service';

@Injectable()
export class UserService {

  private user: User = new User(1, 'Kevin', 'M', '51+', 'M51+', {},
{fruitMet: false, vegMet: false, proteinMet: false, grainMet: false}, false,
'kevin@kevinruse.com');

  currentUser = new BehaviorSubject<User>(this.user);

  getUser(): User {
    if (localStorage.getItem('currentUser')) {
      const user = JSON.parse(localStorage.getItem('currentUser'));
      this.currentUser = new BehaviorSubject(user);
      return user;
    } else {
      return this.user;
    }
  }

  updateUser(user: User): void {
    user.id = 1;
    user.registered = true;
    user.reqsStatus = {fruitMet: false, vegMet: false, proteinMet: false,
grainMet: false};
    this.currentUser.next(user);
  }

  static storeUserLocal(user) {
    localStorage.setItem('currentUser', JSON.stringify(user));
  }

  constructor(@Optional() private userStatusService: UserStatusService) {
    if (this.userStatusService) {
      this.userStatusService.getUserStatus(this.user);
    }
}
```

This is from the advanced section of a previous chapter so it may not be in your file. It is okay if you have an empty constructor here.

Notes

The defaultUser is created for new users, hence the fruitMet, vegMet, proteinMet and grainsMet properties are set to false, because the user has not registered or kept track of any of the food they have eaten. A default name is supplied ('New User') and the registered property is set to false.

The currentUser property is assigned to a new BehaviorSubject of type User and passed the defaultUser).

The getUser method checks to see if the user has already been stored in localStorage and returns that stored user, otherwise the currentUser is returned.

The updateUser method receives a user object (the newly registered user) and flips the registered property to true and sets the reqsStatus values which keeps track of the foods eaten, to false. Finally, the currentUser BehaviorSubject runs the next() method passing the updated user. The next() method is the callback to receive notification of type next from the observable with a value.[5]

Finally, the static method, storeUserLocal() stores the currentUser in the browser's localStorage.

The app.component will use the user.service to invoke the subscribe method.

Step 2 Open app.component.ts and refactor the code using a currentUser as shown below.

```
export class AppComponent implements OnInit {

  currentUser: User;

  constructor(private userService:UserService , private titleService: Title) {
  }
```

Step 3 Refactor the ngOnInit method to invoke the subscribe method on the current user. Pass a function that accepts the user as a parameter and assigns the supplied user object to the component classes' current user property.

```
ngOnInit() {
    this.titleService.setTitle("Welcome to FoodPlate!");
    this.userService.getUser();
    this.userService.currentUser.subscribe(user => this.currentUser = user);
}
```

Step 4 Remove the user binding in app.component.html, uncomment the main component and comment the todays-goal component.

```
<div id="wrapper">
  <fp-header></fp-header>
  <fp-nav></fp-nav>
  <!--<fp-todays-goals></fp-todays-goals>-->
  <fp-main [user]="user"> </fp-main>
  <fp-footer></fp-footer>
</div>
```

[5] http://reactivex.io/rxjs/class/es6/MiscJSDoc.js~ObserverDoc.html

Now that we have a BehaviorSubject (currentUser), we need to make use of it in the other components that need the user object.

The reactive form's `FormGroup` and `FormControl` have a `valueChanges` method that returns an observable that emits the forms latest values. Because it is an Observable, we can subscribe to it whenever we need the forms property changes. At this point we can see the changes, by logging them to the console. But, more importantly, the currentUser will subscribe to the BehaviorSubject and pass the user to the currentUser property of the register.component.

Step 5 In the register.component.ts, inside the ngOnInit method, log the form's changes and Subscribe to the BehaviorSubject.

```
constructor(private userService: UserService, private router: Router, private
fb: FormBuilder) {
...
    }

ngOnInit() {
    this.userService.currentUser.subscribe(user => this.currentUser = user);
    this.regForm.valueChanges.subscribe(value => console.log(value));
  }
```

Step 6 Refactor the `onSubmit` method for the forms submit button, by adding a call to the user.service's `updateUser` method.

```
onSubmit(formValues): void{
    this.userService.updateUser(formValues);
    UserService.storeUserLocal(formValues);
}
```

The plate component also references the user object. It looks at the user's fruitMet, vegMet, proteinMet and grainsMet property to determine which plate image to display. For example, if the user has met their daily fruit requirement, the image on the right will be display, if not, the image on the left will be displayed. The plate component needs to be refactored to use the currentUser BehaviorSubject.

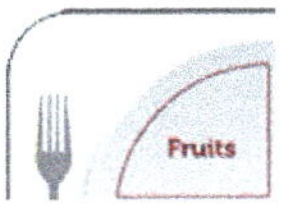

Step 7 If necessary, return the constructor function's FormGroup argument to updateOn **blur** as shown below in bold.

```
  constructor(private userService: UserService) {
        this.regForm = new FormGroup({
              firstName: new FormControl(null, {validators:
Validators.required}),
              email: new FormControl(null, [Validators.required,
Validators.email]),
              gender: new FormControl(null, [Validators.required]),
              ageGroup: new FormControl(null, [Validators.required])
        }, {updateOn: 'blur'});
  }
```

Step 8 Save and test the file. The home button is missing its label and the console shows the following error message:

```
▶ERROR TypeError: Cannot read property     HomeBtnComponent.html:1
'registered' of undefined
    at Object.eval [as updateRenderer] (HomeBtnComponent.html:4)
    at Object.debugUpdateRenderer [as updateRenderer] (core.js:147
35)
```

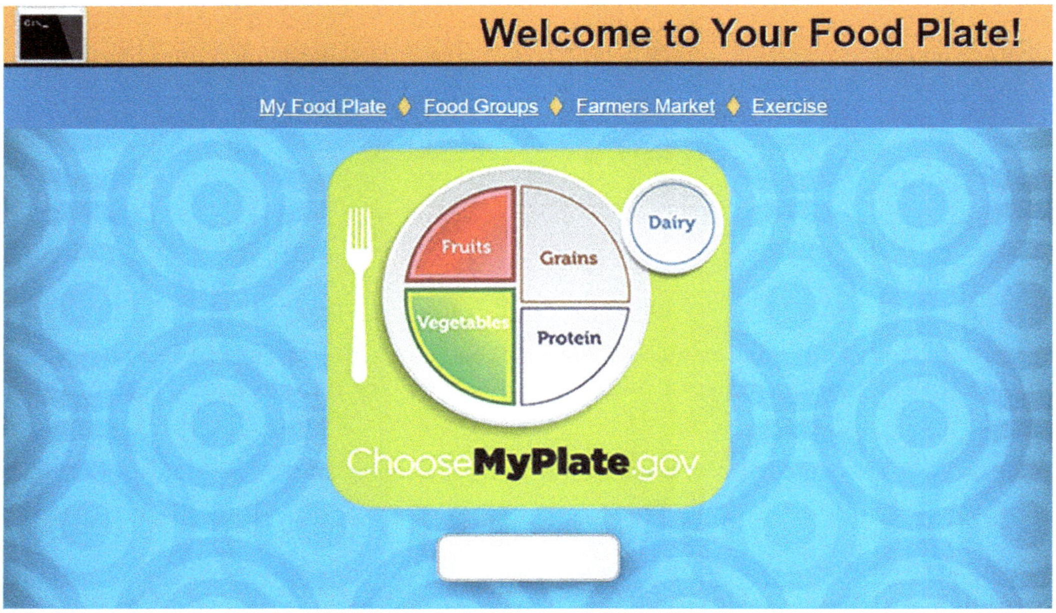

You will fix this error in the next challenge exercise.

13 –Challenge Exercise: Refactor component communication to use observables

In this exercise you refactor the plate component, so the user data is shared by way of an observable instead of the parent/child communication you learned using @Input.

Simple Instructions

- Refactor the plate component so that it utilizes (subscribes to) the user service.
- Refactor the plate template's image src bindings to the currentUser object.
- Refactor the homeBtn component so that it utilizes the currentUser object.

Step by Step Instructions

Step 1 Open plate.component.ts and do the following:

- add the currentUser property
- remove the @Input user: User
- modify the ngOnInit content
- confirm the t UserService has been imported and injected into the constructor

The finished plate.component.ts code is shown below with the relevant modifications shown in bold.

```
import { Component, OnInit } from '@angular/core';

import { User } from '../models/User';
import { UserService } from '../services/user.service';

@Component({
  selector: 'fp-plate',
  templateUrl: './plate.component.html',
  styleUrls: ['./plate.component.css']
})
export class PlateComponent implements OnInit {

  @Input()
  user: User;
  currentUser: User;

  plateImgPath = '../../assets/images/plateImages/';
  fruitEmpty = `${this.plateImgPath}fruit-empty.png`;
  grainDairyEmpty = `${this.plateImgPath}graindairy-empty.png`;
  proteinEmpty = `${this.plateImgPath}protein-empty.png`;
  vegEmpty = `${this.plateImgPath}veg-empty.png`;
  fruitFull = `${this.plateImgPath}fruit-full.png`;
  grainDairyFull = `${this.plateImgPath}graindairy-full.png`;
  proteinFull = `${this.plateImgPath}protein-full.jpg`;
  vegFull = `${this.plateImgPath}veg-full.jpg`;


  constructor(private userService: UserService) {
  }
```

```
  ngOnInit() {
    this.userService.currentUser.subscribe(user => this.currentUser = user);
  }
}
```

Step 2 Open plate.component.html and refactor the plate logic to use currentUser. The relevant code is shown below in bold. Remove the user binding from the `<fp-message>` element.

```
...
     <div id="colwrap1">
       <img [src]="(currentUser?.reqsStatus.fruitMet) ? fruitFull :
fruitEmpty" id="fruit"/>
       <img [src]="(currentUser?.reqsStatus.vegMet) ? vegFull : vegEmpty"
id="veg"/>
     </div>
     <div id="colwrap2">
       <img [src]="(currentUser?.reqsStatus.grainMet) ? grainDairyFull :
grainDairyEmpty" id="grain"/>
       <div id="logoContainer" class="clearFloat"></div>
       <img [src]="(currentUser?.reqsStatus.proteinMet) ? proteinFull :
proteinEmpty" id="protein"/>
       <div class="clearFloat"></div>
     </div>
  <!--<fp-message [user]="user"></fp-message> -->
...
```

The button component makes use of the user service when it changes the label of the button from "Register" to "Check In" depending upon whether the user has registered or not.

Step 3 Open and refactor the home-btn.component.ts file to make use of the BehaviorSubject. Be sure to import the necessary classes.

```
export class HomeBtnComponent implements OnInit {

  @Input()
  user: User;

  currentUser: User;

  constructor(private userService: UserService) {
  }

  ngOnInit() {
    this.userService.currentUser.subscribe(user => this.currentUser = user);
  }
```

Step 4 Refactor the home-btn.component.html as shown below in bold.

```
<input type="button" id="button" class="fpButton"
[value]="(currentUser.registered) ? 'Check In' : 'Register'">
```

Step 5 Remove the `[user]` binding from the fp-home-btn in main.component.html as shown in the strikethrough below.

```
<main>
  <router-outlet name="foodGroupOutlet"></router-outlet>
```

```
  <router-outlet></router-outlet>
  <a routerLink="register">
    <fp-home-btn [user]="user" [hidden]="this.router.url === '/register'">
    </fp-home-btn>
  </a>
</main>
```

Step 6 Confirm the `<fp-message>` component in plate.component.html has been commented and that message component is no longer linked to the user via the @Input() user binding. At the end of this exercise is a challenge exercise to refactor message to use the new BehaviorSubject.

Step 7 Open main.component.ts and remove the `@Input() user: User`.

Step 8 In main.component.ts add the ngOnInit and constructor methods as shown below. Don't forget to import the UserService.

```
export class MainComponent implements OnInit {
  router: Router;
  currentUser: User;

ngOnInit() {
    this.userService.currentUser.subscribe(user => this.currentUser = user);
}

constructor( private _router: Router, private userService: UserService){
    this.router = _router;
}
```

Note After refreshing Chrome, open the DevTools Application tab and remove any data in LocalStorage. Refresh the page after removing the data in LocalStorage.

Removing the LocalStorage data from Chrome

1. Open the DevTools
2. Click the Application Tab and use the right-side navigation and select LocalStorage → http://localhost:4200
3. Highlight the currentUser and click the X to the left of the Filter input field.

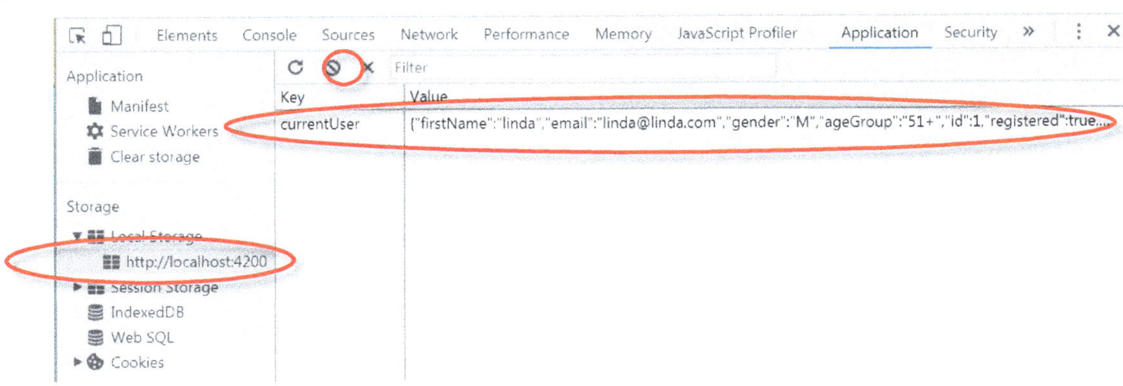

Step 9 Save and test the file in a web browser. Click the "Register" button and register using the form. Then click the "My Food Plate" link in the top navigation bar. The button's label should now show "Check In." Click the "Check In" button and it still goes to the register form. Let's fix that now.

The route attached to the button is configured in main.component.html and is shown below.

```
<main>
```

```
  <router-outlet name="foodGroupOutlet"></router-outlet>
  <router-outlet></router-outlet>
  <a routerLink="register">
    <fp-home-btn [hidden]="this.router.url === '/register'"></fp-home-btn>
  </a>
</main>
```

The link needs to be dynamic: if the user needs to register, the click of the button should take the user to the register form; if the user has already registered and needs to check in, the button should take them to the myPlate route.

Step 10 Open main.component.ts and add a `routerLink and currentUser` properties and a `getRoute()` method to handle the dynamic routing of the home-btn.component. Delete the router property which will be created with the constructor's private parameter in step 18.

```
...
  currentUser: User;
  routerLink: string;
  router;
...

getRoute(): string {
    if (!this.currentUser.registered) {
      this.routerLink = 'register';
    }
    else if (this.currentUser.registered) {
      this.routerLink = 'myPlate';
    }
    return this.routerLink;
}
```

Note There are numerous ways to code step 10 (see one alternative below). Always strive for a balance between using your companies code styling guide and human readability.

```
getRoute(): string {
   const link = (this.currentUser.registered) ? 'myPlate' : 'register';
   return this.routerLink = link;
}
```

Step 11 Open main.component.html and refactor the route as shown below in bold.

```
 <a [routerLink]="getRoute()">
    <fp-home-btn [hidden]="this.router.url === '/register'"></fp-home-btn>
  </a>
```

Step 12 Save and test the file in the browser. You may need to go into localStorage and delete the user you registered earlier.

Click the "Register" button and register using the form. Then click the "My Food Plate" link in the top navigation bar. The button's label should now show "Check In." Click the "Check In" button and it should no longer navigate to the register form.

After registering and clicking the "Check In" button, your screen should match the image below.

Note app.component.ts should call getUser() from the ngOnInit() lifecycle hook.

Possible Solution code

Home button view template

```
<input [value]="(currentUser.registered) ? 'Check In' : 'Register'"
       class="fpButton"
       id="home_btn"
       type="button">
```

Home button component class

```
import { Component, OnInit } from '@angular/core';
import { User } from '../models/User';
import { UserService } from '../services/user.service';

@Component({
  selector: 'fp-home-btn',
  templateUrl: './home-btn.component.html',
  styleUrls: ['./home-btn.component.css']
})
export class HomeBtnComponent implements OnInit {

  currentUser: User;

  constructor(private userService: UserService) {
  }

  ngOnInit() {
    this.userService.currentUser.subscribe(user => this.currentUser = user);
  }
}
```

Plate view template

```
<section id="plate">
  <div id="foodPlateWrapper">
    <div id="colwrap1">
      <img [src]="(currentUser?.reqsStatus.fruitMet) ? fruitFull : fruitEmpty" id="fruit"/>
      <img [src]="(currentUser?.reqsStatus.vegMet) ? vegFull : vegEmpty" id="veg"/></div>
    <div id="colwrap2">
      <img [src]="(currentUser?.reqsStatus.grainMet) ? grainDairyFull : grainDairyEmpty"
id="grain"/>
      <div class="clearFloat" id="logoContainer"></div>
      <img [src]="(currentUser?.reqsStatus.proteinMet) ? proteinFull : proteinEmpty"
id="protein"/>
      <div class="clearFloat"></div>
    </div>
    <img alt="" id="text" src="../../assets/images/plateImages/text.png"/>
  </div>
  <!--  <fp-message></fp-message>-->
</section>
```

Plate component class

```
import { Component, OnInit } from '@angular/core';
import { User } from '../models/User';
import { UserService } from '../services/user.service';
```

```
@Component({
  selector: 'fp-plate',
  templateUrl: './plate.component.html',
  styleUrls: ['./plate.component.css']
})
export class PlateComponent implements OnInit {

  currentUser: User;

  plateImgPath: string = '../../assets/images/plateImages/';
  fruitEmpty: string = `${this.plateImgPath}fruit-empty.png`;
  grainDairyEmpty: string = `${this.plateImgPath}graindairy-empty.png`;
  proteinEmpty: string = `${this.plateImgPath}protein-empty.png`;
  vegEmpty: string = `${this.plateImgPath}veg-empty.png`;
  fruitFull: string = `${this.plateImgPath}fruit-full.png`;
  grainDairyFull: string = `${this.plateImgPath}graindairy-full.png`;
  proteinFull: string = `${this.plateImgPath}protein-full.jpg`;
  vegFull: string = `${this.plateImgPath}veg-full.jpg`;

  constructor(private userService: UserService) {
  }

  ngOnInit() {
    this.userService.currentUser.subscribe(user => this.currentUser = user);
  }

}
```

Register component class

```
import { Component, OnInit } from '@angular/core';
import { FormBuilder, FormGroup, Validators } from '@angular/forms';
import { Router } from '@angular/router';
import { User } from '../models/User';
import { UserService } from '../services/user.service';

@Component({
  selector: 'fp-register',
  templateUrl: './register.component.html',
  styleUrls: ['./register.component.css']
})
export class RegisterComponent implements OnInit {

  currentUser: User;
  ageGroups = ['select your age group', '2-3', '4-8', '9-13', '14-18', '19-30', '31-50',
'51+'];
  regForm: FormGroup;

  constructor(private userService: UserService,
              private fb: FormBuilder,
              private router: Router) {
    this.regForm = fb.group({
      'firstname': [null, [Validators.required]],
      'email': [null, Validators.compose([Validators.required, Validators.email])],
      'gender': [null, [Validators.required]],
      'ageGroup': [null, [Validators.required]],
    }, {updateOn: 'submit'});
  }

  ngOnInit() {
    this.userService.currentUser.subscribe(user => this.currentUser = user);
```

```
    this.regForm.valueChanges.subscribe(value => console.log(value));
  }

  onSubmit(formValues): void {
    this.userService.updateUser(formValues);
    UserService.storeUserLocal(formValues);
  }

}
```

user service

```
import { Injectable, Optional } from '@angular/core';
import { BehaviorSubject } from 'rxjs/index';

import { User } from '../models/User';
import { UserStatusService } from './user-status.service';

@Injectable({
  providedIn: 'root'
})

export class UserService {

  private user: User = new User(1, '', '', '', '', {}, {
    fruitMet: false,
    vegMet: false,
    proteinMet: false,
    grainMet: false
  }, false, 'kevin@kevinruse.com');

  currentUser = new BehaviorSubject<User>(this.user);

  constructor(@Optional() private userStatusService: UserStatusService) {
    if (this.userStatusService) {
      this.userStatusService.getUserStatus(this.user);
    }
  }

  static storeUserLocal(user) {
    localStorage.setItem('currentUser', JSON.stringify(user));
  }

  getUser() {
    if (localStorage.getItem('currentUser')) {
      const user = JSON.parse(localStorage.getItem('currentUser'));
      this.currentUser = new BehaviorSubject(user);
      return user;
    } else {
      return this.user;
    }
  }

  updateUser(user: User) {
    user.id = 1;
    user.registered = true;
    user.reqsStatus = {fruitMet: false, vegMet: false, proteinMet: false, grainMet: false};
    this.currentUser.next(user);
  }
}
```

Homework: Refactor Message component to use the BehaviorSubject and currentUser property

If you do not attempt this challenge exercise, you will need to comment the message component from the plate.component.html as shown below with the strikethrough.

```
  <div id="foodPlateWrapper">
    <div id="colwrap1">
      <img [src]="(currentUser?.reqsStatus.fruitMet) ? fruitFull :
fruitEmpty" id="fruit"/>
      <img [src]="(currentUser?.reqsStatus.vegMet) ? vegFull : vegEmpty"
id="veg"/></div>
    <div id="colwrap2">
      <img [src]="(currentUser?.reqsStatus.grainMet) ? grainDairyFull :
grainDairyEmpty" id="grain"/>
      <div id="logoContainer" class="clearFloat"></div>
      <img [src]="(currentUser?.reqsStatus.proteinMet) ? proteinFull :
proteinEmpty" id="protein"/>
      <div class="clearFloat"></div>
    </div>
    <img src="../../assets/images/plateImages/text.png" id="text" alt=""/>
  </div>
  <fp-message [user]="user"></fp-message>
</section>
```

Step 1 Remove the comment around `<fp-message>`.

Step 2 Remove the `[user]` binding frOm the `<fp-message>` element.

Step 3 Refactor all the necessary files so that the message component uses the same `BehaviorSubject` as the rest of the application.

Chapter summary

Observables are:

- An alternative way to handle asynchronous operations
- A collection of values over time
- Are utilized by Angular in Http Client and other parts of the framework
- Are implemented by Angular via the RxJS library

In this chapter, you learned what observables are and how they can be used to simplify the passing of data. You learned the limitation of Promises (return only one value, cannot be cancelled) and how to overcome those limitation by using Observables. You also got a brief look at RxJS and some of its many operators.

See http://reactivex.io/documentation/operators.html#alphabetical for a list of its 100+ operators.

Chapter 13 Quiz

https://tinyurl.com/uwm4n7o

1) What are some of the fundamental differences between promises and observables?

2) What is wrong with the code below?

data.service.ts

```
getProducts() {
        this.http.get(this.productUrl)
}
```

data.component.ts

```
constructor(dataService: DataService) {}

getProducts() {
    this.dataService.getProducts()
}
```

data.component.html

```
...
<li *ngFor="let product of products">{{ product.description}}</li>
```

3) What code is missing from this code snippet?

```
import { take, map, combineAll } from 'rxjs/operators';
import { interval } from 'rxjs';

// emit every 1s, take 2
const source$ = interval(1000).take(2);
```

Next chapter

In the next chapter you will learn all about getting data by making HTTP requests using Angular's HTTPClient module.

Chapter 14
Http

Chapter 14: HTTP

Objectives

- Understand today's options for making HTTP requests
- Explore the limitations of today's options
- Describe how HTTPClient module uses observables
- Get data by making an HTTP get request
- Create a service that returns an observable
- Build a master-detail page

Introduction

In this chapter, you learn how to make Http requests, but we also take a deeper dive in to Observables and the role they play in streaming data and services that use Http.

14.0 Getting data into the application: Current methods

Most enterprise web applications make requests to the server for data. Getting data into your application typically involves one or more of the following techniques.

- Ajax calls
- WebSockets
- IndexDB
- LocalStorage
- ServiceWorkers

14.0.1 AJAX : Current methods

AJAX calls have historically been a common technique to get data into an application. Past methodologies for making these Ajax requests include:

- XMLHttpRequest object
- Promises API
- Fetch API

Each of these methods have some drawbacks. For example, promises can't be cancelled. If a user triggers a Http request and then leaves the page or component that made the request, the call is still made. This is just one example, when the ability to cancel an Http request would come in handy. Promises also add complexity to code that is dealing with multiple value responses. The XMLHttpRequest object code easily becomes lengthy and complex when using callbacks to handle the asynchronous response. And finally, all techniques would benefit from the ability to easily transform the incoming data. The combination of the HttpModule and Observables help overcome these limitations.

14.1 Building an HTTP Service class

The components in your application should never directly access the data they need via the HTTP module. This approach would quickly become difficult to maintain and the components as well as the data could not be easily shared. Instead, you should create a service. The job of the service will be to access and return the data. The service will be injectable so that it can be easily shared among components.

A reminder about services from the Angular documentation.

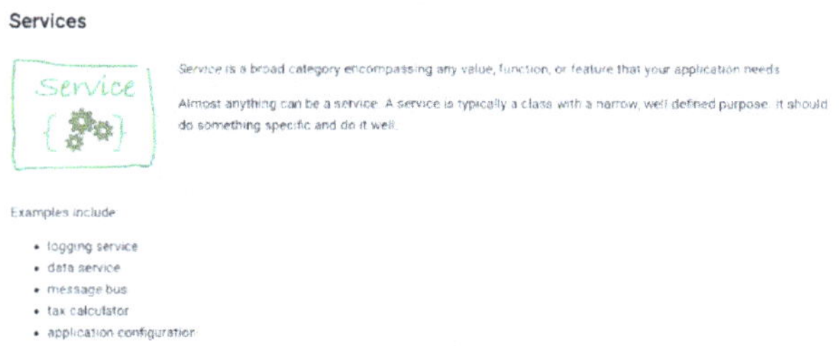

Services

Service is a broad category encompassing any value, function, or feature that your application needs.

Almost anything can be a service. A service is typically a class with a narrow, well defined purpose. It should do something specific and do it well.

Examples include:

- logging service
- data service
- message bus
- tax calculator
- application configuration

14.1.1 Version 2 vs. Version 4

Angular 2 used the HttpModule to make Http requests. Angular 4 has maintained this module but has reimplemented it with new features in a module called HttpClientModule. The new module is available in the package '@angular/common/http' and it will be used in this chapter. The basic steps include:

Import the HttpClientModule in the application's root module (app.module.ts).

- This makes the HttpClient available to the applications components.

To use the HttpClientModule in a component you inject it in the class constructor.

- This makes it possible, within the component class, to use get, post, put, delete, patch, head and jsonp methods.

14.1.2 Importing the HttpClientModule

To use the HttpClient you will first need to import the HttpClientModule that provides it. This is typically done via the application module as shown in the code snippet below.

```
…
@NgModule({
      imports: [BrowserModule, HttpClientModule],
})
export class AppModule {}
```

14.1.3 Injecting the HttpClient

The HttpClient is a service and therefore is injected into any components or services that require it. An example of dependency injection in action appears in the code snippet below which shows the HttpClient being injected into a component via the constructor function.

```
constructor(private http: HttpClient) {}
```

14.1.4 Making Http requests

Making Http requests is simply a matter of calling the correct method of the HttpClient as shown below.

```
ngOnInit(): void {
      this.http.get('/api/food');
}
…
```

4.2 HttpClientModule and Observables

You can fetch data with any of the API's already mentioned: Fetch or Promises. Both APIs will invoke the Http request and return promises. However, promises are different from Observables (which are returned by Angular's Http modules).

14.2.1 Promises vs. Observables

Angular's Http modules all use an RxJS observable-based API. In short, making Http calls made within Angular's framework return an Observable. Observables are basically inert, meaning they are inactive. The observable is triggered by a method called subscribe which activates the stream. See the previous chapter for more information about the differences between promises and observables.

14.2.2 Helpful information about Http Observables

- Nothing happens when you create an observable; you must subscribe to it
- Each subscription to an observable, triggers a new HTTP request
- If the Http request fails, the observable emits an error
- Observables can be easily composed after subscribing to them with methods like map and filter
- Severable observables can create a combined observable
- Observables can be cached
- A second http call can be invoked that uses the observable returned by the first http call

42—Guided Exercise: Making a get request with HttpClient

In this exercise, you get a json file from the server via an http get request.

Step 1 Confirm that the src/assets/server folder contains the requirements.json. If not, copy "angular-class-files/foodPlate-files/assets/server/requirements.json" to the foodPlate-cli project's src/assets/server folder. This is the json file that you will get via HttpClient in this guided exercise.

Step 2 Open app.module and include the HttpClientModule with the other imports at the top of the file as shown below.

```
import { HttpClientModule } from '@angular/common/http';
```

Step 3 Add the HttpClientModule to the imports array as shown below.

```
...
@NgModule({
  imports: [
    CommonModule, BrowserModule, FoodGroupsModule, AppRoutingModule,
FormsModule, ReactiveFormsModule, HttpClientModule
  ]
```

Step 4 Using a terminal, create a service using the cli command shown below.

```
ng g s services/requirements
```

Step 5 Modify the service as shown below in bold.

```
import { Injectable } from '@angular/core';
import { HttpClient } from '@angular/common/http';

@Injectable({
  providedIn: 'root'
})

@Injectable()
export class RequirementsService {
  private requirementsUrl: string = 'assets/server/requirements.json';

  constructor(private http: HttpClient) {
  }

  getRequirements(): void {
    this.http.get(this.requirementsUrl);
  }
}
```

Step 6 Open app.component.ts and inject the service. Don't forget to import the service as well.

```
constructor(private userService: UserService, private titleService: Title,
private reqsService: RequirementsService) {}
```

Step 7 Inside of a console log statement, call the service's `getRequirements()` method from the `ngOnInit()` lifecycle hook method.

```
  ngOnInit() {
    this.titleService.setTitle('Welcome to FoodPlate!');
```

```
    this.user = this.userService.getUser();
    this.userService.currentUser.subscribe(user => this.currentUser = user);
    console.log(this.reqsService.getRequirements());
}
```

Step 8 The console should now log "`undefined`" for the get request, because the request is not made until it is subscribed to. Return to the requirements.service.ts and modify the getRequirements method as shown below in bold.

```
getRequirements() {
    this.http.get(this.requirementsUrl).subscribe();
}
```

Step 9 Now that you have subscribed to the get request, check the application in Chrome with the Network tab of the DevTools open to trace the network traffic. Your results should look like the screenshot below.

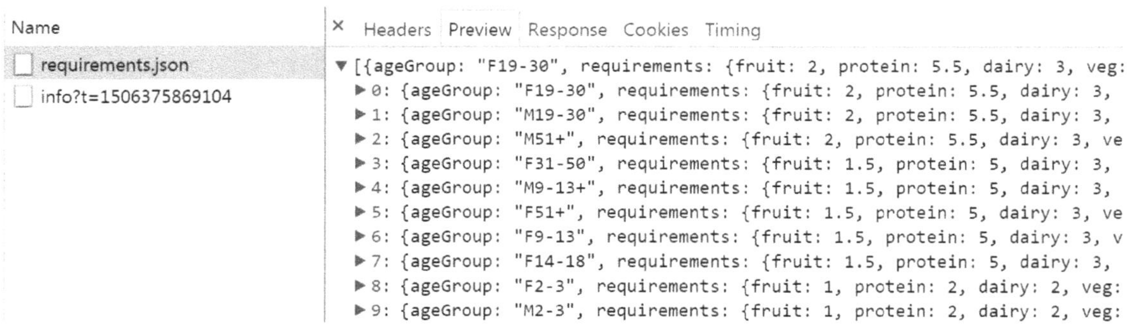

Step 10 In the following step you store the results of the request to requirements.json. In preparation for this, create a file called requirement.ts inside of the "models" folder as shown below. This interface file will describe the abstract type "Requirement" and will not contain any code (like a class does). The CLI command is:

```
ng g i models/requirement
```

```
export interface Requirement {
    ageGroup: string;
    requirements: object;
}
```

Step 11 To store the results of the requirements.json, give the app.component a "requirements" property datatyped to an Array of Requirements

```
private requirements: Array<Requirement>;
```

Step 12 Modify the getRequirements method in requirements.service.ts so that it returns an observable that holds an array of Requirement objects. Remove the subscribe() method. Remember to import both the Observable and Requirement classes.

```
getRequirements(): Observable<Requirement[]>{
        return this.http.get<Requirement[]>(this.requirementsUrl);
}
```

Due to the use of the Observable, you need to import from rxjs via the import statements below. Note you also need to import the Requirement from models.

```
import {Observable} from 'rxjs/index';
import {Requirement} from '../models/requirement';
```

You will get a warning in your IDE to import the Requirement object, so you will create that next.

Step 13 Make sure you have removed the subscribe method from the getRequirements method per step 1. The response will now be handled in app.component.ts. Open and modify app.component.ts as shown below. The relevant changes are shown in bold

```
import { Component, OnInit, ViewEncapsulation } from '@angular/core';

import { User } from './models/User';
import { UserService } from './services/user.service';
import { RequirementsService } from './services/requirements.service';
import { Requirement } from './models/Requirement';

@Component({
  selector: 'fp-app',
  templateUrl: './app.component.html',
  styleUrls: ['./app.component.css'],
  encapsulation: ViewEncapsulation.None

})
export class AppComponent implements OnInit{

    currentUser: User;
    private requirements: Array<Requirement>;

    constructor(private userService: UserService, private reqsService:
RequirementsService) {
    }

    ngOnInit() {
     this.titleService.setTitle('Welcome to FoodPlate!');
      this.userService.currentUser.subscribe(user => this.currentUser = user);
      this.reqsService.getRequirements().subscribe(
            reqs => {
                 this.requirements = reqs;
                console.log(this.requirements);
               console.log(this.requirements[1].ageGroup);
            });
    }
}
```

Step 14 Save and test the application in Chrome with the DevTools console open and examine the log statements.

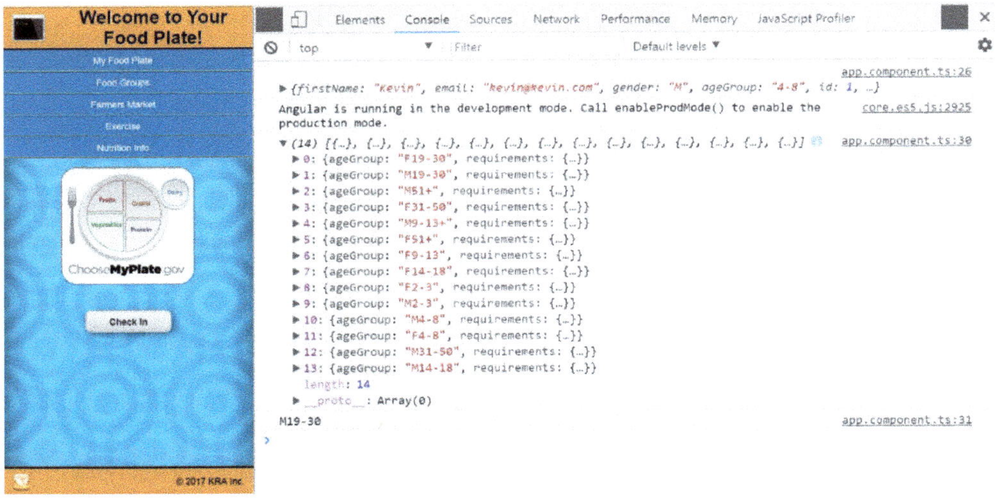

Later in the course, you will make use of this data. For now, consider it your introduction to HTTP as we continue to learn and use the HttpClient module.

43—Guided Exercise: Starting a mock server to store data

For this chapter, you will need to get data from a server. You will be retrieving food nutrition data including the amount of protein, calories, vitamins, minerals and various nutrients found in a large database of food products. There is a small food data file called food-short.json and a much larger file called food.json (both files store the data in JSON format). You will be installing and using a free utility that creates "a full fake REST API with zero coding" called JSON Server. If you are unable to install json-server, you can use the local files provided.

To prepare for the upcoming lessons on HTTP, install the JSON server using the steps below.

Step 1 Install JSON-server from node.js or in the Terminal of your IDE with the command shown below.

```
npm install json-server -g --save-dev
```

Step 2 Confirm the assets folder contains a server folder with food-short.json.

Step 3 Using node.js or a command line terminal, navigate to the src/assets/server folder and test the json-server with the start command and the database json file shown below.

```
cd src\assets\server
json-server food-short.json -p 3004
```

Step 4 If the install is successful, the response should match the screen below.

```
Terminal
+ Local  Local (1)  Local (2)
x

C:\foodPlate-cli\src\assets\server>json-server food-short.json --port 3004

  \{^_^}/ hi!

  Loading food-short.json
  Done

  Resources
  http://localhost:3004/foodItems

  Home
  http://localhost:3004
```

Step 5 Test the json-server by opening a web browser and going to the following url:

http://localhost:3004

Step 6 If the json-server is up and running you should see the following screen.

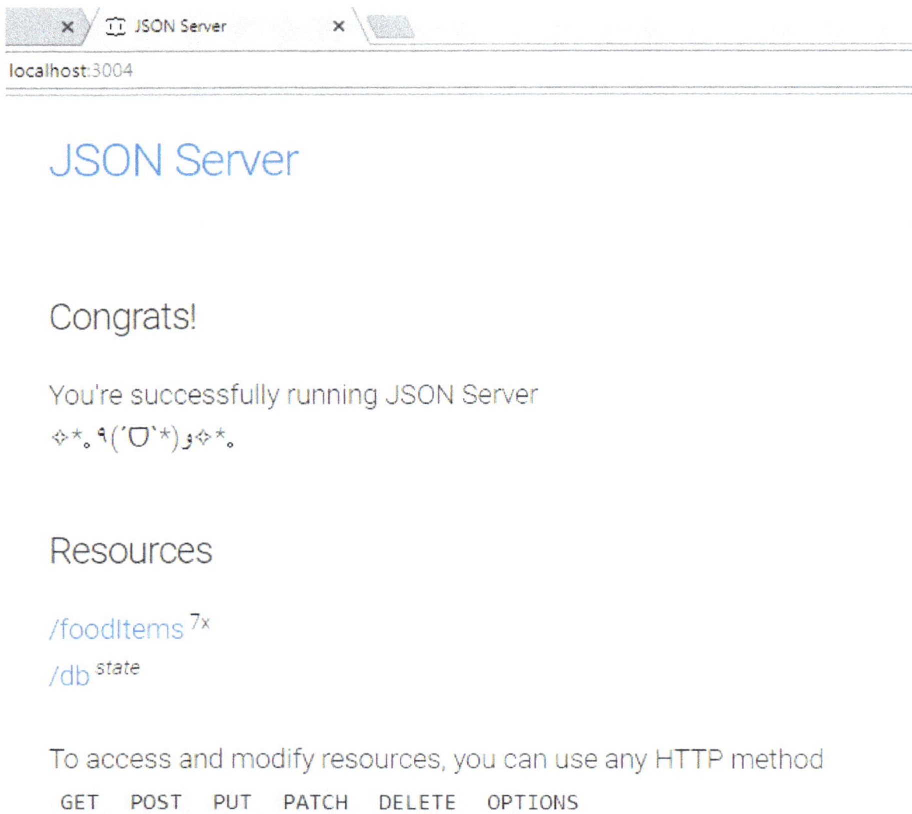

Step 7 Click on the /foodItems list to see the returned json. The food-short.json file contains just a snippet of seven food items while the food.json file is much longer and will be used later in this chapter.

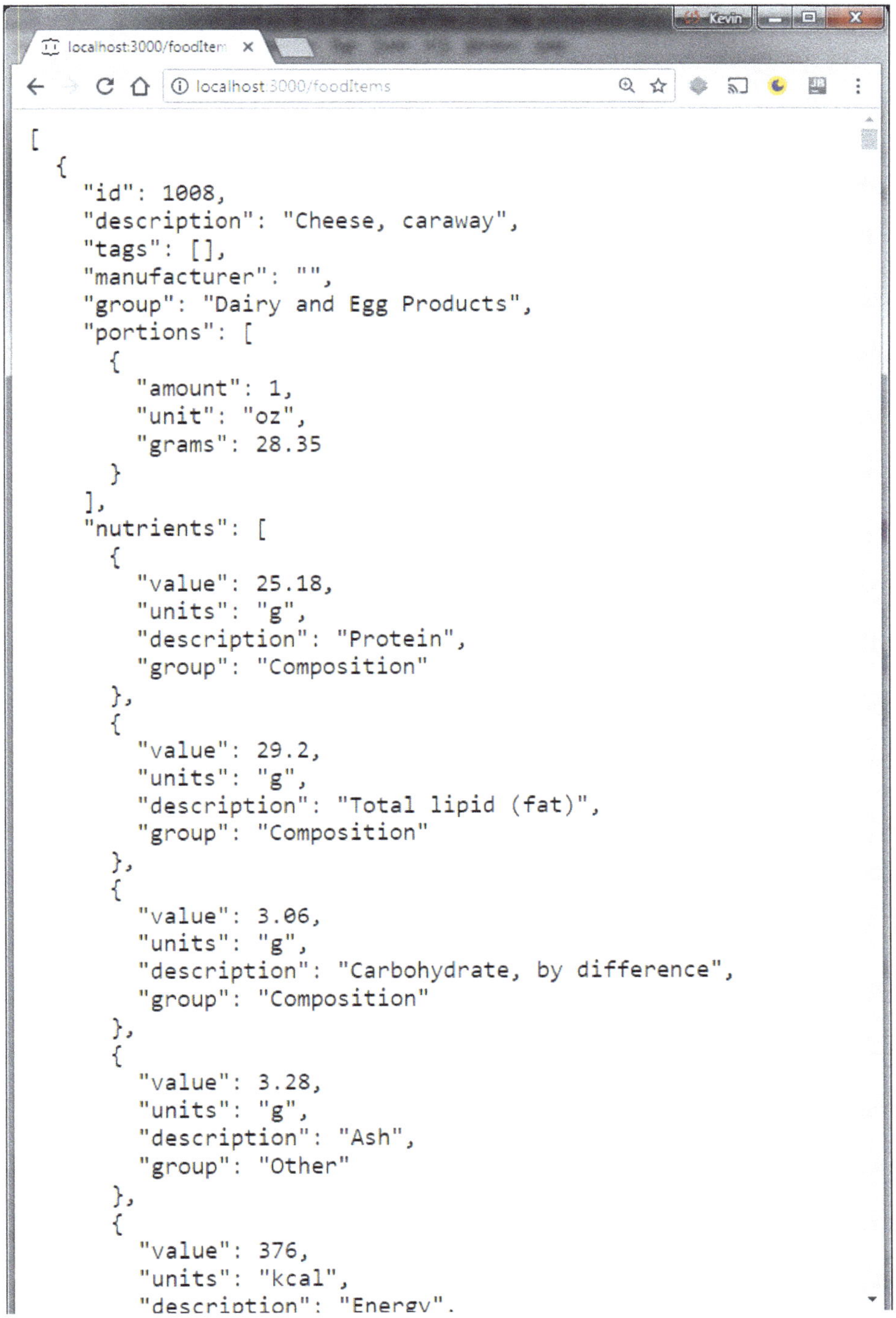
localhost:3000/foodItem
localhost:3000/foodItems
Kevin
[
  {
    "id": 1008,
    "description": "Cheese, caraway",
    "tags": [],
    "manufacturer": "",
    "group": "Dairy and Egg Products",
    "portions": [
      {
        "amount": 1,
        "unit": "oz",
        "grams": 28.35
      }
    ],
    "nutrients": [
      {
        "value": 25.18,
        "units": "g",
        "description": "Protein",
        "group": "Composition"
      },
      {
        "value": 29.2,
        "units": "g",
        "description": "Total lipid (fat)",
        "group": "Composition"
      },
      {
        "value": 3.06,
        "units": "g",
        "description": "Carbohydrate, by difference",
        "group": "Composition"
      },
      {
        "value": 3.28,
        "units": "g",
        "description": "Ash",
        "group": "Other"
      },
      {
        "value": 376,
        "units": "kcal",
        "description": "Energy",

44—Guided Exercise: Create a service that returns an Observable

In this exercise, you create the service that will fetch the nutrition data while learning more about the http calls return type: Observable.

Step 1 Create a typescript file called food.service.ts using the Angular-cli command.

```
ng g s services/food
```

Step 2 In the food.service.ts, add the necessary class to create an injectable service using the HttpClient.

```
import { Injectable } from '@angular/core';
import {HttpClient} from '@angular/common/http';
```

Step 3 Declare the url used to fetch the data. The json-server defaults to port 3000, but this can be changed with the command: `$ json-server dataFileName.json --port 3004.` This was done in the previous exercise.

```
private foodUrl: string = 'http://localhost:3004/foodItems';
```

Step 4 Inject the `HttpClient` in the constructor.

```
constructor(private http: HttpClient) {
}
```

Step 5 Declare the method that will make the http get request for the nutrition data.

```
loadFood() {
     return this.http.get(this.foodUrl);
}
```

Step 6 Next create the food.component.ts file that will display the nutrition data.

```
ng g c food -m app
```

Step 7 Open nav.component.html and add a link to the nav bar called Nutrition Info.

```
    …<li><a routerLink="exercises"
routerLinkActive="active">Exercise</a></li>
    <li><a routerLink="nutritionInfo" routerLinkActive="active">Nutrition
Info</a></li>
</ul>
…
```

Step 8 Add the route to app.routing.module.ts and remember to import the module.

```
…
{ path: 'exercises', component: ExercisesComponent },
{ path: 'nutritionInfo', component: FoodComponent },
...foodGroupsRoutes,
…
```

Step 9 Confirm the FoodComponent has been declared in the app.module.ts as shown below in bold.

```
…
declarations: [ AppComponent, HeaderComponent, FooterComponent,
MainComponent, PlateComponent, MessageComponent, HomeBtnComponent,
```

```
NavComponent, RegisterComponent, FarmersMarketsComponent, ExercisesComponent,
FoodGroupsComponent, FruitDetailComponent, ProteinDetailComponent,
VegetableDetailComponent, GrainsDetailComponent, TodaysGoalsComponent,
FoodComponent ],
...
```

Step 10 Modify the food.component.ts file as shown below in bold.

```
import { Component, OnInit } from '@angular/core';
import {FoodService} from '../services/food.service';

@Component({
  selector: 'fp-food',
  templateUrl: './food.component.html',
  styleUrls: ['./food.component.css']
})
export class FoodComponent implements OnInit {

  constructor(private foodService: FoodService) { }

  ngOnInit() {
    console.log(this.foodService.loadFood());
  }
}
```

Step 11 Save all the files and run the application in Chrome with the console open. After clicking on the Nutrition Info link, examine the results of the console.log statement you added in step 10.

```
▼ Observable {_isScalar: false, source: Observable, operator: MapOperator}
  ▶ operator: MapOperator {thisArg: undefined, project: ƒ}
  ▼ source: Observable
    ▶ operator: FilterOperator {thisArg: undefined, predicate: ƒ}
    ▼ source: Observable
      ▶ operator: MergeMapOperator {concurrent: 1, project: ƒ}
      ▶ source: Observable {_isScalar: false, _subscribe: ƒ}
        _isScalar: false
      ▶ __proto__: Object
      _isScalar: false
    ▶ __proto__: Object
    _isScalar: false
  ▶ __proto__: Object
```

You should now see observable returned by loadFood(); The next step is to prepare the food component to subscribe to the observable.

45–Guided Exercise: Subscribe to an observable

In this guided exercise, you subscribe to the observable returned by the loadFood method in the food service.

Step 1 Add subscribe method to the food.component.ts as shown below in bold.

```
ngOnInit() {
    console.log(this.foodService.loadFood());
    this.foodService.loadFood()
        .subscribe();
}
```

Step 2 Pass the success handler to the subscribe method as shown below in bold.

```
ngOnInit() {
    console.log(this.foodService.loadFood());
    this.foodService.loadFood()
        .subscribe(
            data => console.log(data)
))
```

Now that you have invoked subscribe the get request is triggered.

Step 3 Save the file and run the application in Chrome with the console open and you should see the data logged from the success handler: `data => console.log(data);`

```
                              food.component.ts:15
▶ Observable
  {_isScalar: false, source: Observable, operator
                              food.component.ts:18
▼ (7) [{…}, {…}, {…}, {…}, {…}, {…}, {…}]
  ▶ 0: {id: 1008, description: "Cheese, caraway",
  ▶ 1: {id: 1009, description: "Cheese, cheddar",
  ▶ 2: {id: 1018, description: "Cheese, edam", tag
  ▶ 3: {id: 1019, description: "Cheese, feta", tag
  ▶ 4: {id: 1028, description: "Cheese, mozzarella
  ▶ 5: {id: 1029, description: "Cheese, mozzarella
  ▶ 6: {id: 1038, description: "Cheese, romano", t
    length: 7
  ▶ __proto__: Array(0)
```

In this exercise, you learned how to get the data from the injected service and pass it to a component property. Eventually, you will display the data in the component's view template. But first, let's look at how we can track the progress of the Http request.

46—Guided Exercise: Track the progress of an Http request

In this exercise, you track the progress of an Http request. You will change the url of the JSON data so that it returns a much longer file (over 6,300 food items!).

Step 1 Modify the food service as shown below in bold.

```
import { Injectable } from '@angular/core';
import {HttpClient, HttpRequest} from '@angular/common/http';

@Injectable()
export class FoodService {
  private foodUrl:string = 'http://localhost:3004/foodItems';
  foodRequest = new HttpRequest('GET', this.foodUrl, {reportProgress: true});
```

Step 2 Stop the json-server running on port 3004 and restart it with the following commands:

```
CTRL + C
Y

json-server food.json -p 3004
```

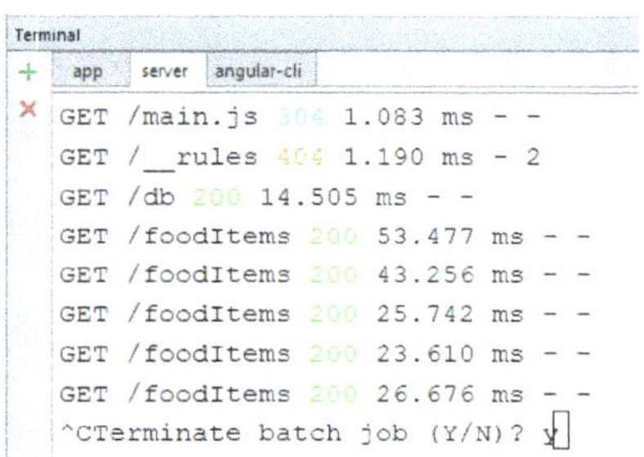

Step 3 Write a `getFoodsProgress()` method in the food.service.ts. file. This method will call the foodRequest Http get request you created in step 1. The added argument config object {reportProgress: true} will allow the tracking of the download progress via the bytes loaded and bytes total properties of the DownloadProgress event.

```
getFoodsProgress() {
    this.http.request(this.foodRequest).subscribe(event => {
      if (event.type === HttpEventType.DownloadProgress) {
        const percentDone = Math.round(100 * event.loaded / event.total);
        console.log(`File is ${percentDone}% downloaded.`);
      } else if (event instanceof HttpResponse) {
        console.log('File is completed downloaded');
      }
    });
}
```

Step 4 Be sure to import the necessary classes in food.service.ts as shown below.

```
import {HttpClient, HttpEventType, HttpRequest, HttpResponse} from
'@angular/common/http';
```

Step 5 Modify the food.component.ts so that it logs the new `getFoodsProgress` method instead of `loadFood`.

```
ngOnInit() {
    console.log(this.foodService.getFoodsProgress());
   /* this.foodService.loadFood()
      .subscribe(data => console.log(data)); */
}
```

Run the file in Chrome and the console will log undefined in response to the code you added above.

Note This will not work because the server must send the Content-Length header so that the request can be measured. The json-server we are using provides the injection of middleware which could be used to add an X-Content-Length header. Therefore, we can implement one of two solutions:

- Step 6: Hard-code the total bytes of the download
- Step 6A: Inject middleware and refactor getFoodsProgress

Step 6 Modify the code to hard-code the total bytes with the value 53370429.

```
getFoodsProgress(): void {
    this.http.request(this.foodRequest).subscribe(event => {
      const totalBytes = 53370429;
      if (event.type === HttpEventType.DownloadProgress) {
        const percentDone = Math.round(100 * event.loaded / totalBytes);
        console.log(`File is ${percentDone}% downloaded.`);
      }
      else if (event instanceof HttpResponse) {
        console.log('File is completed downloaded ');
      }
    })
  };
```

Optional To implement step 6A, follow the lettered instructions below.

a. Shut down the json-server via Control + C followed by Y for yes.
b. Restart the server via the command:
   node content-length-header.js
c. Refactor the getFoodsProgress() method as shown below.
d. You may need to install json-server locally.

```
getFoodsProgress(): void {
   let totalBytes: number;
   this.http.request(this.foodRequest).subscribe(
        event => {
                  if (event.type === HttpEventType.ResponseHeader) {
                 console.log(event.headers.keys().map(key => `${key}:
${event.headers.get(key)}`));
               totalBytes = Number.parseInt(event.headers.get('x-content-
length', 10));
    }
    else if (event.type === HttpEventType.DownloadProgress) {
        const percentDone = Math.round(100 * event.loaded / totalBytes);
```

```
            console.log(`File is ${percentDone}% downloaded.`);
                }
        else if (event instanceof HttpResponse) {
        console.log("File is completed downloaded")
            }
    })
}
```

e. Refactor the `foodUrl` string to port 3005 as shown below in bold.
   private foodUrl:string = 'http://localhost:**3005**/foodItems';

Step 7 Run the application with the console open and you should see the progress logged as shown below. The food.json file is very large and will be slow to load. If you are testing a short file and/or your connection is fast, you can throttle it from the DevTools Network panel as shown below.

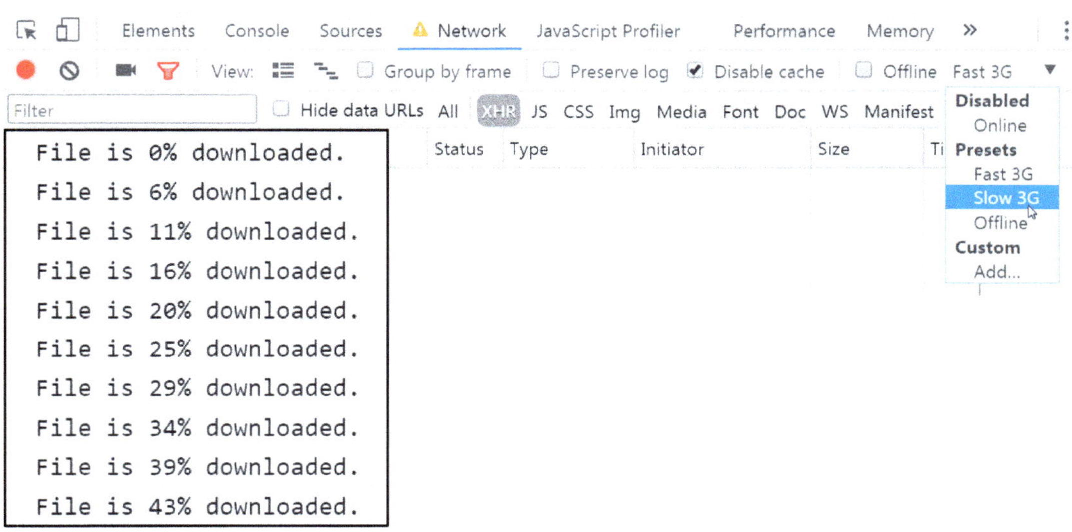

Step 8 If you used the step 6A solution, be sure to return the code back to the Step 6 solution.

Exercise summary

In this exercise, you reworked the initial request by writing it in a property called foodRequest. Using the HttpRequest constructor function, you created a get request. You called the request from the getFoodsProgress method and subscribed to it. At the subscription level, you checked the event.type property to see if it was a DownloadProgress event. Because you passed the reportProgress property with a value of true, you could then access the event's total and loaded properties represent total number of bytes and bytes loaded, respectively. After a bit of simple math, you logged the progress to the console. Finally, you checked for the HttpResponse to log that the file download had completed.

47–Guided Exercise: Displaying the data in the view

In this exercise, you display the data provided by the service in the food component's view template. The basic steps include:

- Create a food class data model to hold the array of food items that come back from the service.
- Modify the food component's css to accommodate the new food items.
- Refactor the food.service.ts to return an Observable of Food Items.
- Modify the food.component with the necessary code to handle the following
  - The status of the http service
  - An error message and error handling for the http service

Step 1 Create a data model called Food.ts in the "models" folder. Use the command:

```
ng g i models/food
```

The data model is shown below.

```
export interface Food {
    id: number;
    description: string;
    tags: Array<string>;
    manufacturer: string;
    group: string;
    nutrients: Array<object>;
    portions: Array<object>;
}
```

Step 2 Open the food.component.ts file and add properties to:

- Track the loading status of the http request
- Handle any errors returned by the http service
- Hold the list of foods coming back from the service as an array of Food Items

```
...
export class FoodComponent implements OnInit {
  isLoading: boolean = true;
  errorMessage: string;
  foodList: Food[];
...
```

Step 3 Import the Food class in food.component.ts.

```
import { Food } from '../models/food';
```

Step 4 Prepare the food component to display the food items, by modifying the view template in food.component.html as shown below.

```
<section>
  <select name="foods" id="foods" size="10" class="selectList">
    <option *ngFor="let item of foodList">{{item.description}}</option>
  </select>
</section>
```

Step 5 Modify the food component styles in food.component.css. You can copy and paste this code from assets/css/ food-component-css.css.

```
#foods {
    width: 80%;
}

.selectMenu {
    padding: .45em;
    margin: 0 auto;
    margin-bottom: 1em;
    border: 1px solid #d4d4d4;
    border-radius: .35em;
    line-height: 1.5em;
    box-shadow: inset 0 2px 2px #ececec;
    display: block;
    width: 40%;
    text-align: center;
}

.selectList {
    border: 1px solid #ccc;
    border-radius: .45em;
    width: 60%;
}

.errMessage, .loadingMessage {
    background-color: #fff;
    font-size: 1em;
    font-weight: 700;
    margin: 1em auto;
    padding: 1em;
    border: 1px solid #ccc;
    border-radius: .35em;
    text-align: center;
}

.loadingMessage {
    animation: pulse 1.75s infinite;
}

@keyframes pulse {
    0% {
        background-color: #333333;
        color: #fff;
    }
    100% {
        background-color: #f00;
        color: #000;
    }
}
```

In step 6 below, you refactor the `loadFood` method of the food.service so that it returns an Observable. The Observable may be typed (at least) two ways: `Observable<Any>` which removes any type or safety checking via TypeScript or `<T>`. The `<T>` datatype serves as a variable that will hold the type we don't know at this time. The type will be supplied later by the caller of the function.

Step 6 Refactor the loadFood method of the food.service so that it returns an Observable of Food objects.

```
loadFood<T>(): Observable<T> {
    return this.http.get<T>(this.foodUrl);
}
```

- Rename the loadFood method `getAllFoods()`.
- Write a method called `OnInit` that calls `getAllFoods()`.
- Call the OnInit method from the constructor function.

The entire food.service.ts is shown below with the refactoring shown in bold.

```
import { Injectable } from '@angular/core';
import {HttpClient, HttpEventType, HttpRequest, HttpResponse} from
'@angular/common/http';
import {Observable} from 'rxjs/Observable';

import {Food} from '../models/Food';

@Injectable({
  providedIn: 'root'
})

export class FoodService {

  private foodUrl:string = 'http://localhost:3004/foodItems';
  foodRequest = new HttpRequest('GET', this.foodUrl, {reportProgress: true}
 );


  constructor(private http: HttpClient)  {
         this.getAllFoods();
  }

  getFoodsProgress(): void {
    this.http.request(this.foodRequest).subscribe(event => {
      if (event.type === HttpEventType.DownloadProgress) {
        const totalBytes = 53370429;
        const percentDone = Math.round(100 * event.loaded/totalBytes);
        console.log(`File is ${percentDone}% downloaded.`);
      }
      else if (event instanceof HttpResponse) {
        console.log("File is completed downloaded")
      }
    })
  };


  getAllFoods<T>(): Observable<T> {
    return this.http.get<T>(this.foodUrl);
  }
}
```

Step 7 In food.component.ts, write a `getFood()` method that subscribes to the food service's observable.

```
getFood(): void {
this.foodService.getAllFoods<Food[]>()
        .subscribe(
             (food) => {
               this.foodList = food;
             },
             (error) => {
               this.errorMessage = error.message;
               this.handleError(this.errorMessage);
             },
             () => this.isLoading = false
        );
}
```

Step 8 Write an error handling in the event the http request fails.

```
handleError(err): void {
  console.log(err);
}
```

Step 9 Refactor the `ngOnInit()` method as shown below. Comment the call to `getFoodsProgress()`.

```
ngOnInit() {
     this.getFood();
     // console.log(this.foodService.getFoodsProgress());
}
```

Step 10 Modify the view template so that it displays the correct content based on the success or failure of the http request. The relevant code is shown below in bold.

```
<section class="loadingMessage" *ngIf="isLoading && !errorMessage">
  WAIT!!! ...Retrieving Nutrition Data...
</section>

<section *ngIf="!isLoading">
  <select name="foods" id="foods" size="10" class="selectList">
    <option *ngFor="let item of foodList">{{item.description}}</option>
  </select>
</section>

<section class="errMessage" *ngIf="errorMessage">
  {{errorMessage}}
</section>
```

Step 11 Run the app in the web browser and you should first see the "WAIT! ... Retrieving Nutrition Data..." message, followed by the food data displayed in the view template.

1–Optional Exercise: Using header information

If you would like to see the header of the get request, you can modify the `get()` method.

Step 1 In the food.service.ts file, comment the code inside the existing getAllFoods() method. Rewrite the get request in the `getAllFoods()` method as shown below in bold.

```
getAllFoods<Food>(): Observable<Food> {
  // return this.http.get<Food>(this.foodUrl);
  return this.http.get(this.foodUrl, {observe: 'response'});
}
```

The code will no longer compile.

Step 2 Run the app in Chrome (be sure to go the Nutrition Info section) and examine the DevTools. You should see the error message shown below.

```
▶ERROR Error: Cannot find a differ supporting object '[object Object]' of type    FoodComponent.html:7
'object'. NgFor only supports binding to Iterables such as Arrays.
    at NgForOf.webpackJsonp.../../../common/@angular/common.es5.js.NgForOf.ngOnChanges (common.es5.js:1
```

This is because the data is now in the body property of the Http response. To see the response data, modify the food.component.ts file to assign the foodList property to the data.body property of the response object. First, move the code into its own function called handleFood().

Compare the first getAllFoods shown below. It returns an Observable of Food objects, but the refactored get method will now return an HTTPResponse object.

```
getAllFoods<Food>(): Observable<Food> {
    return this.http.get<Food>(this.foodUrl, {observe: 'response'});
}
```

The HttpResponse object needs to be handled in the component that gets the data – the food.component.ts

Step 3 Open the food.component.ts and modify the `ngOnInit()` method to call `handleFood()`.

```
ngOnInit() {
    this.handleFood();
}
```

Step 4 Comment the getFood() method in food.component.ts.

Step 5 Write the `handleFood` method and pass the error and complete handlers. You will need to provide the `errorMessage` property to the component as well. The exported class is shown below, with the modifications in bold.

```
export class FoodComponent implements OnInit {
    errorMessage:string;
    foodList: any = [];
    isLoading:boolean = true;

    constructor(private foodService:FoodService) { }

  ngOnInit() {
    console.log(this.foodService.loadFood());
    this.handleFood();
```

```
  }

  handleFood(): void {
      const food$ = this.foodService.getAllFoods()
          .subscribe(
              (data) => {
                  console.log(data);
                  this.foodList = data.body;
              },
              (err) => this.errorMessage = err,
              () => this.isLoading = false
          );
  }
}
```

Step 6 Before testing in the browser, remove the <Food>[]> datatyping from the commented getFood() method in food.component.ts as shown below with a strikethrough.

```
getFood() {
    this.foodService.getAllFoods<Food[]>()
      .subscribe(
        (food) => {
          this.foodList = food;
        },
...
```

Step 7 Test the file in the browser and view the HttpResponse object returned by the console log statement.

Step 8 Delete the added line of code from step 1 in the `getAllFoods()` method with the `{observe: 'response}` and remove the comments from the original `getAllFoods()` method content (the one shown below).

```
return this.http.get<Food>(this.foodUrl);
```

Step 9 Comment the `handleFood()` method of the food.component.ts and remove the comments from getFood() and refactor as shown below in bold.

```
getFood(): void {
    this.foodService.getAllFoods<Food[]>()
        .subscribe(
            (food) => {
              this.foodList = food;
```

```
                },
                (error) => {
                  this.errorMessage = error.message;
                  this.handleError(this.errorMessage);
                } ,
                () => this.isLoading = false
          );
    }
```

Step 10 Refactor ngOnInit() to call getFood().

```
ngOnInit() {
    this.getFood();
}
```

Step 11 Return the foodList property to its original datatype.

```
foodList: Food[];
```

Step 12 Refactor the getAllFoods() method in food.service.ts as shown below.

```
getAllFoods<Food>(): Observable<Food> {
    return this.http.get<Food>(this.foodUrl);
    //return this.http.get(this.foodUrl, {observe: 'response'});
}
```

Step 13 Save all files and test in Chrome.

48–Guided Exercise: Create a master/detail page

In this exercise, you provide further details regarding the food items with a master/detail page using the json-server's REST API that currently provides the food data. See the finished product below which shows the new master/detail interface. A drop-down menu will allow the user to select foods from certain food groups. After filtering the groups on the list, the user can then drill down further to find nutrition data about each specific food item. For this exercise, you will simply log the nutrition data to the console. You can practice your UI skills by building the UI for the nutrition data, but that will not be part of this exercise.

Step 1 Open food.component.ts and create a property that will hold the food groups which will be retrieved from the http request made in the previous exercise.

```
foodGroups: Set<string> = new Set<string>();
```

Step 2 Write the method that will get the food groups.

```
getFoodGroups(food): void {
        food.forEach(food => {
          const group = food.group;
          this.foodGroups.add(group);
      });
      console.log(this.foodGroups);
}
```

Step 3 Open food.component.html and create a drop-down menu that displays the food groups. Place the code below the section element with the *ngIf directive as shown below in bold.

```
<section *ngIf="!isLoading">
    <select class="selectMenu" name="foodGroup" id="foodGroup">
      <option value="allFoods" selected>Select a food group</option>
      <option *ngFor="let group of foodGroups"
value="{{group}}">{{group}}</option>
    </select>
    <select name="foods" id="foods" size="10" class="selectList">
      <option *ngFor="let item of foodList">{{item.description}}</option>
    </select>
</section>
```

Step 4 In the food.component.ts `getFood()` method, call the `getFoodGroups()` method as shown below in bold.

```
getFood(): void {
    this.foodService.getAllFoods<Food[]>()
        .subscribe(
            (food) => {
              this.foodList = food;
              this.getFoodGroups(this.foodList);
            },
            (error) => {
              this.errorMessage = error.message;
              this.handleError(this.errorMessage);
            } ,
            () => this.isLoading = false
        );
  }
```

Next, we need to ensure that the foods displayed in the list, reflect the food choice shown in the new drop-down menu that was added in step 3.

Step 5 Create a property in food.component.ts to hold the food list that is displayed in the list control. This property will reflect the foods currently in the list, for example all the foods, or just the vegetables.

```
foodListByGroup: Food[] = this.foodList;
```

Step 6 Add the displayFood() method to the food.component.ts.

```
displayFoods(group): void {
        if (group === 'allFoods') {
            this.foodListByGroup = this.foodList;
        } else if(group !== 'allFoods') {
            this.foodListByGroup = this.foodList.filter((foods)=> {
                return foods.group === group;
            });
        }
}
```

Step 7 Call display foods in food.component.ts after the call to getFoodGroups that you added in step 4. The method call is shown below in bold.

```
getFood(): void {
    this.foodService.getAllFoods<Food[]>()
        .subscribe(
            (food) => {
              this.foodList = food;
              this.getFoodGroups(this.foodList);
              this.displayFoods('allFoods');
            }, ...
```

Step 8 In the `ngOnInit()` method of food.component, call `displayFoods()` and pass in the string 'allFoods'.

```
  ngOnInit() {
    this.getFood();
    this.displayFoods('allFoods');
  }
```

The only step left to wire the food groups drop-down menu to the correct display of food items is to add an event handler and have the list display only

Step 9 In food.component.html modify the select menu for the food groups as shown below in bold.

```
...
<select class="selectMenu" name="foodGroup" id="foodGroup"
(change)="displayFoods($event.target.value)">
    <option value="allFoods" selected>Select a food group</option>
    <option *ngFor="let group of foodGroups"
value="{{group}}">{{group}}</option>
<select name="foods" id="foods" size="10" class="selectList">
    <option *ngFor="let item of foodListByGroup">
          {{item.description}}
    </option>
  </select>
...
```

Step 10 Be sure that you have returned the `getAllFoods()` method in the foods.service.ts files to its original state, as shown below.

```
getAllFoods<Food>(): Observable<Food> {
        return this.http.get<Food>(this.foodUrl);
}
```

Step 11 Save and test the application in Chrome. Initially, the list should show all food groups. Select a food group from the drop-down menu and the list should be filtered to only show foods in the selected group.

Step 12 Add a `showNutrients()` method to the food component.

```
showNutrients(food): void {
        console.table(food.nutrients);
}
```

As stated in the introduction to this exercise, we will just be logging the nutrition information to the console.

Step 13 Call the showNutrients() method from the food.component.html using the option list as shown below in bold.

```
<select name="foods" id="foods" size="10" class="selectList">
  <option *ngFor="let item of foodListByGroup"
            (click)="showNutrients(item)">
```

```
            {{item.description}}
    </option>
</select>
```

Notice the binding on the click event that calls the `showNutrients()` method passing in the item clicked.

Step 14 Save and test the files in Chrome. Click on a food item and examine the console.

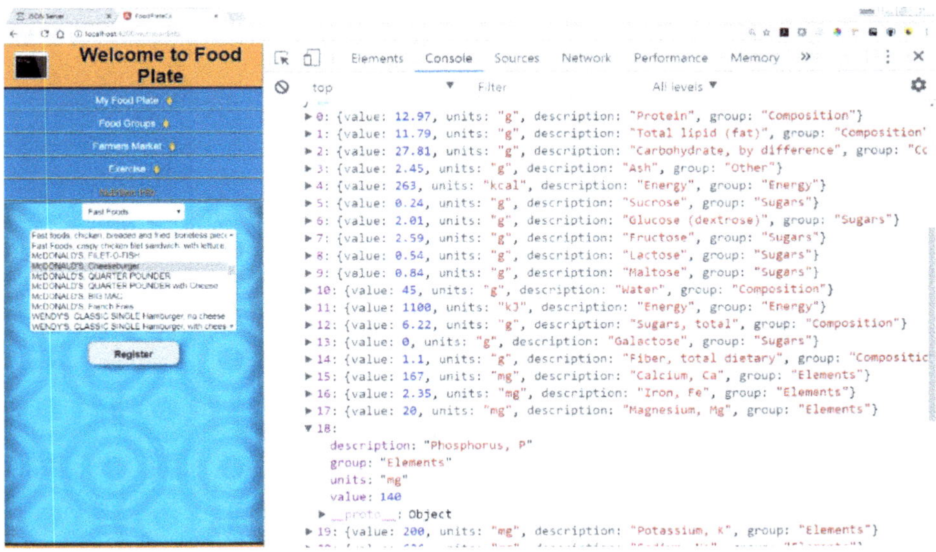

14.3 The Angular Material Component Development Kit

In the previous exercise, when activating the food groups drop down menu you will notice a perceivable lag in displaying the associated food groups in the list of foot items below the dropdown. A common solution for this lag time involves using the Angular Material Component Development Kit (CDK). The CDK is a set of tools the implement common user-interaction patterns that are presentation agnostic. The functionality is abstracted from the view. This CDK provides a scrolling package that can increase performance during scroll events. A tool in this package that can help the response time of the food list is the Virtual scrolling tool.

14.3.1 Virtual Scrolling

The <cdk-virtual-scrolling-viewport> displays large lists of elements in a performance enhancing way. Unlike the current state of the FoodPlate application's food list, the virtual-scrolling-viewport will render only the items that fit on the screen. Thus, 100's of items will be rendered dynamically during the scroll event. The height of the container element is made the same as the height of the total number of elements to be rendered and then renders only the items that fit in that view.

For more information about virtual scrolling as well as the Angular CDK, visit https://material.angular.io/cdk/categories.

49—Guided Exercise: Optional: Implement Virtual Scrolling

Step 1 Install the Angular CDK from the command line/terminal in your IDE.

```
npm install @angular/cdk --save
```

Step 2 Import the ScrollingModule in app.module.ts

```
import { ScrollingModule } from '@angular/cdk/scrolling';
...
  imports: [
            AppRoutingModule,
            BrowserModule,
            CommonModule,
            FormsModule,
            HttpClientModule,
            ReactiveFormsModule,
            ScrollingModule
  ],
```

Step 3 Open the food.component.html view template and comment the existing Food List `<select>` and `<option>` elements as shown below in bold.

```
<!--  <select name="foods" id="foods" size="10" class="selectList">
        <option *ngFor="let item of foodListByGroup"
                (click)="showNutrients(item)">
        {{item.description}}
        </option>
      </select>  -->
```

Change the select menu to an unordered list with a cd-virtual-scroll-viewport inside. Use an `ng-container` element to run the for loop through the foodListByGroup array. Be sure to add index as i.

```
<ul class="list">
    <cdk-virtual-scroll-viewport style="height: 180px" itemSize="15" >
      <ng-container *cdkVirtualFor="let item of foodListByGroup; index as i">
            <li (click)="showNutrients(item, i)" [ngClass]="{'active':
selectedIndex === i}"> {{item.description}} </li>
        </ng-container>
    </cdk-virtual-scroll-viewport>
</ul>
...
<section class="errMessage" *ngIf="errorMessage">
    {{errorMessage}}
</section>

<ng-container #foodDetailContainer></ng-container>
```

The `*cdkVirtualFor` is analogous to the `*ngFor`. The height style reflects the height of the total number of displayed items. This will take some trial and error as you write the CSS for the container element itself. The [ngClass] binding will apply a background color to the selected item. The click event handler will use the index to determine which item has been clicked or "selected." You will write the event handler in the next step.

Step 4 Open the food.component.ts and modify the showNutrients method to include the code that will highlight the selected item.

The additional code is shown below in bold. The added code includes two new properties: protein and selectedIndex.

```
  foodItem: Food;
  protein;
  selectedIndex: number;
...
```

Step 5 Add the select function and refactor the showNutrients method as shown below in bold.

```
  foodItem: Food;
  protein;
  selectedIndex: number;
...
  select(index: number): void {
    this.selectedIndex = index;
  }
...
  async showNutrients(food, index): Promise<any> {
    this.select(index);
    this.protein = food.nutrients[0].value;
    console.log(food.nutrients);
    console.log(this.protein + food.nutrients[0].units);
    this.foodItem = food;
    console.log(this.foodItem);
    this.foodDetailContainer.detach();
    await this.lazyLoadNutritionDetail();
  }
```

Step 6 Angular 9 allows the lazy loading of components (as opposed to lazy loading modules). Add the lazyLoadNutritionDetail method shown below. Note the use of the Angular component factory as introduced in the advanced directives section of this course.

```
private async lazyLoadNutritionDetail(): Promise<any> {
    const { NutritionDetailsComponent } = await import('../nutrition-
details/nutrition-details.component');
    const nutritionDetailFactory =
this.cfr.resolveComponentFactory(NutritionDetailsComponent);
    const { instance } =
this.foodDetailContainer.createComponent(nutritionDetailFactory, null,
this.injector);
    instance.foodItem = this.foodItem;
}
```

Step 7 Inject the ComponentFactoryResolver and Injector in the food.component.ts constructor function as shown below. Be sure to import the necessary classes.

```
constructor(private foodService: FoodService,
            private cfr: ComponentFactoryResolver,
            private injector: Injector) {
}
```

Step 8 Still inside food.component.ts, add the foodDetailContainer as a view child via the @ViewChild decorator and import the necessary classes.

```
@ViewChild('foodDetailContainer', {read: ViewContainerRef})
foodDetailContainer: ViewContainerRef;
```

Step 9 Create the lazy-loaded component called nutrition-details using the CLI.

```
ng g c nutrition-details -m app
```

Step 10 Create the following view template for nutrition-details. Note the data-bindings shown in bold.

```
<h2>Nutrition Details</h2>
<section>
    <table>
        <thead>
            <tr>
                <th>Protein</th>
                <th>Carbohydrate</th>
                <th>Total Lipid (Fat)</th>
            </tr>
        </thead>
        <tbody>
            <tr>
                <td>{{ foodItem.nutrients[0].value }} {{
foodItem.nutrients[0].units }}</td>
                <td>{{ foodItem.nutrients[2].value }} {{
foodItem.nutrients[2].units }}</td>
                <td>{{ foodItem.nutrients[1].value }} {{
foodItem.nutrients[1].units }}</td>
            </tr>
            </tbody>
    </table>
</section>
```

Step 11 Copy the CSS for the nutrition-details.component.css from the assets/css/ nutrition-detail-css.css file.

The nutrition details will have its foodItem input from its parent and logged to the console for in-class debugging. See the nutrition-details.component.ts file shown below with added code shown in bold.

```
import { Component, Input, OnInit } from '@angular/core';

@Component({
  selector: 'fp-nutrition-details',
  templateUrl: './nutrition-details.component.html',
  styleUrls: ['./nutrition-details.component.css']
})
export class NutritionDetailsComponent implements OnInit {

  @Input()
  foodItem;
```

```
  constructor() { }

  ngOnInit(): void {
    console.log(this.foodItem);
  }
}
```

Note In prior versions of Angular, lazy-loaded components were declared in `entryComponents` array property as opposed to eagerly-loaded components which were declared in a modules `declarations` array property. Angular 9 does not required the `entryComponents` property.

Step 12 Add the new component to the food component's view template and test the file in Chrome. Select a food group

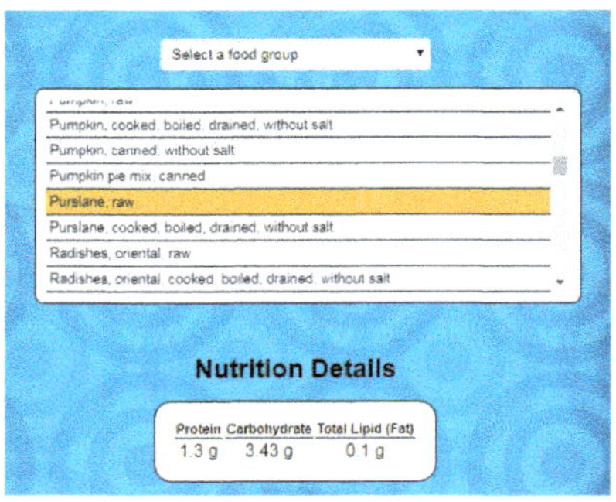

(there should be no lag time now). Select an item on the list.

Homework: Add a view template

Create a view template for the nutritional information.

2–Optional Exercise: Challenge: Fetch and display data in a component using HttpClient

Step 1 Refactor the FarmersMarkets component adding the following functionality

a. Make an HTTP request for the fm-sm.json file which contains information about Farmers Markets in the U.S.
b. Display the returned data in the view template including:
   i. MarketName
   ii. City, State and Zip
   iii. Credit Cards

Step 2 Use the following file for the Farmers-Market view template:
`assets/code-snippets/farmers-markets-html.html`

Step 3 Use the following file for the farmers-markets stylesheet:
`assets/css/farmers-markets-css.css`

Step 4 Start the farmers-markets REST api via the json server command:

```
json-server fm-sm.json -p 3006
```

Step 5 Use the following file for the farmers-markets data model:
`assets/code-snippets/farmers-markets.ts`

Step 6 The finished exercise should look like this:

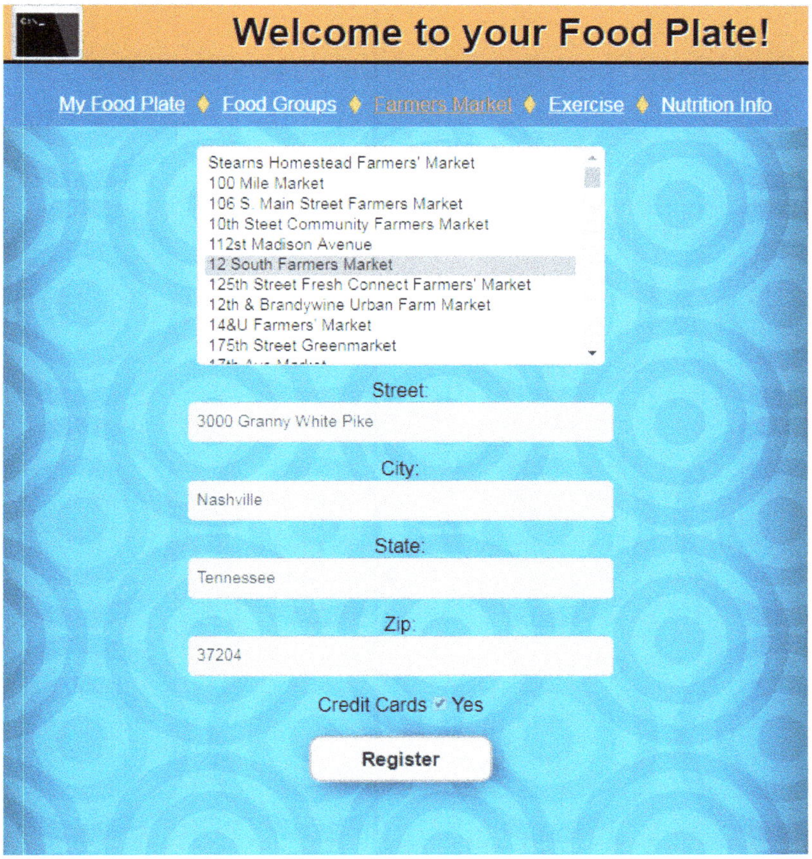

Extra Credit: Highlight the selected market with the same orange color used in the nutrition data. Will you need to refactor any CSS to reuse those style rules? Where should you write that CSS?

Possible Solution to Optional Farmers Market Exercise

farmers-markets.component.html

```
<section class="loadingMessage detailsForm" *ngIf="isloading && !errorMessage">
  WAIT!! Farmers Markets Data is Loading...
</section>

<section *ngIf="!errorMessage" class="detailsForm">
  <select name="markets" id="markets" size="10" class="selectList">
    <option *ngFor="let market of markets" (click)="showDetails(market)">{{ market.MarketName
}}</option>
  </select>
</section>

<section *ngIf="errorMessage" class="message detailsForm">
  {{ errorMessage }}
</section>

<section class="detailsForm">
  <label for="street">Street: <input type="text" id="street" #streetInput></label>
  <label for="city">City: <input type="text" id="city" #cityInput></label>
  <label for="state">State: <input type="text" id="state" #stateInput></label>
  <label for="zip">Zip: <input type="text" id="zip" #zipInput></label>
  <label for="cc">Credit Cards<input type="checkbox" id="cc" #ccInput>Yes</label>
</section>
```

farmers-markets.component.ts

```
import { Component, ElementRef, OnInit, ViewChild } from '@angular/core';
import { FarmersMarket } from '../models/farmers-market';

import { FarmersMarketsService } from '../services/farmers-markets.service';

@Component({
  selector: 'fp-farmers-markets',
  templateUrl: './farmers-markets.component.html',
  styleUrls: ['./farmers-markets.component.css'],
})
export class FarmersMarketsComponent implements OnInit {

  markets: Array<FarmersMarket>;
  isloading = true;
  errorMessage: string;

  @ViewChild('streetInput') streetInputRef: ElementRef;
  @ViewChild('cityInput') cityInputRef: ElementRef;
  @ViewChild('stateInput') stateInputRef: ElementRef;
  @ViewChild('zipInput') zipInputRef: ElementRef;
  @ViewChild('ccInput') ccInputRef: ElementRef;

  constructor(private marketsService: FarmersMarketsService) {
  }

  ngOnInit(): void {
    this.marketsService.getMarkets()
      .subscribe(markets => {
          this.markets = markets;
          console.table(this.markets);
          console.log(this.markets[1].MarketName);
        },
        (error) => {
          this.errorMessage = error.message;
          this.handleError(this.errorMessage);
```

```
      },
      () => this.isloading = false);
  }

  handleError(err): void {
    console.log(err);
  }

  showDetails(market: void {
    console.log(market);
    this.streetInputRef.nativeElement.value = market.street;
    this.streetInputRef.nativeElement.disabled = true;
    this.cityInputRef.nativeElement.value = market.city;
    this.cityInputRef.nativeElement.disabled = true;
    this.stateInputRef.nativeElement.value = market.State;
    this.stateInputRef.nativeElement.disabled = true;
    this.zipInputRef.nativeElement.value = market.zip;
    this.zipInputRef.nativeElement.disabled = true;
    this.ccInputRef.nativeElement.checked = market.Credit;
    this.ccInputRef.nativeElement.disabled = true;
  }

}
```

farmers-markets.service.ts

```
import { HttpClient } from '@angular/common/http';
import { Injectable } from '@angular/core';
import { Observable } from 'rxjs';
import { FarmersMarket } from '../models/farmers-market';


@Injectable({
  providedIn: 'root'
})
export class FarmersMarketsService {

  private marketsUrl: string = 'http://localhost:3006/markets';

  constructor(private http: HttpClient) {
  }

  getMarkets(): Observable<FarmersMarket[]> {
    return this.http.get<FarmersMarket[]>(this.marketsUrl);
  }

}
```

Chapter summary

In this chapter, you were introduced to Angular's HttpClientModule. You retrieved data from the server and showed the headers. You learned how to view the progress of an Http get download. You also used a REST API to fetch data. Observables were used with the HttpClient module and you learned how components can subscribe to the observables that are fetching the data from the server. You also saw how to return an HttpResponse object if needed.

Next chapter

In the next chapter, you will learn how to format displayed data with Angular Pipes.

Chapter 15
Understanding Pipes

Chapter 15: Understanding Pipes

Objectives

- Define a pipe and its use case
- List some of Angular's built-in pipes
- Use one of Angular's built-in pipes to format content
- Combine more than one pipe to format content (chain pipes)
- Add parameters to pipes to further refine the formatting of content (add options)
- Transform the display of data using a custom pipe
- Compare pure vs. impure pipes

Introduction

In this chapter, you learn how to format content in the view by using pipes. You will increase your ability to format content by chaining pipes and adding parameters. You will also create a custom pipe.

15.0 What are pipes

As web developers, we often work with data formats that are not user-friendly. For example, a common date string might look like this: Fri Oct 13 2017 15:50:30 GMT-0700 (Pacific Daylight Time), while the user might prefer to see: 10/13/2017. Angular pipes provide transformation mechanisms that can be declared in the HTML. Pipes are ideal solutions for transforming the display of data that appears often in different parts of your application. The Angular docs liken pipes to styles. Angular comes with built-in pipes for standard transformations like dates, currency and so on. Below is a list of Angular pipes.

15.0.1 Angular's Built-in Pipes

Date pipe
  - Displays a data with a pre-specified format

Decimal pipe
  - Format display of decimal including min and max values

Currency pipe
  - Formats currency using ISO 4217 currency codes and decimal pipe

Lowercase pipe
  - Formats strings as lowercase

Uppercase pipe
  - Formats strings as uppercase

JSON pipe
  - Formats an object to display as JSON

Percent pipe
  - Converts a number to a percentage and adds the % symbol

Slice pipe
  - Converts an array similar to JavaScript's Array.prototype.slice()

Async pipe
  - Subscribes to an Observable or Promise and returns the latest value it has emitted. When the component gets destroyed, the async pipe unsubscribes automatically to avoid potential memory leaks.

Figure #32: Angular Pipe API documentation at https://angular.io/api?type=pipe

15.1 How to use pipes

Basically, a pipe takes data as input and transforms it to more desirable output for display. Syntactically, the pipe is a common symbol in many programming languages. In Angular, pipes will primarily be used in view templates and should not be confused with TypeScript's union operator or a JavaScript bitwise `or` operator. Basically, the pipe accepts data as input, transforms and outputs the data. The pipe character | signifies the pipe to be used. Below is a sample currency pipe.

```
<p>Total: {{subtotal | currency:'USD':true}}</p>
```

In this example, the subtotal property is formatted with the currency pipe. The pipe accepts a symbol display property. When the symbol display property is set to true the currency symbol (example: $) is display; if set to false, the symbol will not be displayed.

```
<p>total in INR: {{b | currency:'USD':false:'4.2-2'}}</p>
```

In this example, the currency code parameter is passed, the currency symbol, which will not be used due to the "false" value passed and the digit information (`digitInfo`).

`digitInfo` is a string which has a following format:
`{minIntegerDigits}.{minFractionDigits}-{maxFractionDigits}`
`minIntegerDigits` is the minimum number of integer digits to use. Defaults to 1.
`minFractionDigits` is the minimum number of digits after fraction. Defaults to 0.
`maxFractionDigits` is the maximum number of digits after fraction. Defaults to 3.

15.2 Adding parameters to pipes

Pipes may accept optional parameters that help in formatting the input data. To add parameters to a pipe, follow the pipe name with a colon and then the parameter value. Multiple parameter values are separated by more colons.

Example: `DecimalPipe`

```
var num = 12.23456;
```

With pipe:

```
{{num | number}}
```

With no parameters passed, the following defaults are used:

Minimal integers = 1

Minimal fractional digits = 0

Maximum fractional digits = 3

Resulting in:

```
{{num | number }} // = 12.234
```

Now, the pipe is used with parameters.

```
{{num1 | number:'3.2-5'}}
```

Resulting in:

```
{{num | number }} // = 12.23456
```

15.3 Chaining pipes

A single property may use more than one pipe. For example, you may want to combine a slice pipe with an uppercase pipe. The syntax to use more than one pipe is to use more than one | character. In the example below, the `today` property is formatted as a date and displayed in uppercase.

```
{{ today | date | uppercase}}
```

15.4 Custom Pipes

Developers can create their own custom pipes for custom formatting. A custom pipe will require a transform method that provides the formatting instructions (per the PipeTransform's interface). In addition, you will supply a pipe name so that you can implement the pipe within template expressions. You can use an Angular CLI command to generate a pipe which is just a class decorated with the pipe metadata. You will create a custom pipe in a subsequent exercise in this chapter.

15.5 Pipes and change detection

Angular looks for data changes after each change detection process that is run (by Angular) after every DOM event. This could potentially create a performance issue with pipe-induced data changes, so Angular takes a different approach to change detection when it comes to pipes.

15.6 Pure and Impure pipes

Angular distinguishes pipes as pure and impure. Pipes are pure by default.

15.6.1 Pure Pipes

A pure pipe is one that Angular executes only when it detects a pure change. A pure change is either a change to a primitive input value (String, Number, Boolean, Symbol) or a changed object reference (Date, Array, Function, Object). For example, if your pipe changes an input month, or adds an item to an input array, or even updates a property of an input object, it is not considered pure and Angular will not call a pure pipe when such changes are made. Pure pipes don't undergo the same change detection as impure pipes. This can be beneficial to performance because an object reference check is much faster than a deep check for object property changes. Therefore, Angular can skip a pipe execution upon changes within (composite) objects. For instance, pushing a new item to an array that uses a pipe will not refresh your template. For more aggressive change detection, the pipe must be made impure.

15.6.2 Impure Pipes

Angular executes an impure pipe during every component change detection cycle. An impure pipe is called often, as often as every keystroke or mouse-move.

Setting the pipe to impure is shown below with the relevant line of code shown in bold.

```
@Pipe({
  name: 'pipeName',
  pure: false
})
```

See the following resource for a working example, of pure and impure pipes: https://stackblitz.com/angular/vjyvpgdbply

50—Guided Exercise: Using a built-in pipe

In this exercise, you format a date to a more user-friendly format. You will use the seed project for this exercise.

Step 1 Open the child-component.ts file and add a property called todays-plate and initialize it to a new Date object. The code is shown below in bold.

```
export class ChildComponent implements OnInit {
  todaysPlate: Date = new Date();
```

Step 2 Open the child.component.html file and display the new property as shown below in bold.

```
<p (click)="loginOutput(true)">Output Login Status</p>
<p>Today's Plate: {{ todaysPlate }}</p>
```

Step 3 Open app.component.html and add a child-component as shown below in bold.

```
<div>
    <app-header [user]="user"></app-header>
    <app-child></app-child>
    <app-login></app-login>
```

Step 4 Add the data pipe inside of the interpolation as shown below in bold.

```
<p>Today's Plate: {{ todaysPlate | date}}</p>
```

Step 5 Open app.component.html and add an app-child component. Comment the app-login component. Save and test the file in Chrome.

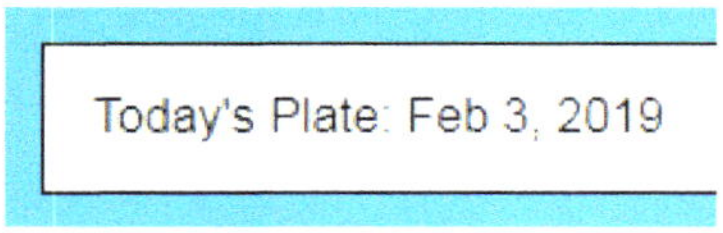

Step 6 Add parameters to the date pipe as shown below in bold.

```
<p>Today's Plate: {{ todaysPlate | date:"MM/dd/yy" }}</p>
```

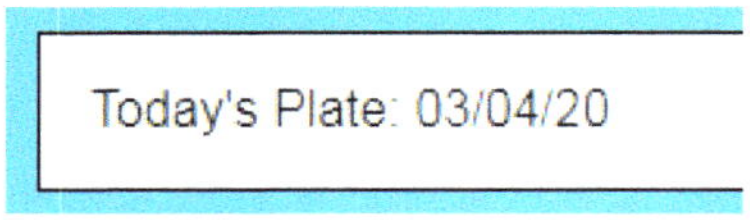

Step 7 Remove the parameters you added in step 6.

Step 8 Using the `todaysPlate` property, chain the date and uppercase pipes.

```
<p>Today's Plate: {{ todaysPlate | date | uppercase }}</p>
```

Step 9 Save and test the file in Chrome.

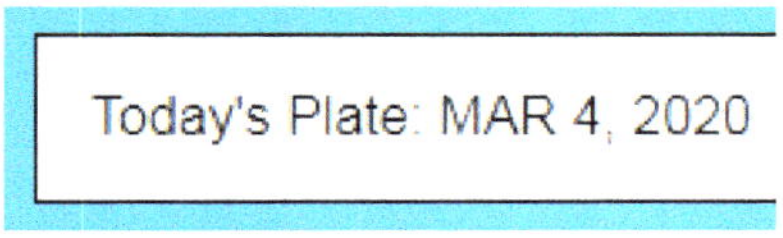

15.7 Custom pipes Review

Recall from section 15.5 that in addition to using Angular's built-in pipes, you can also create your own custom pipes. A custom pipe file requires:

1. Importing the necessary classes from @angular/core
    a. `Pipe` and `PipeTransform`
2. Using the `@Pipe()` annotation and naming the pipe
    a. via the `name` property passed into the `@Pipe()` function
    b. name must be a valid JavaScript identifier
3. Exporting a class
    a. That implements the `PipeTransform` interface
        i. Using the `transform()` method
4. Use the pipe just like a built-in pipe

51–Guided Exercise: Create and use a custom pipe

In this exercise, you create a simple custom pipe that will double a value passed to it.

Step 1 Open protein-detail.component.ts. and add a new property called `proteinSample`. Set the value to an object with the properties, "calories" and "protein."

```
proteinSample = {
  'calories' : 120,
  'protein'  : 9
};
```

Step 2 Open the protein-detail.component.html and add the following HTML. The completed file can be copied and pasted from angular-class-files. The HTML is shown below as well. If you are using Emmet you can type: `section>h1{Protein}+table>tr>th*3^tr*2>td*3`

```
<section>
  <h1>Protein</h1>
  <table>
    <tr>
      <th></th>
      <th>Calories</th>
      <th>Protein (grams)</th>
    </tr>
    <tr>
      <td>Single Serving</td>
      <td></td>
      <td></td>
    </tr>
    <tr>
      <td>Double Serving</td>
      <td></td>
      <td></td>
    </tr>
  </table>
</section>
```

Step 3 Add the following CSS to protein-detail.component.css.

```
table {
  background-color: #fff;
  border: 1px solid #000;
  border-radius: .5em;
  padding: 1em;
  margin: 0 auto;
  display: block;
  width: 65%;
}
```

Step 4 Create a folder called "shared". Create the custom pipe file in the new "shared" folder. Name it "double.pipe.ts."

```
ng g p shared/double --skip-import
```

Step 5 Confirm the name of the pipe is "double" and the file exports a class called "DoublePipe".

Step 6 Modify the transform method as shown below in bold.

```
import { Pipe, PipeTransform } from '@angular/core';
@Pipe({
  name: 'double'
})
export class DoublePipe implements PipeTransform {
  transform(value: number): number {
    return value * 2;
  }
}
```

Step 7 Return to the view template and add the bindings using the pipes. The content added is shown below in bold.

```
...
    <tr>
      <td>Single Serving</td>
      <td>{{ proteinSample.calories }}</td>
      <td>{{ proteinSample.protein }}</td>
    </tr>
    <tr>
      <td>Double Serving</td>
      <td>{{ proteinSample.calories | double }}</td>
      <td>{{ proteinSample.protein | double }}</td>
    </tr>
  </table>
</section>
```

Step 8 In the previous exercise, you did not have to declare the date or uppercase pipes because Angular's built-in pipes are pre-registered. Custom pipes must be registered. Open food-detail.module.ts and declare the custom pipe as shown below in bold.

```
import {DoublePipe} from '../shared/double.pipe';

@NgModule({
  imports: [
    CommonModule
  ],
  declarations: [FruitDetailComponent, GrainsDetailComponent,
ProteinDetailComponent, VegetableDetailComponent, DoublePipe
  ]
})
export class FoodDetailModule { }
```

Step 9 Save and test the file in Chrome.

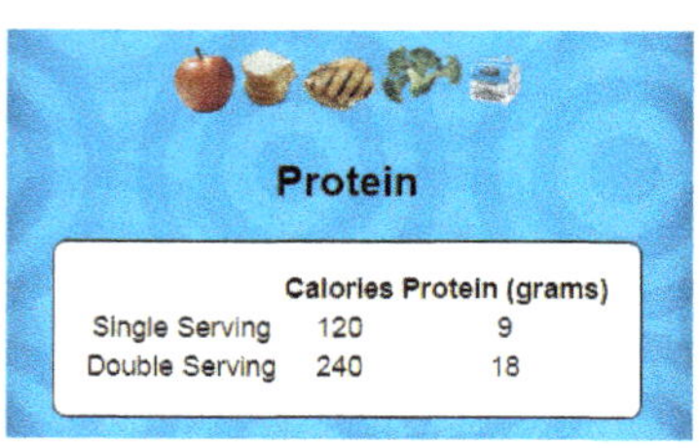

10 – Practice Exercise: Create and use a custom pipe

In this practice exercise, you create and use a pipe that executes a standard conversion formula that converts dry ounces to grams.

Simple Instructions

- Refactor the vegetable-detail view template as shown below.

```
<section>
  <h1>Vegetable Sample</h1>
  <p>Bowl of Peas</p>
  <p>Ounces: <span> </span></p>
  <p>Grams: <span> </span></p>
</section>
```

- Create a pipe called ouncesToGrams that converts ounces to grams
  - Formula: Multiple (dry) ounces by 28.35 to get grams.
- Add bindings to the span tags in the vegetable detail view template to display the ounces and grams.
- The finished file as seen in the browser is shown below.

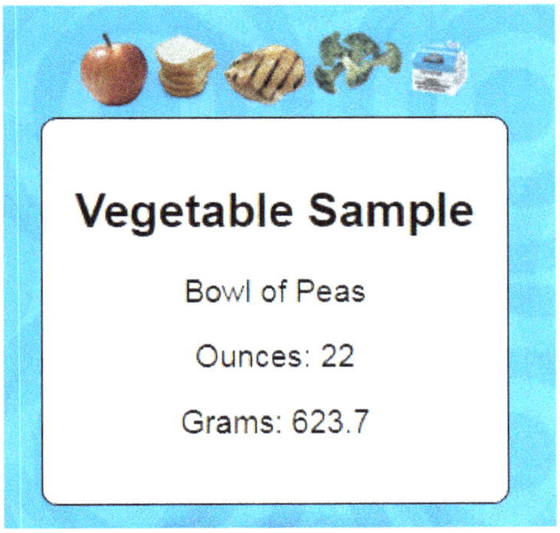

Step by step instructions

Step 1 Open vegetable-detail.component.ts and add a `vegetableSample` property with the value shown below.

```
vegetableSample = {
    'ounces': 22
};
```

Step 2 Modify the view template as shown below.

```
<section>
    <h1>Vegetable Sample</h1>
    <p>Bowl of Peas</p>
    <p>Ounces: <span> </span></p>
    <p>Grams: <span> </span></p>
</section>
```

Step 3 Add the following CSS in the proper location.

```
section {
    background-color: #fff;
    border: 1px solid #000;
    border-radius: .5em;
    padding: 1em;
}
```

The view shows a sample vegetable (bowl of peas) which will be converted from ounces to grams. The conversion formula is shown below.

Conversion Factor

Multiple (dry) ounces by 28.35 to get grams.

Step 4 Create the pipe and name it ouncesToGrams.pipe.ts. Name the pipe itself “ouncesToGrams” and name the class “OuncesToGrams.”

Step 5 When the pipe is done, return to the view template and add the bindings.

Step 6 Test your work in Chrome.

Possible solution code

vegetable-detail.component.ts

```
import { Component, OnInit } from '@angular/core';

@Component({
  selector: 'fp-vegetable-detail',
  templateUrl: './vegetable-detail.component.html',
  styleUrls: ['./vegetable-detail.component.css']
})
export class VegetableDetailComponent implements OnInit {

  vegetableSample = {
    'ounces': 22
  };

  constructor() { }

  ngOnInit(): void {
  }
}
```

vegetable-detail.component.html

```
<section>
    <h1>Vegetable Sample</h1>
    <p>Bowl of Peas</p>
    <p>Ounces: <span>{{ vegetableSample.ounces }}</span></p>
    <p>Grams: <span>{{ vegetableSample.ounces | ouncesToGrams}}</span></p>
</section>
```

ouncesToGrams.pipe.ts

```
import { Pipe, PipeTransform } from '@angular/core';

@Pipe({
        name: 'ouncesToGrams'
})

export class OuncesToGramsPipe implements PipeTransform {
  transform(ounces: number): number {
    const MULTIPLIER: number =  28.35;
    return ounces * MULTIPLIER;
  }
}
```

Chapter summary

In this chapter, you learned all about using pipes to format content. You learned and used some of Angular's built-in pipes and created your own custom pipe. To add more functionality to pipes, the process of chaining pipes was explored. To further customize the pipe's transform method, you were introduced to adding parameters to the pipe.

Chapter 15 Quiz

https://tinyurl.com/rn8qtgd

1) What will the following code display? (using the collection below)

```
collection: string[] = ['a', 'b', 'c', 'd'];)

<ul>
   <li *ngFor="let i of collection | slice:1:3">{{i}}</li>
</ul>
```

____

____

____

2) What will the following code display?

Hint: This date falls on a Monday.

```
birthday = new Date(2020, 9, 28);
{{  birthday | date:'fullDate' | uppercase}}
```

____

____

____

Next chapter

In the next chapter, you revisit Routing and learn how to prevent routes from loading as well as how to inform a user before a route is exited.

Chapter 16

Advanced Routing

Chapter 16: Advanced Routing

In this chapter, you learn how to block users from entering pre-defined routes. You also learn how to prevent users from leaving a pre-defined route. In standard server-side, non-single-page applications, the server typically determines if a user is authorized to view a page or if certain conditions have been met to allow a page to be served. Based on the business logic used, the server may redirect the user or show a "page not found" or "permissions error." Single page applications like Angular, can provide the same behavior, albeit implemented differently. Angular applications load the view-templates of components as routes and these routes can contain logic that can either prevent a component route from loading or ask for user permission before leaving a component route.

16.0 Router Guards

In Chapter 12, routes were defined, and the various exercises involved creating a routing module and using routes in diverse ways to load and unload a component from the view. In this chapter, we continue the discussion of routes by learning how to block a route from loading. Angular provides a mechanism called a router guard for this purpose.

16.0.1 What is a Router Guard?

A router guard is a function that returns true if a user can activate a route and false if they cannot. The route can also return a promise or observable that will later resolve to a boolean. This is because the logic that determines if they can activate the route is dependent on an asynchronous operation like an HTTP request for permission. Because the boolean value is not available immediately the function returns a promise or observable instead of true/false.

16.0.2 Angular's router guards

`canActivate` checks to see if a user can visit a route

`canActivateChild` checks to see if a user can visit a child route

`canDeactivate` checks to see if a user can exit a route

`resolve` gets data required to show the route, before the route is activated

`canload` checks to see if a user can route to a module that is lazy-loaded

16.1 How to implement a router guard

Route guards may be written as class files or as a service. Either way, the logic that allows or disallows the route is created in a function that returns either a true or false value or a promise or observable that will later return a true or false value. The function is called canActivate and the class or service must import the CanActivate class from the @angular/router barrel. The last step is to add the guard to the route. This is done via the canActivate property which is passed one or more guards. Notice the array notation in the sample below. A route may have more than one guard, in which case, all the guards are tested in the order they appear and only if all guards return true will the route be executed.

```
{ path: login, component: LoginComponent, canActivate: [ LoginGuard ] },
```

52—Guided Exercise: Create and implement a router guard with CanActivate

In this exercise, you create and implement a router guard. First you create a guard that really doesn't guard anything. In other words, it's a guard that allows a route to activate as opposed to one that prevents a route from loading. This approach will help to describe the basic steps involved in creating a route guard.

Step 1 Open app.routing.module.ts and add the following class. It is important that this class be declared prior to the routes constant. The added code is shown below in bold.

```
import { NgModule } from '@angular/core';
import {CanActivate, Route, RouterModule, Routes} from '@angular/router';
...
class AllowFullAccessGuard implements CanActivate {
    canActivate(): boolean {
        console.log('FullAccessGuard has been activated.');
        return true;
    }
}
...
```

Step 2 Add the route guard to the "myPlate" route as shown below in bold.

```
const routes: Routes = [
    {
        path: '',
        children: [
            { path: 'myPlate', component: PlateComponent, canActivate: [
AllowFullAccessGuard ] },
            { path: 'register', component: RegisterComponent },
            { path: 'farmersMarkets', component: FarmersMarketsComponent },
            { path: 'exercises', component: ExercisesComponent },
            { path: 'nutritionInfo', component: FoodComponent },
            ...foodGroupsRoutes,
            fallbackRoute
        ]
    }
];
```

Step 3 Provide the AllowFullAccessGuard in the providers array of the app.routing.module.ts as shown below in bold.

```
@NgModule({
    imports: [
        RouterModule.forRoot(
            routes)
    ],
    exports: [
        RouterModule
    ],
    providers: [ AllowFullAccessGuard ]
})
```

Step 4 Refresh the page in Chrome. Be sure to open the DevTools. If you have a user in localStorage, delete it.

Step 5 Active the 'myPlate' route from the "My Food Plate" link in the nav component and examine the console in the DevTools. You should see the log statement from the `canActivate()` method.

```
FullAccessGuard has been activated.                    app.routing.module.ts:16
```

Next, you will create a route guard than prevents the user from going to the plate component/myplate-route, unless they have registered. If they have not registered, they will be redirected to the register page.

Step 6 Create a register.guard.service.ts using the CLI tool with the command below.

```
ng g s services/registerGuard
```

Step 7 Modify the code in register.guard.service.ts as summarized below.

- Import the `CanActivate` and `Router` classes
- Import the `User` class
- Create a `currentUser` property typed as a `User`
- Inject the `UserService` and the `router` into the constructor
- Refactor the provider based on using Angular 4-5 or Angular 6
- Add the necessary code to the `canActivate()` method that
  - Gets the current user
  - Determines if the current user has not registered
  - Sends the user to the register page if they have not registered
  - Alerts the user that they have not registered and will be redirected
  - Allows the myPlate route to execute if they have registered

```
import { Injectable } from '@angular/core';
import { CanActivate, Router } from '@angular/router';

import { UserService} from './user.service';
import { User } from '../models/User';

@Injectable({
  providedIn: 'root'
})

export class RegisterGuardService implements CanActivate {
  currentUser: User;

  constructor(private userService: UserService, public router: Router) {
  }

  canActivate(): boolean {
      this.currentUser = this.userService.getUser();
      console.log(this.currentUser);
      if (this.currentUser.registered === false) {
      this.router.navigate(['register']);
      alert(`You haven't registered yet! You will be redirected to the
register page.`);
      return false;
    }
    return true;
  }
}
```

Step 8 Provide the new service to app.routing.module.ts and import it.

```
...
import {FoodComponent} from './food/food.component';
import { RegisterGuardService } from './services/register-guard.service';

@NgModule({
    imports: [RouterModule.forRoot(routes)],
    exports: [ RouterModule ],
    providers: [ AllowFullAccessGuard, RegisterGuardService ]
})
```

Step 9 Replace the "AllowFullAccessGuard" on the myPlate route with the new "Register Guard" as shown below.

```
const routes: Routes = [
    {
        path: '',
        children: [
            { path: 'myPlate', component: PlateComponent, canActivate: [
RegisterGuardService ] },
...
```

Step 10 Import the RegisterGuardService in app.routing.module.ts as shown below in bold.

```
import {FoodComponent} from './food/food.component';
import { RegisterGuardService } from './services/register-guard.service';
```

Step 11 Save the files and refresh the page in Chrome. Before testing the code, make sure that localStorage isn't holding a user object. Then, perform the following steps to check your router guard.

a. Make sure you haven't already registered by checking localStorage from the DevTools Application panel.

b. After going to the home page, click on the "My Food Plate" link in the nav bar. You should see the alert box shown below.

c. Click the OK button and you should be redirected to the Register Form page.

d. Fill out the form and click the "Register" button.

e. Click the "My Food Plate" link in the nav bar and you should see the Plate component.

53—Guided Exercise: Create and implement a child router guard with CanActivateChild

In this exercise, you create and implement a router guard to prevent child routes from loading under specific conditions. The expected outcome of the exercise is shown below.

If the user clicks on a food-group in which they have eaten all their daily requirements, the route will not execute. In this example, the assumption is that all the fruit for the day has been eaten, but the user still needs to consume vegetable servings.

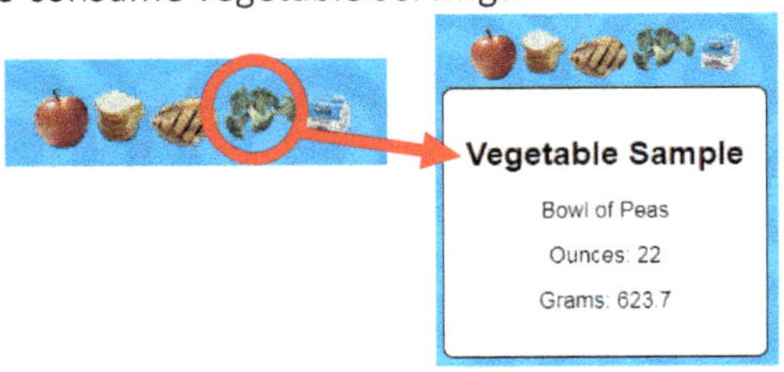

So, if the user clicks on the vegetable, they see the screen below. If they have eaten all their protein and click the protein, they will see the alert box below.

To implement this functionality our guard will need access to the currently logged-in user and look at the reqsStatus property value and its properties: vegMet, proteinMet, grainMet and fruitMet.

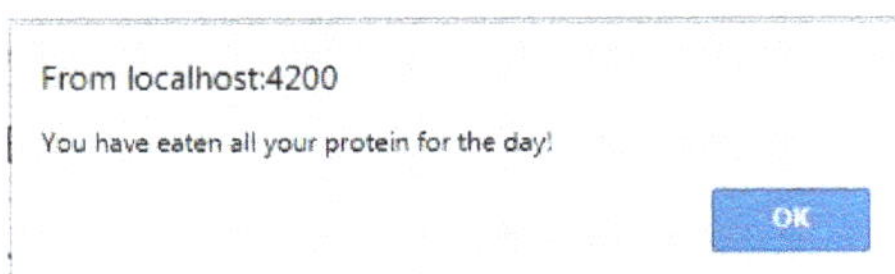

Step 1 Create a new service called food-group-guard.service.ts which will contain the router guard. Use the CLI command shown below.

```
ng g s services/FoodGroupsGuard
```

Step 2 The router guard will implement the `CanActivateChild` which is used for child routes. Add "implements" to the exported class as shown below in bold. You should receive an error on compilation because we have not yet implemented `CanActivateChild`.

```
@Injectable({
  providedIn: 'root'
})
export class FoodGroupsGuardService implements CanActivateChild {
...
```

Step 3 Update the imports at the top of the file as shown below in bold.

```
import { CanActivateChild } from '@angular/router';
import { Injectable } from '@angular/core';
```

Step 4 Because we will need access to the currentUser, create a user property and import the User class and UserService. You will need to know the current route as well as the food group, so add the additional properties shown below in bold.

```
import { CanActivateChild } from '@angular/router';
import { Injectable } from '@angular/core';

import { UserService } from './user.service';
```

```
import { User } from '../models/User';

@Injectable()
export class FoodGroupsGuardService implements CanActivateChild {
    currentUser: User;
    currentRoute: ActivatedRoute;
    group: string;
```

Step 5 Add the constructor function to setup the dependencies.

```
constructor(private userService: UserService, private router: Router, private
activatedRoute: ActivatedRoute) {
        this.currentRoute = this.activatedRoute;
}
```

Step 6 Import the necessary classes.

```
import {ActivatedRoute, CanActivateChild, Router} from '@angular/router';
```

Step 7 Write the `canActivateChild` method with the following summarized steps:

- Declare a variable to hold the group query Param.
- Get the user via the user service.
- Create a value called `valueMet` that will be used to reference the reqsStatus properties: `vegMet`, `grainsMet`, `fruitMet` and `proteinMet`.
- Log the new `valueMet` variable to the console to see if it returns the correct string.
- Pass in the two objects described below.

ActivatedRouteSnapshot

Contains the information about a route associated with a component loaded in an outlet at a moment in time. ActivatedRouteSnapshot can also be used to traverse the router state tree.[6] It is recommended that you read the documentation associated with this class as it can prove very helpful in achieving many route and route-guard related tasks.

RouterStateSnapshot

Represents the state of the router at a moment in time. RouterStateSnapshot is a tree of activated route snapshots. Every node in this tree knows about the "consumed" URL segments, the extracted parameters, and the resolved data.[7] This class contains a helpful property called url which holds the url from which the snapshot was created.

```
canActivateChild(route: ActivatedRouteSnapshot, state: RouterStateSnapshot):
boolean {
    console.log(route);
    console.log(route.queryParams);
    console.log(state.url);
    this.group = route.queryParams.group;
    this.currentUser = this.userService.getUser();
    const valueMet = this.group + 'Met';
    console.log(valueMet);
    return true;
}
```

[6] https://angular.io/api/router/ActivatedRouteSnapshot

[7] https://angular.io/api/router/RouterStateSnapshot

To understand this code, you must know about the `ActivatedRouteSnapshot`. Note that you are logging it to the console. In addition to the route, you are logging the `queryParams`.

Step 8 Be sure to add the new imports.

```
import {ActivatedRoute, ActivatedRouteSnapshot, CanActivateChild, Router,
RouterStateSnapshot} from '@angular/router';
```

Note **If you are using Angular 5 or lower**, the file can't be tested yet, because the service has not been provided. Open the app.module and import and provide the service.

```
import {FoodGroupsGuard} from './services/food-group-guard.service';
...
providers: [UserService, FoodGroupsGuardService ]
```

Step 9 Using food-groups.routing.ts, add the `canActivateChild` property before the array of children routes as shown below.

```
export const foodGroupsRoutes: Routes = [
    {
        path: 'foodGroups',
        canActivateChild: [ FoodGroupsGuardService ],
        children: [
...
```

Step 10 Add the necessary imports to food-groups.routing.ts.

```
import { FoodGroupsGuardService } from './services/food-groups-guard.service';
```

Step 11 Open food-groups.component.ts and add the code shown below in bold. The `queryParams` are a property of the `ActivatedRouteSnapshot` and this particular route comes from the food-groups.component.ts. The relevant code from this file is shown below for reference. Notice the router objects navigate method contains the route instructions and include the `queryParams`.

```
showGroup(group): void {
        this.router.navigate([group.name], {relativeTo: this.route,
queryParams: {group: `${group.name}`}
        });
}
```

The group object comes from the foodGroups Service which is utilized by the food-groups.component. The food-group.component.html is shown below with the relevant code in bold.

```
<section>
  <img *ngFor="let group of foodGroups"
       src="{{group.icon}}"
       alt="{{group.name}}"
       [ngStyle]="iconStyles"
       (click)="showGroup(group)">
</section>
```

Step 12 Before you can test, you need to set the user's fruitMet and proteinMet properties to true. Open the user.service.ts and add the code shown below in bold. **See the note below the code before you make these changes.**

```
getUser() {
    if(localStorage.getItem('currentUser')) {
        const user = JSON.parse(localStorage.getItem('currentUser'));
        this.currentUser = new BehaviorSubject(user);
        return user;
    }
    else {
            // remove after route-child-guard test
            this.user.reqsStatus.fruitMet = true;
            this.user.reqsStatus.proteinMet = true;
            // user.reqsStatus.vegetablesMet = true;
            // user.reqsStatus.grainsMet = true;
            return this.user;
}
...
    updateUser(user:User) {
        user.id = 1;
        user.registered = true;
        user.reqsStatus = {fruitMet: true, vegMet: false, proteinMet: true,
grainMet: false};
        this.currentUser.next(user)
    }
```

Note Alternatively, you can change properties of the user object at runtime using the Augury Chrome extension. *Some versions of Augury can be buggy at this step. If using Augury does not work complete step 12.

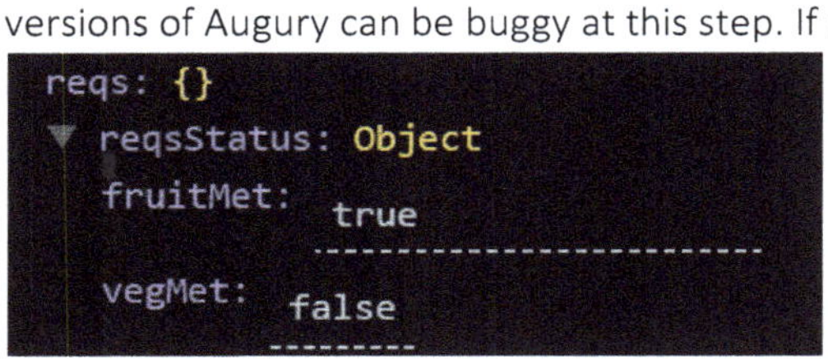

Step 13 Save your changes and recompile the application. Examine the refreshed file in Chrome, with the DevTools console open. Navigate to the Food Groups link from the home page. Then, click the apple. You should see the console log

```
                                                     food-group-guard.service.ts:32
▶ ActivatedRouteSnapshot {url: Array(1), params: {…}, queryParams: {…}, fragment: undefined,
  data: {…}, …}
▶ {group: "fruit"}                                   food-group-guard.service.ts:33
/foodGroups/fruit?group=fruit                        food-group-guard.service.ts:34
```

statements shown below.

Step 14 Take a moment to examine the ActivatedRouteSnapshot. Then look in the console at the result of the line of code shown below from food-groups.service .

```
console.log(route.queryParams);
```

Now that you know where the queryParams come from, it's time to use them in the router guard.

Step 15 Save and refresh in Chrome. Activate the FoodGroups link and then, click the apple, bread, chicken and broccoli. Confirm the log statements in the console which should read:

```
group=fruit
```

```
group=grains
group=protein
group=vegetables
```

Step 16 Refactor the `canActivateChild` method. Now that `canActivateChild` contains all the values needed, pass the control of the guard to a new function called `getRoute()` and remove the "return true" as shown below. Notice the use of the valueMet variable.

```
console.log(valueMet);
return this.getRoute(this.group, this.currentUser.reqsStatus[valueMet]);
```

Step 17 Write the getRoute method as shown below.

```
getRoute(group, metValue): boolean {
   if (metValue === true) {
         alert(`You have eaten all your ${group} for the day!`);
         return false;
   } else {
          return true;
   }
}
```

Note Be sure to remove the currentUser object from localStorage before proceeding to step 19.

Step 18 Save and refresh the file in Chrome and test. You will need to fill out and submit the register form before you can activate the "My Food Plate" link. Click on the "My Food Plate" link to confirm the new property values are correct. The fruit and protein portions of the plate should be in color (red and purple).

Click on the "Food Groups" link. Then click on the vegetable link. The vegetable route should execute. Click on the protein. The router guard should execute resulting in the alert box and the route block. The grain link should work, and the fruit link should not work.

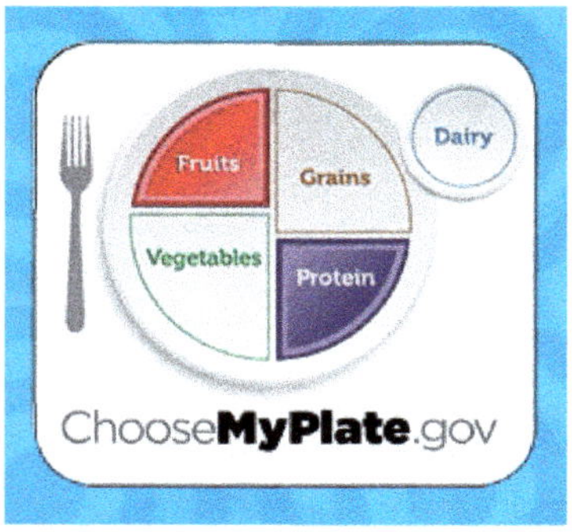

54—Guided Exercise: Create and implement a router guard with CanDeactivate

In this exercise, you create and implement a router guard to prevent the user from leaving a route. When the exercise is completed, if the user fills out the registration form but does not submit it, they will be warned before leaving the page (route) that there are unsaved/submitted changes to the form.

Step 1 Open register.component.ts. Create a `canDeactive` method in the register component that determines if it has unsaved changes.

```
canDeactivate(): boolean {
        console.log(!this.regForm.touched);
        return !this.regForm.touched;
}
```

Step 2 Create a new guard called leaveRegisterGuard.

```
ng g s services/leaveRegisterGuard
```

Step 3 Implement CanDeactivate which should expect a RegisterComponent and write the `canDeactivate()` method passing in the RegisterComponent.

```
import { Injectable } from '@angular/core';
import { CanDeactivate } from '@angular/router';

import { RegisterComponent } from '../register/register.component';

@Injectable({
  providedIn: 'root'
})

export class LeaveRegisterGuardService implements
CanDeactivate<RegisterComponent> {

  canDeactivate(component: RegisterComponent): boolean {
    console.log('LeaveRegisterGuard');
      return component.canDeactivate() || window.confirm('Are you sure you
want to leave the form?');
  }
}
```

The CanDeactivate class is imported as is the RegisterComponent. The canDeactivate method logs the "LeaveRegisterGuard" message to the console and returns the canDeactivate method written in the RegisterComponent in step 1 that will allow the route to execute if it's true or pop-up a confirm box if it is false.

Step 4 In the register component constructor, the `{updateOn: 'blur'}` must be removed so that the form will add the "ng-touched" property as soon as the user adds data to any form field.

```
constructor(private userService: UserService) {
        this.regForm = new FormGroup({
            firstName: new FormControl(null, {validators:
Validators.required}),
```

```
            email: new FormControl(null, [Validators.required,
Validators.email]),
            gender: new FormControl(null, [Validators.required]),
            ageGroup: new FormControl(null, [Validators.required])
        }, {updateOn: 'blur'});
}
```

Step 5 Add the new router guard to app.routing.module.ts.

```
...
const routes: Routes = [
    {
        path: '',
        children: [
            { path: 'myPlate', component: PlateComponent, canActivate: [
RegisterGuardService ] },
            { path: 'register', component: RegisterComponent, canDeactivate: [
LeaveRegisterGuardService] },
            { path: 'farmersMarkets', component: FarmersMarketsComponent },
...
```

Note **If you are using Angular 5 or below,** provide the new service in app.routing.module.ts.

```
providers: [ RegisterGuardService, LeaveRegisterGuardService ]
```

Step 6 Save and test the file in Chrome with the DevTools console open. Be sure to remove any previous registration by deleting it in the Applications panel as shown below.

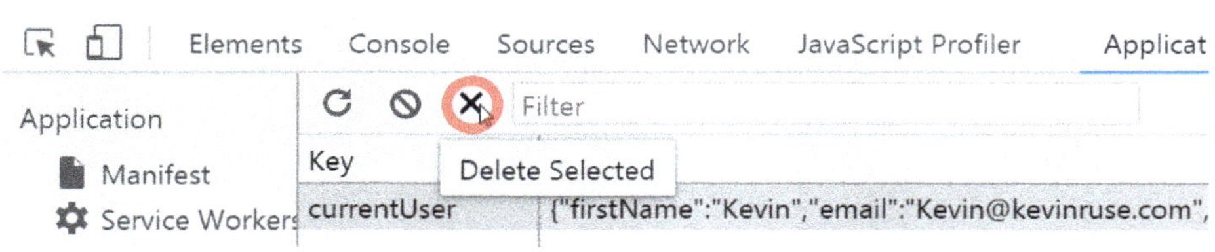

Step 7 Start at the home page and click the "Register" button. Fill out the form, but do not click the "Register" button. Attempt to go to another route such as the "Farmers Market." You should see the confirm dialog box shown below.

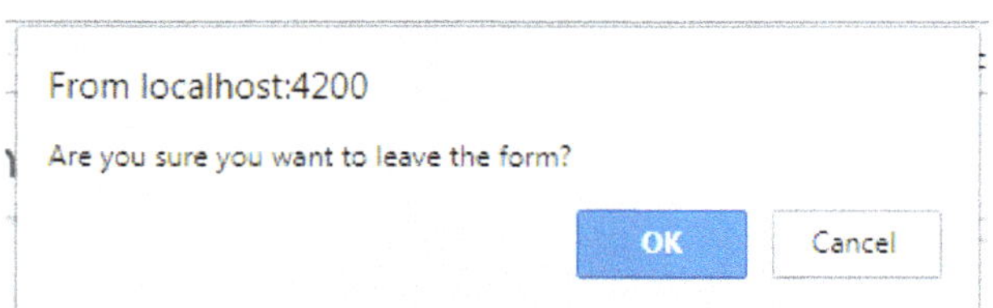

If you return to the form, fill it out and click the "register" button, you will still see this alert.

The following steps will redirect the user to the plate page after registering.

Step 8 In register.component.ts add a submit property. Refactor the `canDeactivate()` function in register.component.ts so the alert box does not pop up when the register form is completed and submitted.

```
...
ageGroups = ['2-3', '4-8', '9-13', '14-18', '19-30','31-50', '51+'];
```

```
submit: boolean;
router: Router;
...
constructor(private userService: UserService,  private router: Router) {
        this.regForm = new FormGroup({
...
   canDeactivate() {
        console.log(!this.regForm.touched);
        return !this.regForm.touched || this.submit;
    }
```

Step 9 Modify the onSubmit() method in the register.component.ts file so the user is navigated to the "My Plate" route after registering.

```
onSubmit(formValues): void {
        this.submit = true;
        this.userService.updateUser(formValues);
        UserService.storeUserLocal(formValues);
        this.router.navigate(['myPlate']);
}
```

Step 10 Save and test again in Chrome. Be sure the clear the current user from localStorage. Start at the home page and click the "Register" button. Fill out the form and click the "Register" button. After clicking "OK" on the alert box, you should be directed to the plate page.

16.2 Lazy Loading Modules

As Angular applications (like all web applications) get larger, their startup time suffers as all the necessary code takes longer to load. Developers can choose to startup the application with a minimum of necessary modules loading at startup. The remaining modules may be loaded at runtime when they are needed or called for by user interaction. This is called lazy-loading modules. Up to this point in the course, all the modules have been eagerly loaded. They are loaded at startup by our app module. In the next exercise, you learn how to lazy-load modules.

16.3 Code Splitting

Code splitting is the act of breaking up your application into various feature modules. This is the preferred method of development. Ideally, as new features are created, they are added to modules that contain all the code relevant to the new feature. Then, the new feature can be loaded eagerly or lazy-loaded. In addition, because all the code related to the features is in a single module, it can be easily maintained, updated and shared. For example, if a given feature required several pipes, various components and services, each of these would be declared or imported from the feature module itself (as opposed to the app module or some other feature module).

55—Guided Exercise: Lazy load a module

In this exercise, you add code that prevents a module (FoodGroupsModule) from loading at startup and instead loads the module only when the user navigates to that module's components. At the same time, you split the code that was lazy-loaded into a feature module.

Step 1 Open app.module.ts. To lazy-load a module, you cannot import it at startup (loading a module at startup is called eager loading), so you must remove the import of the FoodGroupsModule as shown below with the strikethrough.

```
...
@NgModule({
  imports: [
    CommonModule, BrowserModule, FoodGroupsModule, AppRoutingModule,
FormsModule, ReactiveFormsModule, HttpClientModule
  ],
...
```

Step 2 Open app.routing.module.ts. It is in this file that instructions are provided to the router that a module should be lazy loaded. We must also indicate where to find the module. Refactor app.routing.module.ts by adding the code shown in bold.

```
{ path: 'nutritionInfo', component: FoodComponent },
...foodGroupsRoutes,
{ path: 'foodGroups',
              loadChildren: () => import('./food-groups/food-groups.module')
                  .then(mod => mod.FoodGroupsModule)
},
fallbackRoute
```

Step 3 Replace the existing routing module for food-group routes (called food-groups.routing.module.ts) with the code shown below. Alternatively, you can copy and paste this file from assets/code-snippets/lazy-load-food-groups-routing-ts.txt.

```
import { NgModule } from '@angular/core';
import { RouterModule, Routes} from '@angular/router';

import {FoodGroupsGuardService} from '../services/food-groups-guard.service';
import {FoodGroupsComponent} from './food-groups.component';
import {ProteinDetailComponent} from '../food-detail/protein-detail/protein-
detail.component';
import {FruitDetailComponent} from '../food-detail/fruit-detail/fruit-
detail.component';
import {VegetableDetailComponent} from '../food-detail/vegetable-
detail/vegetable-detail.component';
import {GrainsDetailComponent} from '../food-detail/grains-detail/grains-
detail.component';
```

```
export const foodGroupsRoutes: Routes = [
    {
        path: '',
        canActivateChild: [ FoodGroupsGuardService ],
        children: [
            {
                path: '',
                component: FoodGroupsComponent,
                outlet: 'foodGroupOutlet'
            },
            {
                path: 'protein',
                component: ProteinDetailComponent,
            },
            {
                path: 'fruit',
                component: FruitDetailComponent
            },
            {
                path: 'vegetables',
                component: VegetableDetailComponent
            },
            {
                path: 'grains',
                component: GrainsDetailComponent
            }
        ]}
];

@NgModule({
    imports: [
        RouterModule.forChild(
            foodGroupsRoutes)
    ],
    exports: [
        RouterModule
    ],
})

export class FoodGroupsRoutingModule {
}
```

Note If you did not make the child route guard "FoodGroupsGuardService," you will need to remove or comment the line shown below:

```
// canActivateChild: [ FoodGroupsGuardService ],
```

Step 4 Remove the import of this routing file from app.routing.module.ts as shown with the strikethrough below.

```
...
{ path: 'exercises', component: ExercisesComponent },
{ path: 'nutritionInfo', component: FoodComponent },...
{ path: 'nutritionInfo', component: FoodComponent },
...foodGroupsRoutes,
{ path: 'foodGroups', loadChildren: './food-groups/food-groups
...
```

Step 5 If you save and refresh in the browser, the "Food Groups" link will not work.

Open the food-groups.module.ts and import the new food-groups routing module as shown below in bold.

```
...
import { FoodGroupsRoutingModule } from './food-groups.routing.module';

@NgModule({
  imports: [
    CommonModule, FoodDetailModule, FoodGroupsRoutingModule
  ],
```

Note Because we are bundling the food group component as a feature module, it should import all its required modules. Notice what the food-groups.module imports.

Step 6 Remove the AllowFullAccessGuard from the providers array in app.routing.module.ts because it is not being used.

```
class AllowFullAccessGuard implements CanActivate {
    canActivate() {
        console.log('FullAccessGuard has been activated.');
        return true;
    }
}
...
```

Step 7 Stop the client app in the command prompt with the command:

`Control + C`, followed by "`y`" for yes.

Step 8 Serve the application via the command: `ng serve`

Step 9 Save and refresh the file in Chrome. The food-groups link should work but we want to make sure it is being lazy-loaded. Test the page using the following steps.

a. Open the DevTools and activate the Network Panel. Click the "JS" button as shown below.

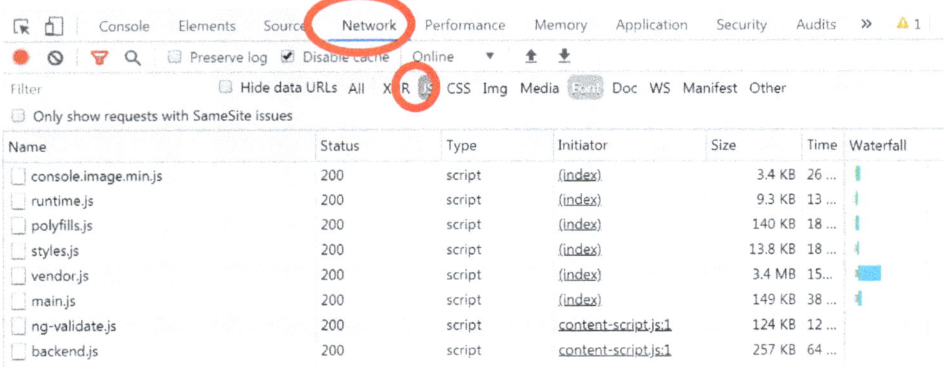

b. Refresh the page in Chrome.

c. Click on the "Exercises" link. The network panel should indicate no further loading of JavaScript files. The same should be true of the "Farmers Markets" and "My Food Plate" links. Now click the "Food Groups" link. A new JavaScript file called "food-groups-food-groups-module.js" should appear in the Network tab of the Chrome DevTools. The module has lazy-loaded!

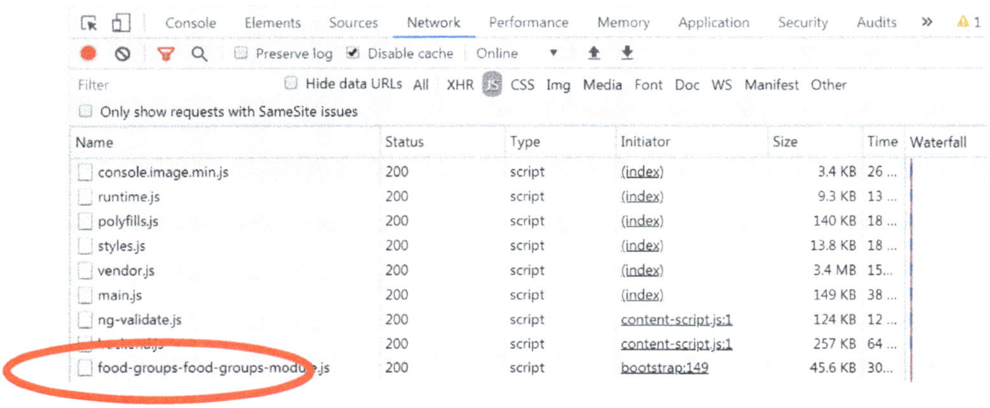

16.4 Lazy Loading and Services

Before we review lazy loading and services in Angular 10, look at the summary for dependency injection provided by the Angular documentation. See below (per the Angular documentation):

DI is wired into the Angular framework and used everywhere to provide new components with the services or other things they need. Components consume services; that is, you can inject a service into a component, giving the component access to that service class.

To define a class as a service in Angular, use the @Injectable() decorator to provide the metadata that allows Angular to inject it into a component as a dependency. Similarly, use the @Injectable() decorator to indicate that a component or other class (such as another service, a pipe, or an NgModule) has a dependency.

- The injector is the main mechanism. Angular creates an application-wide injector for you during the bootstrap process, and additional injectors as needed. You don't have to create injectors.
- An injector creates dependencies and maintains a container of dependency instances that it reuses if possible.
- A provider is an object that tells an injector how to obtain or create a dependency.

For any dependency that you need in your app, you must register a provider with the app's injector, so that the injector can use the provider to create new instances. For a service, the provider is typically the service class itself.

16.4.1 Angular 5 and lower: providing services

If you used Angular version 5 or lower, you would have provided services in the providers array property of @NgModule as shown below.

```
@NgModule({
  declarations: [ AppComponent,
                  DefaultComponent,],
  imports: [
             AppRoutingModule,
             BrowserModule],
  bootstrap: [ AppComponent ],
  providers: [ DataService,
               ...]
})
```

16.4.2 Angular 6: providing services

After Angular 6, services were provided by the service class itself via the `providedIn` property of the @Injectable decorator as shown below.

```
@Injectable({
  providedIn: 'root'
})
```

This approach allowed for 3 significant changes within the Angular framework.

1. Services became tree-shakable.
2. Services became singletons application-wide including lazy loaded modules.
3. There was no need to add to a "providers" array as the service provided itself.

16.4.3 Angular 9 services

As of Angular 9, services can now be provided via the providedIn property passed to the @Injectable() decorator with values other than 'root'. 'platform' and 'any' are two new approaches to defining where a service should be resolved. They are defined as follows:

`providedIn` value	Description	Creates
`platform`	This is a special singleton platform injector shared by all applications on the page. It makes the service available between multiple applications or Angular elements.	providedIn the platform injector creates a singleton for all applications including lazy-loaded modules (this approach is reflected when running multiple Angular applications within the same window or using Angular elements shared by more than one application)
`any`	Provides a unique instance in every module (including lazy modules) that injects the token.	Results in multiple instances of the same service. Each lazy-loaded module has its own instance of the service. Eagerly loaded modules share one instance of the service provided by the root module.
`root`	The application-level injector in most apps.	One instance, provided in app.module

Angular provides two injector hierarchies:

1. `ModuleInjector`
2. `ElementInjector` (NodeInjector in Ivy)

The hierarchy of injectors looks like this

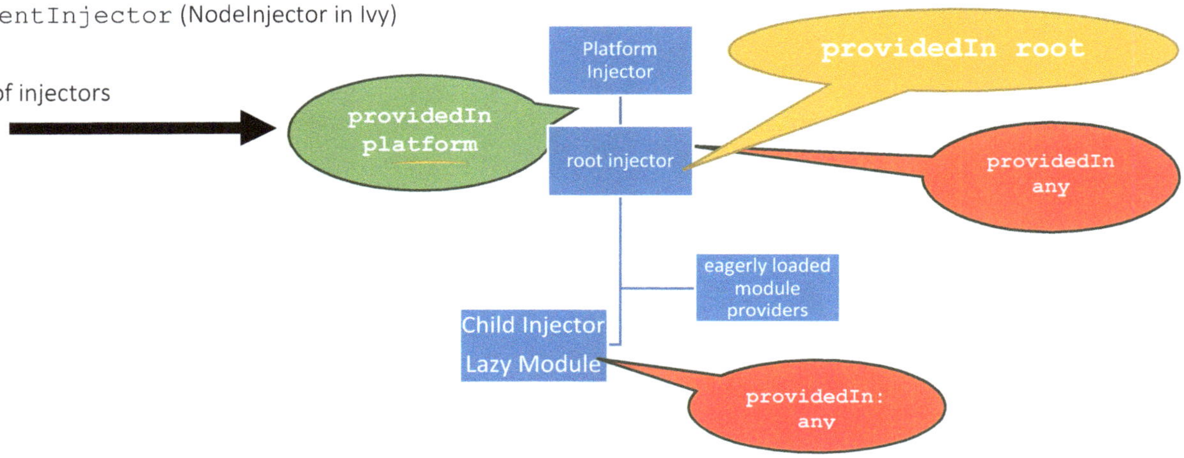

The services you create will be in one of these injectors, typically the root injector. Special or shared services that are used by multiple applications would use the Platform Injector. (a DOM sanitizer is a good example of a service that is used by multiple applications). The root injector is the primary location for all eagerly loaded module providers. LazyModule injectors are used for all lazy loaded modules which always create a child injector. 'any' is a good option if you need to enforce a singleton within the boundaries of a module.

56—Guided Exercise: Understanding Provided Services

We need two lazy loaded modules to better examine how Angular 9 handles the creation and resolution of services.

Basic Steps:

1. Create a module for the exercises feature
2. Lazy load the exercises module
3. Create an interface to be used with a token that will be injected via a new service
4. Create a new service
5. Inject the new service into both the foodGroups and Exercises components
6. Use the new service in FoodGroups and Exercises
7. Create a token to be injected into the application at various places
8. Create an interface for the token
9. Inject the token into the new service
10. Provide the token in the app module
11. Provide the token with different values to FoodGroups and Exercises Modules

Step 1 Create a new module for the exercise feature of the FoodPlate application via the CLI tool.

```
ng generate module exercises
```

The CLI tool should create a TypeScript file called exercises.module.ts and put the file in the exercises folder of the application. Confirm this by examining your project folder.

Step 2 Confirm that the exercises module declares the exercises.component and remove the declaration of exercises from the app.module.

Step 3 To lazy load the exercises module, create an exercise.routing.module.ts file in the exercises folder.

```
import { NgModule } from '@angular/core';
import { Routes, RouterModule } from '@angular/router';

import { ExercisesComponent } from './exercises.component';

export const exerciseRoutes: Routes = [{ path: '', component:
ExercisesComponent }];

@NgModule({
    imports: [RouterModule.forChild(exerciseRoutes)],
    exports: [RouterModule]
})
export class ExerciseRoutingModule { }
```

Step 4 Import the ExercisesRoutingModule in the exercises module.ts file.

```
@NgModule({
  declarations: [ ExercisesComponent ],
  imports: [
    CommonModule,
    ExerciseRoutingModule
  ],
```

Step 5 Refactor the app.routing.module to lazy load the exercises and food-groups components as defined by the Angular 9 documentation. The changes are shown below in bold. (Don't forget to remove the original exercises route.)

```
const routes: Routes = [
    {
        path: '',
        children: [
            {path: 'myPlate', component: PlateComponent, canActivate:
[RegisterGuardService]},
            {path: 'register', component: RegisterComponent, canDeactivate:
[LeaveRegisterGuardService]},
            {path: 'farmersMarkets', component: FarmersMarketsComponent},
            {path: 'nutritionInfo', component: FoodComponent},
            {path: 'foodGroups', loadChildren: () => import('./food-
groups/food-groups.module').then(m => m.FoodGroupsModule)},
            {path: 'exercises', loadChildren: () =>
import('./exercises/exercises.module').then(m => m.ExercisesModule)},
            fallbackRoute
        ]
    }];
```

Step 6 Create an interface that will be used with an injectable token. Name the file TestInterface.ts and save it in the models folder.

```
export interface ITest {
    testString: any;
}
```

Step 7 Create the token to be injected into components. Name the file test.token.ts and save it in the models folder.

```
import { InjectionToken } from '@angular/core';
import { ITest } from './TestInterface';

export const testToken = new InjectionToken<ITest>('test token');
```

Step 8 Create a new service that will use the token. Name the service test.service.ts.

```
import { Inject, Injectable } from '@angular/core';
import { testToken } from '../models/test.token';
```

```
import { ITest } from '../models/TestInterface';

@Injectable({
  providedIn: 'root'
})
export class TestService {

  constructor(@Inject(testToken) private test: ITest ) {
    console.log("%cnew instance of FoodGroupsService created", "color: red");
  }

  getValue(): ITest {
    return this.test;
  }
}
```

The service uses dependency injection to inject a testToken called "test." The %c before the console log string is used to color the console log statement in red. This will make it easier to find when the file is tested. The getValue() method simply returns the token.

Step 9 Inject the new service in the exercises component and log the value of the token to the console as shown below.

```
  constructor(private testService: TestService) { }

  ngOnInit(): void {
    console.log('%cfrom exercises.component:', 'color: red');
    console.log(this.testService.getValue());
  }
```

Step 10 Inject the new service in the food-groups component and log the value of the token to the console as shown below.

```
constructor(private foodGroupsService: FoodGroupsService,
             private router: Router,
             private testService: TestService,
             private route: ActivatedRoute) {
  }

    ngOnInit(): void {
      console.log('%cfrom foodGroups.component:', 'color: red');
      console.log(this.testService.getValue());
      this.foodGroups = this.foodGroupsService.getFoodGroups();
  }
```

Step 11 Notice the error message shown below for reference.

```
▸ERROR Error: Uncaught (in promise): NullInjectorError: R3InjectorError(FoodGroupsModule)   core.js:5845
[TestService -> TestService -> InjectionToken test token -> InjectionToken test token -> InjectionToken
test token]:
  NullInjectorError: No provider for InjectionToken test token!
NullInjectorError: R3InjectorError(FoodGroupsModule)[TestService -> TestService -> InjectionToken test
token -> InjectionToken test token -> InjectionToken test token]:
  NullInjectorError: No provider for InjectionToken test token!
```

The application is expecting a value for the injected token (test token) but there is no provider.

Step 12 Open the app module and provide a test value as shown below. Note how the providers array provides the token as well as the value creator.

```
export const testValue2: ITest = {
    testString: 'AppModuleTestValue'
};
...

bootstrap: [ AppComponent ],
  providers: [{
      provide: testToken, useValue: testValue2
  }]
})
```

Step 13 Test the file in Chrome with the DevTools Network panel open. Click the Food Groups link and see the lazy-load.

Step 14 Click the Exercises link and see the lazy load as shown below in the network tab of the DevTools.

runtime.js	200	script	(index)
polyfills.js	200	script	(index)
styles.js	200	script	(index)
vendc	200	script	(index)
main.j	200	script	(index)
ng-validate.js	200	script	content-script.js:1
backend.js	200	script	content-script.js:1
common.js	200	script	bootstrap:149
food-groups-food-groups-module.js	200	script	bootstrap:149
exercises-exercises-module.js	200	script	bootstrap:149

http://localhost:4200/styles.js

Step 15 Open the DevTools console, return to localhost:4200 and refresh the page.

Step 16 Click the Food Groups link and notice the red console line shown below.

```
new instance of FoodGroupsService created
from foodGroups.component:
▸{testString: "AppModuleTestValue"}
```

A new instance of the TestService has been created and the test string has been returned from the value supplied to the app module.

Step 17 Click the Exercises link and notice the red console line shown below.

```
new instance of FoodGroupsService created
from foodGroups.component:
▶ {testString: "AppModuleTestValue"}
from exercises.component:
▶ {testString: "AppModuleTestValue"}
```

The same instance of the test service is used returning the same test token.

Step 18 Provide each module (Exercises module and FoodGroups module) a different token value as shown below. First open the Exercises module. The relevant code changes are shown in bold.

```
import { NgModule } from '@angular/core';
import { CommonModule } from '@angular/common';

import { testToken } from '../models/test.token';
import { ITest } from '../models/TestInterface';
import { ExerciseRoutingModule } from './exercise.routing.module';
import { ExercisesComponent } from './exercises.component';

export const testValue: ITest = {
    testString: 'exercisesModuleTestValue'
};

@NgModule({
  declarations: [ ExercisesComponent ],
  imports: [
    CommonModule,
    ExerciseRoutingModule
  ],
  providers: [{
    provide: testToken, useValue: testValue
  }]

})
export class ExercisesModule { }
```

Step 19 Do the same for the FoodGroups module, shown below for reference.

```
import { NgModule } from '@angular/core';
import { CommonModule } from '@angular/common';

import { testToken } from '../models/test.token';
import { ITest } from '../models/TestInterface';
import { FoodDetailModule } from './food-detail/food-detail.module';
import { FoodGroupsComponent } from './food-groups.component';
```

```
import { FoodGroupsRoutingModule } from './food-groups.routing';

export const testValue2: ITest = {
  testString: 'foodGroupsModuleTestValue'
};

@NgModule({
  declarations: [ FoodGroupsComponent ],
  imports: [
    CommonModule,
    FoodDetailModule,
    FoodGroupsRoutingModule
  ],
  providers: [{
    provide: testToken, useValue: testValue2
  }]
})

export class FoodGroupsModule {
}
```

Step 20 Repeat steps 16 and 17 to test the values passed to the modules. Again one TestService is instantiated and the value passed is still from the app module.

```
new instance of FoodGroupsService created
from foodGroups.component:
▶ {testString: "AppModuleTestValue"}
from exercises.component:
▶ {testString: "AppModuleTestValue"}
```

This is where providedIn: any will help. Sometimes you will need two or more instances of your service and would like components to receive different values from the injected token. In other words, there are times when each module should have their own instance. This is common with lazy-loaded modules.

Step 21 Open the TestService and change the providedIn property from `'root'` to `'any'` as shown below.

```
@Injectable({
  providedIn: 'any'
})
```

Step 22 Test the file in Chrome. The console should now look like this:

```
new instance of FoodGroupsService created
from foodGroups.component:
▶ {testString: "foodGroupsModuleTestValue"}
new instance of FoodGroupsService created
from exercises.component:
▶ {testString: "exercisesModuleTestValue"}
```

16.5 Lazy Loading Components

Prior to Angular version 9, only modules could be lazy loading. Due to Angular 9's new compilation and rendering capabilities (via the code name "Ivy" – the older compiler and runtime is known as "View Engine"), Angular can now lazy load components. By now, you should understand the power of modules and their significance in the compilation process. Modules declare components, directives and pipes and provide services. Without Modules, the compilation process as we know it today cannot take place. Before Angular 9, the compiler known as "View Engine" adds to the modules all of the required component metadata such as the selector, any inputs and outputs used, as well as variables and constants. Ultimately compiling a version of your components template with all of its functionality intact. Angular 9 which uses the "Ivy" compiler and runtime now uses a concept called "locality" which allows a component to exist without a module, essentially bundles our component code, a factory that can instantiate the component and all of the components' metadata such as type, selectors and son on. In addition, Ivy adds a template function which is the compiled version of the HTML along with instructions to create the DOM. This is a somewhat reverse version of the way the older View Engine worked. View Engine iterated through our code and executed it. Ivy triggers Angular to execute allowing the component to live independent of a module. This change also allows the Angular core library to be tree shakable.

Ultimately Angular compilation is required because the component code we write is declarative in that it declares our components, our bindings and so on, they do not indicate how Angular will perform change detection on our bindings for example. Browsers do not understand this declarative code, thus Angular provides a compiler that will convert this declarative code to the imperative code the browser does understand which results in the DOM methods that create our templates.

16.5.1 Compilation: Just In Time

Angular can use Just In Time or JIT compilation which means that in addition to transpiling TypeScript to JavaScript, decorators such as @Component that invoke the compiler, do so truly just in time. In other words, when the field is read. This results in compiled code that potentially may not ever run. The decorators become part of the transpiled bundled JavaScript run in the browser. The decorators call the compiler at runtime. At this point, the declarative code is converted to imperative code: at runtime or "Just In Time."

16.5.2 Compilation: Ahead Of Time

Ahead Of Time compilation known as AOT, executes at build time using (ngc) what JIT executes at runtime, thus avoiding the cost of runtime compilation. AOT takes the decorators and pre-compiles them into the imperative instructions needed at runtime. This happens "Ahead of Time."

16.5.3 How to lazy load components

To lazy load components, they must first be added via a container on the parent component. This container can be an HTML element like a div or an Angular-specific element like ng-container. Some developers prefer a separation of concerns around this choice. Since there is no compelling or semantic need for another HTML element, the ng-container is sometimes preferred. This approach can minimize CSS errors as well because there is no risk of accidentally styling an otherwise unnecessary HTML element.

The parent component class now needs a reference to the container tag which can be accomplished with a template variable combined with an @ViewChild decorator which reads the template variable as a ViewContainerRef. A ViewContainerRef represents a container where one or more views can be attached to a component.

The next step is to use a ComponentFactoryResolver (introduced in the directives chapter) that acts as a registry that maps Components to generated ComponentFactory classes that have been used to create instances of components.

16.5.4 How does Angular lazy load components?

Angular uses the ECMAScript import function to lazy load components. This function returns a promise that can be handled with JavaScript's async await method.

Async/Await[8]

The word "async" before a function means one simple thing: a function always returns a promise. Other values are wrapped in a resolved promise automatically.

The keyword await makes JavaScript wait until that promise settles and returns its result.

The ComponentFactoryResolver then invokes the resolveComponentFactory method on the lazy loaded component, followed by the container which invokes the createComponent method using the injector. The createComponent method instantiates a single component and inserts its host view into this container. It returns the new component instance, containing the host view. It requires the following properties:

1. The (component) factory to use.
2. The index at which to insert the new component's host view into this container. If not specified, appends the new view as the last entry.
3. The injector to use as the parent for the new component.

The instance component created by the createComponent method can be passed any @Input properties it requires.

[8] https://javascript.info/async-await

57—Guided Exercise: Lazy Load a Component

In this exercise, you lazy load a new component called Nutrition Detail. You will need to start the food.json server on port 3004. After the food items load in the browser, the user can click on a food item from the list and see the new nutrition detail component as shown below.

Step 1 Open nutrition-details and add an input property called foodItem which represents the selected food item. The code is shown in bold below.

Note The nutrition-details component was made in the optional exercise called "Implement Virtual Scrolling," step 9 from Chapter 14.

```
import { Component, Input, OnDestroy, OnInit } from '@angular/core';
import { Food } from '../models/food';

@Component({
  selector: 'fp-nutrition-details',
  templateUrl: './nutrition-details.component.html',
  styleUrls: ['./nutrition-details.component.css']
})
export class NutritionDetailsComponent implements OnInit {

  @Input()
  foodItem: Food;

  constructor() { }

  ngOnInit(): void {
    console.log(this.foodItem);
  }

}
```

Step 2 Copy the assets/css/nutrition-detail-css.css file to the nutrition-detail/nutrition-detail.component.css file.

Step 3 Copy the assets/code-snippets/nutrition-details-html to the nutrition-details/nutrition-details.component.html file. The relevant code is shown below in bold.

```
<h2>Nutrition Details</h2>
<section>
    <table>
        <thead>
            <tr>
                <th>Protein</th>
                <th>Carbohydrate</th>
                <th>Total Lipid (Fat)</th>
            </tr>
        </thead>
        <tbody>
            <tr>
                <td>{{ foodItem.nutrients[0].value }} {{
foodItem.nutrients[0].units }}</td>
                <td>{{ foodItem.nutrients[2].value }} {{
foodItem.nutrients[2].units }}</td>
                <td>{{ foodItem.nutrients[1].value }} {{
foodItem.nutrients[1].units }}</td>
            </tr>
            </tbody>
    </table>
</section>
```

Step 4 Open the nutrition-details parent component, food.component.ts and add the following code shown below in bold.

```
...
foodListByGroup: Food[] = this.foodList;
foodItem: Food;  // references the foodItem selected
protein;         // test property for log statements
```

Step 5 Return to the parent HTML file, food.component.html and add an ng-container to hold the lazy-loaded component. The additional code is shown below in bold.

```
<section class="errMessage" *ngIf="errorMessage">
    {{errorMessage}}
</section>

<ng-container #foodDetailContainer></ng-container>
```

Step 6 Open the parent component class file: food.component.ts and add a reference to the ng-container via @ViewChild.

```
@ViewChild('foodDetailContainer', {read: ViewContainerRef})
foodDetailContainer: ViewContainerRef;
```

Step 7 Create the showNutrients method which will call the lazyLoadNutritionDetail() function via async await.

```
async showNutrients(food): Promise<any> {
    this.protein = food.nutrients[0].value;
    console.table(food.nutrients);
    console.log(this.protein + food.nutrients[0].units);
    this.foodItem = food;
    console.log(this.foodItem);
    this.foodDetailContainer.detach();
    await this.lazyLoadNutritionDetail();
}
```

Step 8 Add the lazyLoadNutritionDetail function shown below.

```
async showNutrients(food): Promise<any> {
    this.protein = food.nutrients[0].value;
    console.table(food.nutrients);
    console.log(this.protein + food.nutrients[0].units);
    this.foodItem = food;
    console.log(this.foodItem);
    await this.lazyLoadNutritionDetail();
}
```

Step 9 Write the LazyLoadNutritionDetail method.

```
private async lazyLoadNutritionDetail(): Promise<any> {
    const { NutritionDetailsComponent } = await import('../nutrition-
details/nutrition-details.component');
    const nutritionDetailFactory =
this.cfr.resolveComponentFactory(NutritionDetailsComponent);
    const { instance } =
this.foodDetailContainer.createComponent(nutritionDetailFactory, null,
this.injector);
    instance.foodItem = this.foodItem;
  }
```

Step 10 Save and test in the browser with the DevTools Network panel open. Make sure the food server is running on port 3004. Click the Nutrition link, then click a food item.

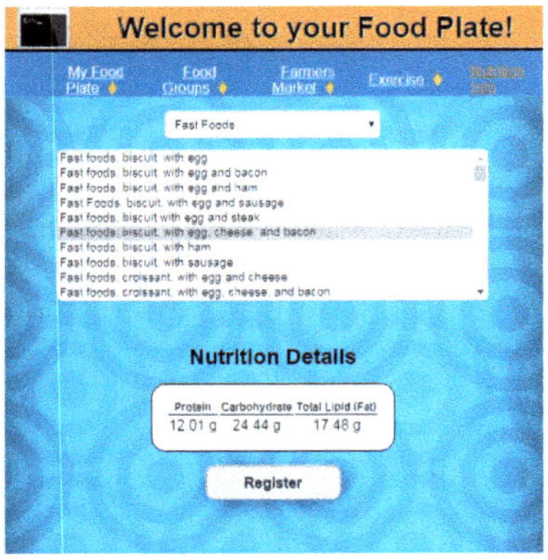

runtime.js	200	script
polyfills.js	200	script
styles.js	200	script
vendor.js	200	script
main.js	200	script
ng-validate.js	200	script
backend.js	200	script
nutrition-details-nutrition-details-component...	200	script

Step 10 Click another food item and you will see an additional component. The user should see only one food-detail component at a time.

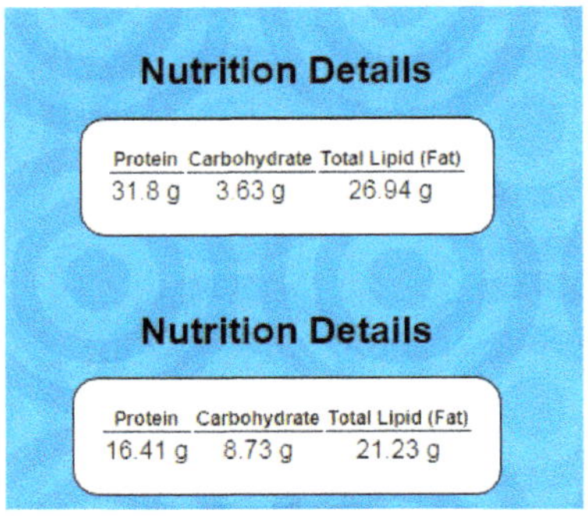

Step 11 Before lazy loading any food-detail components, you can detach the component in the container from the DOM to solve this problem. Add the code shown below in bold.

```
async showNutrients(food): Promise<any> {
  this.protein = food.nutrients[0].value;
  console.table(food.nutrients);
  console.log(this.protein + food.nutrients[0].units);
  this.foodItem = food;
  console.log(this.foodItem);
  this.foodDetailContainer.detach();
  await this.lazyLoadNutritionDetail();
}
```

Step 13 Confirm that the nutrition-detail component is not being eagerly loaded. If necessary, open app.module and remove it from the declarations array.

Step 14 Save and test again, note the network panel showing the lazy loaded component.

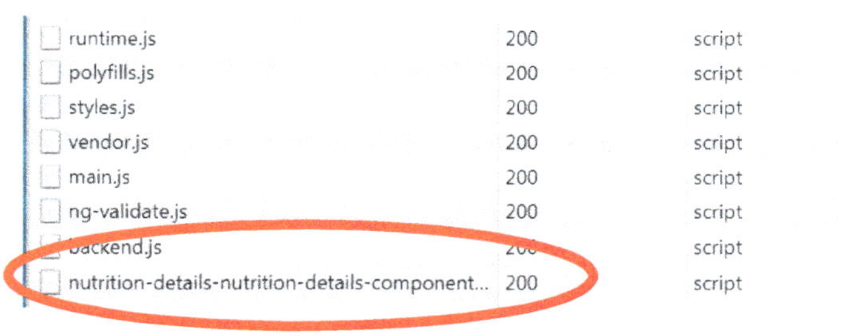

Chapter 16 Quiz

Online Quiz: https://tinyurl.com/4rpdkxx6

1) Which of the following are route guards?
   a) canAuthorize()
   b) canActivate()
   c) canDeactivate()
   d) canLoad()
   e) resolve()

2) True/False
   CanActivate() can return an observable or a promise.

3) True/False
   Angular does not provide a method that prevents a user from leaving a route.

4) True/False
   By default, NgModules are eagerly loaded.

Next chapter

In the next chapter, you revisit HTTP to create a simple CRUD (create, read, update, delete) section for the FoodPlate application.

Chapter 17

HTTP CRUD

Chapter 17: HTTP CRUD

Objectives

- Create a form to collect user goals
- Understand the architecture of Reactive Forms
- Keep track of goals reached
- Create new goals
- Read goals
- Update goals
- Delete goals

Introduction

CRUD is the popular acronym for applications that deal with data from the server. Data items are created, read, updated and deleted, thus C-R-U-D.

17.0 Reactive forms and CRUD

Reactive forms help us create forms that facilitate a reactive style of programming.

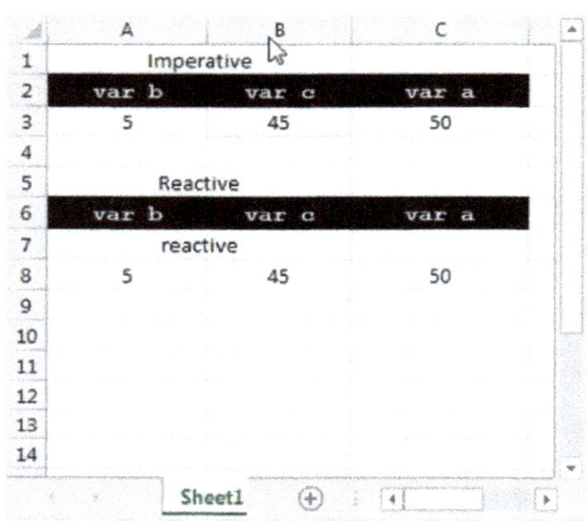

Similar to the way that a spreadsheet reacts to changes in different cells, reactive programming also concerns itself with changes in data streams in a declarative manner. In a previous chapter on Observables, you learned about asynchronous data streams and how they can be handled via observables. This is reactive programming in the sense that you are creating “streams” of data out of just about anything including mouse clicks, variables, user input, properties and so on and reacting to that stream. To review, we respond to th stream by listening and we listen by subscribing. The functions that act on the stream are observers and the stream is the observable. By using this approach, our code can react to any propagated changes without additional code concern around how those changes propagate. This demonstrates yet another separation of concerns that facilitates code maintenance.

Combined with reactive forms, the observer pattern described above can listen for FormControl value changes. See the snippet from angular docs below (https://angular.io/api/forms/AbstractControl#statusChanges).

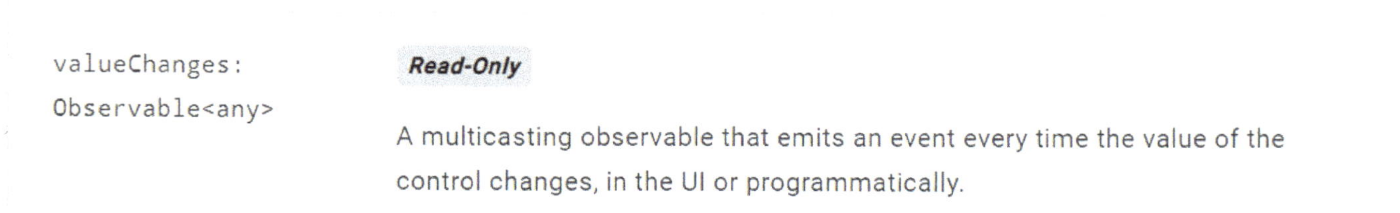

valueChanges: Observable<any>

Read-Only

A multicasting observable that emits an event every time the value of the control changes, in the UI or programmatically.

Figure #33: The valueChanges observable as seen in the Angular documentation.

17.1 The Reactive Model

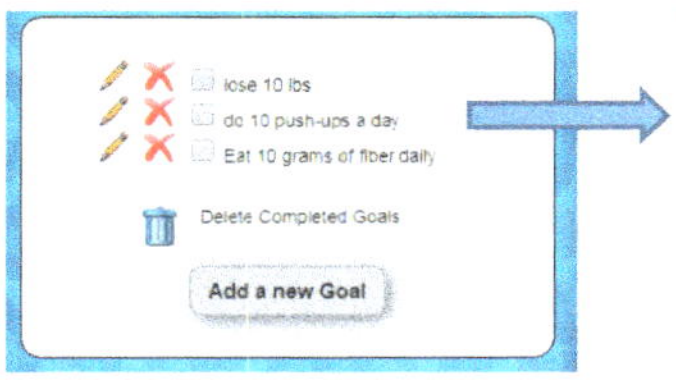


```
[
  {
    "id": 8,
    "goalTitle": "lose 10 lbs",
    "goalDeadline": "12/31/2017",
    "didIt": false
  },
  {
    "id": 9,
    "goalTitle": "do 10 push-ups a day",
    "goalDeadline": "12/12/2020",
    "didIt": false
  },
  {
    "id": 12,
    "goalTitle": "Eat 10 grams of fiber daily",
    "goalDeadline": "1/1/2018",
    "didIt": null
  },
  {
    "id": 14,
    "goalTitle": "yet another one",
    "goalDeadline": "1/2/2019",
    "didIt": null
  }
]
```

There is a mapping between the data model and the user interface as shown above.

```
createForm() {
  //the form model
  this.goalForm = this.fb.group({
    id: [''],
    goalTitle: ['', Validators.required],
    goalDeadline: ['', Validators.required],
    didIt: ['']
  })
}
```

The component class creates and manipulates form control objects and is the pure source of original values.

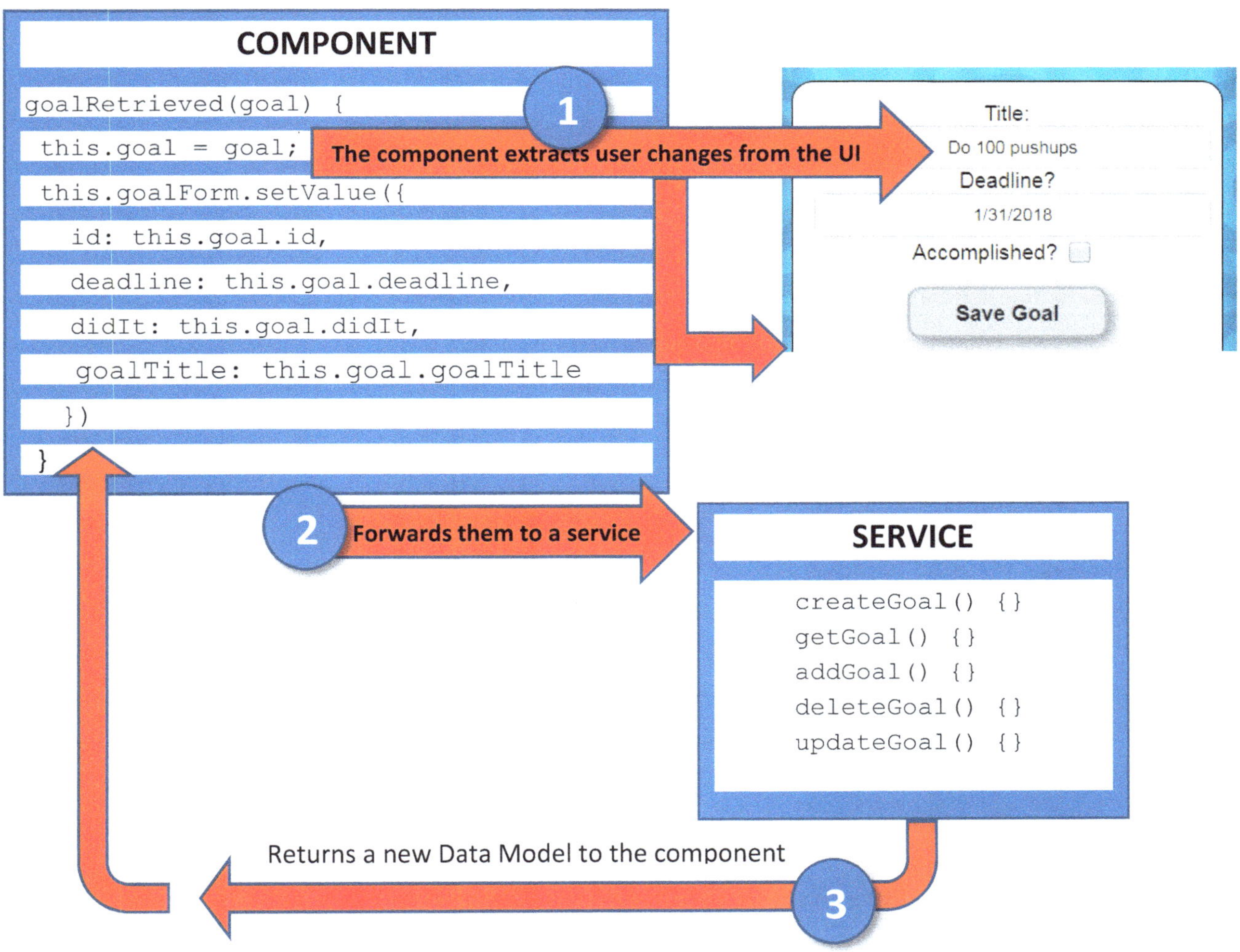

58–Guided Exercise: Create a component for CRUD operations

In this exercise, you create the component that will display goals.

Step 1 Create a new component called "goals" via `ng g c goals -m app.`

Step 2 Add the view template to "goals.component.html" as shown below. You can copy and paste this file from assets/code-snippets/goals-component-html.html

```
<section class="initScreen">
  <ul>
    <li>
      <div>
        <img src="assets/images/icons/pencil.png"
             id="editIcon"
             class="icon buffer">
        <img src="assets/images/icons/delete.png"
             id="deleteIcon"
             class="icon buffer">
        <input class="checkboxLg" type="checkbox">
        <label> </label>
      </div>
    </li>
  </ul>
  <section class="trashIcon">
  <img src="assets/images/icons/trash-icon.png"><span>Delete Completed
Goals</span>
  </section>
  <button class="fpButton" >Add a new Goal</button>
</section>
```

Step 4 Add the CSS for the new component. You can copy and paste from goals-component.css in the assets/css folder.

Step 5 To create the goal component, you need to complete the following steps:

- Use dependency injection to access the **`FormBuilder`** class
- Create a **`FormGroup`** object and name it **`goalForm`**
- Write a **`createForm`** method that uses the FormBuilder to create a form with the following fields:
    - **`id`**
    - **`goalTitle`** (required)
    - **`deadline`** (required)
    - **`didIt`**
- Call the **`createForm`** method from the constructor
- Import the necessary classes

```
import { Component, OnInit } from '@angular/core';
import { FormBuilder, FormControl, FormGroup, Validators } from
'@angular/forms';

@Component({
  selector: 'fp-goals',
  templateUrl: 'goals.component.html',
  styleUrls: ['goals.component.css']
})
```

```
export class GoalsComponent implements OnInit {
  goalForm: FormGroup;

  createForm(): void {
    this.goalForm = this.fb.group({
      id: [''],
      goalTitle: ['', Validators.required],
      deadline: ['', Validators.required],
      didIt: ['']
    });
  }

  constructor(private fb: FormBuilder) {
      this.createForm();
  }

  ngOnInit(): void {}
}
```

Step 6 Add the new component link to the nav component.

```
...
<li><a routerLink = "goals" routerLinkActive= "active">My Goals</a></li>
...
```

Step 7 Add the route in app.routing.module.ts for the new Goals component and import the component.

```
import {GoalsComponent} from './goals/goals.component';
...
{ path: 'nutritionInfo', component: FoodComponent },
{ path: 'goals', component: GoalsComponent },
...
```

Step 8 Confirm the Goals module has been declared in the app.module.ts.

Step 9 Start a new JSON server using the goals.json file with the following command. Be sure you are inside the server folder, shown below, before typing the command.

```
cd src/assets/server
json-server goals.json -p 3006
```

Step 10 Save and test the app in Chrome. It should match the screenshot below.

59—Guided Exercise: Create the service with the CRUD operations

In this exercise, you create the service that will contain the CRUD operations for creating new goals, deleting goals, updating goals reading goals.

Step 1 In the "models'" directory, create a Goal data model (to store the goal data) and name it goal.ts. The code is shown below the CLI command.

```
ng g class goal - -type model
```

```
export class Goal {
    id: number = 0;
    deadline: string;
    didIt: boolean = false;
    goalTitle: string;
}
```

Step 2 Create a new service called goals.service.ts via `ng g s services/goals`.

Step 3 Add the following private properties: `goalUrl` to store the location of the Goals API (via json-server) and jsonContentTypeHeaders to store the header type used in the Http requests. Don't forget to import the necessary classes.

```
goalUrl = 'http://localhost:3006/goals';
jsonContentTypeHeaders = {
    headers: new HttpHeaders().set('Content-Type', 'application/json'),
};
errorMessage: string;
```

Step 4 Inject the HTTPClient dependency in the constructor function. Don't forget to import the new HTTPClient module from the @angular/common/http.

```
constructor(private http: HttpClient) {
}
```

Step 5 Add the http verb methods as shown below.

```
getGoals(): Observable<Goal> {
    const results: Observable<Goal> = this.http.get<Goal>(this.goalUrl);
    console.log(`getGoals() returned ${results}`);
    return results;
}

getGoalById(goalId: string): Observable<Goal> {
    const results: Observable<Goal> =
this.http.get<Goal>(`${this.goalUrl}/${goalId}`);
    console.log(`getGoals(${goalId}) returned ${results}`);
    return results;
}

addGoal(goal: Goal): Observable<Goal> {
    const results: Observable<Goal> =
      this.http.post<Goal>(this.goalUrl, goal, this.jsonContentTypeHeaders);
    console.log(`addGoal(${goal}) returned ${results}`);
    console.log(typeof goal.id);
```

```
    return results;
}

updateGoal(goal: Goal): Observable<Goal> {
    const results: Observable<Goal> =
      this.http.put<Goal>(`${this.goalUrl}/${goal.id}`, goal,
this.jsonContentTypeHeaders);
    console.log(`updateGoal(${goal}) returned ${results}`);
    return results;
}

deleteGoalById(goalId: string): Observable<Goal> {
    const results: Observable<Goal> =
this.http.delete<Goal>(`${this.goalUrl}/${goalId}`);
    console.log(`deleteGoalById(${goalId}) returned ${results}`);
    return results;
}
```

Notice that each method returns an Observable of Goal object.

Step 6 In goals.service.ts, be sure that you have imported all the necessary classes.

```
import { Injectable } from '@angular/core';
import { HttpClient, HttpHeaders} from "@angular/common/http";
import { Observable} from 'rxjs/index;
import { Goal } from '../models/Goal';
```

Step 7 Open goals.component.html and add a databinding to the goal.title in the goal view template file as shown below in bold.

```
...
<input class="checkboxLg" type="checkbox">
        <label> {{ goal.goalTitle }} </label>
      </div>
...
```

Save the file and test the app in Chrome. You should receive an error message indicating that goal is undefined as shown below.

```
▶ERROR TypeError: Cannot    ng:///AppModule/Goal…ent.ngfactory.js:22
read property 'goalTitle' of undefined
    at Object.eval [as updateRenderer] (ng:///AppModule/Goal…ent.ngf
actory.js:36)
```

Step 8 Inject the goals.service in the constructor function.

```
...
import {GoalsService} from '../services/goals.service';
...
constructor(private fb: FormBuilder, private goalsService: GoalsService) {
    this.createForm();
  }
```

Step 9 Add an allGoals property to the component as shown below in bold and import the Goal class.

```
goalForm: FormGroup;
allGoals;
errorMessage: string;
isLoading: boolean;
```

```
goal: Goal;
```

Step 10 Call the `getGoals()` method from `ngOnInit()`.

```
ngOnInit() {
        this.goalsService.getGoals()
        .subscribe((res: any) => {
          this.allGoals = res;
          console.log(this.allGoals);
          this.isLoading = false;
        }, err => {
          this.errorMessage = err;
          console.log(this.errorMessage = err.message);
          this.isLoading = false;
        });
}
```

Step 11 Modify the view template as shown below in bold.

```
<section class="initScreen" *ngIf="errorMessage">{{errorMessage}}</section>
<section class="initScreen" *ngIf="allGoals?.length > 0">
  <ul>
    <li *ngFor="let goal of allGoals">
      <div>
        <img src="assets/images/icons/pencil.png"
             id="editIcon"
             class="icon buffer">
        <img src="assets/images/icons/delete.png"
             id="deleteIcon"
             class="icon buffer">
        <input class="checkboxLg" type="checkbox">
        <label>{{goal.goalTitle}}  </label>
      </div>
    </li>
  </ul>
  <section class="trashIcon">
  <img src="assets/images/icons/trash-icon.png"><span>Delete Completed
Goals</span>
  </section>
  <button class="fpButton" >Add a new Goal</button>
</section>
```

Step 12 Save the files and test the app in Chrome. It should look like the image below.

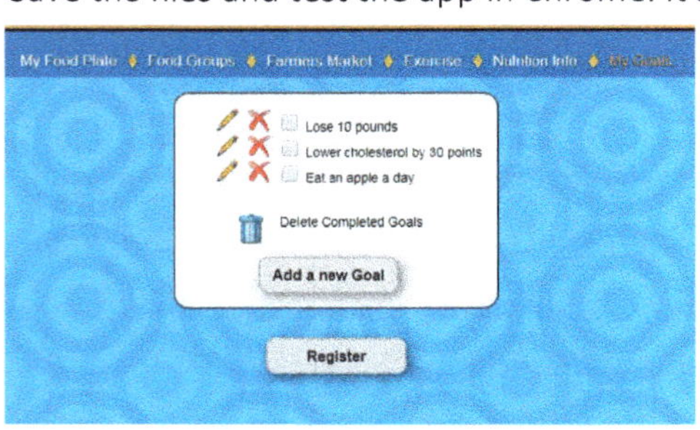

Note In the next exercise you will add the delete, edit and add functionality.

60—Guided Exercise: Add the CRUD functionality to the component

In this exercise, you add behaviors to the edit and delete buttons in the view template. You also add the functionality to the "Save Goal" button and make other updates as needed to the UI.

Step 1 Open the goals.component.html and add the event hooks as shown below in bold. Also add the class binding to the goal title's label element.

```
<section class="initScreen" *ngIf="allGoals?.length > 0">
  <ul>
    <li *ngFor="let goal of allGoals">
      <div>
        <img src="assets/images/icons/pencil.png"
             id="editIcon"
             class="icon buffer"
             (click)="showEditGoalForm(goal)">
        <img src="assets/images/icons/delete.png"
             id="deleteIcon"
             class="icon buffer"
             (click)="deleteGoal(goal)">
        <input class="checkboxLg" type="checkbox"
(click)="toggleGoalComplete(goal)">
        <label [class.completed]="goal.didIt"> {{goal.goalTitle}}  </label>
      </div>
    </li>
  </ul>
  <section class="icon trashIcon" (click)="deleteCompleted()">
   <img src="assets/images/icons/trash-icon.png">
   <span>Delete Completed Goals</span>
  </section>
  <button class="fpButton" (click)="showAddGoalForm()">Add a new Goal</button>
</section>
```

Step 2 In the goal component class, add the goal property and its datatype, Goal as shown in bold below. Add the `newGoalView` property and initialize it to `'false'`. Add the activeGoal property. Be sure to import the Goal class.

```
...
goal: Goal;
activeGoal: Goal;
newGoalView = false;
```

Step 3 In the goal component class, add the methods added in the view template in step 1.

```
showEditGoalForm(goal: Goal): void {
    this.newGoalView = true;
    this.getGoal(goal.id);
    this.showGoalAddEditForm(true);
}

toggleGoalComplete(goal: Goal): void {
    goal.didIt = !goal.didIt;
}

showAddGoalForm(): void {
    this.showGoalAddEditForm(true);
    this.resetGoalService();
```

```
}

showGoalAddEditForm(showForm: boolean): void {
   this.newGoalView = showForm;
  }

getGoal(id): void {
    this.goalsService.getGoalById(id)
      .subscribe(
        goal => this.goalRetrieved(goal),
        error => console.log(error)
      );
}

deleteGoal(goal): void {
    this.goalsService.deleteGoalById(goal.id)
        .subscribe(goal => this.goalsService.getGoals());
}

goalRetrieved(goal): void {
    this.goal = goal;
    this.goalForm.setValue({
      id: this.goal.id,
      deadline: this.goal.deadline,
      didIt: this.goal.didIt,
      goalTitle: this.goal.goalTitle
    });
}

resetGoalService(): void {
    this.goalForm.reset();
}

deleteCompleted(): void {
    const completedGoals = this.allGoals.filter(goals => goals.didIt ===
true).map(goals => this.deleteGoal(goals));
    console.log(completedGoals);
}
```

Step 4 Open goals.component.html and add the form that will be used to add and update goals. Add the form code below the existing HTML. You can copy and paste this file from assets/code-snippets/add-goal-form-html.html.

```
...
<section class="initScreen" *ngIf="newGoalView">
  <form [formGroup]="goalForm" novalidate>
<!--    <label for="id">ID</label>
    <input type="text"
            id="id"
            formControlName="id"
            value="{{activeGoal?.id}}">-->
    <label for="goalTitle">Title:</label>
    <input type="text"
            id="goalTitle"
            autofocus
            formControlName="goalTitle"
            value="{{activeGoal?.goalTitle}}">
```

```
    <label for="deadline" style="display: block">Deadline?</label>
    <input type="text"
           id="deadline"
           formControlName="deadline"
           value="{{activeGoal?.deadline}}">

    <label for="didIt">Accomplished?</label>
    <input type="checkbox"
                id="didIt"
                formControlName="didIt"
                (click)="toggleAccomplished()"
                class="checkboxLg checkboxSpacer">
    <input type="button" class="fpButton blk"
            value="Save Goal"
           (click)="submitGoal(goalForm.value)"/>
  </form>
</section>
```

The formGroup is a reactive form directive that associates the formgroup instance with an html element. The formControlName binds the html control to the angular formGroup and the formControl property in the component class.

Step 5 As part of the learning experience, add the following elements below the closing form element.

```
</form>
  <p>Form Value: {{ goalForm.value | json}}</p>
  <p>Form Status: {{ goalForm.status | json}}</p>
  <p>Goal Deadline pristine state: {{ goalForm.get('deadline').pristine}}</p>
  <p>Goal Deadline touched state: {{ goalForm.get('deadline').untouched}}</p>
  <p>Goal Form dirty state: {{ goalForm.dirty}}</p>
</section>
```

Step 6 Return to goals.component.ts and write the insert and update methods.

```
insertGoal(goal: Goal): void {
    this.goalsService.addGoal(goal)
        .subscribe(goal => {
                this.goalsService.getGoals();
            },
            (error) => console.log(error)
        );
}

updateGoal(goal: Goal): void {
    this.goalsService.updateGoal(goal)
        .subscribe(goal => this.goalsService.getGoals());
}
```

Step 7 Finally, write the toggleAccomplished method which toggles the checkbox's checkmark if the goal has been accomplished.

```
toggleAccomplished(): void {
        console.log(`toggleAccomplished called`);
        this.goalForm.patchValue({didIt: true});
}
```

Step 8 In goals.component.ts, add the `submitGoal()` method.

```
submitGoal(goal): void {
    console.log(`submitGoal() called`);
    if (this.goalForm.invalid) {
      console.log('submitGoal(): this.goalForm.invalid = true ');
      return;
    }
    this.showGoalAddEditForm(false);
    // Insert
    if (goal.id === null || goal.id < 1) {
      this.insertGoal(goal);
    }
    // Update
    else {
      this.updateGoal(goal);
    }
}
```

The `submitGoal()` method will invoke either an update or a create via the put or post method in the service.

Step 9 Save all files and refresh the page in Chrome. Test the file with the following steps:

a. From the home page, click the "My Goals" link.
b. Edit the first goal to: "Lose 5 lbs" by clicking the pencil icon and making the change.
c. After making the change, click the "Save Goal" button.
d. Delete the "Eat 1 apple a day" goal by clicking the "x" icon.
e. Click the "Add a new Goal" button and add "Eat 1 banana a day" and a deadline of 12/12/2020.
f. Click the "Save Goal" button.
g. Click the checkbox to the left of the "Lose 5 pounds" goal.
h. Click the Trash can icon.

14 –Challenge Exercise: Add a title to the edit goal page

In this challenge exercise, you add the necessary code to achieve the result shown below.

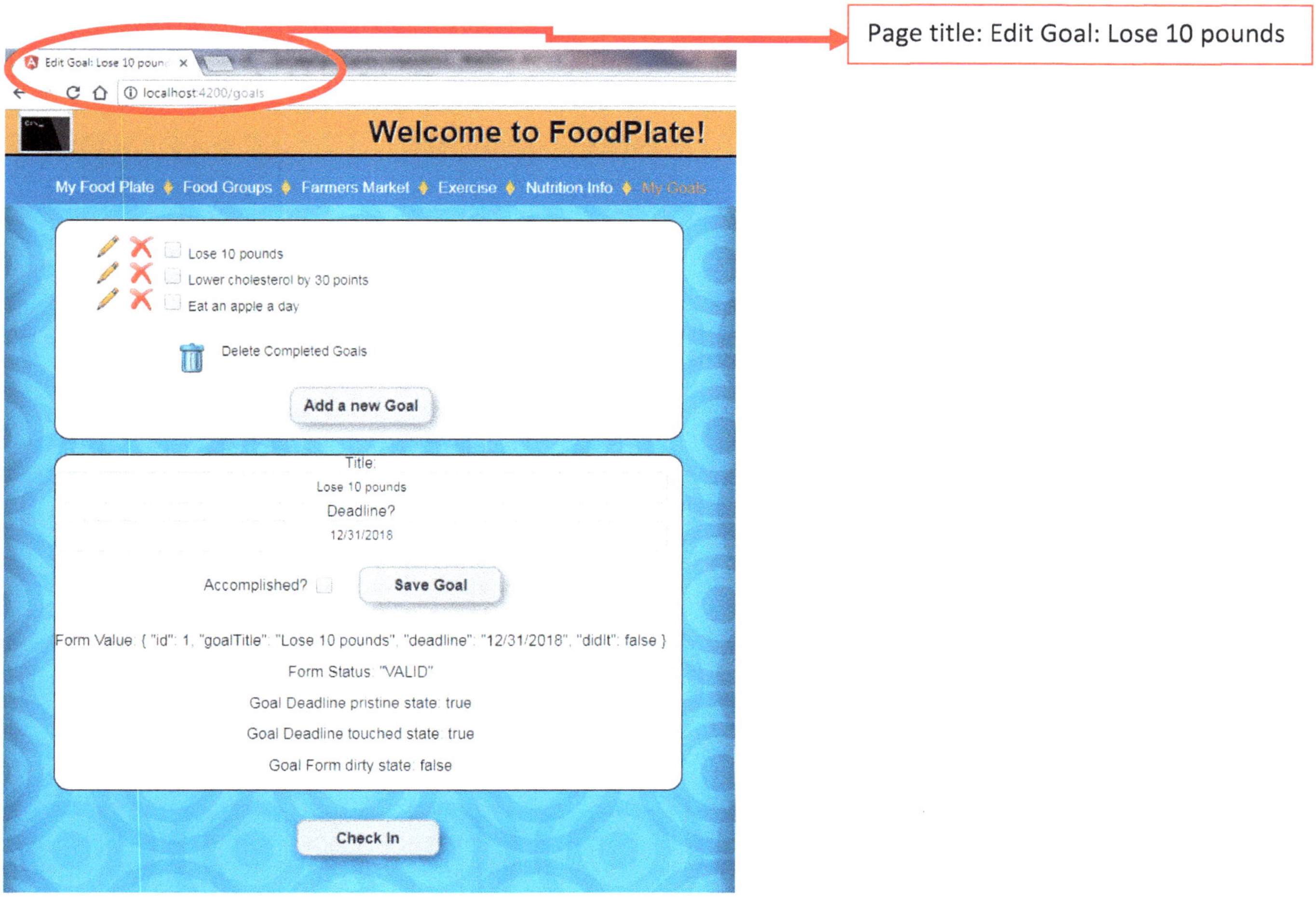

Possible solution: Goal.component.ts

```
  setTitle(newTitle: string) {
    this.titleService.setTitle(newTitle);
  }

  constructor(private goalsService: GoalsService, private fb: FormBuilder, private
titleService: Title) {
    this.createForm();
  }


  goalRetrieved(goal) {
    console.log('getRetrieved() called');
    this.goal = goal;
    this.setTitle(`Edit Goal: ${this.goal.goalTitle}`);
    this.goalForm.setValue({
      id: this.goal.id,
      deadline: this.goal.deadline,
      didIt: this.goal.didIt,
      goalTitle: this.goal.goalTitle
    })
  }

  showAddGoalForm() {
    console.log('showAddGoalForm() called');
    this.showGoalAddEditForm(true);
    this.resetGoalService()
  }
```

Chapter 17 Quiz

1) True/False
   The code that creates the CRUD methods is typically found in the component class.

Chapter summary

In this chapter, you added create, read, update and delete functionality to the application utilizing a REST API and HTTP calls from the client to the server. The Goals component was added so that the user could read goals, edit goals, add goals and delete goals. You further explored the use case for observables in the CRUD functionality.

Next Chapter

The remaining chapters of the course explore miscellaneous features that are common to web application development including Testing, using 3rd party libraries and UI frameworks like BootStrap and Angular Material.

Chapter 18

Introduction to Angular Testing

Chapter 18: Introduction to Angular Testing

Objectives

- Describe the role of testing in front-end web development
- Explain why testing is valuable
- List the different types of tests available
- List the testing tools used in the Angular framework

Introduction

In this chapter, the testing process is examined beginning with why developers should test their applications and ending with how to test Angular applications using tools and API's provided by the framework. This chapter will define unit testing vs. end-to-end testing. The testing tools and frameworks used with Angular will be covered as well as exercises in creating and running tests.

18.0 Why Test?

The benefits of testing web applications are widely known, but if you still need convincing visit the following sites:

- https://jrsinclair.com/articles/2016/gentle-introduction-to-javascript-tdd-intro/
- https://codeburst.io/testing-your-javascript-code-95c171c71647
- Udacity Lesson 1 from JavaScript Testing (free course) https://classroom.udacity.com/courses/ud549

To very briefly summarize some of the benefits of testing, see the list below.

- Testing adds clarity to the code base. Many developers acquaint themselves with a project by first reading the test code. Reading the test helps developers know the code authors intent when writing the code.
- Testing encourages developers to favor decoupling in the code they write, either in anticipation of testing or in the case of test-driven development (test is written prior to the code) before the code is written.
- While writing tests, developers can more easily identify overly complex code, thus test writing helps encourage code simplification.
- Testing doesn't prevent new code from breaking old code, but it helps bring our attention to potential bugs after adding code.
- Tested code is easier to maintain and scale. Code that is easier to test is typically well-written and more loosely coupled than code that is difficult to test, thus the act of testing tends to improve the quality of the code.

18.1 Testing Categories

Before we begin discussing Angular testing specifically, let's look at the two main types of testing that will be covered in this chapter.

- Unit Testing
- Functional Testing

18.1.1 Unit Tests

Unit tests are considered isolated tests because we isolate a single unit of code to test, ideally without requiring any other code to test that one unit. A unit is often identified as the smallest testable part of an application, such as a single function.

18.1.2 Functional Tests

Functional testing sometimes referred to as end-to-end testing or integration testing, tests the flow of the application from start to finish. In other words, testing the inter-dependencies within the application code. The application in its entirety is being tested to ensure that in a real-world environment, users can complete the various tasks provided by the application.

18.1.3 Other Tests

This chapter is highly focused to just a few testing types. Of course, web application development entails a multitude of other testing including but not limited to:

- Functionality testing
  - Does the app function per the specifications?
- Usability testing
  - Typically carried out by a dedicated testing team and includes testing of:
    - Navigation
    - Content
    - Images
- Accessibility testing
  - Does the test meet the expected Accessibility standards and priorities?
- Interface
  - Does the applications requests send correctly?
  - Is the data output correctly?
  - Is the web server handling all application requests without any service denial?
  - Do the queries sent to the database give expected results?
- Performance testing
  - Does the application meet performance standards set in the requirements?
  - Does the site perform sufficiently under low bandwidth? At peak loads?
- Security testing
  - Has the site been tested for unauthorized access?
  - Are page restrictions honored?
  - Are session automatically ended after prolong inactivity by the user?
  - Is the application served securely from the server?
- UI Testing
  - Do the images load properly?
  - Does the UI meet the design expectations?

18.2 Testing Types

Tests can be further defined by what they tests. For example, isolated tests typically test a component class or a service class without HTML. Basically, testing only. the classes properties and functions. Shallow tests test only a single component as opposed to a component and its child components. Finally, there are integrated tests which test multiple components.

18.3 Testing Angular Applications

Testing Angular applications is best done with the tools recommended (and in some cases installed) by the Angular team. The Angular framework provides a robust testing environment for testing Angular applications. The Angular CLI tool will download and install everything needed to test your application using specific tools and libraries.

18.3.1 Tools and frameworks used by Angular

- Jasmine
- Karma
- Protractor

18.4 Introduction to Unit Testing with Jasmine

In this section, we explore the Jasmine unit testing framework and how to implement it within the Angular ecosystem, specifically using the Angular CLI tool. You will learn what Jasmine code looks like along with the terminology used with this (and many other) testing frameworks.

18.4.1 What is Jasmine?

Angular uses the Jasmine unit testing framework to test Angular classes (pipes, components, services, etc.). You can learn more about Jasmine at https://jasmine.github.io/. Jasmine is described as follows:

"Jasmine is a behavior-driven development framework for testing JavaScript code. It does not depend on any other JavaScript frameworks. It does not require a DOM. And it has a clean, obvious syntax so that you can easily write tests."[9]

18.4.2 Behavior Driven Development

Behavior-driven development was derived from test-driven development. It utilizes short development cycles in which the tests are written prior to writing the code. Thus, the code is written with a clear objective: passing the test. The test then is an implementation design for the code. The short development cycle stems from the fact that the code is frequently refactored to pass additional test requirements. In the end, you have functions that are focused, single-task oriented and easily tested and re-tested after more code is added.

Behavior driven-development is defined by its human readability using natural language constructs in the tests. The tests read as sentences that confirm the business objective or behavior of the code being tested.

18.4.3 Jasmine Code and Testing Terminology.

Unit testing involves certain terminology such as the previously defined "test." A definition that lends itself nicely to the testing terms you are about to learn is to simply think of a test as a validation of an expectation. Jasmine, like most unit testing frameworks have additional terms that will be helpful.

Test	A single test function (a validation of an expectation) also known as a spec.
Test Suite	A group of tests.
Expectation	The expectation portion of the validation.
Matcher	An expression that represents the expectation.

[9] https://jasmine.github.io/

18.4.4 Anatomy of an Angular Jasmine Test

Test your knowledge and understanding of a Jasmine test file here: http://kevinruse.com/resources/angular-microlearning-modules/root-folder/unit-test.html

In the next section, we will look at where this code is run within the Angular development environment.

```
import { TestBed, async } from '@angular/core/testing';

import { AppComponent } from './app.component';

describe('AppComponent', () => {

    beforeEach(async(() => {
        TestBed.configureTestingModule({
      declarations: [
        AppComponent
       ],
      }).compileComponents();
}));

it('should create the app', async(() => {
    const fixture = TestBed.createComponent(AppComponent);
    const app = fixture.debugElement.componentInstance;
    expect(app).toBeTruthy();
}));
```

The test suite

Test Setup

*there is also a test teardown: `afterEach()`

The test

The expectation

The matcher

18.5 What is Karma?

KARMA

Karma is a test running framework that executes our tests and displays the results. It comes from the Google team. Karma is run via a command line interface. It is a robust and helpful test runner because it does more than just create and run the HTML page that displays the test results It can also watch our tests and automatically run them when changes are made and can be configured via the karma.conf.js file.

18.6 What is Protractor?

Protractor is an integration testing framework for Angular. Protractor uses Selenium web-driver for conducting end-to-end testing that includes Angular hooks. Protractor uses Jasmine syntax.

18.7 Testing with Angular tools and files

The Angular CLI tool provides "out-of-the-box" configuration for testing Angular applications with the tools mentioned above (Jasmine, Karma, and Protractor). In other words, the setup for testing is done when the project is created/scaffolded, and Angular's built-in tests are ready to run. When using the Angular CLI tool to create pipes, services, components and so on, the CLI creates corresponding unit tests using the naming convention:

- component-name.component-type.spec.ts
- Example: app.component.spec.ts

Of course, you are free to edit these tests as well as create your own. All of which can run immediately, due to the configuration and setup of testing tool and frameworks by the Angular CLI tool.

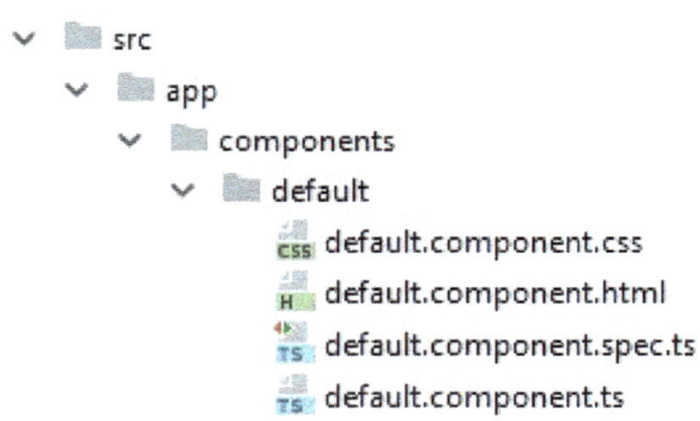

Figure #34: The cli-generated default component shown with the automatically generated unit test called default.component.spec.ts.

18.8 Angular's Testing Config Files

When the Angular CLI tool scaffolds a new project with `ng new projectName`, it creates several configuration files for testing.

karma.conf.js	This file configures the test runner called Karma
protractor.conf.js	This file configures end-to-end tests created with Protractor. This configuration refers to test files found in the e2e folder that is also created with the Angular CLI tool.

18.9 Testing Guidelines

The following guidelines should be considered when writing unit tests.

1. One assertion per test.
2. Name the test for: what is being tested, the test conditions, the expectation.
3. Make tests simple. No loops or code branching.
4. Maintain normally accepted coding best practices. Be DRY and optimize.
5. A good practice to avoid code duplication on our specs is to refactor repetitive code into the setup.

? add more guidelines here. List some of your company's policies here:

61–Guided Exercise: Examine the CLI-generated tests.

In this exercise, you open and review some of the spec files created by the Angular CLI tool.

Step 1 Open the file src/app/components/default/default.component.spec.ts and identify the following parts:

A. What are the required imports?
B. What component is being tested? Identify the line number in the code that helps answer this question.
C. Which line number represents the beginning of the test suite?
D. Which line number represents the beginning of a test?
E. Which line number represents a setup function?
F. Which line number represents a teardown function?
G. Which line number represents an expectation?
H. Which line number represents a matcher?

```
1. import { async, ComponentFixture, TestBed } from
   '@angular/core/testing';

2. import { DefaultComponent } from './default.component';

3. describe('DefaultComponent', () => {
4. let component: DefaultComponent;
5. let fixture: ComponentFixture<DefaultComponent>;

6. beforeEach(async(() => {
7. TestBed.configureTestingModule({
      declarations: [ DefaultComponent ]
8. })
9. .compileComponents();
10.   }));

11.   beforeEach(() => {
12.   fixture = TestBed.createComponent(DefaultComponent);
13.   component = fixture.componentInstance;
14.   fixture.detectChanges();
15.   });

16.   it('should create', () => {
17.   expect(component).toBeTruthy();
18.   });
19.   });
```

1. Required components: DefaultComponent
2. DefaultComponent; line 5 and 22
3. Suite: Line 5: describe()
4. Test: Line 22 it()
5. Setup: Lines 9, 16
6. Teardown: none
7. Expectation: Line 23
8. Matcher: line 23: toBeTruthy()

Step 2 Add the letter "f" in front of the describe function as shown below in bold.

Step 3

```
import { DefaultComponent } from './default.component';

describe('DefaultComponent', () => {
  let component: DefaultComponent;
  let fixture: ComponentFixture<DefaultComponent>;
```

Using a command line, enter the command shown below and wait for Karma to launch a web browser and display the results of the test.

```
ng test
```

The test results are shown below.

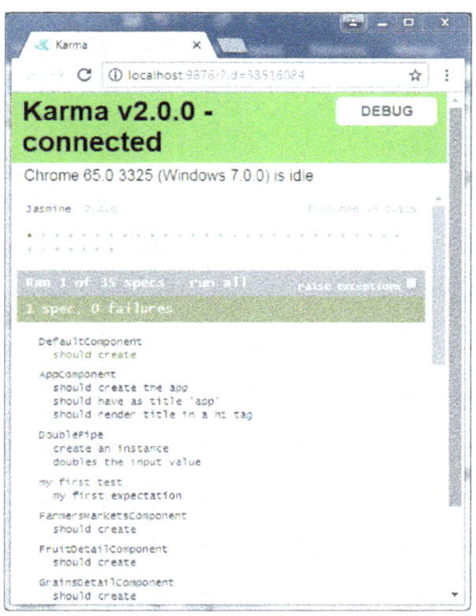

Step 3 Return to the spec file and remove the letter "f" that was added in step 2.

Step 4 Open src/app/services/todays-goal.service.spec.ts and compare it to the previous test.

Step 5 Answer the following questions:

What additional classes are being imported and why?

What is different about the setup function?

What is the test specifically testing for?

Step 6 Open src/app/double.pipe.spec.ts and compare it to the previous two tests and answer the questions below.

What is happening in the setup function?

What is the test spec testing for?

62—Guided Exercise: Write a test for a pipe.

In this exercise, you create a test for a pipe by building on the existing spec created by the CLI tool when the Pipe class was created.

Step 1 Open double.pipe.spec.ts.

Step 2 Add the following code to the file.

```
import { DoublePipe } from './double.pipe';

describe('DoublePipe', () => {
  let pipe;
  beforeEach(() => {
    pipe = new DoublePipe();
  });

  it('create an instance', () => {
    const pipe = new DoublePipe();
    expect(pipe).toBeTruthy();
  });
  it('doubles the input value', () => {
    expect(pipe.transform(2)).toEqual(4);
  });
});
```

Step 3 Add the letter "f" before the `describe()` function to run the test.

63—Guided Exercise: Write a test for a component

In this exercise, you create a test for a component by building on the existing spec created by the CLI tool when the component class was created.

Step 1 Delete the auto-generated test for header component.

Step 2 Write the test.

```
import { async, ComponentFixture, TestBed } from '@angular/core/testing';

import { HeaderComponent } from './header.component';
import { AppComponent } from '../app.component';

fdescribe('HeaderComponent', () => {
  let component: HeaderComponent;
  let fixture: ComponentFixture<HeaderComponent>;

  beforeEach(async(() => {
    TestBed.configureTestingModule({
      declarations: [ HeaderComponent ]
    })
    .compileComponents();
  }));

  beforeEach(() => {
    fixture = TestBed.createComponent(HeaderComponent);
    component = fixture.componentInstance;
    fixture.detectChanges();
  });

  it('should create the component', () => {
    expect(component).toBeTruthy();
  });
  it(`should have a title of 'Welcome to FoodPlate!'`, async(() => {
      // const fixture = TestBed.createComponent(HeaderComponent);
      // const app = fixture.debugElement.componentInstance;
      expect(component.title).toEqual('Welcome to FoodPlate!');
  }));
  it('should render title in a h1 tag', async(() => {
      // const fixture = TestBed.createComponent(HeaderComponent);
      // fixture.detectChanges();
      const compiled = fixture.debugElement.nativeElement;
      expect(compiled.querySelector('h1').textContent).toContain('Welcome to
FoodPlate!');
  }));
});
```

Step 3 Save and run the test.

18.10 Introduction to End to End Testing (e2e)

End to end tests simulate user interactions and confirms the correct response. End to end tests can test an application process or feature in its entirety: end to end. Unlike unit tests, e2e tests focus on the overall functionality of an application as opposed to a specific piece of code (or function).

18.11 Using Protractor for End to End Testing

The Protractor e2e testing framework requires three files for testing.

1. Page Object File

   This is a helper file for dealing with components in your tests. It is a class the describes a high-level view of a component or a "page." It includes logic that describes:

   a. How to find all the elements on the component
   b. How to navigate to the page

   The benefit of this file is that it decouples the DOM from the tests because DOM elements can change, but your test code will remain the same.

   The Page Object File is a class with functions that return elements found on components like buttons, inputs, text and anything you need to execute a test.

2. e2e Test Spec File

   This file with initialize the page object and contains the test code.

3. Protractor Configuration File called protractor.conf

   This file is located at the root of the project file and allows configuration of the Protractor testing framework.

18.11.1 The Protractor Runtime

Protractor e2e tests run inside of a web browser where the runtime behaves like an end-user, performing actions like button clicks, text input and form submission.

Chapter 18 Quiz

1) True/False
   The default unit testing framework generated by the Angular CLI is Jasmine.
2) What is the name of the test running framework used by Angular?
3) What would be the name of the auto-generated unit test for a component call login?
4) What does Angular's default component test file actually test?
5) What is the purpose of the TestBed interface in Angular?
   a) Configures and initializes environment for unit testing.
   b) It automatically generates a unit test for a given component.
   c) It provides methods for creating components and services in unit tests.
   d) It is a fixture for debugging and testing a component.

Appendix

Appendix A: The Angular Ecosystem

- Google
- Angular community
- Angular Extensions
- IDE plug-ins
- Browser plug-ins/extensions

A.1 Google

Discussion Group:
- https://groups.google.com/forum/#!forum/angular

Comprehensive list of Google Angular resources
- https://angular.io/resources

Angular documentation
- https://angular.io/docs

Angular CLI tool and Schematics
- https://github.com/angular/angular-cli/wiki
- https://www.youtube.com/watch?v=LZxbDp1nOVo&feature=youtu.be&t=8m57s
- https://www.youtube.com/watch?v=ZKyz0lb0GjA

Angular Dev Kit
- https://github.com/angular/devkit

Angular Component Development Kit
- https://github.com/angular/material2/tree/master/src/cdkAsdf

A.2 Angular Community

https://www.reddit.com/r/angular/
https://www.reddit.com/r/angularjs/comments/3dltmj/freenode_chat_dedicated_to_get_angular_2_support/
https://www.madewithangular.com/

A.3 Asking questions

Google search tip:
- Add `site:angular.io` to your google search

Slack Channel
- https://www.reddit.com/r/Angular2/comments/4j6c13/slack_official_channel/

Stack Overflow
- https://stackoverflow.com/questions/tagged/angular

A.4 IDE plug-ins

Visual Studio: Angular snippets (Dan Whalin)
- https://marketplace.visualstudio.com/items?itemName=danwahlin.angular2-snippets

Visual Studio Code: Angular snippets (John Papa)
- https://github.com/johnpapa/vscode-angular-snippets

Sublime Text: Angular snippets
- https://dotsway.com/2017/04/05/sublime-text-3-angular-4-snippet/

A.5 Browser plug-ins/extensions

- Angular Augury
  - https://augury.angular.io/
- Redux Extension
  - https://github.com/zalmoxisus/redux-devtools-extension

Appendix B: Angular Versioning

B.1 Semantic Versioning

When Angular version 2 was released in September of 2016, the team also announced that they would be using Semantic Versioning or SEMVER. Semantic versioning involves a numbering convention for versioning your software. The entire specification can be found at semver.org. See the graphic below for a sample version number that conforms to the Semantic Versioning rules.

Figure #35: An example of semantic versioning.

For learning Angular, we will simply summarize the following basic rules as follows:

Given the version number: `2.3.1`

- Changing the first digit (2) is considered a major revision which includes incompatible API changes.
- Changing the second digit (3) is considered a minor revision where functionality is added that is backwards-compatible.
- Changing the last digit (1) is considered a patch (backwards-compatible bug fixes).

Because the Angular framework is comprised of libraries, various parts of the framework (libraries) are at different versions.

@angular/core	v2.3.0
@angular/compiler	v2.3.0
@angular/compiler-cli	v2.3.0
@angular/http	v2.3.0
@angular/router	**v3.3.0**

Figure #36: Version numbers for Angular packages are out of synchronization

B.1.1 Semantic Versioning Rules

Want the latest patch for version 2.1?

- 2.1
- 2.1.x
- ~2.1.0

Want the latest release of 2?

- 2
- 2.x
- ^2.0.0

Want the latest major release?

- *

B.1.2 Why Not Version 3?

Again, per Igor Minar: "Due to this misalignment of the router package's version, the team decided to go straight for Angular v4. In this way, again, all the core packages are aligned which will be easier to maintain and help avoid confusion in the future."

This announcement may be seen at:

YouTube: https://www.youtube.com/watch?v=aJIMoLgqU_o&feature=youtu.be

Short Link: https://youtu.be/aJIMoLgqU_o.

B.2 Angular's Tentative release schedule

Version 4	March 2017
Version 5	September/October 2017
Version 6	March 2018
Version 7	September/October 2018

Figure #37: Angular's historical release schedule.

Notice from the historical chart above, the Angular team is planning on major release every 6 months!

B.3 Angular's Current release schedule

DATE	STABLE RELEASE	COMPATIBILITY
October/November 2019	9.0.0	^8.0.0
May 2020	10.0.0	^9.0.0

Compatibility note: The primary goal of the backward compatibility promise is to ensure that changes in the core framework and tooling don't break the existing ecosystem of components and applications and don't put undue upgrade/migration burden on Angular application and component authors.

Support policy and schedule

All of our major releases are supported for 18 months.

- 6 months of *active support*, during which regularly-scheduled updates and patches are released.
- 12 months of *long-term support (LTS)*, during which only critical fixes and security patches are released.

The following table provides the status for Angular versions under support.

VERSION	STATUS	RELEASED	ACTIVE ENDS	LTS ENDS
^8.0.0	Active	May 28, 2019	Nov 28, 2019	Nov 28, 2020
^7.0.0	LTS	Oct 18, 2018	Apr 18, 2019	Apr 18, 2020
^6.0.0	LTS	May 3, 2018	Nov 3, 2018	Nov 3, 2019

Angular versions ^4.0.0 and ^5.0.0 are no longer under support.

Figure #38: Angular's tentative release schedule (https://angular.io/guide/releases#release-schedule).

This courseware has been tested with Angular version 4.4.3 and higher.

Appendix C: AngularJS vs. Angular 2 and higher

C.1 What is AngularJS?

AngularJS is a JavaScript MVC-like framework for creating Web applications. It was created in 2009 by Misko Hevery and is maintained by a community of individuals and corporations.

AngularJS is:

- a toolset for building a framework most suited to your application development
- fully extensible
- a framework that works well with other libraries
- a framework with features that can be modified or replaced
- a framework that lets you extend the HTML vocabulary for your application

AngularJS moves display logic from the server (as in PHP, JSP, etc.) into the browser using Angular templates (partial html files), leaving the model business logic on the server, accessed via RESTful web services.

AngularJS moves application logic into JavaScript controllers that coordinate the view (html partials) and the data model and uses two-way data binding to manipulate the DOM.

AngularJS facilitates the creation of applications that use a single page architecture.

C.2 Where did Angular come from?

Work on Angular began in 2009 by Misko Hevery, while at Brat Tech LLC, but was eventually released as an open source code library. The first release of Angular was in 2010. Angular is now developed by Google and a very active community of developers.

C.3 Why Angular 2?

While extremely popular, the AngularJS framework is not without its detractors (see Google trends below). The following websites explore some of the framework's pain points.

- https://medium.com/@mnemon1ck/why-you-should-not-use-angularjs-1df5ddf6fc99#.i6s6i4a8j
- https://medium.com/este-js-framework/what-i-would-recommend-instead-of-angular-js-62b057d8a9e#.jkpma6dix
- https://larseidnes.com/2014/11/05/angularjs-the-bad-parts/
- http://www.quirksmode.org/blog/archives/2015/01/the_problem_wit.html
- https://medium.com/este-js-framework/whats-wrong-with-angular-js-97b0a787f903#.n47dsegr2

Angular 2 is an attempt to remedy some of AngularJS's less desirable syntax, behavior, and performance issues. It is also an attempt to improve the framework by taking advantage of new browser features, HTML APIs and the latest version of ECMAScript.

See: https://my.visme.co/projects/90yywgvk-angularjs-and-beyond

In addition to addressing some of the concerns web developers reported while attempting to use the framework, the Angular team, was eager to take advantage of current trends in web development. Trends that were facilitated by the rise in HTML5 APIs, new ECMAScript features and the increase in browser support of these new features.

As you can see from the timeline below, a lot of helpful APIs and language features like promises and classes and much more were developed after the release of AngularJS. Therefore, these features never made it into the framework, nor was the framework created with these features in mind. Angular 2 not only takes advantage of these new capabilities, but it has been developed with an eye to the future and includes support for features soon to be released in ECMAScript 2017.

The initial news regarding the release of Angular 2 was that there would be no clear migration path from Angular 1 to 2. This, naturally, caused much concern from developers who were deeply entrenched in projects built in Angular 1 but eager to enjoy the benefits promised by Angular 2. As the chart above indicates, API's that can radically change the way applications are built were released after Angular's release.

C.3.1 What's changed in Angular 2?

There have been numerous changes to the Angular framework as discussed in the previous section and you should now have an idea as to how and why those changes were made. This section will take a deeper look into both the changes themselves and their implementation.

The differences between Angular 1 and Angular 2 can be summarized as follows:

- Angular 2 is very component-based.
- Angular 2 enjoys better performance in the browser in the areas of UI rendering and application API.
- Angular 2 supports ES2016, ES2016 and TypeScript.
- Developers no longer must deal with scope hierarchies and the general complexities behinds scope when using Angular 2.
- Angular 2 provides one method only for dependency injection.
- Two-way data binding is now turned off by default in Angular 2.
- Angular 2 change detection mechanism is faster.
- Angular 2 uses a new rendering architecture using native UI components as well as the ability to run a renderer for iOS and Android.

C.3.1.1 Topics covered in this section

- List of major changes implemented in Angular 2
- List of constructs removed from Angular 2
- Angular directives
- Components
- Filters
- Change detection
- Routing

C.3.2 Major changes implemented in Angular 2.x

Below is a breakdown of the main changes to the Angular framework.

- Directives
  - now have two parts with clearly defined roles:
    - Components
      - Provide an API to define the UI of our application
    - Directives
      - Attach behavior to a DOM element/component
  - Components contain views
  - Directives do not contain views
  - Directive syntax differs from AngularJS
- Filters
  - are now called Pipes
- Change detection mechanism
  - has been enhanced with new capabilities and better performance
- Routing mechanism
  - is now component-based
  - includes new capabilities
  - syntax differs from AngularJS

C.3.3 Constructs Removed in Angular 2

Some of the fundamental features and concepts in Angular 1 have been removed in Angular 2 including:

- $scope
- jqLite
- angular.module

Some features and concepts have not been removed, but are implemented differently including:

- Controllers
- Directives
- Filters

C.3.3.1 Components

- Components are the main building blocks of an Angular application's user interface.
- If you are familiar with AngularJS, it might be helpful to understand that components extend directives.
- Components provide the view by way of an attached template.
- Templates may hold expressions and have their own controllers.
- Use a single component per DOM element so...
    - Elements are used as selectors

```
<food-plate> </food-plate>
```

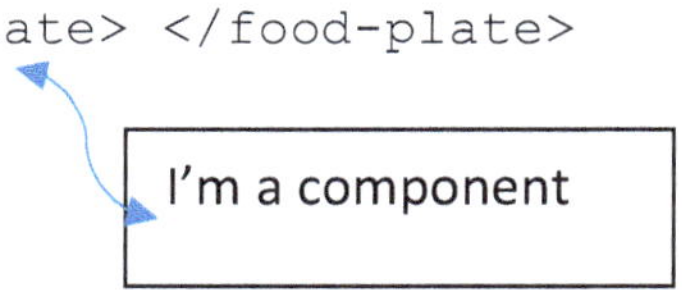

- Component example (written in TypeScript):

```
@Component({
  selector: 'food-plate',
  styles: [`
              h1 {
                    color: #f00;
                    padding: 1em;
                 }
          `]
  template: '<h1 id="FoodPlate">Welcome {{ user }}</h1>'
})
export class FoodPlate {
  user: string;
  constructor() {
     this.user = "New User";
  }
}
```

- The component implementation would look like this:

```
<food-plate> </food-plate>
```

C.3.3.2 Directives

- Directives are used to attach behavior to the DOM by extending it with custom logic that is defined in a class file.
- The class file may be written in ES2015, ES2016 or TypeScript.
- Angular has new built-in directives including:
    - ngFor similar to ng-repeat
- Angular adds new data binding semantics
    - <h1 ng-something = "someValue">
    - ng-something is a directive
    - someValue could be a:
        - literal value

        - expression
        - callback function
        - microsyntax (a syntax inside of a syntax!)
    - in propertyName = “someValue” syntax
        - Angular expects/accepts a string value. SomeValue undergoes no further processing by Angular
    - In [propertyName] = “expression”
        - Angular expects/accepts an expression and Angular handles it accordingly.
    - In (click) = “doSomething()”
        - Angular expects/accepts an event handler which will be triggered on the click event.
- Angular directives are typically created using ES2016 decorators.
- You can have multiple directives on a single element, so...
    - Attributes are used as selectors
    - <div foodGroup = “fruit” status = “completed”>

C.3.3.3 Filters

Filters are now called pipes and are created with ES2015 decorators, similar to the way that Angular 2 creates directives and components.

```
@Pipe
```

To which a name and data-formatting logic are added.

Plunker Pipe example by Cory Rylan at http://plnkr.co/edit/3WnMwD56lEAOUh1jlgn2?p=preview

```
import {Pipe} from 'angular2/core';

@Pipe({
    name: 'ellipsis'
})
export class EllipsisPipe {
    transform(val, args) {
        if (args === undefined) {
            return val;
        }

        if (val.length > args) {
            return val.substring(0, args) + '...';
        } else {
            return val;
        }
    }
}
```

C.3.3.4 Change Detection

Change detection has been enhanced with the capability to create custom optimized algorithms. To understand the fundamental difference, make sure you understand AngularJS change detection as described below.

C.3.3.5 AngularJS Change Detection

Before we discuss the change detection, $scope life cycle and the digest loop, let's review some basic terminology.

C.3.3.6 Review of scope terminology

Binding

tells Angular that it should evaluate an expression and insert the result into the DOM in place of the binding

- Syntax:
  - <h2>User Name: {{ userName }} </h2>
- a binding will result in efficient continuous updates whenever the result of the expression evaluation changes

- Expression
  - is a JavaScript-like code snippet that is evaluated by Angular in the context of the current model scope, rather than within the scope of the global context (window).
- $scope
  - just a simple JavaScript object with a small API designed to detect and broadcast changes to its state

$scope provides an API called $watch that will observe changes in the model. To understand the scope life cycle, you must understand the digest loop.

Consider this example:

```
<label for="firstName">Enter your first name:
</label>
<h1>Hello {{firstName}}</h1>
```

and in the browser:

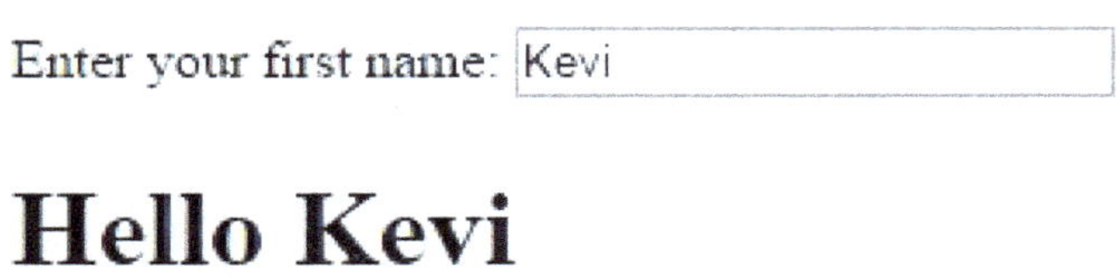

As you type your first name, the expression in the <h1> element displays what you type. This is due to the data-binding. But how do you get this instant and magical result?

Angular watches are added to bindings with behavior associated with the braces {{ binding }}.

Angular 2 has made radical changes to the digest loop. In Angular 2 change detection, $scope.apply is no longer needed. Events which take place outside the framework are now achieved using a JavaScript library called zone.js This library allows Angular or JavaScript to intercept asynchronous browser events and involve the digest loop only once and at the right time. In addition, Angular 2 uses "Differs" that allow developers to extend the change detection mechanism.

C.3.3.7 Routing

- Angular 2 routing is now component-based.
- Only components can be rendered by a router.
- The developer must bear in mind that Angular 2 directives do not hold templates.
- Angular 2 routing includes support for nested views (like ui-router)

Appendix D: Angular new features

D.1 Angular 4 New Features (released in March 2017)

The course may be used with Angular version 4.0. Features introduced in version 4 are shown in the list below.

Angular 4 was the first major release after Angular 2 (see the section above regarding the missing Angular 3). While there are a lot of changes in Angular 4, there are relatively few breaking changes. Additions to Angular 4 include:

- Ahead of Time Compilation – Angular "compiles" templates during the build as opposed to JIT compilation in the browser. A nice side effect of this is runtime errors now display at compile time. In addition, compiling ahead of time means you no longer have to send the Angular compiler to users resulting in a faster startup.
- Universal –Additional work was done on the "Universal Project" for server-side rendering.
- Animations –are now in their own package.
- Template tag is deprecated: use `ng-template` instead.
- Syntax changes:
  - @ngIf can use an else syntax
  - As keyword to store a result in a variable of the template
- New Pipes and Validator:
  - Pipe: titlecase
  - Validator: email
- Simplified search parameters to an HTTP request
- Meta service to easily get or update meta tags.
- New Interface to represent the parameters of a URL: `ParamMap` instead of `queryParamMap` or `queryParams`.

D.2 Angular 5 New Features (released in November 2017)

The course may be used with Angular version 5.0. Features introduced in version 5 are shown in the list below.

While Angular 4 added new syntax and features for developers, this upgrade was focused largely around performance gains but also includes some new features for

- Server-side rendering of apps
- Router life-cycle events
- Form submission

D.2.1 A build optimizer in the Angular CLI Tool – performs optimizations on the build process (by default) designed to remove dead JavaScript code (tree-shaking) thereby reducing the bundle-size of the compiled JavaScript. The build optimizer removes Angular decorators which are used by the compiler but unnecessary at runtime. The improved tree-shaking results in smaller bundle size in the finished production application code.

D.2.2 Angular Universal State Transfer API and DOM Support – Angular Universal is designed to aid developers who want server-side rendering of their applications. Added to this project in version 5.0 is the ServerTransferStateModule and the BrowserTransferStateModule which allow you to generate information as part of the server-side rendering and then transfer that information to the client. Thus, reducing an initial HTTP request for data as it will arrive with application from the server to the client.

D.2.3 Compile Improvements – The Angular compiler now supports incremental compilation which can provide faster rebuilds. The new compiler includes a TypeScript transform. TypeScript transforms' take place when the compiler takes the TypeScript Abstract Syntax Tree and transforms it to a JavaScript Abstract Syntax Tree. The compiler now supports TypeScript 2.4

D.2.4 New Number, Date and Currency Pipes – results in increased standardization across browsers the eliminate the need for localization polyfills. The new pipes handle internationalization of numbers, dates and currency values as opposed to handling through the browser's i18n API.

D.2.5 Reduced dependency on polyfills – like the new pipes above, additional polyfills have been removed including Reflect polyfill. Prior versions of Angular use a Reflective Injector for instantiating and injecting classes which is dynamic and requires map files and polyfills. Angular 5 uses a Static Injector which is more performant because it does not require dynamic decision making.

D.2.6 HttpModule has been deprecated – the @angular/http library has been deprecated and replaced with the improved @angular/common HttpClient module.

D.2.7 updateOn blur/submit – it is now possible to do both validation and update values on the "blur" and "submit" events.

D.2.8 RxJS 5.52 – Angular now supports the use of RxJS version 5.5.2 or higher which includes pipeable operators. It is distributed by default with the Angular CLI tool using ECMAScript modules. This has the effect of reducing the bundle size. This upgrade changes the import code (for better tree-shaking). See the example below.

```
import 'rxjs/add/operator/filter'
import 'rxjs/add/operator/retry'
```

Can now be written as: `Import { scan, retry } from 'rxjs/operators'`

D.2.9 New Router Lifecycle events – Angular has added new lifecycle events to the router that allow developers to track the cycle from the very start including running route guards right through to the completion of the router activation. This allows the developer to tap into routing events such as the initial checking for a guard, the final guard check and the end of the route activation.

D.2.10 Export components with multiple names – Angular can now export your components with multiple names. This can ease migration of code by eliminating some refactoring.

D.3 Angular 6 New Features

The course may be used with Angular version 6.0. This upgrade includes new features that center largely around tooling.

D.3.1 Tooling

- CLI commands
- Libraries

D.3.2 Better development experience

- Components export to custom elements
- Updated to use v6 of RxJS

D.3.3 Some new features for:

- Component Development Kit

D.3.4 Performance

- Tree shaking
- Removed polyfills

D.3.5 New code:

- Providers are now provided in the component that uses the service

D.3.6 ng update

- New CLI command
- Analyzes package.json and recommends updates
  - Get the right dependencies
  - Keep dependencies in sync
  - Uses npm or yarn under the hood
- Example: ng update @angular/core
  - updates all the Angular framework packages
  - Updates RxJS and TypeScript (and if they have schematics, will update their dependencies)
  - Installs the rxjs-compat automatically to run RXJS 6 with less problems

D.3.7 ng add

- uses your package manager to download new dependencies
- invoke an installation script (implemented as a schematic) which can update your project with configuration changes
- add additional dependencies

Examples

Command	Description
`ng add @angular/pwa`	Turn your application into a PWA by adding an app manifest and service worker
`ng add @ng-bootstrap/schematics`	Add ng-bootstrap to your application
`ng add @angular/material`	Install and setup Angular Material and theming
`ng add @angular/elements`	Add the needed document-register-element.js polyfill and dependencies for Angular Elements

D.3.8 Angular Elements

- Register your components as custom elements (HTML5)
- Allows developers to export components to be used outside of an Angular app
  - React
  - Vue
  - Vanilla JavaScript

D.3.9 Angular Material + CDK Components

- new tree component for displaying hierarchical data
- come in both styled (Material's mat-tree) and unstyled versions (CDK's cdk-tree)
- https://blog.angular.io/a-component-dev-kit-for-angular-9f06e3b4b3b4
- https://material.angular.io/cdk/categories

D3.10 Multiple workspaces

- Support for multiple workspaces
    - Each CLI workspace has projects, each project has targets, and each target can have configurations.
    - https://github.com/angular/angular-cli/wiki/angular-workspace
- Now use angular.json instead of .angular-cli.json for build and project configuration

D.3.11 Library support

- ng generate library <name>
- creates a library project within your CLI workspace
- configures it for testing and for building
- https://github.com/angular/angular-cli/wiki/stories-create-library

D.3.12 Tree Shakable Providers

- Modules no longer reference services
- Services reference modules

Angular 5: the module

```
@NgModule({
  ...
  providers: [MyService]
})
export class AppModule {}
```

Angular 6: the service

```
import { Injectable } from '@angular/core';
@Injectable({
  providedIn: 'root',
})
export class MyService {
  constructor() { }
}
```

D.3.13 Animation Performance Improvements

- no longer need the web animations polyfill

D.3.14 RxJS 6

- Use ng update
- Including a backwards compatibility package rxjs-compat that will keep your applications working
- More tree shakeable

D.4 Angular 7 New Features

The course may be used with Angular version 7.0. This upgrade includes new features, improvements and upgrades, bug fixes and some new tooling functionality While this release does not include the new Angular compiler/renderer called Ivy, much time was spent on this project which will soon become a part of the Angular ecosystem.

D.4.1 Tooling

- CLI options are now presented as command prompts
- A new Angular Console tool used to generate code and serve projects in a graphical UI using the Angular CLI under the hood.

D4.2 Angular Material Component Development Kit additions

- Scrolling module that allows the dynamic loading of data at runtime. As elements enter and exit the user interface, they can be virtually loaded and unloaded from the DOM.
- Drag and drop module is now part of the Component Development Kit including automatic rendering, drag and drop handlers and the ability to transfer data via drag and drop.

D4.3 Polyfill removals

- Angular continues to remove unnecessary polyfills. In this version, the reflect-metadata polyfill has been removed.

D4.4 Performance Improvements

- New projects now use default Budget Bundles which send notifications when your app is reaching size limits. Notifications include warnings at 2MB and errors at 5MB.

D4.5 Updates on Dependent Libraries

- TypeScript version is 3.1.
- RxJS is version 6.3.
- Node is version 10.

D4.6 Upgrade Path

- To upgrade from Angular 6 to Angular 7 use the following command:
  ```
  ng update @angular/cli @angular/core
  ```

D4.7 Other Improvements

- Improved documentation.
- New life cycle hook for modules that need to bootstrap a component (ngDoBootStrap).
- Better handling of @Output error handling when the property is not initialized.

D.5 Angular 8 New Features

The course may be used with Angular version 8.0. This upgrade includes new features implemented in the framework as well as experimental features that can be optionally implemented.

D.5.1 New Rendering Engine (optional)

The new internal rendering engine is called Ivy and Angular provides experimental support for this rendering engine which is responsible for rendering Angular templates. The Angular team has rewritten Ivy to render Angular applications much faster due to reduced bundle size. The feature is almost fully implemented and therefore not 100% complete and not recommended for mission critical complex applications. More information can be found at https://next.angular.io/guide/ivy.

D.5.2 New Build Tool (optional)

Angular 8 provides experimental support for the build tool called Bazel. This tool controls current build tools like Webpack to optimize the build process workflow and improve speed. Like Ivy, this tool is not fully finished or tested. It can be used on an experimental basis. More information can be found at https://bazel.angular.io.

D.5.3 Differential Loading

Angular 8 CLI now provides multiple production bundles for both modern and legacy browsers. This results in optimized bundles due to browser optimized code and the removal of unnecessary polyfills. Automatic browser detection deploys the correct bundle.

D.5.4 Breaking Changes

Http is no longer supported. You should use @angular/common/http (HttpClient).

D.5.5 @ViewChild

Http @ViewChild now requires the property “static”. When set to True it resolves query results before change detection runs.

Appendix E: How Angular applications bootstrap

E.1 The Root Directory

The root directory that is created from the Angular cli command: ng new [app name] results in the following directory structure. For a description of the files and folder and their role in the Angular application, visit:

http://kevinruse.com/resources/root-folder.html.

E.2 The package.json file

The package.json file holds metadata about the project. This file lists the packages that your project depends, allowing other developers to quickly install libraries and build the application. For a detailed line-by-line explanation of Angular's package.json visit

https://www.kevinruse.com/resources/packagejson.html

E.3 High-level overview of Angular Architecture

Angular applications begin like any other web page being loaded into a web browser, with an HTTP get request. The returned HTML page, however, does not look like a typical index.html. Instead of exposing HTML code that contains the contents of the page, it contains placeholders for data that will be injected at runtime by the accompanying JavaScript. The process is summarized below.

1. Initial HTTP request for index.html
    - Contains placeholders for data
2. JavaScript makes AJAX requests for HTML snippets/partials/templates
3. JavaScript makes AJAX requests for data from a web API
    - Typically, in JSON format
4. Data then populates the templates

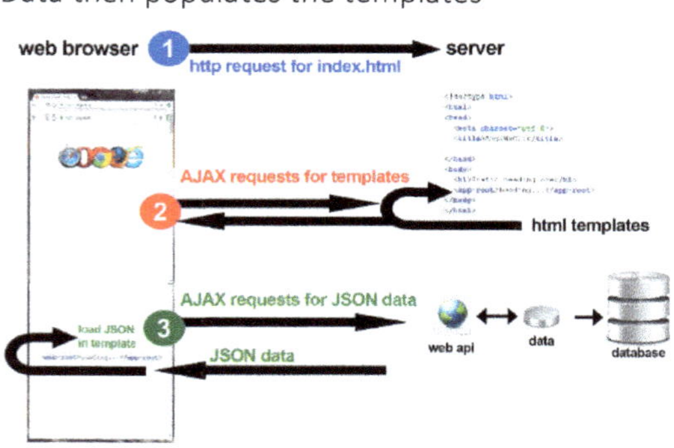

A high-level overview of an Angular application.

For more detailed information, see the documentation at https://angular.io/guide/architecture.

E.4 Which file launches the application?

The application launch occurs by bootstrapping the AppModule in main.ts/main.browser.ts.

The main.browser.ts/main.browser.ts TypeScript files will be transpiled into main.js (a JavaScript file).

```
import { enableProdMode } from '@angular/core';
import { platformBrowserDynamic } from '@angular/platform-browser-dynamic';

import { AppModule } from './app/app.module';
import { environment } from './environments/environment';

if (environment.production) {
  enableProdMode();
}

platformBrowserDynamic().bootstrapModule(AppModule)
  .catch(err => console.log(err));
```

main.ts generated by the Angular-CLI tool, showing the import of the platformBrowserDynamic package.

This file imports the PlatformBrowserDynamic package which contains the Angular features that get the application up and running.

Then, main.ts imports the AppModule which is the applications root module.

```
main.ts
import { enableProdMode } from '@angular/core';
import { platformBrowserDynamic } from
 '@angular/platform-browser-dynamic';

import { AppModule } from './app/app.module';
import { environment } from './environments/environment';

if (environment.production) {
  enableProdMode();
}

platformBrowserDynamic().bootstrapModule(AppModule);
```

main.ts generated by the Angular-CLI tool, showing the import of the application's root module called AppModule.

The application's root module (traditionally called AppModule), imports the necessary classes and tells Angular how to compile and launch the application. It does this via a metadata object which includes:

- Importing of other modules needed by this module (using the "imports" property).
- Listing of all components used by this module (using the "declarations" property).
- Identifying the module used to bootstrap the application (using the "bootstrap" property).

```
import { BrowserModule } from '@angular/platform-browser';
import { NgModule } from '@angular/core';

import { AppComponent } from './app.component';

@NgModule({
  declarations: [
    AppComponent
  ],
  imports: [
    BrowserModule
  ],
  providers: [],
  bootstrap: [AppComponent]
})
export class AppModule { }
```

main.ts

```
import { enableProdMode } from '@angular/core';
import { platformBrowserDynamic } from
 '@angular/platform-browser-dynamic';

import { AppModule } from './app/app.module';
import { environment } from './environments/environment';

if (environment.production) {
  enableProdMode();
}

platformBrowserDynamic().bootstrapModule(AppModule);
```

bootstraps the app!
Renders the root component of the component tree

The app.module.ts file as generated by the Angular CLI tool.

The main.ts file showing the bootstrapModule() method that bootstraps the application and loads the AppModule that renders the root component.

Back in main.js the platformBrowserDynamic is used to tell Angular that this application will run in a Web browser. The bootstrapModule method of the platformBrowserDynamic object is used to bootstrap the application.

E.4.1 Index.html and the bootstrap process

Ultimately, all the TypeScript required to bootstrap and run an Angular application must be compiled to JavaScript and served to the client. Angular uses many JavaScript modules which are bundled together and requested by index.html. Module loaders look for import statements, build a dependency chain and then emits multiple bundles. Developers may choose among several Angular-compatible module loaders. The Angular team currently uses Webpack, however, this may change in the future.

For more information about Webpack and Angular visit https://angular.io/guide/webpack.

Figure 10 below show the index.html source code generated by the Angular CLI tool with no script tags. Figure 11 shows the "compiled" version (also generated from the Angular CLI tool) which includes http requests for the webpack modules that have been bundled into single requests. Figure 12 is index.html as generated by the Angular seed project, showing the single call to "main.bundle.js."

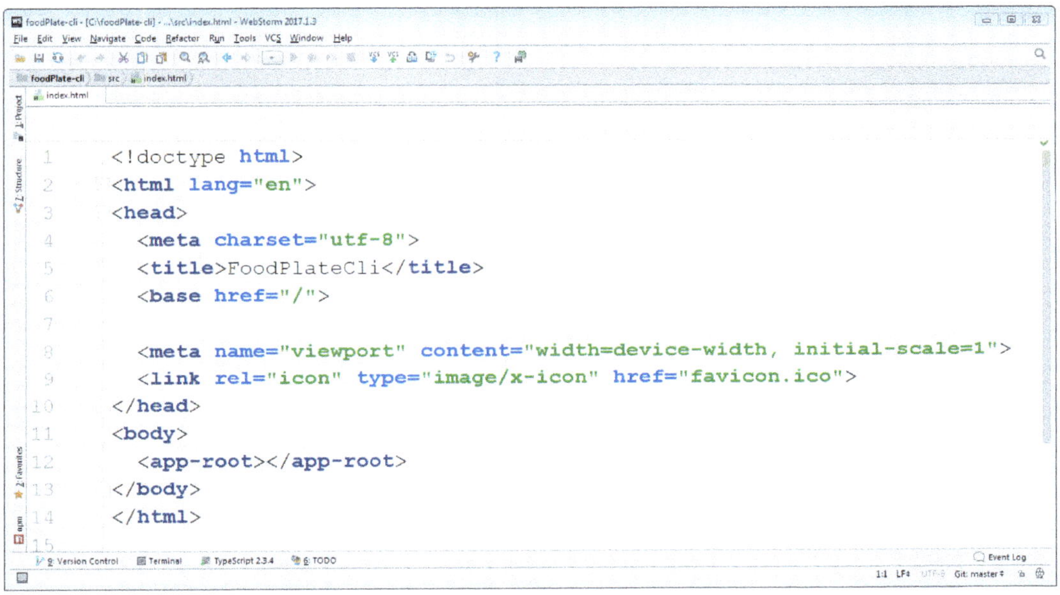

Index.html source code, generated by the Angular CLI tool, as seen in an editor with no Angular script tags

Index.html, generated by the Angular CLI tool, as seen in the Chrome console, with Angular script tags added by Webpack.

index.html

html body

```html
<!DOCTYPE html>
<html>
  <head>
    <meta charset=UTF-8>
    <meta name="viewport" content="width=device-width, initial-scale=1">
    <title>Angular2 Seed</title>
    <base href="/">
  </head>
  <body>

    <app>
      Loading...
    </app>

    <script async src="/main.bundle.js"></script>

  </body>
</html>
```

Index.html, generated by the Angular seed project, shown a single script tag requesting main.bundle.js.

Appendix F: Quiz Answers

Chapter 1

1) Angular may be written in which language(s)?
   E. JavaScript or Dart or TypeScript
2) Which of the following are valid versions of Angular?
   A. AngularJS
   C. Angular 1.0
   D. Angular 2.0
   E. Angular 4.0
3) Angular may be used to develop which of the following?
   E. All the above
4) Which of the following represents a best practice guide for Angular?
   B. John Papa's Style Guide

Chapter 3

1) **True** The Angular Seed project is located at github.
2) As of this publication date the fastest way to install dependencies with the seed project is:
   a. Yarn
3) Write the Angular-CLI command for making a new Class called FoodItem
   `ng g c FoodItem`

Chapter 4

1) The seven keys to Angular are:
   a. Modules
   b. Components
   c. Templates
   d. Databinding
   e. Structure Directives
   f. Services
   g. Dependency Injection
2) An Angular application is a tree of **components**.
3) Angular code is organized in **modules.**
4) What do developers typically name the root module of their application? **app.module.ts**
5) What is a good name for the login component's template file? **login.component.html**

Chapter 5

1) Angular application code is organized into logical blocks of functionality called **modules**?
2) An Angular application is a tree of **components** made from class files.
3) The component class has two commonly used properties: **selector** and **template or templateUrl**.
4) All Angular applications have a root module, typically named **app.module.ts**.

Chapter 6 Quiz

1) Match the CSS style rule with its proper location in the application code.

`background-color` for the entire web app	login.component.css
`background-color` for the login component	styles.css
`background-color` for the admin login only →	login.component.css
`background-color` for components A, B,C, all of which have been declared in the ABC.module.ts with view encapsulation set to none →	abc.component.css

(Arrows: entire web app → styles.css; login component → login.component.css.)

App Structure

main.component

— abc.component

—a.component

—b.component

—c.component

login.component

Chapter 7 Quiz

1) Given the following scenarios choose the correct binding type.
    F. Property binding
    G. Attribute binding
    H. Class binding
    I. Style binding
    J. Event binding

2) You need to style a DOM element based on the boolean value of a property in the component class. **Class binding**
3) You need to bind an `href` attribute to a component class property. **Class binding/attribute binding**
4) You need to bind a DOM element to a CSS class. **Class binding/style binding**
5) You need to bind a `click` event to component class method. **Event binding**
6) You need to set the `className` property for an H1 element. **Class Binding**
7) You need to bind the `colspan` attribute of a <td> element to a component property. **Class binding**

Chapter 8 Quiz

1) **True** or False   Any sort of business logic may be placed in a service file.

2) Below are the steps needed for using a service. Which step is missing?
    a. Make the service has been provided via:
        i. The module's providers property
        ii. The service provides itself via:

```
@Injectable({
        providedIn: 'root',
})
```

Chapter 9 Quiz

1) The app component needs to share data (invoice object) with its child component, details. The code below will not work. See if you can spot the errors.

    a. The invoice object was not passed from parent to child. `[invoice] = invoice`

Chapter 11 Quiz

1) Routing can be *completely* configured by the Angular CLI tool. **false**
2) Correct the error in this route: `{ path: 'home',` ~~`module`~~`: Home' }`
   `{ path: 'home', component: Home' }`

3) Define the following routing objects and their purpose:
    a. Router
        i. Implements the router service, router directives and providers
        ii. Used to implement `navigate()` and `navigateByUrl()`
    b. RouterOutlet
        i. Acts as a placeholder that Angular dynamically fills based on the current router state
        ii. Used to inject content from a route into the template
    c. Routes
        i. Represents a route configuration
        ii. Used to create the array of routes used to navigate the application
    d. RouterLink
        i. Used to link to a specific route in the application
    e. ActivatedRoute
        i. Provides access to information about a route associated with a component that is loaded in an outlet. Use to traverse the RouterState tree and extract information from nodes.
    f. Location
        i. A service that applications can use to interact with a browser's URL.
        ii. Methods include:
            1. `forward(), back(), onUrlChange()`

Chapter 12 Quiz

1) Describe the fundamental difference between template-driven and reactive forms.

   Reactive forms are based on reactive programming with code found in the component class and service files. Template-driven forms are based on declarative programming with code found the view template.
2) Which Angular module is necessary to build a template-driven form? **FormsModule**
3) Which Angular modules are necessary to build a reactive form? **FormsModule, ReactiveFormsModule**
4) What specific class properties are bound by the directive [(ngModel)] **Creates a FormControl instance (from a domain model) and binds it to a form control element in the UI.**
5) Where is form validation code found in a reactive form? Name the file and location.

   The Component that creates the form; in the formBuilder's group() method.

Chapter 13 Quiz

1) What are some of the fundamental differences between promises and observables?
   Observables can be cancelled; promises cannot.
   Promises execute immediately; observables are inert/code ; data cannot be accessed until you subscribe.
   Observables can provide multiple values; promises typically supply only one value
   Observables have built in methods to retry; promises do not.
2) What is wrong with the code below?

   data.service.ts

```
getProducts() {
        this.http.get(this.productUrl)
}
```

   data.component.ts

```
constructor(dataService: DataService) {}

getProducts() {
     this.dataService.getProducts()
}
```

   data.component.html

```
...
<li *ngFor="let product of products">{{ product.description}}</li>
```

   The observable does not invoke the subscribe method.

3) What code is missing from this code snippet?

```
import { take, map, combineAll } from 'rxjs/operators';
import { interval } from 'rxjs';

// emit every 1s, take 2
const source$ = interval(1000).(take(2));
// map each emitted value from source to interval observable that takes 5 values
const example$ = source$.pipe(
```

```
        map(val =>
          interval(1000).map(i => `Result (${val}): ${i}`),
            take(5)
          )
        )
      );
```

The pipe method of the RxJS Observable object.

```
const source$ = interval(1000).pipe(take(2));
```

Chapter 15 Quiz

1) What will the following code display? (using the collection below)

```
collection: string[] = ['a', 'b', 'c', 'd'];)

<ul>
  <li *ngFor="let i of collection | slice:1:3">{{i}}</li>
</ul>
```

<li>b</li>
<li>c</li>

2) What will the following code display?

```
birthday = new Date(2020, 9, 28);
{{ birthday | date:'fullDate' | uppercase}}
```

MONDAY, OCTOBER 28, 2020

www.ingramcontent.com/pod-product-compliance
Ingram Content Group UK Ltd.
Pitfield, Milton Keynes, MK11 3LW, UK
UKHW052009041026
15590UKWH00008B/2244